More praise for *A Girl Stands at the Door*

"Before reading this I would have imagined that nothing new could be said about the struggle to desegregate schools—I would have been wrong. Rachel Devlin has uncovered a neglected history of how parents and, importantly, children braved rejection, hostility, even assault to insist on their right to a decent education. Possibly most surprising, these courageous students were mostly girls, a finding that challenges some assumptions about risk-taking behavior. Not least, the book is a great read."

—LINDA GORDON,
author of *The Second Coming of the KKK*

A GIRL STANDS
at the DOOR

A GIRL STANDS
at the DOOR

———

The Generation of Young Women
Who Desegregated America's Schools

Rachel Devlin

BASIC BOOKS
New York

Basic Books
Hachette Book Group
1290 Avenue of the Americas, New York, NY 10104
www.basicbooks.com

Printed in the United States of America

First Edition: May 2018

Published by Basic Books, an imprint of Perseus Books, LLC, a subsidiary of Hachette Book Group, Inc. The Basic Books name and logo is a trademark of the Hachette Book Group.

The publisher is not responsible for websites (or their content) that are not owned by the publisher.

Print book interior design by Jeff Williams.

Library of Congress Cataloging in Publication Control Number: 2017055188

ISBNs: 978-1-5416-9733-1 (hardcover), 978-1-5416-1665-3 (ebook)

LSC-C

10 9 8 7 6 5 4 3 2 1

In Memory of
Betta Jean Bowman
1947–2016

Rubye Nell Singleton Stroble
1947–2010

Contents

Introduction

O N THE MORNING OF APRIL 13, 1947, fourteen-year-old Marguerite Daisy Carr went with her father to Eliot Junior High School, the white middle school closest to her home in Washington, DC, and attempted to enroll. The principal, tipped off that she was on her way, met her on the steps. As she stood facing him, the white students pressed up against the windows to see what would happen. Across the street, teachers, students, janitors, the Parent-Teacher Association (PTA), and the principal from Carr's black middle school, Browne Junior High, lined the sidewalk. "To their minds it was something made up, something fantastic. But here this child is just coming on," Carr, now Marguerite Carr Stokes, remembers. In gauging this situation, she relied on what her parents had taught her about how to behave in the presence of adults. "And so," she says, "I smiled nicely, because I knew how to act in polite company." When the principal told her "you don't want to come here," she responded, respectfully but firmly: "I *do* want to come to this school." Carr's response met the contradictory requirements inherent in such confrontations. She smiled, a sign of social reciprocity, trustworthiness, a willingness to engage. On the other hand, she combatively, courageously talked back to a white adult, announcing her intention to break down the legal strictures and social customs that barred her from the newly built citadel of learning two blocks from her home.[1]

Marguerite Carr and her father, James C. Carr, sued Eliot Junior High, and her lawsuit, *Carr v. Corning*, was one of almost a

dozen school desegregation cases—most of them now forgotten—
that were initiated in the immediate aftermath of World War II.
Because these complaints originated with students and parents in
disparate communities, they took shape in individual ways. However, they share a striking feature: all save one of the early school
desegregation lawsuits, which would pave the way for the cases that
became *Brown v. Board of Education*, were filed on behalf of girls.
Young women and girls, almost exclusively, attempted to register
at white schools, testified in court, met with local white administrators and school boards, and talked with reporters from both the
black and white press. This disparity held true in the Deep South,
upper South, and Midwest.[2]

After the Supreme Court ruled on *Brown v. Board* in 1954, the
pattern continued: in the most contested school desegregation battles in the Deep South, girls and young women vastly outnumbered
boys as the first to attend formerly all-white schools. In Little Rock
in 1957, six girls and three boys famously went forward as the Little Rock Nine. In New Orleans in 1960, four girls entered the first
grade at previously all-white schools. In 1963, seven girls and three
boys desegregated the lower and upper schools in Charleston, South
Carolina, and in the same year twenty-two girls and six boys desegregated the high schools in Baton Rouge, Louisiana. In Albany,
Georgia—site of intense civil rights protests and the mass jailing of
young people in the early 1960s—six young women desegregated
Albany High School in 1964. Whether applying to graduate schools
in the 1940s, filing lawsuits with their parents in the immediate
postwar years, or volunteering to desegregate high schools in the
Deep South after *Brown*, girls and young women disproportionately
led the way in the battle to desegregate American public schools in
the mid-twentieth century.[3]

School desegregation could not have happened without those
who were willing to put themselves forward—the "guinea pigs," as
they sometimes called themselves—willing to incur the wrath of

local white officials and at times backlash from within their own communities. Shifting the lens from the legal arguments against segregation and the lawyers who made them reveals what has heretofore been invisible: the largely young, feminine work that brought school desegregation into the courts, that helped make school desegregation central to the American political imagination of the postwar period and, with less success but equal meaning, that made integrated schools possible.[4]

The story that has been told about *Brown* is that the National Association for the Advancement of Colored People (NAACP) was the engine behind the cases: desegregation cases began to be filed in 1950 only after the NAACP made them its top priority, litigants were recruited and vetted, and many if not most plaintiffs were prevailed upon by NAACP lawyers to file desegregation cases. Following Richard Kluger's timeline in his magisterial 1975 book *Simple Justice: The History of Brown v. Board of Education and Black America's Struggle for Equality*, the history of *Brown* is told—in countless museum exhibits and textbooks—as a story that began in Clarendon County, South Carolina, with *Briggs v. Elliott*, then took a detour through Texas with the law school case *Sweatt v. Painter*, found its way to a Charleston federal appeals court, where Judge Julius Waties Waring contributed a galvanizing dissent in 1951, and then proceeded with cases in Delaware, Virginia, Kansas, and Washington, DC, all filed between 1949 and 1951.[5]

Much about this tidy conceptualization, however, is belied by the geography of the many previously unknown postwar cases and the manner in which they came to the attention of the NAACP. Indeed, the NAACP had little to do with the sudden rash of cases that presented themselves all at once in the aftermath of World War II. As Thurgood Marshall complained in 1968,

> People are not yet convinced that we never had a program . . . from the beginning to the end there was no plan on any of these cases.

None. The best proof of it is that once we won the law school and the graduate school the next case should have been college, then junior college, then high school, then elementary school. It ends up the next case was elementary school. Well obviously there was no plan. And we, we were kind of peeved. We didn't really want it. We didn't want it, but we had it. We wanted to bring it down, bring it down one to the other. . . . We had been going at it this long, lets take a couple more years. Then all of a sudden, here we go.

Indeed, *Brown v. Board* was the end result of an onslaught of un-solicited cases, initiated by parents and students, which came as a surprise to the national office and ultimately convinced NAACP lawyers to litigate on the grade school level. The road to *Brown* was a grassroots movement spearheaded by girls and young women, whose words, actions, and public commitment brought school de-segregation to the fore in the postwar era. These girls and young women legitimized school desegregation in the eyes of an often du-bious public and then volunteered to be "firsts" at formerly all-white schools in the early 1960s.[6]

———

After World War II, municipalities faced a dire need for better school facilities, and across the country bonds were issued to fi-nance construction, with new schools opening their doors in 1947 and 1948. Black students found themselves excluded from the building boom, and black schools—always underfunded—looked even shabbier by comparison to the sleek, modern accommodations increasingly available for their white counterparts. African Ameri-can parents and students responded with a range of protest tactics, including picketing in front of inadequate black schools, staging walkouts, filing equalization suits (in which boys made up a slight majority of plaintiffs), and going to white schools to announce their intention to immediately enroll. Arriving at the schoolhouse door was the more radical approach: It made for good theater and announced a sense of ownership over existing state institutions. It also conveyed a profound sense of urgency, suggested immediate alternatives to the status quo, and forced white school officials and parents to face racial inequities they preferred to ignore. Such moments of confrontation also yielded results. Long-awaited improvements to black schools were often procured in the aftermath of a "school visit." But the goals of these visits and subsequent lawsuits were more far-reaching. Attempting to walk into a white school was not only bold, it also announced the presumption of full equality and integration, no matter how futile the gesture might have seemed at the time. The trip to the front office—or however far one got—was just the beginning, and white officials could not pretend otherwise. Notice had been served.[7]

The 1940s was an exciting and propitious time to play a role in the fight for school desegregation. Membership in the NAACP, founded in 1909 by a small, interracial group of activists to fight for racial justice, surged during the war years, creating an organization with tens of thousands of members stretching from Maine to California. The organization was composed of individual branches, both small and large, each of which exercised a fair amount of autonomy in tackling local issues, from teacher salaries to securing representation for criminal trials to housing discrimination. Field officers from New York fanned out across all regions to spread news from the main office and gauge the animating concerns and activities of its members. At the same time, the organization held fast to its defining goals: antilynching legislation, equality before the law, equal pay and educational opportunities, voting rights, the enforcement of fair labor contracts, and the eradication of Jim Crow. Legal and legislative battles—as opposed to street protest or boycotts—were the driving force of the organization. In 1939, the NAACP established the Legal Defense and Education Fund, Inc.—at first called the "Inc. Fund" and later referred to as the LDF—as a separate entity within the NAACP. While the larger organization worked on legislative action against lynching and promoted antidiscrimination in the military, war industries, and federal programs, the LDF pursued constitutional protections and civil rights in the courts. By the late 1940s, discrimination in education was the LDF's most prominent pursuit.[8]

Charles Hamilton Houston, a "radical visionary" who led the legal division of the NAACP in the 1930s, laid the groundwork for the legal campaign for school equity and desegregation that would blossom after World War II. He made his mark in the field of education when he argued in front of the Supreme Court to have Lloyd Gaines admitted to the University of Missouri Law School. In *Gaines v. Canada*, the court decided that states must provide graduate education for black applicants "as soon as it does for all other residents." The 1938 ruling helped ignite the long battle to desegregate American schools from top to bottom. In 1936, Houston hired Thurgood Marshall to help with the growing caseload of the LDF. When Houston moved to Washington, DC, in 1939, Marshall became the first director counsel for the LDF in New York. Marshall won a series of high-profile cases in the 1940s, including *Alston v. School Board of City of Norfolk*, a salary equalization suit for public school teachers; *Smith v. Allwright*, a Supreme Court decision outlawing the exclusion of black voters in primaries in Texas; and *Shelley v. Kraemer*, another Supreme Court victory that rendered "restrictive covenants"—legally binding agreements between white neighbors not to sell homes to African Americans—illegal.[9]

World War II was a political watershed for African American men. After returning from the front, many veterans risked their lives attempting to vote in the South. The "feeling," as historian Neil Wynn puts it, was "that participation in the war effort would be rewarded." Black men made huge strides in attaining greater parity for the race as a whole after the war: they held elected offices, desegregated baseball, ascended the ranks of the Democratic and

Republican parties, became presidents of academic associations, and held presidential appointments. Meanwhile, with his eye firmly on the black voting bloc in the North, President Harry Truman convened the first panel to investigate the state of civil rights in the United States. Black men famously went on to lead a range of protest movements in the fifties and sixties. African American men— young and old—would make up two-thirds of the rank-and-file Freedom Riders in the 1960s. Young men and boys would also lead high school walkouts and protests in the late sixties, demanding the adoption of black history curricula, the creation of black student unions, and reforms to dress codes.[10]

For many girls and young women, school desegregation was *their* call to arms, a mission they felt to be their own. Those who participated uniformly shared a perception that segregated public schools were a political and moral crisis. In 1988, then Detroit mayor Coleman Young asked Ada Lois Sipuel Fisher why she agreed to "become the guinea pig" in the case that led to the desegregation of the University of Oklahoma College of Law in 1949. Wasn't she aware that the state would resist with all of its resources, that there could be intimidation, harassment, and even physical harm? "Look," she responded, "the law was wrong." Doris Raye Jennings Brewer and Doris Faye Jennings Alston, twins who attempted to desegregate a high school in rural Texas as teenagers in 1947, used the word "natural" to describe their youthful commitment. "I just thought it was the natural thing to do and it had to be done," Brewer says. "Like mopping the floor. Some things need to be done and to us that was one of the things that needed to be done to get to the next place." Marguerite Carr Stokes uses almost identical language when reflecting on her lawsuit: "Somebody has to step up. And I was the one to step up. So I stepped up. It [was] not idealistic . . . we were taught that . . . if you see something needs to be picked up, pick it up!" In looking back, these women likened their desegregation lawsuits more to a household chore than a political salvo. There is a nagging sense of personal responsibility in their words, one that exists separately from self-interest—an obligation incurred as a (female) member of a household or community. These women perceived their actions as those of a person who, because she has seen an injustice, has incurred a burden. The obligation to correct a profound inequity appeared obvious, natural, "not idealistic." At the same time, it is not insignificant that these women invoked domestic chores to describe the work they were doing. It is possible that they felt an obligation to their race that stemmed from their sense of themselves as women.[11]

One way to understand young women's disproportionate sense of obligation to school desegregation is to compare it to similar feelings inspired in young men during World War II. These girls and young women felt an ethical compulsion to act at a young age—just like those boys (some of whom were not yet eighteen) who went and signed up for the army after Pearl Harbor. They were called to fight both by the government draft and by their own conscience. Similarly, there was, in the post–World War II era, a strong, though unstated, cultural assumption that the war to end school desegregation was a girls' war, a battle for which young women and girls were especially suited. Some girls were drafted, others volunteered, but in general girls were influenced by a pervasive sense that they were obligated to participate in this struggle. The faith placed in them by adults and their own commitment helped them to fight to desegregate the schools and, once inside formerly all-white schools, to survive.[12]

Indeed, many saw desegregation firsts as soldiers. In some cases, adults enlisted girls to fight for school desegregation by using martial analogies. Melba Pattillo Beals, who desegregated Little Rock's Central High School in 1957, writes in her memoir that after a particularly violent and demoralizing day at school, her grandmother found her crying. "This will be your last cry," her grandmother said, "because you are a warrior . . . [and] warriors don't cry." Other plaintiffs and desegregation firsts remember their mothers and fathers giving them similar directives: to be tough, to hold back tears, to be

stoic in the face of physical and psychological violence. Many desegregation firsts who volunteered also thought of themselves as soldiers in a war that they had chosen to fight. Rubye Nell Singleton
Stroble, who desegregated Albany High School in 1964, remembered, "I never felt afraid . . . it was just like . . . when you see people
[who] know they've got a *job* to do. Just like those people—they go
in the war and fight. . . . They go over there to fight for their country!
Well, same sense. I'm going for equal rights, equal opportunities. . . .
And regardless of the outcome, that's what you go for."[13]

Girls as young as six exhibited a sense of obligation to lead, no
matter the consequences, danger, or pain inflicted. NAACP field organizer Jean Fairfax was still marveling, twenty years after the fact,
over a young girl she encountered in Leake County, Mississippi, in
the mid-1960s. The night before the schools were to be integrated
"the whites went out and harassed everybody." Everyone backed out
except one family; they were still considering their options when
Fairfax sat down at their kitchen table to speak with them. "There
was this silence" Fairfax remembers, "then the daughter, Deborah,
who was 6, said, 'Well, what's everybody waiting for, I'm ready to
go.'" Gayle Vavasseur Jones, who desegregated Baton Rouge High
School in 1963 over the objections of her mother, recalls, "I just felt
in my heart, in my soul, that it was something I had to do. I *had* to
do. If I didn't do it, who was going to do it?"[14]

—

Though the desegregation of America's public schools may seem
a self-evident objective, in the 1940s and early 1950s it remained
a radical, divisive idea. There was no consensus about how best to
attack educational inequality. Segregated schools existed in almost
every state—even in states where segregation was prohibited. A
range of laws governed the racial practices of school boards. Some
state constitutions made no mention of separate schools, such as
California, Iowa, Oregon, and Wisconsin. Other states, including

Michigan, Massachusetts, New Jersey, and Rhode Island, banned separate schools. A third group—Indiana, New York, Wyoming, and Kansas—had "permissive" laws on school segregation, meaning that counties and cities were permitted to segregate as they saw fit. Finally, there were the states that made school segregation mandatory: all of the states of the former Confederacy as well as Arizona, Delaware, and Washington, DC. Though some states had no laws concerning segregation and others prohibited it, de facto segregation existed, in some form, in every state. For example, New Jersey, where segregation was outlawed, and California, where it was not mandatory, still had extensively segregated schools throughout the twentieth century.[15]

Since the end of the Civil War, American grade schools had been an arena of ongoing litigation, including lawsuits filed by African American, Mexican, Chinese, and Native American students. Between 1865 and 1935, 113 recorded legal cases involving school segregation and inequality were filed in twenty-nine states. Parents and students sought to contest segregated schools, they sued to stop school boards from allocating funds to a white school when there was no appropriation for black schools, and they filed lawsuits to "obtain identical facilities" for "colored students." In many places, there were simply no schools—especially high schools—for black students. In California in the nineteenth century there were segregated grade schools for black and white students, but none for Chinese students.[16]

Prior to World War II, most school cases were filed by fathers (as head of household) on behalf of their minor children. In cases where an adult sued on behalf of a single plaintiff, or a lead plaintiff who represented "others similarly situated," girl plaintiffs outnumbered boys two to one. In the most prominent cases—those that were appealed to a state supreme court or the Supreme Court of the United States—girls were almost always the lead plaintiff. This preference for female school desegregation plaintiffs held true across age, region, and even race. The earliest school desegregation case, *Roberts v. City of Boston* in 1850, was filed on behalf of African American five-year-old Sarah Roberts, who had to pass several white schools close to her home in order to reach a school assigned to black students. In California in 1884 (*Tape v. Hurley*), and again in Mississippi in 1927 (*Lum v. Rice*), Chinese American parents filed lawsuits on behalf of daughters who wished to attend segregated white schools. The first successful school desegregation lawsuit in California was *Mendez v. Westminster* in 1947, filed on behalf of Sylvia Mendez and other Mexican children "similarly situated." The plaintiff Mamie Tape (of *Tape v. Hurley*) was described in terms that foreshadowed descriptions of black girl plaintiffs in the mid-twentieth century. She was poised, friendly, and carefully dressed in Western attire for her day in court, with a large white bow at the end of her black braid. A white bow could signal many things: sexual innocence, cleanliness, a white flag in the midst of racial hostilities. Parents would want to convey all of those messages about their children to the white male judges who would be deciding their daughter's—and by extension their race's—educational future.[17]

There was enormous debate—starting in the 1930s and extending through the postwar era—over whether school desegregation or the equalization of facilities and teacher salaries was the better path forward. In a special issue of the *Journal of Negro Education* on segregation published in 1935, the famous black educator Horace Mann Bond looked at the history of school segregation since its inception and found that everywhere "the basis for the separate school is apparently an unwillingness of the white population to accept the Negro as a full participant in the life of our Democracy." Segregation, he wrote, "has not been done because [black children] do not need any education . . . but because black children were deemed unfit associates of whites, as school companions." Laws pertaining to school segregation noted the "unassimilability" of black children and excluded them "as one would take from a school those with measles or chicken-pox, or diphtheria." The fear, everywhere, was that "black is catching." Because racism predominated even in integrated schools, where black students were often made to sit in the back row or endure lectures on the inferiority of the race, "Negroes [were] willing," he wrote, "to accede to the institution of separate schools as quickly as possible."[18]

W. E. B. Du Bois, a founder of the NAACP and its most famous intellectual, lent his imprimatur to the notion that black schools should be valued as a form of protection for black children against white teachers who did not treat them like human beings, and that black children ought not to be used "as a battering ram" against segregation. (Though Du Bois did send his own daughter to a white boarding school.) Gladys Tignor Peterson, who wrote an overview of different approaches to segregated and unequal schooling, listed going North, seeking the ballot, and appealing "to the fair-mindedness" of one's "white neighbors." But, she wrote, "the process of educating both groups, each to a tolerance of the other, is a slow and tedious one." It was this slow and tedious work that black girls were tasked with when they filed desegregation lawsuits and that they assigned themselves when they volunteered to desegregate schools after *Brown*. By approaching white universities, speaking with white officials, and engaging with white students on campuses in the 1940s; by testifying in court and responding to inquiring white reporters in the 1950s; and by choosing to enroll in previously all-white schools in the 1960s, girls and young women initiated and enacted school desegregation so that others might be able to envision themselves doing the same.[19]

———

In 2012, President Barack Obama hung the Norman Rockwell painting *The Problem We All Live With* in the West Wing of the White House, further cementing the painting's important place in American history and culture. The painting—of a six-year-old black girl, dressed in white from the bow on her head to the shoes on her feet, and accompanied on her way to school by four US Marshals—is thought to be a depiction of Ruby Bridges. It is more likely a composite of the four girls who desegregated two schools in New Orleans in November 1960: Gail Etienne, Leona Tate, Tessie Prevost Williams, and Ruby Bridges. The small girl in white is contrasted with the ugly stains and graffiti on the wall behind her. Her head only reaches the men's elbows. The sentimental appeal of the picture stems from the fact of witnessing a solitary, vulnerable black girl surrounded by large white men in the act of bridging a racial divide. But if the contemporary viewer sees this girl as innocent, it is important to point out that this is not how white Americans in the early 1960s South, and indeed much of the country, saw her.[20]

The most important difference between white and black girlhood in the mid-twentieth century—especially in the South—was that black girls were afforded none of the public protections that were extended to middle-class white girls, such as the assumption of dependence, the notion that children ought to be free of economic exploitation, or security from public violence and sexual harassment. Black girls were regularly targeted by gangs of white boys on the way to and from school. White men in the South were known to strike black girls if they did not give up their seats fast enough on a train or bus. The Ku Klux Klan—masked and robed—broke up a black Girl Scout meeting in Alabama in 1948 because some of the counselors were white. And when six black girls enrolled at Fremont High School in Los Angeles in 1947, they were kicked, punched, and spat on by both male and female classmates. Later, the students rioted and hung the girls in effigy. When Lydia and Sandra Nelson attempted to integrate a school in Indianapolis in 1947, and when a group of nine girls and four boys tried to enroll at a white school in East St. Louis in 1949, the white students responded with strikes, angry street protests, and physical threats. Any notion that black girls would somehow be more acceptable to whites, or that they would not provoke or be subjected to violence, ignores the facts as they were known and widely disseminated in the postwar era. When black girls desegregated high schools after *Brown*, they were subjected to far more violence than young men. Ernest Green, one of the Little Rock Nine, remembers, "The girls got it the most. . . . People took their femininity as a weakness and attempted to take advantage of that." Green's point is reinforced by girls' experiences elsewhere. Women who desegregated high schools in Baton Rouge in 1963, for instance, recall far more violence directed at them than men.[21]

Some historians have assumed that white parents were afraid that school desegregation meant black boys would mix with white girls. Yet fears about interracial sex were usually described with abstract terms like "amalgamation" or "miscegenation"—with the gender of the participants left unstated. And while some of the most sensational anti–civil rights propaganda of the fifties and sixties deployed images of black men with white women, when it came to school desegregation the record shows that judges and lawyers spoke more about the innate promiscuity of black girls. In a desegregation lawsuit brought against the East Baton Rouge School Board in 1956, the defense produced poster-board-sized charts detailing "Illegitimate births by Race . . . Mothers 10-14 Years of Age" and "Venereal Diseases by Race . . . Per 1,000 Population" (the second chart referencing fears of promiscuity within the black race as a whole). In a Supreme Court conference proceeding for *Brown v. Board of Education*, Tom C. Clark, a justice from Texas, spoke about the problem of black girls within the context of school desegregation. "The problem [in Texas]," he said, "is as acute as anywhere. Texas also has the Mexican problem. [A] Mexican boy of 15 is in a class with a negro [*sic*] girl of 12. Some negro girls get in trouble (pregnant)."[22]

In fact, for centuries, the most common sort of interracial, nonconsensual sex in the South involved white men and boys and black women and girls. That young black women gave birth to mixed-race children far more often than young white women was a social fact universally known and understood in the South. That is why men, in their positions as judges and lawyers, addressed it in court as a legitimate social concern in the event of the desegregation of public schools. As Nell Irvin Painter, Deborah Gray White, Darlene Clark Hine, and other historians of black women have shown, black girls and women were both sexually vulnerable and viewed as sexually dangerous. This is not to say that black boys and young men were not seen by whites as sexually threatening, but simply that sexualized stereotypes also followed black girls when they desegregated schools. Black girls were not met with more equanimity from white parents when they desegregated schools because of their gender.[23]

Ultimately, fears of black children—as black *people*—tended to be thoroughgoing and nonnegotiable. The most common fears voiced by white parents in the fifties and sixties were exactly those that Horace Mann Bond had identified in the earliest school segregation statutes of the nineteenth century. An incoherent but omnipresent perception of contagion underlay the irrational passions of white parents confronted with the possibility of black children in "their" schools. As one white mother in Alabama claimed in 1965, "N—s in our schools will ruin my children morally, scholastically, spiritually and every other way." And as Louisiana state senator William Rainach put it, "School desegregation will plunge the white school children of Louisiana into moral and intellectual chaos and would seriously jeopardize their health."[24]

———

Why, then, did so many young women and girls file school desegregation lawsuits and volunteer to desegregate schools? What allowed them to look at the edifice of a white school and say—to themselves, their parents, a lawyer—*Yes, I can go there and talk to that hostile, white principal. I can hold my own with those white students.* There were not a lot of girls who thought this. But there were enough to get the job done.

School desegregation differed from other civil rights battles—such as the desegregation of lunch counters, public transportation, and parks—in that interacting with white people was not, as legal scholar Derrick Bell has explained, fleeting or "fortuitous," but central to the project itself. School desegregation required sustained interactions with white school officials and students. This fact called for a different approach than other forms of civil rights activism. Attempting to desegregate interstate travel or to extend voting rights in the Deep South called for, above all, physical courage—the willingness to put one's life on the line. School desegregation, on the other hand, demanded both physical courage and exceptional social finesse. Attempting to desegregate a school was both an act of provocation and an uncomfortable appeal for social acceptance. This appeal, of course, was not met—and it was in the nimbleness with which girls navigated social hostility that they excelled. They spoke with school officials, lawyers, and black and white reporters, all of whom asked them impossible questions about their intentions, whether they believed they would "make friends" in white schools, and why they sought to leave their own schools and communities. Young women managed—time and time again—to find ways to respond to these queries. They were artfully vague, they were diplomatic, they were patient, and they found ways to parry with those who stood between them and access to white schools. Once inside formerly all-white schools, those few who volunteered managed to eventually "tune out" (as they put it) the roars of angry crowds and the epithets that were hurled at them in class. They found ways to speak up for themselves, even when white teachers refused to call on them—deploying what some called "sass" or a "smart mouth." Desegregating schools was a social high-wire act, and a disproportionate number of young women and girls proved to be especially able and willing to do it.[25]

Of the experiences that allowed these desegregation firsts to feel somewhat prepared for the psychological complexity and social nuance required of them, domestic service was the most common and, in the South, definitive. During the first half of the twentieth century, the vast majority of African American women, no matter their social class or educational background, worked in domestic service at some point in their lives. African American domestic laborers brought their daughters to work with them from the time they were four or five in order to teach them how to interact with white people of all ages and both genders. As a domestic worker explained, "She took you with her so you'd not *act out* or wrong. She showed you how you was expected to be" (emphasis added). Another said that, above all, a domestic worker had to learn "how you had to act with them all." The expectation was that these forms of learned self-governance would be put to use in girls' future working lives. What is important here is that black women used the word "act" or "acting" to describe their most common work experiences with white people—a skill that would be vitally important when attempting to gain access to and survive inside white schools.[26]

Girls' experiences in white homes were not simply lessons in deference and self-control. They also learned how and when they could strategically confront and verbally defy their white employers. For instance, desegregation plaintiffs Doris Raye Jennings Brewer and Doris Faye Jennings Alston described an encounter their mother, Ella Mae Jennings, had with her white employer as the inspiration for their own ability to calmly stand behind their desegregation lawsuit years later. Alston recalls:

My mother worked as a maid in a white home. One day . . . we had gone with her. And the white owner came into the kitchen. And she said:

"Ella Mae, by the time you get ready to retire your girls will be ready to come and work in your place."

And she says "No ma'am."

"They can't work for me?"

"No ma'am. They will NOT be working in your house."

And that was the end of that.

This exchange taught Jennings's daughters skills they would later deploy in confrontations over school desegregation. Jennings was polite—using the honorific "ma'am," answering questions in a direct manner—while emphatically contradicting her employer. From experiences like these, many black girls learned the nuances of maintaining an ongoing relationship with whites that was at once accommodating and confrontational.[27]

Plaintiffs and firsts also remember shopping expeditions with their mothers as formative. Like white women, black women managed their families' consumer needs. They went to grocery stores and downtown department stores. They opened their front doors to traveling salesmen. All of these encounters were fraught. In their numerous interactions with rude and condescending salespeople, black women fought back with the only tools they had: a sharp retort or stubbornly insisting on respect by whatever means necessary short of violence. Peggy King Jorde, who desegregated a lower school in Albany, Georgia, recalls her regular trips to the A&P with her mother:

> As a kid, it's very exciting. . . . You like to pick out your cereal. . . . But then as you got to the end of your shopping experience, [you were] thinking, "OK, now we're getting to the checkout. Is the checkout girl going to call my mother by her first name? Is she going to engage in some sort of behavior that's going to try to diminish or degrade my mom? And if she did, we knew that my mother would either demand to see the manager or speak to her. Or carry out some form of resistance. . . . As a kid it's kind of tough to handle when everybody in all the other aisles are looking at you. [But] you learn from the experience. . . . As you get older you look back and [realize] *I took my cues from my parents.*"

Many black women believe that witnessing these daily encounters gave them their survival skills—especially those deployed inside formerly all-white schools.[28]

Black girls were never free from harassment, especially sexual harassment—whether in white homes, from the man of the house or his sons, or on the streets of southern cities, where police officers were just as likely as other men to insult them. To help girls defend their dignity, and secure some measure of safety, community elders lectured them endlessly on cleanliness, civilized behavior, and decorum as a way to telegraph a self-possession that might deter—to whatever degree possible—unwanted sexual attention. Black women also, as historian Evelyn Brooks Higginbotham has shown, were tasked with contributing to the "assimilationist" goals of the race and thus were taught to be "ever-cognizant of the gaze of white America." Black girls were instructed by their parents, pastors, teachers, and social workers to be always aware of their presentation in public. Older girls monitored younger girls' public conduct as well. As historian LaKisha Michelle Simmons explains, midcentury girls used the word "nice" to describe their ideal—they aspired to be "nice girls." As Simmons notes, girls of all ages, but especially those in middle and high school, associated the word "nice" with high standards of public morality: abstaining from "fights, alcohol and hanging around boys alone," as well as maintaining good posture, being well dressed, and always appearing composed. In courtrooms and in schools, girls used their deep practice in decorum, poise, and manners as a weapon against white hostility. An unflappable self-possession was key to managing the relentless scrutiny inherent in the school desegregation process, and many black young women and girls arrived at the schoolhouse door with those skills already in place.[29]

In addition to social grace, many black girls and young women brought another feminine attribute to school desegregation: a finely calibrated projection of warmth in their dealings with white administrators and students. They were not effusive about forging interracial bonds. Rather, they offered small gestures and succinct statements that communicated a positive perspective on the prospect of interracial accord. Almost all desegregation pioneers smiled. Others offered words—not to be confused with acts—of friendship, or a perspective that signaled their acceptance of the reciprocal obligations inherent in entering white institutions. Such signs were a subtle but consistent component of girls' public personae in the earliest desegregation cases and then later in places where *Brown* was most fiercely contested. The impulse to *appear* socially open was modeled by adult black women, who, as the twentieth century wore on, increasingly engaged in people-oriented work—teaching, nursing, and social work. In these professions, it was necessary to radiate friendliness, sincerity, and openness. African American girls, too, were explicitly taught that extending themselves to others was a vital component of their femininity. Black advice literature aimed at girls and young women regularly directed them to be "personable" at all times. Smiling and appearing friendly was not only polite but also a form of protection—it threw white students and officials off guard. As Albany, Georgia, desegregation first Beverly Plummer Wilson explains, "When you stand and smile, [that] smile will kill anything. Because they're looking for you to retaliate. So with six [girls] against five hundred [white students] . . . you do it, just smile and stand!"[30]

Ideas about girls' public presentation on behalf of the race were championed overtly by black women leaders such as Mary McLeod Bethune, who spoke about the special role of women in bringing the races together. Bethune, former director of Negro affairs of the National Youth Administration under President Franklin D. Roosevelt and one of the most politically powerful, visible, and ubiquitous black leaders of the mid-twentieth century, had been speaking since the 1920s about what she called the "unique responsibility" of the "Negro girl": "cleanliness, beauty and thoughtfulness." Girls, Bethune wrote, must be taught to enact these qualities so that the "Negro boy . . . is tolerated." After World War II, Bethune grafted her prewar ideas about girls' capacity for decorous display in the service of racial rapprochement onto more bold language about equal rights. In a speech she gave across the country to large audiences, Bethune declared, "These are the days when we must bridge the chasms that stand between man and man.... I feel very deeply that the responsibility rests very largely upon the women of America ... that the influence that we shall send out ... will tend to bring men quickly to realize the democratic policy ... that we are all yearning for in our deepest hearts." While the method by which women would "bridge" the races was left unstated in this speech, Bethune continued to assert the unique responsibility and implicit capacities of women to conduct the inherently social mission of establishing interracial trust.[31]

Bethune often addressed mixed crowds of black and white women at YWCAs, usually in larger cities. Black women, and occasionally white women, were open to her call to work for interracial comity. Few white women acted, but those who did stepped outside the usual strictures on women in the 1940s and displayed a willingness to lead. Decades before the resurgence of feminism in the late 1960s, and during a conservative era in which women's leadership was rare, a range of women spoke out against school segregation. One young white woman tried to register at a black high school in Washington, DC, in 1948, and when she was ejected from the school filed a desegregation lawsuit. Other white women led demonstrations on college campuses. In 1948 in a small town in Kansas, Esther Brown, a twenty-three-year-old Jewish woman, helped lead a yearlong school strike and desegregation lawsuit that would bring NAACP leaders to the state and help convince them to pursue the lawsuit that would become *Brown v. Board.*

But the most numerous and consequential contributions to the school desegregation movement were made by African American young women and girls. These girls were expected to enact interracial accord by serving as the advance guard in the earliest stages and most difficult battles of school desegregation. And though not every female plaintiff or first succeeded, there was a pattern to the performances of girls and young women in front of both black and white audiences. They hewed to a script of interracial possibility, even in places where their own communities did not necessarily share their vision. They imagined what school desegregation might look like before any template—social, legal, or political—for desegregation existed. And they devoted every waking moment to their cause for many years of their young lives. The social expectations that girls be pleasing, that they embody assimilationist aspirations, and that they be able to handle thorny social confrontations made these young women ripe candidates for early attempts at desegregation. Once inside formerly all-white schools, those who weathered the ordeal were fortified by a deep conviction that desegregation was politically necessary: not for themselves (though some wanted the better facilities and new textbooks) but for the larger civil rights movement, the nation, and society writ large. They believed that spending eight hours a day, five days a week, nine months of the year in a room with white students could help lead the way to a more equal society. And with every foray into—or at the door of—a white school, it became easier for blacks and whites, for the NAACP top brass and the grassroots on the ground, to envision a future with desegregated schools.

I

Roots of Change

Lucile Bluford's Long Crusade

LLOYD GAINES HAD BEEN A local hero in Kansas City, Missouri, since 1935 when he first initiated an NAACP-sponsored lawsuit against the University of Missouri (MU) for denying him admission to the law school. When, on December 12, 1938, the nation heard the news that the Supreme Court had ruled that the university must admit him "in absence of other [graduate] training within the state," the announcement was met with surprise and celebration in many quarters. Gaines and the newspaper that had faithfully backed him over the course of his long lawsuit—the *Kansas City Call*—were flooded with congratulatory telegrams, including one from NAACP president Walter White. Gaines, "the Victorious Youth," was a native son who worked his way through Vashon High School, graduated valedictorian from a class of fifty in just three years, and then went on to Lincoln University in Jefferson City, Missouri, where he graduated as an honors student and president of the senior class. Gaines—resplendent and serious in his large photo in the *Call*—lent his "brilliance," his youth, his academic achievements, and his political fervor to the cause of school desegregation. In a telegram to the *Call*, he wrote: "Organized pressure has opened another great gate for our people. . . . May we all see that this Golden Opportunity is never neglected, Lost or Forgotten." The newspaper and its readers were justifiably proud of their local hero. And they were sorely disappointed, less than a year later, when he disappeared under mysterious circumstances with his challenge to segregation at MU still unresolved. By then, however, another desegregation activist had stepped forward, answering Gaines's call by applying to the University of Missouri School of Journalism, the oldest and one of the most respected journalism schools in the country. That graduate school candidate and plaintiff was none other than the *Kansas City Call*'s own, twenty-eight-year-old managing editor, Lucile Bluford.[1]

In the heady days following the *Gaines v. Canada* decision, black graduate students sought admission to state universities in Arkansas, Georgia, Kentucky, Missouri, North Carolina, South Carolina, and West Virginia.[2] Only Bluford managed to keep her case alive in the courts. In all, she would apply to the University of Missouri School of Journalism *eleven* times, and her court case would span three years, from 1939 to 1942. As she performed the work of a plaintiff, she also worked as a journalist on the beat—chronicling every step of the way in the pages of her newspaper.

In 1942, the University of Missouri shut down its prestigious graduate school rather than admit Bluford. She had pursued the school so relentlessly—in court, on campus, in editorials, and in an endless letter-writing campaign—that the school's lawyer, William Hogsett, attempted to have her formally branded a legal "nuisance." Undeterred, Bluford turned her penetrating gaze to other desegregation and social justice efforts. By 1955, she was editor in chief and publisher of the *Kansas City Call*. Until she suffered a stroke in the 1990s, Bluford put in long hours every day, her only vacations were trips to NAACP conventions, and she never failed to put the paper to bed on Thursday nights. The newspaper covered every issue of importance to the black community in Kansas City during these years, including lunch-counter sit-ins, redlining, civil rights legislation, housing segregation, and the leaders and political aspirations of the civil rights movement. Her head-on, thorough, and hard-hitting reporting led her to be called the "conscience of the community" and helped the paper become the Midwest's largest circulation weekly. Local journalists, citing her deep commitment to civil rights and uncompromising reporting, compared her to Ida B. Wells. But while Wells was most passionate about lynching, Bluford's most ardent concern was the fight against segregated education. She believed that segregated schools were the great scourge of her time. She would commit her formidable energy and truth-telling ways to this cause above all others, from the inception of her own desegregation lawsuit, *Bluford v. Canada*, in 1939 to *Brown v. Board*—a close-to-home lawsuit on which her handprints can, from the right angle, be recognized.[3]

No story was too remote, too small, or too messy for Bluford to cover. Nor did she shy away from the more controversial aspects of both segregated schooling and the divisive fight to dismantle it. Using scorching language, she refused to be vague about the ugly realities of impoverished black schools. She railed against "the four months' schooling, the underpaid teacher, the unsanitary cracker-box schools standard in many places 'because it costs too much to educate Negroes.'" She exposed more than a few black leaders and professionals when they made compromises with local politicians or accepted bribes to the detriment of black students. A front-page article she published in 1939, "Langston U. Head Quits in [One] Day," detailed the corruption that the new president found on his arrival at the only black college in Oklahoma. Many of the top positions were filled (simultaneously) by one man, a man whom State Senator Louis Ritzhaupt referred to as his "campaign manager" or, with a pat on the back, "Jimmy." Indeed, all of the top administrators at Langston were in Ritzhaupt's pocket, and Bluford printed all of their names. It was an act that set the *Call* apart from other black newspapers, which tended to shy away from intra-racial conflict on educational matters as much as possible. The *Call* also reported on desegregation lawsuits that other papers missed or chose to ignore. It was the *Kansas City Call*, rather than the local *Houston Informer*, that broke news of the *Jennings* desegregation lawsuit in Hearne, Texas, in 1948, which was the first grade school desegregation case that Thurgood Marshall argued (not *Briggs* as historians believe). And it was the *Call* that first reported on a 1948 desegregation case in rural Kansas, *Webb v. District No. 90*, as well as the many other local cases that would eventually lead the NAACP to conclude that the push to desegregate grade schools was a growing, grassroots phenomenon that it could not ignore.[4]

———

Lucile Bluford inherited her commitment to education from her parents and her maternal grandmother, Mariah Harris. Bluford was born in Salisbury, North Carolina, on July 11, 1911. Her mother, Viola Harris Bluford, was a graduate of Oberlin College, and her father, John H. Bluford, held degrees from Howard and Cornell Universities and worked as a professor of agriculture at North Carolina A&M in Greensboro. Viola Bluford died when Lucile was only four years old. Two years later, after remarrying, her father, seeking "better educational opportunities" for his children, gave up his position at North Carolina A&M and moved to Kansas City with Lucile's two older brothers, John Jr. and Guion. Lucile, six years old at the time, elected to stay with her grandmother, whom she adored and credited with teaching her "everything" she knew about life. But two years later her grandmother died, and Lucile made the move to Kansas City to join her father and brothers.[5]

As a child, Lucile spent most of her time reading. As she described later, "My neighbors used to say I read all day long. [They] said I'd sit out on the swing and read." Her stepmother, Addie Alston Bluford, bucked gender stereotypes by allowing Lucile, the only daughter, to spend her time as she pleased. "Now my mother didn't have me helping much in the house or in the kitchen," she later said, "so most of my time I would read." She would often go to the library at the nearby white high school, where she was allowed to take out books. Addie Bluford must have approved of the way her stepdaughter was spending her time and, by freeing her of household responsibilities, nurtured what would become a life-long relationship with the written word—and a disdain for the domestic arts. "I never did learn how to cook till after college," Bluford recalled with a chuckle.[6]

As a teenager, Bluford attended NAACP meetings with her father, who for a number of years was secretary of the Kansas City branch. She also attended NAACP conventions with him in the summertime, where she heard Walter White and Charles Houston speak, "and later on, people like Thurgood Marshall when he was young." The "NAACP message," she recalled, "would not have gotten across to the bulk of the black population except for the black press. Their message was carried to the people not through the radio, or television, or anything, but through the black press around the country." Her affection for journalism started young. Her brothers "used to throw [deliver] the [*Kansas City*] *Journal Post*," which provided free reading, but one paper was not enough for Bluford. She read all of the local papers: the *Kansas City Star*, *Kansas City Times*, and of course, her favorite, the *Kansas City Call*. She particularly admired Roy Wilkins's column for that paper, "Talking It Over." Wilkins, she said, "was always talking about some interesting thing that happened in the community, some kind of discrimination or something interesting. And I'd always pick up the *Call* and say, 'Well, let's see what Roy is talking about this week.' I guess he was kind of a role model for a little while."[7]

John Bluford taught at Lincoln High School, an esteemed high school in Kansas City that attracted top-notch faculty from around the nation. It was at Lincoln High that Lucile Bluford first practiced journalism. She worked on the school paper, the *Lincolnite*, with the encouragement of her English teacher, Trussie Smothers. She later recalled that Smothers "got me interested in staying after school and gathering and writing articles for the *Lincolnite*. . . . I didn't mind staying after school because [I] liked it and it was enjoyable." After finishing work on the *Lincolnite*, Bluford made a habit of walking down 18th Street, home to the humming black business district in Kansas City, and stopping in at the office of the *Call*, where she befriended founder and editor Chester A. Franklin and her erstwhile role model, Roy Wilkins. Wilkins, a Kansas City native, would go on to become editor of the NAACP publication the *Crisis* in 1934 and eventually executive secretary of the NAACP in 1955. Like so many in the arts, Bluford got her start in journalism by simply hanging around, making herself useful, and striking up conversations when she could. Bluford knew that, as a teenage girl, spending her free time at an all-male office was unusual. "At the time I was coming along," she recalled, "the only professions black girls entered were, traditionally, schoolteaching [*sic*], nursing and social work. I didn't really like any of those." Dorothy Johnson, who worked for Bluford at the *Call*, recalled that "her mother's friends were scandalized. Nice girls weren't supposed to go to work on 18th street . . . but for Lucile, 18th street was . . . comfortable. . . . Lucile was not afraid to go anywhere or ask any question of anybody."[8]

Bluford graduated valedictorian of her senior class and had her hopes set on attending Howard University like her father. But John Bluford preferred she stay closer to home, and he ultimately prevailed. The University of Missouri did not accept black students, but the state did give black residents partial scholarships to attend state universities elsewhere, so she attended the University of Kansas (KU) in Lawrence. She immediately set about majoring in journalism. According to Bluford, a former student named Marie Ross "paved the way" for her. "She was the first black student in the School of Journalism and they gave her a hard time. Dean Flint told her in so many words or point blank, 'There's no point in your studying journalism because there's nowhere for you to work and you're just

wasting your time. You shouldn't be here.' Tried to get her to withdraw." Ross was determined and refused to back down:

> But she wouldn't [withdraw]. Oh no, she wouldn't. She came down
> here and told Roy Wilkins what the dean had said. And they got
> together a stack of black newspapers, about two hundred, you
> know, that we got on exchange. And . . . Marie took them up there
> and showed them to Dean Flint. He had never heard of a black
> newspaper. Never heard of it. . . . She was very persistent. So when
> I went I was the only black student in the journalism school, too,
> all the time I was there. But I got along fine . . . Marie paved the
> way for me.

Ross was doing the tedious work of educating the other race—in
precisely the way that Gladys Tignor Peterson had described. The
level of ignorance about black accomplishment that Ross encountered is a good indicator of how difficult the educational process
would be for Bluford in the 1930s. Bluford's experience at the University of Kansas was not all smooth sailing, despite her later recollections. But she always credited Ross with opening up the school of
journalism. It was a debt that she felt bound to acknowledge when
anyone inquired about her past.[9]

Bluford made it her daily mission to break down what segregation
remained both on campus and in Lawrence. While the cafeteria was
not segregated, there was no seating for blacks at the student union.
She and her friend Mary Louise Chapman "had to break that up" as
Bluford described it, as if it was merely an item on a checklist. Bluford and another friend, Anna Jean McCampbell, attempted to sit in
the "white's only" section of a Lawrence movie theater. McCampbell
was so light skinned she could pass for white, so she bought the
tickets. Then the two young women, instead of going to the balcony,
found a seat in the middle of the main floor. "And the ushers saw us
but they lost us," Bluford said. "In the dark they couldn't find us, and

they walked all up and down the aisle." When that failed, the ushers turned on the lights momentarily. "So they came over and tried to get us to move. And we acted like we didn't know what they were talking about and kept looking at the picture. We never did move." In Bluford's later recollections in 1989, she sounded most passionate about the fact that segregation persisted in the University of Kansas cafeteria, even though no official rules forced black and white students to sit apart. "As it happens now," she said, "black students kind of congregated together . . . and I wish they didn't. They used to do that in the cafeteria. But every time I'd see a bunch, I'd go sit someplace else." It sounds exhausting, routinely moving away from your friends and actively looking for another table. Bluford understood why it wasn't attractive to others. "You're segregating yourself and you do it because you know your friends are there. But I just didn't think it was a good idea." It was rare for anyone in the mid-twentieth century to complain about self-segregation (though Thurgood Marshall did on occasion). And while Bluford understood it, she openly deplored it.[10]

Bluford might sound like a bit of a loner, searching the cafeteria for mixed seating, but her closest bonds were with black women. Black students were not allowed to live on campus, and so several women got together sophomore year and moved into the first black sorority house at KU, Alpha Kappa Alpha (AKA). Mary Louise Chapman described Bluford as someone who "had a good sense of humor, but very serious. She lived in that journalism building." Everyone in the house pitched in and cooked—except Bluford. Everyone cared about fashion and self-image—except Bluford. "The ongoing joke when we were in college was: Style be hanged when it came to Lucile." Which is not to say that she did not have her own, unique look. "I recall a little green leather jacket she wore all the time," Chapman said. "She loved that green leather jacket." Bluford recalled that "it had good pockets" and she "wore it . . . until it got worn out and my friends thought I looked terrible. I think they finally took it and burned it up." She also refused to wear a hat—an even more radical act for the early 1930s. Her sorority sisters were shocked when, as president of the AKA chapter in Lawrence, she went to a national meeting hatless. "She went all the way to New York and didn't wear a hat!" she remembered them saying. A lot of people, Bluford admitted, "thought that was real strange."[11]

From early on, it was clear that Bluford would not be constrained by the dominant standards of femininity in the 1930s. Her inattention to women's fashion and her willingness to enter male spaces and speak to all people regardless of gender or rank suggest a person who was unusually comfortable contravening gender norms. Indeed, in later years she would adopt a masculine pseudonym, Louis Blue, for her more political stories in the *Call*. This unconventional approach informed her journalistic practice and perspective. Being an outsider to both masculine and feminine worlds may have also informed her commitment to school desegregation. She saw the limitations of rigid group identity, grasped the need for social understanding, and possessed a highly critical view of the status quo. Chapman would later note Bluford's unusual position when she told a reporter in 1987 that the *Call* was "[Bluford's] life, her husband, her child and everything else." Clearly Bluford's friends accepted, even celebrated, her unusual standing as a woman free from the responsibilities of a feminine, heterosexual life, and connected this freedom to her formidable skills as a crusading journalist and editor. Bluford's only allegiance was to the truth as she saw it—an allegiance that was more clear-eyed and critical than most.[12]

During college, what mattered most to Bluford—even more than her classes—was the KU newspaper, where she worked as a writer, telegraph editor, and copy editor. She made Phi Beta Kappa, and she impressed the "other [white] women" in the journalism program, who nominated her for membership in Theta Sigma Phi, which later became the Association for Women in Communications. "But the national organization balked," Chapman remembered. "Theta

Sigma Phi did not admit blacks." Bluford had begun to write for the *Call* when she was an undergraduate, sending the paper articles about events in Kansas. It seemed a foregone conclusion that she would segue from the KU journalism building to the offices of the *Call*, but first she took a job at the *Atlanta Daily World* for four months. When she moved back home, she started at the *Call* as a full-time writer. By the time she attempted to enroll at the University of Missouri, she had become managing editor.[13]

———

On a snowy day in late January 1939, Bluford began her fight to enter the University of Missouri. Accompanied by local NAACP lawyer Carl Johnson (her father was terrified and insisted that she not go alone), she traveled two hours from Kansas City to the campus in Columbia; attempted to enroll; interviewed students, professors, administrators, and passersby on campus; drove back; and wrote— in what must have been a fervid all-nighter—two lengthy front-page articles that went to press soon after. In "M.U. Rejects Woman Student" and "Nothing Will Happen when Negro Student Is Admitted to M.U.," Bluford did not dwell on the fact that she was denied admission, nor did she say anything about her legal status as a state resident applying to a public institution. Instead, she described the small exchanges and interactions she had with people on campus, all of them strangers. She wrote that "Dean Martin was very cordial," and that a member of the faculty said, "We are here to teach the students who come here. It makes no difference to us who they are." She even got a plug for her newspaper from a graduate student she interviewed: "A journalism student who is correspondent for a press service asked whether I worked for *The Call*. When I told him I did, he said 'It's the best weekly in the state.' Surprised that he knew of *The Call*, I asked, 'Do you read it?' He answered, 'Of course.'"[14]

Bluford even managed to defang S. W. Canada—the vilified registrar named in *Gaines v. Canada* (and eventually in *Bluford v.*

Canada)—using her encounter with him as another example of local connection and individual courtesy. When Bluford arrived at the registrar's office, the secretary summoned Canada, who stepped out of his office to read a statement from the board of curators proclaiming that *Gaines* had not been fully resolved and that in the meantime she should apply to the black school Lincoln University, which did not have a journalism program. Bluford went on to describe the rest of her encounter—a conversation with a man who appeared to be nothing more than a low-level functionary on a topic so picayune that, for most reporters, it would merit no column space at all. "The registrar and I chatted for quite a while. He said he was sorry I was disappointed in not being able to enroll, but that he was glad I came from Kansas City and not St. Louis because he had just learned that a car bringing students to Columbia from the Mound City had been stuck in the snow on the highway. 'I'm glad you arrived safely,' he said." Then he offered that "perhaps by September the matter would be straightened out and that I might be able to enroll then."[15]

While such reporting could sound merely folksy, for Bluford it represented a deeply considered perspective—one she had been experimenting with and reflecting on since her days in the cafeteria at the University of Kansas. For Bluford, the human details of her experience at the university were as worthy of reporting as the blunt fact that she had been rejected. She found significance in small acts of decency and mutual acknowledgment in everyday encounters. Central to the story she wished to tell was that everyone had far more in common than not. Basic civility was born of the natural, local connections that brought people together. A shared newspaper, a shared snowstorm—this was the common ground upon which human exchanges might transpire. That intimated the possibility, in philosopher Danielle Allen's memorable phrase, of "political friendship": not an emotional tie but the simple acknowledgment of a "shared life." The courtesy with which she and the white students, faculty, and administrators at the University of Missouri managed to address one another functioned as examples of what desegregation, ideally, would look like—one encounter at a time.[16]

Bluford did not see these encounters as a portent for the immediate future but for the long term. They proved both the absurdity of Jim Crow and the propensity—even if for no other reason than a self-interested desire to get through the day without incident—for members of a community to get along. Bluford articulated this point explicitly in an editorial she wrote a month later. "To admit Negroes to white schools will be less revolutionary than it appears," she wrote. "Personal and civic decency will make the others share the state schools with Negroes from their home towns, especially since they already tolerate colored people from Asia." Bluford did not mention constitutional rights, the courts, or any other apparatus of the state. Instead she invoked an ideal: "Personal and civic decency." The perception of civic decency seems to have evolved from her visit to the University of Missouri campus, as well as her earlier experiences in Kansas, where some people were able to connect in ways that bridged the racial divide. Bluford did not believe these interactions made legal action unnecessary; rather, she chose to see these fine-grained social choices as integral to her identity not only as a legitimate student, but also as a neighbor and state resident. In Bluford's telling, individual white citizens were already willing, in 1939, to exhibit their own best principles by acknowledging what they shared with their longtime neighbors.[17]

Which is not to say that the path forward would be easy. It was Bluford herself, in her capacity as a journalist, who initiated conversations with people on campus, sought out students to interview, questioned the registrar, and approached professors. Of course, Bluford had been practicing for this day since her years at the University of Kansas. But how many African Americans, in a segregated society, could imagine interacting with so many white people, all in a day's work? And there is no question Bluford excised negative information from her reports: no African American went to an all-white campus in 1939 without inspiring hostile curiosity. (She later admitted that the encounter with Canada's secretary was uncomfortable, and that a student handing out registration cards "flushed" when he saw her.) Bluford made an editorial choice to communicate positive exchanges, it would appear, not because she failed to understand the breadth and depth of racism. Rather, in her reporting she modeled and embodied the attitude and behavior required of any black applicant and desegregation first. Any such pioneer would have to go looking for "civic decency," to inspire and accept "cordial" toleration as the best that could be expected, a small achievement at the cost of a great deal of interpersonal effort. She was, in effect, modeling what early desegregation efforts would look like. The vast majority of her readers would never set foot on the MU campus—or any college campus for that matter. Bluford was describing terra incognita, and if she tended to exaggerate small successes it was in the venerable tradition of war correspondents trying to boost the morale of folks back home, or of diplomats seeking to keep lines of communication open with hostile foreign powers.[18]

Bluford's stance anticipated the firsts who would come after her, including, famously, Jackie Robinson. Robinson was described in many ways: he was stolid, courageous, and an astonishing athlete who could concentrate under enormous pressure. But the word used most often was "diplomatic." Whatever difficulty he had with white players—whether on the field or in the locker room—he never discussed it with the press. And he had this to say to a reporter: "It wasn't a question of the players getting along with me. I was on the spot to see if I could get along with them." The burden— disturbingly unfair—was on the pioneer to prove her trustworthiness to those who overtly objected to her presence. This was the ugly responsibility that Bluford willingly took on with every trip she made to the University of Missouri over three years. The hope was that once the first had paved the way—someone like Marie Ross or Lucile Bluford or Jackie Robinson—the burden would not be so great for the second, third, or one hundredth person, and on down the line.[19]

In February 1939, having taken the measure of the Supreme Court's decision on *Gaines*, as well as Bluford's application, the Missouri state legislature attempted to pass a bill (House Bill 195) to build a law school for Lloyd Gaines, along with funds to begin building a comprehensive black graduate program at Lincoln University. Bluford immediately went to work writing, printing, and distributing petitions against House Bill 195, popularly known as "the Taylor Bill" after the representative who introduced it. "We strongly urge you, our representatives in the sixtieth Missouri legislature," the petition read, "to vote against House Bill 195 ... for the reasons set forth in the articles printed on this petition." On the back of the petition were two of Bluford's editorials from the *Call*, denouncing the impossible costs and insincerity of segregated graduate training and arguing for the inherent ability of the races to coexist on campus. Bluford printed hundreds of these petitions at the *Call* and then sent them to her agents—mostly boys who "threw" the paper—in cities and towns across Missouri. They collected thousands of signatures, which were sent back to the main office and then delivered to legislators in Jefferson City.[20]

In an article she wrote for the *Crisis*, Bluford described the events surrounding the Taylor Bill and eviscerated the notion of equalization put forth by the Missouri legislature. To illustrate the corrupt nature of House Bill 195, she began by explaining exactly who had proposed it. "The bill was introduced by John D. Taylor, lawyer from Keytesville ... whose anti-Negro record is common knowledge. ... Taylor is the man who once described himself as an 'unreconstructed rebel.'" His fellow legislators had to prevail upon him to stop using the N-word on the floor of the house, though when he was in his hometown he continued to refer to "his Negro constituents as 'my darkies.'" Bluford then described the schools that Taylor was responsible for in Keytesville:

Taylor has been president of the school board for years. Although he and the board have continued, year by year, to improve the white school . . . Negro children . . . attend the same old dilapidated, unpainted, frame two room shack that their parents attended 50 years ago, the same old scarred desks of 1880 vintage are there. They use the same out of door unsanitary toilets that their parents used and that the health officials of the county have condemned. Until this year, the children drank from a germ infested well, which was closed only when the county health officers ordered it so.

Obviously, Taylor could not "be sincere" in proposing "equal higher education for the Negro."[21]

The initial Taylor Bill hadn't even appropriated any funds. A few weeks after the first bill, Taylor introduced a separate appropriations bill, which allocated $200,000 in special funds for the "expansion" of Lincoln. The same bill gave the University of Missouri $3,000,000. "But the 'joker' in the whole situation," Bluford wrote, "comes in the words 'special fund.' We in Missouri are accustomed to special funds, which turn out to be 'no funds.'" Special funds consisted of whatever was left over after the state's regular budget had funded all other state functions. Such funds, promised year after year to Lincoln, rarely materialized. Even if the $200,000 was appropriated to Lincoln, Bluford wrote, it would never be enough money to create a school of journalism equal to that of the University of Missouri.[22]

As Bluford would highlight again and again in her reporting, a central problem with these funds was not just that they were unreliable, but that they constituted a form of corruption. There was no accountability or oversight governing the state's allocation to black schools. As segregated schools, they existed in a no-man's-land outside the legitimate concerns of the state. The special monies, when they appeared, were distributed through white school boards, which were also corrupt. White school boards would accept paltry or nonexistent sums for the black children in their districts, either because they did not believe in black education or because they preferred to look the other way. School board members wanted to work with people who would not question the status quo, and thus sought out the most cynical black school administrators they could find. This dynamic, Bluford held, was at work wherever segregated education existed. Other women activists after her would make the same charge. It was an unpalatable truth, one that implicated black school officials alongside the white school boards, and was therefore almost never discussed. Few had the stomach for it.[23]

When the Taylor Bill was being debated, two hundred African Americans showed up at the capitol building to protest. They were happily surprised when a hitherto unknown ally, a legislator from Hickory County, gave an impassioned speech on the floor, saying, "We denounce Hitler for his unjust discrimination against Jews. Our university's discrimination against Negroes is even less defensible." Unlike Germany, he argued, the United States guaranteed protection against discrimination in its Constitution. "Why," he asked, "exclude the children of Negro citizens of the state when the school is open to Japanese? I would rather have children of mine associate with those who have been good citizens of Missouri." (He had apparently been reading Bluford's editorials.) The speech fell on deaf ears, however, and the Taylor Bill passed.[24]

But the protests continued. By August 1939, the front page of the *Call* had become a war zone, as Bluford continued to attempt to register at the university and, simultaneously, the Lincoln University School of Law was established in the old Poro building on Pine Street in downtown St. Louis. Poro College, as it was once known, had been founded by entrepreneur Annie Malone to train agents to sell her cosmetics and other beauty products. Bluford fulminated against the "ruse" of a black law school. "Keep Fighting!" she urged, even as thirty students lined up to enroll. The new law school, as Bluford colorfully described it, was like a jerry built shack on a construction job, [it] is not the equal of Missouri University's school of law. The latter is the work of years and millions. The other can only be what any new school is. . . . Negroes naturally want to move into their larger citizenship. But law is slow. Decision will follow decision before the course of proper conduct will be clearly defined. In the meantime, patience! And keep your powder dry! The rights the courts declare are the Negro citizens' must be fought for until granted![25]

A group calling themselves the "Colored Clerks' Circle of St. Louis" formed a picket line in front of the Poro building, trying to dissuade students from registering. As these events unfolded, Bluford ran two front-page stories on August 4, 1939, side by side. One, "Name Dean for L.U. Law School: W.E. Taylor of Howard U. to New Post," praised the accomplishments of the new faculty of the law school. The second column, abutting the first, with an equally large headline, read "Picket New University Law School." As the two sides squared off in downtown St. Louis and on the front page of the *Call*, Bluford did not shrink from the potential dissonance this battle created for her readers, nor from the intra-racial conflict it revealed. "The Colored Clerks' Circle of St. Louis is still picketing the law school," she wrote in October 1939, "the signs on the backs of the youthful pickets calling the school a subterfuge." She continued, "Pickets also are around the home of Frank L. Williams, principal of the Vashon High School, who is a member of the Lincoln University Board of Curators. 'Were you the ninth person to vote for this Jim-Crow school, Mr. Williams?' it asks." Williams was one of the most respected black educators in the state, with a long list of local achievements, government posts, and public honors. Bluford made herself a powerful enemy when she published this story, accompanied by large photos of the protest. It reflected not simply her journalistic integrity but also her willingness to embarrass black leaders—mostly men—when they stood in the way of school deseg-regation efforts.[26]

In the autumn of 1939, school desegregation activists had more reason for disappointment when Lloyd Gaines suddenly disappeared. The NAACP, through the black press, put out calls for any information about the whereabouts of their client. Rumors began to circulate—that he had been bought off, that he was in the river, that he had been seen in New York and Mexico. In 2009, the *New York Times* ran a brief story about his disappearance, with the strong intimation that he was likely murdered. The feeling at the time, however, was that he simply left St. Louis, searching for the privacy he had lost when he became a guinea pig for the NAACP. He seemed "troubled" to those who knew him, was having "financial difficulties," and had grown increasingly disturbed by the case, his role in it, and the unsought fame it conferred. The NAACP was deeply disappointed. In a telling interview with an *Ebony* reporter, St. Louis lawyer Sidney Redmond said, "He had cooperated with us fully on the case, and at that time it was almost impossible to get anyone who would be willing to take part in that kind of lawsuit. Even some of the lawyers we first asked were a little reluctant to be associated with it. It was that kind of thing." Gaines had been at the University of Michigan in 1939 doing graduate work in economics while the LDF continued to press for his admission to MU and as the *Call* did battle with the state over the Taylor Bill and the Lincoln law school. He was last seen in public in March 1939 in St. Louis, where he gave a speech to a crowd of over a thousand at the Pine Street YMCA. (Bluford invited him and made the arrangements.) His last words—both to the public and in a letter to his mother—tell the story of someone who was in a great deal of pain.[27]

His speech was one of barely suppressed outrage: fury at how little had changed for African Americans since 1865 and frustration that more people were not involved in fighting for civil rights. "We were freed almost 80 years ago," he told the crowd, but "according to public policy we are still outside the pale of humanity. We are still jim-crowed and segregated." Why, he asked, were people not doing more? "It has been the policy of man all the way down the line to let George do it ... but there are some things that you must do for yourselves." Most painful, surely, to him, was the lack of support from his own friends. "Speaking of his own case," the *Call* reported, "Gaines said that he had to stand the criticism of personal friends and many acquaintances who told him that he was wrong in wanting to go to M.U.... 'Why didn't I go to some university which admitted Negroes ... they wanted to know why I wanted to start so much noise about entering M.U.'" In the following decades, most school desegregation plaintiffs would experience such criticism. Of all the burdens that desegregation pioneers had to shoulder—endless court battles, unsettled plans, humiliating comments from white school officials, media scrutiny—criticism from friends and neighbors was often the most painful part of the ordeal. There was so much division on the question of desegregation within black communities that hostility toward desegregation activists was inevitable. Yet many desegregation plaintiffs were surprised and deeply hurt by the level of anger directed at them by members of their own race.[28]

After the speech, Bluford put Gaines on a train to Chicago. She was the last person to see him in Missouri. He disappeared from Chicago a few weeks later. He left his rented room at the YMCA, telling the landlady that he was going out to buy stamps. He never came back to pick up his clothing or other personal items. But before he went missing, he sent two letters to his mother. The first was eight pages long. "As for my publicity relative to the university case," he wrote, "I have found that my race still likes to applaud, shake hands, pat me on the back and say how great and noble is the idea ... and there it ends." He wished he did not appear in the papers. He wished he did not have to make this "sacrifice—almost the 'supreme sacrifice'" alone. "I wish," he ended the letter, "I were just a plain, ordinary man whose name no one recognized." After this, there was one more letter—a postcard as sparse as the previous one had been overflowing. "Goodbye," he wrote. "If you don't hear from me anymore, you know I'll be all right." Asked in 1951 whether her son disappeared because of the case, his mother had this to say: "I do know he never intended going there [MU] He said he wasn't. . . . I remember once I asked him if he was going to that school, and he said 'No.'" The family never filed a missing persons report or a death certificate. Which is not to say definitively that Gaines did not meet foul play, but there is a great deal of evidence that he wanted, needed, and intended to walk away.[29]

There was hand-wringing and second-guessing all around. "The Strange Disappearance of Lloyd Gaines," made for good headlines, and the *Chicago Defender*, the *Pittsburgh Courier*, and the *Call* ran many of them. Pauli Murray—civil rights activist and eventual lawyer, feminist, and the first black female Episcopal priest—knew about Bluford's attempts to enroll at MU and was aware of her position at the *Kansas City Call*.[30] Murray had been attempting to enroll at the University of North Carolina since 1938. (The NAACP refused to take her case after Murray wrote one too many editorials to the *Tarheel*, the UNC campus newspaper; LDF lawyers decided that she looked too much like a radical agitator.) Murray sent Bluford an editorial about Gaines's disappearance for publication in 1940. But before that, she sent Gaines a letter. The day the Supreme Court decision was announced, Murray wrote to Gaines imploring him to follow through and attend the University of Missouri. That Murray understood how painful it would be for Gaines indicates what is now somewhat difficult to grasp—how tortuous attending a white school in 1938 would be. "I do hope you will accept your admission to the University of Missouri, even if it means a temporary sacrifice. The example you will set for other young Negroes of the South who need leadership and guidance will more than repay you for the torture endured."[31]

Murray's editorial for the *Call* complained of the same issues Gaines had been speaking of in his last public and private moments. Bluford put the piece on the front page. In "Who Is to Blame for Disappearance of Lloyd Gaines?" Murray, described as "The Girl Who Tried to Enter North Carolina," wrote, "I do not think . . . that Gaines is entirely to blame even if he permitted himself to be scared away. I am convinced that if he had been able to lean upon the Negro masses, he would have neither been intimidated nor bought off." Gaines, she said insightfully, "was almost a solitary figure in a tremendous conflict, raising issues not raised so fundamentally since the War between the states. The Gaines decision . . . was an attack on the basic institutions of the Civil War South." The willingness on the part of black educators and prospective students to accept the Lincoln University School of Law, she wrote, must have been profoundly demoralizing for him to watch. "What actually happened after the Decision was handed down? . . . He saw no unity of purpose anywhere within the race; he saw frightened Negro leaders . . . rush to the aid of a Negro law school, which was being erected to evade the Supreme Court mandate. Most disappointing of all he witnessed the indifference of the . . . Negro population."[32]

She imagined—perhaps from her own experience—how he felt. "How much fellowship did Gaines have within his own group? How many negroes [sic] were there to stand behind him every step of the way, with funds, with letters, telegrams and demonstrations?" She continued, "Not a single mass demonstration [was] held anywhere in the country!" Murray urged young people to apply to graduate schools across the nation, to accept nothing less, "dollar for dollar," than what the white universities had. Like Bluford, she lambasted education officials, including a North Carolina college administrator who had accepted funding for a proposed segregated law school, which never materialized. "We will sell our birthright for the mess of porridge to be found in Negro 'make-shift' graduate schools. If this happens we will have forfeited one of the greatest opportunities in our lifetime to achieve a body *blow to inequality.*" She ended her editorial with two lines, separated from the last paragraph: "Find Lloyd Gaines, if he can be found. If not, finish the job he left uncompleted."[33]

Murray was a powerful, unique writer. She was a visionary destined to make groundbreaking intellectual contributions to both civil rights and feminist causes. As early as 1939 she argued that African Americans ought to follow in the footsteps of Gandhi's anti-colonial protests in India and form a mass movement. But there were important overlaps with Bluford's writing, too—and connections to future women school desegregation activists. Chiefly, she was not afraid to get in the ring with specific black administrators who were fighting against her. "Last Spring," she reported, "the president of the North Carolina College for Negroes was more concerned with the new buildings on his campus . . . than with the tragic fact that the state . . . was using him as the cat, to pull its 'jim-crow' chestnuts out of a very hot fire." Compare this to Charles Houston's speech in October 1939 complaining of the same problem: "Virginia, Tennessee, Maryland—all of those states in the wake of lawsuits immediately came up with funds for libraries or other improvements at black institutions. [But] you can't buy all of us. Some of us don't need your money. Some of us need it but won't take it." Houston's words expressed the same frustration in terms that were less specific, more above the fray. Houston could position himself in this way, however, in part because Bluford and Murray were busy fighting in the trenches for him. Both women were unafraid to name their adversaries: the president of the North Carolina College for Negroes, and Frank L. Williams, Vashon High School principal and Lincoln board member. It was dirty work, but they believed they had to put a name to the issue, so that readers could see for themselves what was happening. Generalities would not do. Bluford and Murray were no doubt despised by the powerful educators they targeted—and widely admired by young people—especially by those protesting the Lincoln law school in front of Frank L. Williams's house.[34]

In August 1939, Bluford stepped up her efforts to enter the University of Missouri School of Journalism. She reappeared in S. W. Canada's office, she visited Lincoln University to assess progress on the new Lincoln School of Journalism (there was none), and then addressed a series of letters to Henry Bent, dean of the graduate faculty at MU; Frederick A. Middlebush, president of the university; and Frank McDavid, president of the Board of Curators. She updated them all on the status of the journalism school at Lincoln and insisted that she be allowed to enroll at MU immediately. She also conferred with Kansas City lawyer Sidney Redmond, who had worked on *Gaines*. By October, Houston and the LDF had come to terms with the fact that they could not locate Gaines. Houston immediately turned his attention to the Bluford case. He was supportive of Bluford, writing to her that her lawsuit would "focus attention on Negro women" while also serving to "keep public attention focused on the University problem." This was not the first time that Houston had encouraged women to act as desegregation plaintiffs. Murray kept a clipping in her files that reported "more youths, especially co-eds were urged by Charles H. Houston . . . to file applications for admission to lily-white institutions of higher learning." Later, Houston said in a letter to Bluford, "Yours would be the first case of a Negro woman actually being . . . either admitted or refused at a State University." The novelty of a woman applicant, he said, "would have much more publicity value than a man."[35]

Bluford's case did indeed spark the headlines Houston wanted and redirected attention away from the dispiriting news about Gaines. Houston had a two-pronged plan: Bluford would apply for a mandamus—a writ from the court demanding that a public official perform his or her statutory duty (that is, for Canada to immediately admit her)—and a damages suit, to pay her for lost time during which she could have been pursuing her degree. The idea of filing

for damages was to make segregation impossibly expensive for the
state. On October 13, 1939, the *Call's* headline was "File Another
Suit." "Miss Lucile Bluford," it began, "who twice has been denied
admittance to the University of Missouri School of Journalism will
go to Columbia today where attorneys will file in the Boone County
circuit court a petition for a writ of mandamus against the university." The *Chicago Defender* used a large font for the headline, "Barred
Student Files Damage Suit against the University of Missouri," then
again in November for a front-page story, "Girl Sues University
of MO. for $20,000." The *Pittsburgh Courier* put her name in the
headline, "Lucille [*sic*] Bluford Sues for $20,000." Other headlines
made statements about the status of the Gaines case, immediately
followed by information about the Bluford case. "Lloyd Gaines Case
Has Been Dismissed," the *Courier* wrote. But just under the headline, in smaller type, was "Fight for Equal Education in Missouri to
Go On as Group Prepares for Battle in Bluford Suit."[36]

In an editorial entitled "Halted but Not Stopped," Bluford asked
her readers to have patience and remain hopeful. "Though we are
disappointed that Lloyd Gaines . . . is not present to do his part in
the next step of the litigation we are not discouraged. . . . Some day if
not Gaines, another Negro will stand at the bar of justice demanding
equal educational opportunity. In time Negroes will develop cham-
pions, who will match what Nathan Hale did for the revolting col-
onists at the cost of his life." Bluford was in the midst of answering
her own call to action, and, perhaps in her more romantic moments,
saw herself in the colonial soldier that she invoked.[37]

The next few years saw mostly repeated rejections and draining,
nasty legal tactics by the University of Missouri. An unexpected
bright spot, however, emerged in the spring of 1940, when a group
of about 150 white college girls filled the courtroom to overflowing,
arriving en masse to hear Bluford's historic trial. *Call* writer Dorothy H. Davis reported on this surprise showing with undisguised
enthusiasm:

The courtroom was crowded throughout the trial, mostly by students from Stephens College, an exclusive white girls' school of Columbia. They stood four deep in the rear and sides of the room and sat on the floor in front of seats in the front of the room. During noon recesses some of them remained in order to hold their seats, sending out for sandwiches and malted milk for lunch. . . . Early in the trial the students became sympathetic towards Miss Bluford. During the first part of Ms. Bluford's cross examination [an] argument . . . developed. . . . Miss Bluford held her ground so well and with such assurance that the white students in the audience burst into laughter and loud applause. . . . Judge Dinwiddie immediately ordered the courtroom cleared, in an action unprecedented in the history of the Boone County District Court.[38]

The sandwiches, the informal seating, the spontaneous, unruly laughter, the inappropriate applause and general cacophony all give a sense of the women's youthful enthusiasm. Reports of the noisy approbation of Bluford ran for two weeks in the *Call* alongside a large picture of the girls surrounding Bluford. They are all in their late teens and early twenties, looking conservative in smart skirts and jackets, knee socks and saddle shoes, some hugging schoolbooks to their chest, all gazing admiringly at twenty-eight-year-old Bluford. Other black newspapers and the Associated Press also picked up the story. The *Pittsburgh Courier* went with "White Girl Students Banished at MO. Trial: Cheered Efforts of Miss Bluford to Attend MO. Univ." The white Columbia, Missouri, *Daily Tribune*, however, was not amused. Its headline read, "Negro Woman Seeking to Enter University Parries Attorney Question, Seeks to Force Entrance, Obstinate Attitude Starts Applause and Court Order Room Cleared."[39]

Charles Houston was thrilled. When he had come to St. Louis to argue the Gaines case in 1938, the crowd had been disappointingly thin—a fact that had affected everyone's morale, including the plaintiff's. In a memorandum to Walter White, Houston described

Bluford's two-day trial in detail. "The trial was a community event," he enthused. "The courtroom was more crowded than for the Crawford case [the George Crawford murder case in 1932, Houston's most crowded trial to date]. Girl students were sitting on the floor, the aisles and rear of the room were packed." The courtroom full of young people inspired Houston to take a more professorial tack, making Bluford and her associates at the *Call* an object lesson in black accomplishment and readiness to join white students at the University of Missouri. "I tried the case as a social issue as well as a legal issue. . . . This meant explaining each step so the students could understand. That took us two days." As part of his lesson to the students, he read two of Bluford's editorials on segregated education in open court. Then, "by way of impressing the students and the court that this university movement is a ground swell, we went into the qualifications of all our witnesses." By "ground swell," it seems Houston meant both that the desegregation of graduate schools was a grassroots movement and that there was a pipeline of qualified students ready to attend the university on equal footing with white students.[40]

"We started with Lucile, showed how her father had moved from North Carolina . . . to give his children a better chance." Houston elicited from Bluford all of the educational accomplishments of every member of her family. "You could hear the murmur that went over the court room as [Bluford] very quietly and simply recited the facts. The reporters say it made a profound impression." After putting Bluford's colleagues at the *Call* on the stand and having them similarly list their degrees and attainments, Ada Franklin, the wife of *Call* founder Chester A. Franklin, took the stand. Franklin recited her long list of educational achievements and positions of responsibility, at which point "the court room turned out [erupted]." Then, Franklin added that, in addition to all her other responsibilities, she had to take care of the editor of the *Kansas City Call*, too. "This put everybody in a good humor, and in the best of spirits Hogsett [the opposing counsel] smiled and asked her if it was a full-time job. The whole room went into high glee." Hogsett's whole case, Houston then explained, was that Bluford had not applied to MU in good faith but was merely "lending herself to our educational campaign as a straw plaintiff." Bluford "vigorously denied this," and when Hogsett demanded that she produce letters between herself and Houston, she adamantly refused. This was when the girls in the courtroom got rowdy, cheering Bluford's stubborn refusal. When the girls were allowed back in the next day, Houston continued to aim his words at them. "Folks say that my argument was more a sermon than anything else. . . . The courtroom was with me. I took longer than usual, but it was because I was determined that the students should not leave without getting our point of view."[41]

In addition to an education in civil rights law, the girls in the courtroom were also treated to some soaring oratory. In his closing statement, Houston created a compelling picture: "A girl stands at the door and a generation waits outside." By pointing to Bluford's status as a girl, he was making a connection between her and the girls in the audience. In this moment, she was not part of the NAACP or a journalist or an activist. She was—as Mary McLeod Bethune and other black women leaders had advocated—a thoughtful, poised, socially open girl whose job it was to reach out to sympathetic whites on behalf of the race.[42]

It should be noted that Stephens College, the school attended by the white women in the courtroom, was not simply an "exclusive white girls' school." It was one of the oldest women's colleges in the country, with a mandate to educate women stretching back to its founding in 1833. In 1944, it became the first college in the country to offer an aviation program for women. The inclusion of women in professions from which they were otherwise barred was part of the school's mission. Did this mission affect the girls' perspective on Bluford? Why did these particular young white women feel they could be so expressive, so obstreperous and noisy, on the issue of racial justice—in the presence of a county judge and a courtroom full of white officials and professionals? It is difficult to imagine that these young upper-middle-class white women were quite so disrespectful to white officials in any other aspect of their lives. With their laughter and loud comments, they were not only disrespectful to the judge but also registering contempt for the legal system that was oppressing Bluford. It must have been empowering to take a stand, at least until they were barred from the courtroom. Clearly, these women felt some kind of personal connection with Bluford and her fight for admission to MU. Whether it was solidarity based on gender, or a particular calling to the issue of segregated education, it was enough to create a critical mass of girls willing to disrupt the state's business.

Bluford was also moved by the girls' support and shared her surprise and delight with her readers for two weeks running, with large photos and big captions such as "White Girls Want Lucile Bluford to Win" and "We Hope You Get In—We're for You." When looking back on her MU trial fifty-three years later, the applause of the Stephens College girls was one of the first memories Bluford recalled to a reporter. The spirited display by young white women was not simply personally meaningful to Bluford. She seems to have believed that their presence was historically significant and valuable to the postwar school desegregation battle. After this experience, she committed herself to reporting on the activities of white girls and women when they merited attention—a commitment that was highly unusual. Other black newspapers reported on white students who professed progressive racial views, but such reporting was reserved for high-profile undergraduates, such as those who voted to make Levi Jackson captain of the Yale football team in 1949. Bluford, in contrast, wrote about young women who would have otherwise remained anonymous. In "White Girl Deplores Bias at FHA Meet," Bluford wrote about the "sensation" that was created when a teenage girl urged several thousand of her contemporaries "not to be

stampeded into accepting the racial prejudice of the older generations" at a meeting of the Future Homemakers of America. She also
reported on a protest against segregation at the University of Oklahoma in 1948 led by a young woman named Jody Casey, who dramatically burned a copy of the Fourteenth Amendment in front of
the assembled crowd and sent the ashes to President Truman. These
stories, and many others like them, foreshadow Bluford's eventual
alliance with Esther Brown, a young white woman who helped initiate a school desegregation lawsuit in South Park, Kansas, in 1948,
Webb v. District No. 90, that proved to be the forerunner of the bigger trial in Topeka.[43]

Between 1940 and 1942, while continuing to write stories in
the *Call* about both the progress and setbacks in her battle against
MU, Bluford was stage-managing every aspect of her case behind
the scenes. It was a highly coordinated effort, both on legal strategy
and public relations. Bluford kept Houston apprised of every move
by MU and Lincoln University. Houston responded with lengthy
directives, assigning her any and all administrative tasks related to
her case, including arranging his travel details and speaking engage-
ments, and even giving her regular advice about editorials she should
publish. He wrote:

> Here is something else you should do at once. Get the current Uni-
> versity of Missouri catalogue showing the graduate courses offered
> next semester, together with the instructors teaching the same.
> Write the President and Board of Curators of Lincoln University
> and list such courses with names of instructors as the ones offered
> at U. Missouri and as the ones you want at Lincoln; and further say
> that you expect the instruction offered at Lincoln to be substan-
> tially equal to that offered at U. Missouri, and by instructors having
> comparable qualifications and experience. You should state specif-
> ically in this letter that you are writing now to put both Lincoln
> University and the University of Missouri on ample notice. Send a

copy of this letter to Canada. . . . Register both the letter to Lincoln
and the one to Canada.

In another letter, he instructed, "Next I think you should make a trip
to Lincoln University next week. . . . Write an editorial in the *Call*
setting out objectively just wherein Lincoln University fails to offer
substantially the equivalent of the work available in the University
of Missouri."[44]

Bluford was applicant, correspondent, secretary, legal accomplice,
spy, reporter, and editorialist. She procured course catalogs, wrote
detailed letters, met with Lincoln and MU school officials, arranged
to have Houston visit the state, and editorialized about these activities in a large circulation weekly. Any one of these activities would
be onerous. Conducted together over the course of years, they were
Herculean, requiring not only long hours, endless paperwork, time
on the road, and overtime at the office but also a stunning amount
of commitment and emotional effort. It is clear that, while Houston
argued the case in the courtroom, Bluford was making the case to
the public, using words and images far more exciting than lawyerly
minutia.

May and June of 1940 brought bad news. Bluford lost both the
mandamus and the damages case. William Hogsett convinced the
Missouri jury that Bluford was not a genuine applicant and that
she only wished to disrupt the traditional boundaries separating
the races. As such, she was entitled neither to the mandamus nor to
the damages. "Bluford Action Denied," reported the *Courier*. As her
lawsuit dragged on unsuccessfully, through multiple appeals in 1941
and 1942, Bluford began to show signs of frustration and anger—
somewhat like Gaines did in the spring of 1939, when his own lawsuit was several years old. She was certainly done, for the moment,
with keeping quiet about Gaines. While the NAACP maintained a
dignified silence about their missing plaintiff, Bluford began to publish what clues she could collect: "A former schoolmate of Gaines

said that he heard regularly from the Missouri U. Case principal whose letters were postmarked from Mexico, Mo. And then Paris, Ill." She also managed to dig up and report on the postcard he sent his mother. As the second anniversary approached of the founding of what everyone was now calling "the Poro law school," she wrote, "The Poro law school, opened as the result of Gaines' suit against M.U., will open its second term soon. We wonder what Gaines will be doing on enrollment day?"[45]

She also began to speak more about her rights and less about civic decency. Characteristically blunt, and with a gimlet eye trained on the farcical outcomes of Jim Crow schools, Bluford took an angrier tone in interviews given to members of the black press. In a story published in the *Chicago Defender*, she told a reporter that she had visited Lincoln to check on the progress of the journalism school. "She found, however, no buildings, offices, classrooms. . . . The office of the dean of the school of journalism was found to be in a bedroom of one of the instructors in the Science hall." In May 1942, after the University of Missouri shuttered its journalism school, she said to the press, "I refuse to permit my career to be thwarted by the erroneous verdict of a jury egged on by the most vicious appeal to race prejudice [by Hogsett] I have ever heard."[46]

She finally became exhausted. When Missouri closed the journalism school in response to her ongoing lawsuit (the school claimed it was because of wartime shortages), Bluford wrote to Houston that she would like to continue her lawsuit, even though, "to be very frank, I dread another trial and if I considered only my personal feelings . . . I would say that it would be a great relief to withdraw the suit just to escape another grilling from Hogsett and the ordeal of facing another Missouri Jury." Here we see the toll that the courtroom experiences took on her. She was weary and dispirited from experiencing racist posturing in close quarters and facing jurists as they pronounced Lincoln's still-unbuilt school of journalism the equal of MU. And yet, Bluford fought through her own exhaustion and urged Houston to continue, even offering to help fund the law-suit. "I hope the N.A.A.C.P. will be able to continue financing the case," she wrote, "although I realize that the war-time demands upon the association may be too great to warrant putting more funds into the Missouri fight. I will be able to stand some of the expense." But the LDF decided that litigating against a closed journalism school was not a promising use of its time. As Bluford's lawsuit faced its final stage, Houston suggested that she write to Canada and tell him to consider hers as a standing application, and then publish the fact in the *Call*. "With this appearing in this week's *Call* every Negro will take heart, because they all expected you to lose but are thankful for the fight."[47]

———

While Bluford did sound different in her public statements in 1942 than in 1939, the tough talk and the uncompromising reporting had been there from the beginning in her hard-hitting journalism and unusual commitment to publishing stories about intra-racial discord. Bluford was an enormously courageous writer and deseg-regation pioneer. In her forays into the MU campus, she exhibited another quality: social optimism and an unusual ability to connect with white students and faculty. Bluford brought a multilayered set of skills to school desegregation. She was both hardheaded and gre-garious. Tough talk overlapped with warm gestures, the celebration of small gains with impatience for racial progress. She had a perspec-tive that could take into account the importance of civic decency *and* the necessity to do battle in the courtroom, even when that meant parrying with racist lawyers. She used all of these strengths in her many trips the University of Missouri, in her editorializing and po-litical activism, and in her court case.

In 1942, Bluford finally let go of her pursuit of the University of Missouri School of Journalism and turned her energies to track-ing down information on school desegregation lawsuits throughout the South. She continued, too, to hold all school activists—whether white or black, whether fighting for desegregation or equalization—accountable. She would continue to report on school-board corruption, and the painful disputes that cropped up around school litigation continued to make headlines in the *Call*.

In 1984, the University of Missouri awarded Bluford an honorary degree. Such awards mounted as she reached old age and apparently meant little to her. "A handful of her own honors are hung in the newsroom," the *Kansas City Star* reported. But "staffers did it themselves . . . after fruitlessly nagging their boss to do it." According to the *Star*, "Bluford's friend of 40 years," Ellen Yates, stockpiled Bluford's awards for her. "More [awards] sit in the bottom of [my] dresser drawer," said Yates. "We'd go places and they'd give her these awards and then she'd just leave them in the car."[48]

When Bluford went to the University of Missouri campus to receive her honorary degree in 1984, she took it upon herself to look up S. W. Canada, now retired and living just off campus. "I went out to his house," she told a local reporter. "He was kind of slow; he was on a cane. I said, 'I'm Lucile Bluford, remember me?' He smiled and said, 'Oh yes, yes, I remember you, come on in' . . . We had a nice chat. He wanted to make sure I knew there wasn't anything personal about it, and I said, 'Yes, yes, I understand.'" The fault did not lie with Canada, she continued: "It was the university. It was the state. It was the law. They had a *law*." Seeking out Canada remained the most powerful impulse Bluford had. She went to the university that day not only to collect an accolade but also to continue the crusade she had begun forty-five years earlier. She sought out and extended herself to Canada—as she had done the first time she went to campus in 1939—so that he might be able to extend himself back to her. It was yet another opportunity for civic decency. Bluford's message was clear: school desegregation was both a legal and a social endeavor. Acknowledging the second was as important as the first. Indeed, by 1984, the legal questions had been at least temporarily resolved, but, from Bluford's perspective, the social questions had not. It would take ongoing attempts at social connection for the university to become truly desegregated.[49]

Bluford's college friend Mary Louise Chapman captured Bluford's crusading style during her years as a desegregation pioneer: "She has been told she can't eat here, she can't come in here, she can't go to school here, she can't do this and can't do that. But with a steady stare, a friendly little smile and an unnatural calm, she did the things they told her she couldn't do." It was an approach that would be mirrored almost exactly—the same smile, determination, and unyielding patience—by another pioneer of the 1940s, Ada Lois Sipuel.[50]

2

"This Lone Negro Girl"

Ada Lois Sipuel, Desegregation Champion

WHEN ASKED, NEARLY FORTY YEARS later, what inspired the school desegregation lawsuit in her home town of Topeka, activist Berdyne Scott did not mention the conditions of the local public schools or her own participation in the NAACP. She replied simply: "I remember Ada Sipuel came to town with her lawyer." Elaborating on why Sipuel was such an inspirational figure seemed unnecessary. To Scott—as to the rest of her generation—Sipuel was the famous, universally acclaimed school desegregation crusader of the pre-*Brown* era. As law professor Anita Hill recalls, growing up in the 1950s in Oklahoma, "Ada Lois Sipuel Fisher was a larger than life legend." And yet, historians have largely relegated Sipuel to a footnote in the story of *Brown v. Board* and the civil rights movement, and few people today know who she was or what she accomplished.[1]

After World War II, the LDF contacted branches throughout the South announcing a renewed effort—halted during the war—to attack segregated education at the graduate level. It was looking for plaintiffs who would be willing to apply to a segregated state professional school, preferably a law school. Behind the scenes, Thurgood Marshall was hoping to find a plaintiff in Texas, in part because he knew NAACP state coffers were flush and he had long-standing relationships with NAACP officials there. Ultimately, plaintiffs came forward in several southern states.

Ada Lois Sipuel was the first African American person to apply to an all-white graduate school in the United States after World War II, presenting herself and her stellar credentials to the registrar at the University of Oklahoma College of Law on January 14, 1946. In 1948, she became the only graduate student plaintiff to say no—immediately and unequivocally—to the state's offer to set up a separate "Negro law school." When she was finally admitted to the law school, in 1948, she became the only graduate student to pass all of her classes as a segregated "Negro student," and then the only such student-plaintiff to graduate. In 1950, Sipuel—now with the eyes of the nation and world upon her—passed the bar exam and became the first and only practicing black lawyer in the state of Oklahoma who had been trained within its borders.

During the years before she was admitted to the law school, as Sipuel tried many times to register and was turned away, and as she attended countless meetings, public events, fund-raisers, court hearings, and judicial rulings, her case began to be referred to as the "popular Sipuel case," and Sipuel herself as "that brilliant girl." But the press did not follow Sipuel with such avidity merely because she was persistent. What attracted people to Sipuel was the finesse with which she performed the role of school desegregation pioneer. She was engaging, and at times even exuberant, with press. She had both tough words and a ready smile for reporters, and she communicated a disarming excitement about her case alongside a steely determination to vanquish the University of Oklahoma. Her statements to the public were nuanced, perfectly timed, and communicated in such a way as to make her presence on the University of Oklahoma campus appear not only possible but natural. It was no mean feat.[2]

The second reason for Sipuel's popularity was contextual: she refused to consider the state's offer to provide a segregated graduate school at a time when most plaintiffs settled for separate "Negro" professional schools—whether in a stand-alone building, like the Lincoln law school in St. Louis, or attached to an extant black university campus. Most pointedly, Sipuel stood in contrast to Heman Sweatt. Sweatt had an ambivalent attitude toward school desegregation, but the NAACP thrust him into the national spotlight when it named him as plaintiff in a case against the University of Texas law school a few months after Sipuel's case was filed. When the LDF so publicly put the NAACP's resources behind a wavering candidate in Texas, it fostered a public sense of disappointment, a void that Sipuel would step in to fill. The impact of Sweatt's public equivocations about school desegregation illuminates a simple truth about desegregation pioneers: there can be no successful lawsuits without committed plaintiffs. It would fall to the black press to remind the lawyers in New York of this fundamental fact as they set about covering both plaintiffs.

Despite Sweatt's vacillations, Thurgood Marshall would ultimately make legal headway with the 1950 Supreme Court ruling in *Sweatt v. Painter*, which outlawed segregation in graduate education in its entirety. But in the intervening years, "the girl who started the fight," as the black press referred to Sipuel, would ignite the aspirations of those numerous parents, young women, and girls who came forward to follow in her footsteps. For many, the revelation that school desegregation was in their grasp came not from the persuasive power of NAACP officials and lawyers, but from the "young girl" who would not be turned down. It was only with slight exaggeration that Roscoe Dunjee, editor of Oklahoma City's *Black Dispatch*, proclaimed in January 1949 that "this lone Negro girl" had, with her lawsuit, "done more to bring to the attention of the nation the question of educational inequality than any other experience we have had during 1948.... We have learned with the Sipuel case that it takes occasionally a little social dynamite to blast paths of advancement and progress."[3]

———

Sipuel was born in 1924 in Chickasha (pronounced Chick-a-shay), Oklahoma, a small town southwest of Oklahoma City that she proudly described in her autobiography as more "Wild West" than "Old South." Her parents, Martha Bell Smith Sipuel and Travis B. Sipuel, moved from Tulsa to Chickasha after the infamous Tulsa race riot of 1921 that left thirty-five square blocks of its black neighborhood—including the Sipuel home—burned to the ground. Sipuel grew up with stories about the lynching of Dick Rowland, which sparked the violence in Tulsa, as well as the lynching of Henry Argo just northeast of Chickasha in 1930, the last recorded lynching in Oklahoma.[4]

The stories Sipuel heard wove together wrenching details of white violence with black armed resistance. When a married white woman accused Argo of rape (locals of both races later agreed that the two were involved in an ongoing, consensual relationship), Sheriff Matt Sankey had one of his black deputies arrest the nineteen-year-old and place him in the county jail. A large mob subsequently formed around the courthouse. In response, W. A. J. Bullock, a local doctor and pillar of the black community, gathered a group of black men to stand outside the jail to protect Argo. They managed to keep the white mob at bay for two nights, until Sankey convinced them that the danger had passed. Soon after Bullock and his men had departed, however, the mob stormed the jail and stabbed Argo in the chest. The mob then threatened to drag Argo's body through the black section of Chickasha, whereupon Bullock resummoned his men, this time to Minnesota Street, the dividing line between the black and white sections of town. Bullock declared that any white man who tried to cross it "would die in colored town." The white mob dispersed. Fifteen years later, Bullock would come to the Sipuel home seeking a plaintiff to sue the University of Oklahoma.[5]

After the Argo lynching, Martha Sipuel put her first political sign on the family's automobile, which read "To Hell with Matt Sankey." She and the rest of Chickasha's black population coalesced around the slogan "Remember Henry Argo," and they helped to oust the sheriff from office with a two-thousand-vote majority. Thereafter, Martha Sipuel served as part of an informal black caucus, interviewing, vetting, and endorsing political candidates in return for delivering black votes. Eventually, Martha Sipuel became a major political force in Chickasha, brokering deals that led to improvements in the black part of town, including much-needed asphalt roads. She amassed so much power that in 1941 the mayor contributed $100 to a legal defense fund she had created for another Oklahoma black man accused of rape, W. D. Lyons.[6]

The daughter of a mixed-race woman and a white man, Martha Sipuel could easily have passed for white. There were times when she was ordered off the "black car" or sent back to the white part of town by white policemen. Martha Sipuel corrected those who were mistaken about her identity, even when it angered whites—which it often did. When one of her white relatives invited her to visit him at his office—he was an elected official in Arkansas—but cautioned her not to bring her "little pickaninnies" with her, she slammed the phone down on him. These experiences only sharpened Martha Sipuel's political perspective: she was an active member of the NAACP and made sure that her children read the *Chicago Defender*, the *Crisis*, and Dunjee's *Black Dispatch*, which she kept on the coffee table in the living room at all times.

Travis B. Sipuel, a minister of the Pentecostal Church of God in Christ, was the moral leader in the family. He inspired Ada with his speaking ability and charismatic sermons. The son of former slaves in rural Mississippi, Travis Sipuel grew up on the same plantation where his family had lived and labored for generations under slavery and afterward. Fleeing the Deep South, he worked on the railroad, eventually becoming a foreman. Martha Sipuel taught him how to read when they married in 1908, and soon thereafter he became a minister. In 1930, when Ada was six years old, her father was promoted to superintendent of the southwestern Oklahoma districts, and then later to state bishop of Oklahoma. Ada adored her father and found him more lenient and indulgent than her mother. But because he was away a great deal, her mother was left to largely direct the children's upbringing. Travis Sipuel's position in the church also allowed the family to live in relative material comfort. The Sipuels were one of only two black families in town with a phone and a radio. People from the neighborhood came to the Sipuel home to listen to the news, call their employers, or pick up messages.[7]

Even though her mother could be strict, Ada was given a great deal of freedom. She exploited that freedom to its fullest, roaming the neighborhood yards, streets, vacant lots, and railroad tracks with her older brother, Lemuel (the parks were "whites only"). She was, as she called herself, a regular "tomboy." She followed Lemuel everywhere he went, even to school when she was four years old, learning to read and write alongside him and rendering her own first years of school impossibly tedious. Fights regularly broke out on the way home, and Lemuel taught his sister how to help out: "To throw and block punches and move in." Because she was a minister's daughter, some initially thought she was a safe target for taunting without retaliation. "My father may be a preacher," she would tell them, "but I'm not."[8]

In school, Sipuel was unusually confident, competitive, and "smart-mouthed." In the early grades, when she was bored, she was frequently punished for "talking back." Her verbal and physical aggressiveness would find better outlets at Lincoln High School on the debate and basketball teams. Five feet eight inches tall, lithe, and quick, Sipuel was an excellent guard. Her defensive group was so physical that the coach decided to pair them up with the boys' team for practice. She also found time to be a soloist in the school choir and, indeed, a brilliant student, graduating valedictorian of her class. Despite her competitive nature and personal ambition, Sipuel later emphasized that all of the students at Lincoln High School were valued, supported, and taught that they were "special." Though Sipuel realized she could sound sentimental when looking back at her segregated upbringing, her affection for that time stemmed from the belief that her committed teachers, the bonds of family and church, and even her hardscrabble fistfights prepared her well for the difficult battles that lay ahead.[9]

———

Originally, the Oklahoma City branch of the NAACP sought to recruit Lemuel Sipuel to apply to the University of Oklahoma. W. A. J. Bullock met with the family in the fall of 1945. He told them that Lemuel was the ideal candidate: he had proved himself in battle as a soldier in the US Army and had graduated from Langston University, the only black university in Oklahoma, with a 4.0 grade point average. The NAACP needed an applicant who was not only academically proven but someone who could withstand "a long and probably bitter controversy." Bullock recited the facts about the mysterious disappearance of Lloyd Gaines after years of legal and personal trials, and added that it would be necessary for Lemuel to complete his law training in Norman, Oklahoma—a town where African Americans were not permitted after dark. Lemuel had just returned from Europe, where he had fought for three years. He had always planned to attend Howard Law School, and now he was in a hurry. When Lemuel turned Bullock down, Ada immediately started hoping. It is unclear if she volunteered, her mother suggested her, or Bullock asked her. Whatever the case, Bullock left the house with Ada's name instead of Lemuel's to put forward to the NAACP. He warned her that other NAACP officers were fanning out across the state to look for plaintiffs, and she might not be chosen. However, given the NAACP's difficulty in finding plaintiffs in other states to apply to graduate schools, and based on the speed with which Roscoe Dunjee selected Sipuel, it is safe to conjecture that there were few if any other volunteers.[10]

When Sipuel arrived at the University of Oklahoma College of Law in January 1946, the white, and almost exclusively male, law students were made uneasy by her presence. "Normally in enrollment period you have long lines of students, and when I walked up and got in the line there were looks of surprise all around and I would say half the line stepped aside to look at me," she recalled in a 1981 interview. In what would become a characteristically upbeat response to such situations, Sipuel took advantage of the opening and "stepped in front of them and got down to the counter." After her failed attempt to register, Sipuel and Dunjee met with the president of the university, George Cross. Cross later recalled that Sipuel was "chic" and "charming." Sipuel had dressed with care that morning, wearing a smart suit and a fashionable animal pelt draped around her shoulders, perhaps inspired by her own love of hunting. Her clothes and confident demeanor gave her a sophisticated, undaunted air—early evidence of the charisma that would later add to her allure with the national press.[11]

On January 15, 1946, the day after Sipuel's trip to the University of Oklahoma, Dunjee wrote a confident and celebratory letter to Thurgood Marshall, exclaiming, "Here's your case, and I think it's what one would call a 'natural.'" He described their meeting with Cross, where the president noted that "Miss Sipuel's scholastic credits are nearly perfect," and that her "transcript entitled her to enter the law classes of the university without examinations." Dunjee also reported that the president told him confidentially that he would put anything in writing that "you feel will get you into court." "Let me know when you can come down and file the case," Dunjee signed off. It was the first and last optimistic letter he would send to the NAACP's national office.[12]

———

The desegregation lawsuit against the University of Texas School of Law was troubled from the beginning. In July 1945, Austin lawyer and NAACP official Kenneth R. Lamkin wrote to Marshall with the unfortunate news that the prospective law school desegregation plaintiff had "changed his mind about filing at the University of Texas Law School. So that puts us back where we started." In August, Dallas NAACP secretary A. Maceo Smith wrote to Marshall that out of five suggested plaintiffs, only one met the "qualifications" necessary. Everyone knew what those qualifications were. NAACP lawyer William Hastie had written in 1933 that an ideal plaintiff was a person of "outstanding scholarship . . . neat, personable . . . who measure[s] up in every respect to collegiate standards." When in mid-August the organization finally found such a young man, he too had to withdraw because of "opposition [from] his family." Several other prospective plaintiffs—all of them men— were considered but then ruled out for various reasons.[13]

Given the many frustrations and dashed hopes in Texas, both local and national leaders must have been relieved when, in October 1945, Heman Sweatt, a thirty-two-year-old letter carrier, postal union organizer, and part-time reporter for the *Houston Informer*, volunteered. When Houston branch executive secretary Lulu White made an appeal at a meeting at the Wesley Chapel AME Church, Sweatt bravely offered himself as plaintiff. A World War II veteran and a calm, reserved, dapper man, Sweatt had graduated from Wiley College in Texas and completed a year of graduate work at the University of Michigan. The NAACP's nine-month search finally seemed to have come to an end.[14]

But Texas NAACP officials soon began to worry. On January 28, 1946 (fourteen days after Sipuel had applied to the University of

Oklahoma), W. J. Durham wrote to Marshall asking if Sweatt's tran-script was sufficient. "Will you be kind enough to check his credits and advise me whether or not in your opinion his educational quali-fications will meet the test?"[15] Sweatt's transcript from Wiley showed more gentleman's C's than Durham was comfortable with. Sweatt volunteered knowing that his academic record was imperfect— a fact that speaks to the selflessness of the act and perhaps explains why he only stepped in when the NAACP could find no one else. That Marshall signed off on the transcript reflects his deep determi-nation to find a plaintiff in Texas. This was Marshall's first mistake in the Texas case, and it proved to be an unconscionable disservice to Sweatt. It was the LDF's responsibility to locate a plaintiff who fit the necessary criteria. Marshall, unlike Sweatt, knew from expe-rience what kind of scrutiny and public pressure the plaintiff would have to endure, and, if Sweatt was accepted, how difficult the work in law school would be.

Then there was the issue of the Sweatt family's politics. After the announcement that Heman Sweatt would be suing the Univer-sity of Texas, his brother John Sweatt publicly stated that only "Joe Stalin" could open the gates of the university, indicating both a lack of confidence in his brother's lawsuit and radical leftist politics that were anathema to the NAACP in the postwar era. In early Novem-ber 1946, Heman Sweatt wrote a letter to Walter White expressing profuse admiration for communists, while carefully stating that he himself was not a member of the party. Given the lengths that the NAACP went to distance itself from the radical left, it is surpris-ing that Sweatt's proximity to communist politics did not disqualify him. In addition, Sweatt sought, and was granted, funding to cover his expenses during the lawsuit. He was a married man with a mort-gage, and becoming a plaintiff cost him time at work. Requesting support was neither unreasonable nor unheard of, but granting it was against NAACP policy. A plaintiff receiving any payments from the NAACP was compromised in the eyes of both the public and the law. In 1956, the state of Texas would seek to ban the NAACP on the grounds that it had contracted to pay Sweatt $11,000 to support him during the lawsuit and while in law school.[16]

The most glaring red flag, however, should have been Sweatt's ambivalence about aligning himself too closely with the NAACP and with the goal of desegregation—an ambivalence that Sweatt was honest about almost from the outset. On February 26, 1946, Sweatt went to the University of Texas to enroll, accompanied by a committee of African American state leaders with varying outlooks on education. After meeting with University of Texas president Theophilus Painter, Sweatt stated to the Associated Press that he was not "a guinea pig [of] any crusading Negro group" and simply wished to study law, an assertion of personal autonomy to which he would return again and again.[17]

Given these drawbacks, why did Marshall agree to go forward with Sweatt? It appears that Marshall planned on making Texas the testing ground for the desegregation of graduate education, with Sweatt as his most prominent plaintiff. Marshall's stubborn commitment to this plan led him to overlook obvious problems with his plaintiff and to go out of his way to secure every advantage for the case. Marshall left no record stating why he preferred to fight segregated graduate schools in Texas. There were several factors that could have recommended Texas to him: it was a large state with resources, and Marshall had connections to African American leaders in Houston and Dallas. That he preferred not to work in Oklahoma—and with a female plaintiff—is another possibility.

Marshall put enormous pressure on NAACP officers in Texas, explicitly imploring them to stay ahead of Oklahoma in their court filings. On January 24, 1946, ten days after Sipuel attempted to register at the University of Oklahoma, and before Sweatt and the Texas NAACP could make their sojourn to the University of Texas, Marshall wrote to A. Maceo Smith in Dallas, saying, "What in the world has happened to our proposed case against the University of

Texas? ... Oklahoma is going to put the jump on Texas." On March 8, after receiving more queries from Dunjee in Oklahoma, Marshall again chided Texas for lagging behind. He wrote to Durham, "I hope that we will be able to file suit not later than the case which is to be filed in Oklahoma." Marshall did not state why he wanted Texas to stay ahead of or at least keep pace with Oklahoma. In the same letter, he asked Durham for copies of correspondence with the University of Texas and "any other information" on the case he could provide. On March 11, Marshall wrote back to Durham, thanking him for supplying the information and stating that he was immediately handing it over to Roy Wilkins, editor of the *Crisis*, to publicize the case.[18]

A few weeks later, Marshall expressed alarm at reports that a civil war had erupted among the leadership in Texas over the Sweatt case in advance of its first court hearing. Some prominent black leaders in the state wanted to file a desegregation lawsuit solely as a ploy to pressure the Texas legislature to create a bona fide state system for black graduate education. Others wanted to see how far they could get with a desegregation case but would be willing, at some unspecified point, to accept a compromise. A third group firmly backed Marshall and the LDF's plan to accept no comprises and fight the case until Sweatt was accepted at the law school.

On one side was Carter Wesley, editor of the *Houston Informer* and perhaps the most influential African American man in the state of Texas. In 1945, Wesley, with a group of black moderates from a range of southern states, founded the Southern Negro Conference for Equalization. Wesley believed, as historian Merline Pitre puts it, "that true equality could be accomplished under the 'separate but equal' doctrine." Wesley initially agreed to work with Marshall and the Texas NAACP on a proposed desegregation lawsuit, claiming that it was possible to work for both goals at once. But by March 1946, he had begun to state, both publicly and privately, that he wanted to pursue *Sweatt* only "as continuing leverage" to influence the state legislature to establish "a Negro university . . . with Negro regents." In order to facilitate this goal, he, along with members of a group calling themselves the Texas Council of Negro Organizations, met with officials from the University of Texas and Texas A&M to hammer out an agreement for a new black university, the Texas State University for Negroes. Wesley was not a lone supporter of autonomous black institutions; black leaders elsewhere, perhaps most conspicuously in Atlanta, supported what Tomiko Brown-Nagin has called "principled pragmatism"—an approach that "valued black economic independence and reacted skeptically to litigation," particularly litigation on education. These pragmatists wanted to retain black teaching jobs and sought avenues of economic redress that would bolster the black middle class.[19]

Smith—the secretary of the Western Mutual Life Insurance Company and an NAACP leader—took the safe, middle route by pledging fidelity to both sides. When writing to Marshall, he was fully committed to seeing the case through, sending him updates and in general acting like a trusted lieutenant and ally. In a letter to Wesley, however, Smith wrote that "realism dictates that a separate university is about the most we are going to get." Lulu White—a longtime NAACP organizer and, as of March 1946, director of state branches—was a steadfast school desegregationist. "It is unfortunate," she wrote to Marshall, "that some of these persons are leaders and members of the NAACP who are on the one hand . . . fighting to enter the University of Texas and who are also at the same time members of these other organizations who are believing . . . we will never enter the University of Texas." Marshall recognized the danger immediately. "Needless to say I am more than worried," Marshall wrote to Smith upon finding out about the rift, "but from past experience, it has always been possible for we 'Texans' to get together and arrive at a definite program." He then offered to come to Texas on April 10 to help the leadership reach consensus about the lawsuit.[20]

During these same early months of 1946, when Marshall was in a state of high anxiety over the Texas case, Roscoe Dunjee and Oklahoma lawyer Amos Hall found it impossible to reach Marshall or engage him about the Sipuel case in any way. It took Marshall a month to reply to Dunjee's first letter sent in January. When he finally wrote back, it was only to say that he was too busy with other cases to go to Oklahoma. He promised to send his first lieutenant, Robert L. Carter, instead. But Carter had not been in the state for twenty-four hours when Marshall sent a telegram instructing him to return to New York as soon as possible to address another case. Dunjee had to settle for giving a draft of Hall's legal brief to Carter to take to LDF's office in New York and then waiting for whatever comment Marshall might find time to give.[21]

Another month of complete silence emanated from the New York office. On March 9, Dunjee wrote to Marshall again, this time addressing him gingerly as "My dear friend Marshall." "I have just had a talk with Hall and he states he has had no word from the office since he forwarded the rough draft of the petition. . . . When may we expect you to come or send some one to file them?" Dunjee went on to state that he was under enormous pressure from his constituents, "both black and white," and that he was getting letters and phone calls every day asking him about the progress of the suit. "The delay in filing . . . has caused a lot of critics to begin to throw cold water on things," he complained. Offers of funding had begun to dry up. He ended, as he did all of his letters, with a promise to pay for all legal expenses associated with the lawsuit. A few days later, after receiving a telegram from Marshall stating once again that he could not come, Dunjee wrote to Marshall that he was "terribly disappointed" because he had given out "a statement to the Associated Press saying that the Sipuel case would be filed" the next day. Dunjee began to feel humiliated. "A complete let-down in the public eye" was how he put it—a stain not only on his leadership but on the reputation of the NAACP in the state.[22]

On April 6, almost three months after sending his first letter to New York, Hall was forced to submit his brief—written with no input from the national office—to the court in Norman, Oklahoma. It was a simple, unadorned statement of the facts: Sipuel was a resident of Oklahoma. She had applied for admission at the university. The College of Law was the only law school in the state. Sipuel met the requirements for admission in every way, and failure to "admit plaintiff to the first year of the said laws [sic] school solely on the ground of race and color inflicts upon your plaintiff irreparable injury."[23]

Three months later, in anticipation of the next court date, Hall again wrote to Marshall, and, for the third time, received no reply. Dunjee finally resorted to contacting NAACP president Walter White. The two exchanged angry letters, and White accused Dunjee of ignoring the importance of Marshall's other cases. On June 17, 1946, Dunjee apologized to White, saying, "There was nothing intended that would take Thurgood away from the work he is doing." He rather plaintively explained his predicament: Hall "will have to go to trial [by himself] for we have exhausted both of our continuances. . . . I wrote you because, as you note from Mr. Hall's letter, he reported inability to reach Thurgood." Dunjee and Hall were making every attempt to postpone the case until Marshall was available. Marshall, meanwhile, was stalling.[24]

In 1946, Marshall was, no doubt, drawn to the fact that the Houston branch possessed around $7,000 in savings—money that was already on hand to help fund a prolonged court battle. No fund-raising would be necessary. Marshall also had long-standing friendships with Durham, White, and Smith. He got to know these Texans when he worked with the Houston branch to challenge the white primary in *Smith v. Allwright*—a fight that he took to the Supreme Court and won in 1944. During the years when Marshall was fighting *Smith*, membership in the Texas NAACP shot up to twenty-three thousand members. Oklahoma was, compared to Texas, a backwater. Texas had a large, established black elite in

Houston, a growing population in Dallas, and a comparatively cosmopolitan college town as its capital in Austin. But there were also drawbacks to working in Texas, with infighting among the leadership of the Houston branch chief among them. And though Marshall had ties to Carter Wesley, the two had been suspicious of one another for years over their differing approaches to educational equality. It is possible that Marshall's rivalry with Wesley stoked his determination to prove the possibility and efficacy of desegregation on Wesley's turf, and that the plaintiff in the case was of little consequence within the context of what one historian has called "the clash of the titans."[25]

The sex of the plaintiff in Oklahoma would also have been an unsettling factor for Marshall. There were no women—of any race—in law school at the University of Oklahoma, and there were only two white women enrolled at the University of Texas in 1946. Lawyers were the most prestigious black professionals in the 1940s, and the number of black women practicing law was infinitesimal. When Sipuel applied to the University of Oklahoma, there were 1,013 black male lawyers and 172,329 white male lawyers working in the United States. In 1940, there were only thirty-nine black female lawyers practicing law, in part because half of all black women who earned law degrees were forced to find work in other fields. Of those who remained, most worked for male attorneys performing office drudgery rather than representing clients in court. A 1947 article in *Ebony* magazine on "lady lawyers" claimed that most black women found "sex [a] bigger barrier than color," and that this was particularly true in the South where "lady lawyers [were] rarer than elephants."[26]

Practicing law was almost impossible for black women because, as historian Kenneth W. Mack has shown, they met with immediate and overt hostility from judges and their presence at a trial was perceived as "a direct assault on the masculine norms" of the courtroom by the "legal fraternity." Sadie Alexander, one of the few practicing black female lawyers at the time, explained that, in rare instances when judges did not "get irritated the moment they [saw] a woman lawyer," they were so condescending as to undermine women lawyers' professional status in court. Lucia Thomas, who practiced law in Chicago in the mid-1940s, recalled a judge who "stopped the whole prosecution to whisper, 'Young lady, you're acquitting yourself *very* well.'" His words "were heard throughout the courtroom," and Thomas was mortified. For men in the postwar world of lawyering, different rules applied in court than outside, and often "professionalism trumped race." Black male lawyers who earned the respect of white judges and lawyers were eventually treated "as a white man" by the community of male legal professionals. No one was going to accord Sipuel such status, no matter where she earned her degree, and no one would have been more aware of this fact than Marshall, who brilliantly and famously exploited the peculiar bonhomie of the legal fraternity to his advantage.[27]

From the perspective of defending a legitimate candidate for law school—someone who Marshall believed the public could envision as a practicing lawyer, and whose right to an education in preparation for that career was being unjustly denied—a male plaintiff was a safer bet. No doubt this is why the NAACP came looking for Lemuel Sipuel in the first place. Moreover, Dunjee may have damaged the Oklahoma case when early on he voiced doubts about Ada Sipuel. Among his pleas for help in March 1946 was a letter to Marshall saying that he was worried Sipuel was being "influenced" by others who would "inspire demands for money" (though Sipuel received no money from the organization), and that "in addition to being a brilliant girl, she trends towards the neurotic." Sipuel quickly dispelled Dunjee's fears, and he did not voice them again. However, Dunjee's skepticism may have contributed to Marshall's doubts about the case.[28]

Despite the ongoing silence from New York, the *Sipuel* case needed to be funded, so Dunjee and Sipuel got to work. By the time the Supreme Court ruled on *Sipuel v. Board of Regents* in 1948, the case had cost $26,000, with the majority of the money, according to an Oklahoma NAACP official, "given by public-spirited citizens in the low income bracket, farmers, domestic laborers and the common people." Much of it was raised by Sipuel herself, on long road trips with Dunjee from one state line to the other, with occasional forays into Kansas. Sipuel and Dunjee took these grueling trips for over two years, often driving late into the night and finding food and housing where they could. No rural town or hamlet was too small to visit: Ardmore, Boley, Crescent, Elk City, El Reno, Enid, Idabel, Kingfisher, Watonga. As Sipuel put it, "Wherever two or three African Americans might gather, there we were also." The citizens of these towns donated in amounts that suggest a sacrifice of the slimmest of earnings. For instance, in the town of Bristow, Sipuel and Dunjee raised two dollars and fifteen cents. That sum was donated by individuals giving twenty-five and fifty cents apiece. The Landmark Baptist Church was the largest contributor, donating $1.40. When Marshall came to the state in March 1947, larger donations from deeper pockets would be forthcoming. But in 1946 and early 1947, Dunjee and Sipuel were quite literally counting their pennies.[29]

It was through the endless travel and slow work of fund-raising that Sipuel became something of a regional folk hero and gained critical experience in public speaking. By the time she was interviewed by the national press in 1948, she knew exactly how to represent her case because she had been honing her message—in small groups and at large gatherings—for years. At twenty-three years old, she had made the desegregation of the University of Oklahoma her life's work. Her knowledge of the labor entailed, the daily engagement that was necessary to win people over, would go a long way toward making her words worthy of a national audience. By the time her case finally did come to the notice of the national NAACP office and the national press, her commitment to the cause of school desegregation had been thoroughly nourished by the farmworkers and domestics who had sacrificed their hard-won savings to get her into court. A sense of obligation to them would contribute to her informed eloquence when it was most needed.

The long wait for Marshall to appear in Oklahoma also fed Sipuel's palpable excitement about the case. In February 1947, when Sipuel found out that "the famous barrister" was finally coming to argue for her in court, she was so excited "it was like waiting for Christmas." Whether and to what extent Sipuel sensed hesitation on Marshall's part, or his preference for the case in Texas, is an open question. As a recent college graduate in her early twenties, with little experience of the inner workings of the NAACP, Sipuel could not have been fully aware of the politics within the organization. Nor did Dunjee explain to her the reasons for delays in the case. When Marshall failed to materialize during the first year of litigation, Dunjee, Sipuel later remembered, merely counseled patience. However, given the ongoing delays in her case, and the fact that Marshall and other LDF lawyers were in Texas for the *Sweatt* trial on December 17, 1946, it seems unlikely that she remained completely blind to her lawsuit's status within the hierarchy of the organization's concerns prior to 1948. Surely, during those endless hours spent on the road with Dunjee, some of his frustration—even without the details—must have been apparent to her. Sipuel was both book-smart and street-smart, and she may have sensed the tension that was brewing between Roscoe Dunjee, Thurgood Marshall, and Walter White.[30]

Nor could Sipuel have remained unaware of Marshall's attitude toward her and the ways in which he viewed her status as a woman. When Marshall finally showed up for the hearing before the Oklahoma Supreme Court in Norman, none of the NAACP lawyers were able to eat lunch because Norman was an all-white town, with no services—not even backdoor services—for blacks. Sipuel later recalled that Marshall turned to her and said, "I'm going to put you in charge of baloney sandwiches; don't you let this happen no more." Though Sipuel recounted this chiding from Marshall without acrimony, the details stayed fresh in her mind well into old age. An order to make sandwiches after she had already given so much, after she had become a working partner of the male NAACP leaders in her state, must have struck a discordant note.[31]

Sipuel's marginal position within the NAACP—like her need to raise her own funds—may have added fuel to her ferocious determination to succeed. For someone as competitive and scrappy as Ada Sipuel, such treatment must have been, to some extent, a call to arms. The fight to attend the University of Oklahoma College of Law was, for her, a battle with two fronts. She had something to prove, both to the state of Oklahoma and to the NAACP.

———

Without the need for fund-raising, Heman Sweatt made few public appearances, and when he did they were mostly in front of small, private audiences. While the Texas NAACP's financial strength made his job as plaintiff much less arduous, it also insulated him from rank-and-file supporters who desperately wanted to see him enter the University of Texas. Whether because of a lack of connection with his supporters or because of the influence of Carter Wesley, for whom he worked part-time at the *Informer*, Sweatt began to waver on the question of whether he would continue to pursue his lawsuit in the event that Texas created a new, separate law school. In a letter to Lulu White sent on July 25, 1946, Sweatt opened with the arresting statement that although the NAACP had so far achieved certain advantages in the struggle for "equal opportunities . . . we can hope to retain [them] only so far as we are honest enough to face the cold facts of social history." Then, sounding like Wesley and A. Maceo Smith, he began to describe his lawsuit as a way to "threaten the segregation system" in order to "force the greatest possible measures of equality in any accepted compromise within the framework of segregation." He also suggested he would attend a segregated law school. "In the event of the segregated institution materializing on a fair basis," he wrote, "I could not handicap my future. . . . I trust I make myself clear." White immediately forwarded the letter to Marshall. In response, Marshall began to correspond directly with Sweatt, telling him how important he was to the case and encouraging him to reach out should he have any misgivings. "Whenever there is any question whatsoever in your mind, will you please go to Dallas at our expense and discuss it with Durham, and if at anytime you deem it necessary, call me collect."[32]

Sweatt's vacillating position should be read as a sign of the enormous pressure he was under from Wesley, who had become incensed about the ongoing desegregation lawsuit and resorted to ruthless tactics as the case wore on. On December 30, 1946, Walter White sent a memorandum to Marshall saying, "Lula [sic] White telephoned me . . . saying Julius [her husband] insists that she resign because Carter Wesley and Maceo Smith are making the fight a personal one against her." A few days before, Wesley had published an article in the *Informer* in which he claimed Lulu White was a communist, that she and the NAACP were trying to dictate policy to the state, and that she was a troublemaker. It was the opening shot in what would be an ongoing assault on her character and leadership. In a withering editorial written in 1947, Wesley tarnished *Sweatt v. Painter* and White specifically by describing the goal of desegregation as "emotional." The editorial began, "Unfortunately, the leadership of Texas has gotten itself lost in a fog of emotions over the abolition of segregation." After additional complaints about "the pathless moors of emotions," Wesley wrote, "We submit that the NAACP's present point of view is as unrealistic as a little boy's notion that the boards in the tree constitute an airplane that can fly all over the world." Wesley argued from the perspective of someone who saw desperately needed funding for children in the segregated

Texas school system being drained away by the single-minded and questionable pursuit of enrolling one man at the University of Texas. By describing *Sweatt* as "emotional," he was also delegitimizing the goal of desegregation by associating it with a characteristically feminine attribute. If there was any doubt about the feminine nature of Wesley's charge of emotionalism, the "leadership" he was referring to was Lulu White. The attacks eventually took their toll. White hung on to her post for another couple of years, despite her husband's demands and Wesley's determination to discredit her. But Wesley won in the end. White stepped down on June 13, 1949.[33]

If Wesley and Smith were willing to drag White through the mud, one can only imagine their impact on Sweatt, who had no official position within the NAACP and ostensibly no one to turn to if he came in for the same treatment. He also had good reason to worry. His brother's comments about Stalin and his own ties to communists in the state, which Wesley was surely aware of, made him an easy target for red-baiting. Wesley was also his boss. Sweatt was in a very difficult position.

Given Sweatt's privately stated views, and the editorials in the *Informer*, it was probably not a surprise when Sweatt—who had been informed that, in response to his lawsuit, Texas had allocated money for a separate law school—told the national black newspapers that he would "investigate the matter" and that "if the general program is not as good" he would continue his lawsuit. This statement was not criticized in the black press, but neither was it greeted with much enthusiasm. By September 1947, however, Sweatt was back on track with the lawsuit, at least in his correspondence with the LDF. He wrote to Marshall that he felt he could now "shake-off the psychopathic squels [*sic*] of Carter Wesley." Nonetheless, Sweatt began to show signs of distress. He suffered from recurrent illnesses and regularly canceled events, especially large ones, because he was sick. He rarely went out in public as the case wore on, and his wife was overheard wondering aloud if it "was worth it."[34]

Skipping events, however, only earned Sweatt the enmity of the national black press, which expressed subtle and not so subtle disappointment when he did not appear at rallies and marches to support his lawsuit. For instance, when an interracial group, sponsored by the NAACP, picketed to protest segregation at educational facilities at Texas State University in Houston, a *Pittsburgh Courier* reporter wrote that "Heman Marion Sweatt, focal point around whom the fight ... is being waged, was absent from the picket line."[35]

Unsurprisingly, the *Kansas City Call*—with Lucile Bluford now at the helm as editor in chief—fully dramatized the dashed hopes of his supporters. For one important fund-raising event, more than 2,500 people paid twenty-five cents each to see Sweatt at the Moorland YMCA in Dallas. According to the *Call*, the most gripping moment of the event came when an elderly man pushed his way through the tightly packed audience to get a glimpse of the honoree:

> An old man fought his way through the milling crowd in the "Y" lobby, fought his way through the crowd on the winding stairs that led in the gym. Then finally on the gym floor, having exhausted the full weight of his years, he propped himself [up] to take a breath of air.... One of the hostesses said ..."shall I get you a chair?" "No." the old man breathed. "I just want to see him." It seemed that everyone in Dallas wanted to see him that day.... But the little man was not there.... His telegram said he was sorry he couldn't make it to Dallas."

The public wanted to make Sweatt into a school desegregation champion, but it was a role he was unwilling or unable to fully embrace, to the apparent disappointment of a great many African Americans in Texas. Clearly there was enormous excitement about the possibility that an African American might set foot on the beautifully manicured campus of the University of Texas as a student rather than a groundskeeper. This desire was both separate from and entangled with the desire to improve educational opportunities for black children. While there was a bright line between desegregation and equalization for NAACP officials, for those not caught up in the power struggles of the organization the two goals may have seemed less mutually exclusive. Many of those who attended the event for Sweatt, if asked whether they preferred equalization or desegregation, may well have answered "both."[36]

Though the citizens in Texas and the black press became increasingly frustrated with Sweatt, it is important to point out that he was certainly not the only litigant who viewed funding for a separate graduate school as a legitimate outcome of his lawsuit. In 1946, John H. Wrighten sued to enter the University of South Carolina and Charles J. Hatfield III and Viola Johnson sued for admission to Louisiana State University. All three suits ended abruptly when their state representatives passed legislation to fund graduate schools at existing black institutions. Indeed, ever since the *Gaines* decision in 1938, black students had been attempting to enroll at segregated state institutions as a way to force states to uphold the Supreme Court's ruling that states must provide graduate education "no later than it did for white students." The LDF initially announced that the Louisiana and South Carolina cases would, as one press release stated, "open fire on the legal fiction of 'separate but equal.'" When those cases abruptly turned into equalization cases, the national black newspapers aired their disappointment by announcing the results with lackluster headlines such as "Plan State Law School," accompanied by brief reports with little follow-up. The dissonance between the plans of the national NAACP and those of the plaintiffs and lawyers in the South created a situation where expectations were raised about the possibility of access to state institutions with dazzling endowments—and of a foothold in the fight against segregation—only to be replaced with announcements about plans for small, separate institutions.[37]

When Ada Sipuel found out that Thurgood Marshall was going to argue her case in front of the US Supreme Court on January 8, 1948, she traveled—uninvited and with her own funds—to Washington, DC, to witness the event.[38] Only a few days later, in what the *New York Times* called "a move of startling suddenness," the Supreme Court ruled that the "petitioner is entitled to secure legal education afforded by a state institution. . . . The State must provide it for her in conformity with the equal protection clause of the Fourteenth Amendment, and provide it as soon as it does for applicants of any other group." Upon hearing the news, Sipuel immediately flew back to Oklahoma in order to enroll for the spring semester. The local white press rushed to meet her at the airport upon her return on January 15. With a remarkable sense of occasion, Sipuel met the limelight with rhetorical brilliance. She exuded not only unshakable enthusiasm for her cause but also gratitude for the opportunity to pursue it—a sensibility that was as politically savvy as it was irrepressible. Her appreciation, cannily, was not for the opportunity to attend the white University of Oklahoma but for the idea, in her words, that "justice is for everyone" in the United States. Sipuel said to the *Daily Oklahoman*, a white paper, "It's a wonderful Constitution. . . . I'm going to be a lawyer, I'm going to learn." She then added that she had never felt "happier or luckier." With just a few words Sipuel made her case into a victory for herself, her race, and the nation. It was not that she had been vindicated, nor that the NAACP had triumphed; instead it was the Constitution that had been given its day in court and had been proven "wonderful." By connecting her case to the core American value of self-improvement, she linked school desegregation to the nation's democratic progress.[39]

Whether everyone in the press corps liked what Sipuel had to say was, of course, immaterial to the legal outcome of her case. That Sipuel's words were filled with an optimistic faith in American justice, however, imbued her stance with universal appeal. Whatever her true feelings, she displayed a seasoned political acumen. The *Daily Oklahoman* was completely won over. The same paper that had, in 1946, questioned Sipuel's academic credentials and issued the triumphant headline "Negro Barred from Enrolling at University" now published a half-page, flattering picture of Ada and Martha Sipuel embracing, with the headline "It's a Wonderful Constitution Ada Says on Return to State."[40]

When she was interviewed a few weeks after the Supreme Court decision, upon attempting and failing yet again to register at the University of Oklahoma, Sipuel distinguished herself once more as she spoke at length and was quoted extensively in both the black and white press. The *Chicago Defender, Pittsburgh Courier, Atlanta Daily World*, and *Daily Oklahoman* clearly delighted in her hard-headed determination, political finesse, storytelling, and competitive bravado. Referring to five other firsts who had agreed, fleetingly, to sign on to the lawsuit in late 1947, she said, "Six of us decided to apply for various departments at the University of Oklahoma. Everybody backed out, so I nominated myself chief guinea pig." She was overt about her anger at segregated education. "I got mad when I was a junior at college. . . . We had a state official down to ask for better facilities. We showed him all over the campus, what we needed, and he just shrugged his shoulders, said we were lucky to have any school."[41]

Also potentially attractive to both the white and black press, for different reasons, was the clarity with which she announced that her focus would be on studying as opposed to mixing with white students—while at the same time stating that she was open to white friendship. While she "hoped to make friends," she said, speaking on behalf of herself and a few others who joined her in 1948, "we want to learn—we don't care about social life." She added for good measure: "The few on the campus who might call me names—why, I won't even hear them." She managed, in just a few brief sentences, to convey both social openness (she hoped to make friends) and emotional distance (she would not hear racial insults), two attributes that might appear contradictory but in this instance fit the occasion perfectly. Both would be needed to survive at the University of Oklahoma, and together would work to make her an airtight, unstoppable desegregation pioneer. Stating that she would not "hear" hostile speech made explicit what Lucile Bluford had only implied in 1939: she would find a way to factor out overt racism. Sipuel was not pledging forbearance but impenetrability. Whatever one's interpretation of this kind of stance now, in the late 1940s it proved inspiring to a broad range of the public.[42]

Oklahoma responded to the Supreme Court decision by hastily creating a "Negro law school" in three rooms on the fourth floor of the capitol building in Oklahoma City. Sweatt's interest in a segregated law school and the disappointments of the desegregation lawsuits in Louisiana and South Carolina explain why most in the black press assumed that, when Oklahoma offered Sipuel a separate law school as part of Langston University, her suit would change course. "[Now] we will see Miss Sipuel attending law classes as a lone scholar . . . in a room in the State House," Marjorie McKenzie predicted in the *Pittsburgh Courier*, for "we have gotten into the habit of being grateful for small things."[43]

When instead Sipuel, then known by her married name Ada Sipuel Fisher, dismissed the black law school out of hand, the announcement was met with shock and celebration in quick succession. *Newsweek* editors doubted "their man" in Oklahoma when they heard the news and contacted the New York NAACP office to find out if it was true. "NEWSWEEK is reporting that Mrs. Fisher is stating that she will not attend that school. . . . They wish to confirm this statement," legal secretary Marian Wynn Perry reported in a memo to Marshall. (It is unclear whether Marshall could verify the statement or not; it appears Sipuel did not consult him.) The black press, particularly the *Courier*, reveled in it: In addition to front-page headlines announcing the "surprise move," the paper told and retold the story of her "refusal" or "rejection" in seven separate articles from mid-January to April 1948. Banner headlines included "Mrs. Fisher Won't Accept State Jim-Crow Setup" and "Mrs. Fisher Ignores State Jim-Crow Setup." Sipuel's refusal marked a departure, and when the *Courier* later offered an official "salute" to her "for her courage and determination to win equal rights . . . by refusing to attend the makeshift law school," it was making a distinction between Sipuel and other plaintiffs. Her pronouncement to the press that she would not accept the separate law school sounded all the better for being the only such words spoken by a desegregation plaintiff.[44]

Hence it was in the spring of 1948, following her "refusal," that the press began to refer to "the celebrated Ada Lois Sipuel case" and to Sipuel herself as "that brilliant girl." The NAACP began to put her case in bold letters in their advertisements. Oklahoma Republicans predicted black defection from the Democratic Party because of the failure of state Democrats to resolve Sipuel's suit. One humorous and telling anecdote published at the height of her popularity in 1948 recounted how NAACP lawyers in Washington—who had filed a petition with the Supreme Court to halt Oklahoma's move to establish a black law school—wished that Sipuel would hurry up and attend law school so they could ask her advice on how to proceed with her case. "As no word had come last week on the Oklahoma Law School admissions case from the Supreme Court," a *Chicago Defender* reporter wrote, "Thurgood Marshall was figuratively wringing his hands wondering about his next step. One of his legal colleagues in Washington . . . suggested brightly, 'Let's get Ada Sipuel in the school and let her tell us what to do!'" Marshall greeted this unanticipated turn of events by making it his own. In his speeches, he began to sidestep the *Sweatt* case entirely and to frame the assault on segregated graduate education as "support" for "Mrs. Ada Lois Sipuel Fisher in her fight for admission to the law school of the University of Oklahoma."[45]

It had become abundantly clear that Sipuel's unequivocal commitment was no small matter. By 1948, no one—in the NAACP or the black press—was taking it for granted. Roscoe Dunjee and Amos Hall in Oklahoma, meanwhile, understood the magnitude of Sipuel's popularity. Wanting to provide some living expenses for Sipuel, Hall contacted Gloster Current, director of branches at the NAACP national office, to see if there might be a position for her in the organization. "In addition to the time she lost and embarrassment suffered in connection with the lawsuit," he wrote, "she has given unstintingly of her time in making public appearances in the state as an aid to the raising of funds with which to conduct litigation." Current enthusiastically concurred with Hall about Sipuel's potential as an NAACP spokesperson, telling Marshall that "for some time I have been of the opinion that Mrs. Fisher could be used profitably in a nation-wide tour of larger NAACP branches in the states of Tennessee, Kentucky, West Virginia, North and South Carolina, Ohio, Pennsylvania, New York, Illinois, Indiana and Missouri." She might, he added "also be used profitably on the West Coast." Roy Wilkins, assistant secretary of the NAACP, wrote back that while "ALL of us appreciate the sacrifices Mrs. Fisher has made and the dramatic manner in which she has symbolized the struggle for equality in education . . . at this time it does not appear that we will be able to offer any employment." He added in a postscript: "In addition to the above, there is some opinion here that the NAACP should not have on its payroll any person who is a principal in a case which NAACP lawyers are conducting in the courts."[46]

Meanwhile, on the last day of the registration period in 1948, six black students—three women and three men—applied to and were accepted to six different programs at the University of Oklahoma. The university was forced to admit it could not afford to establish that many separate programs. Upon arriving, all six students found themselves segregated within their classrooms. Marshall

immediately named George McLaurin plaintiff in a lawsuit arguing that such segregation was unconstitutional. The NAACP hired
a photographer to accompany McLaurin to class. In the now historic photo, McLaurin was shown sitting alone in an antechamber,
cordoned off from the other students. A month after Marshall filed
McLaurin v. Oklahoma State Regents, Oklahoma City radio station
WKY aired an editorial billed as "Thoughts of a Negro College Student," which author Kenneth Johnson read on air. Johnson ruth-
lessly criticized McLaurin for seeking a seat next to white students.
Echoing Heman Sweatt's letter to Lulu White, Johnson said, "History does not lie. . . . It takes years and years to replace customs and
habits." He goes on to call the lawsuit a "nampbly-pamby [*sic*] . . .
approach to race relations" and argues that "it behooves all Negroes
to act like MEN . . . and to accept a Manly responsibility by rec-
ognizing the TRUTH AS IT IS." McLaurin, a fifty-four-year-old
retired Langston professor, responded to this attack on his mascu-
linity much as Sweatt had responded to similar (but more oblique)
criticism in Texas; he became reluctant to interact with the press and
quietly withdrew the moment the Supreme Court resolved his case.
Later, in a joint interview with her husband, Mrs. McLaurin told a
Washington Post reporter that it had been her idea for him to register
in 1948.[47]

Ada Sipuel Fisher finally arrived as a registered student on the
University of Oklahoma campus during the summer session of 1949.
When she got there, her words were, once again, simultaneously effective and economical. The *Pittsburgh Courier* quoted her as saying,
"I expect to spend the rest of my life demonstrating to the State of
Oklahoma that a mistake was made in attempting to prevent me
from getting a legal education at the state university." The statement,
once again, encapsulated her crowd-pleasing nuance: she was blunt
in her condemnation of the University of Oklahoma at the same
time that she communicated an intention to keep working with it—
by taking it upon herself to *prove* something to the institution and

the state. She succeeded in paying tribute to the mutuality inherent in the desegregation process—she would work hard and Oklahoma would be obligated to honor her achievements—while remaining completely confident in herself.[48]

Sipuel continued to rack up successes and pioneering achievements. When *Ebony* covered her career at the University of Oklahoma College of Law in the spring of 1951, there were no other nationally known desegregation plaintiffs still enrolled in the schools they had desegregated. When *Time* magazine noted that she had passed the bar exam the following summer, it was a similarly singular accomplishment. But the fact that Sipuel took advantage of every opening that came her way—whether by taking her brother's place as a plaintiff or reinforcing the media's image of her as happy to be the only black person and the only woman in her class—does not mean that her road was any less difficult. During the years she pursued her case, she received a constant stream of hate mail, threatening phone calls, and public abuse. One letter reached her home from another state despite the fact that it was addressed only to Ada Lois Sipuel, N—. Her phone was tapped, and she eventually had to conduct all her legal business in person. In a book published in 1948, William H. Murray, the former governor of Oklahoma, intimated that she was bestowing sexual favors on a University of Oklahoma law professor who publicly supported her. He wrote that the professor reminded him of the song "Negro from San Antonio": "I jumped on a pony / And rode to San-an-tony / To see that Brown-skin woman . . . / Choc'lit to the bone / Make a preacher lay his Bible down." Perhaps, he mused, "the Doctor has long ago laid his Bible down."[49]

What has been largely forgotten—because of a lack of photographic documentation and only a passing journalistic reference—is the fact that during her time in law school, Sipuel endured the humiliation of sitting in roped off areas and in chairs with large signs marked "colored." Writing her autobiography almost fifty years later, she still found it difficult to discuss the pain of having to climb up to her "colored" chair in the top tier of seats in the law school classroom. In 1949, however, she minimized her reaction. "Mrs. Fisher said she is not satisfied with [campus] segregation regulations," the *Daily Oklahoman* reported, "but she appeared happy to enroll." And while she kept up a brave countenance when she was on campus in Oklahoma, in a talk she gave in New York City in 1948 at the *New York Herald Tribune* annual forum, she hinted at the personal cost of the lawsuit. "In my effort to get a legal education in the State of Oklahoma," she told the audience, "to the vast majority of people I lost my identity as Ada Lois Sipuel and have become instead a test case." The long, drawn-out lawsuit and Sipuel's status as the foremost school desegregation pioneer had incurred, it seems, a kind of self-alienation that was both difficult to endure and difficult to describe. It shows, too, the extent to which Sipuel was making a calculated decision when she told the press, in 1948, that she was happy to be a guinea pig. Her statement hints, as well, at why Heman Sweatt might have wanted to declare the opposite, to insist from the beginning that he was not anyone's test case or guinea pig—that he was his own man.[50]

Sweatt continued to state that his real goal was to study law. When the *Kansas City Call* caught up with him in April 1950, as his lawsuit was being argued in the Supreme Court, the reporter asked what he would do if he lost his case. He did not say he would keep fighting but that he would study law in the North. As it turned out, Thurgood Marshall and the LDF won the case, which was handed down on June 5, 1950. The Supreme Court stated that a hastily set up black law school could not be equal to the University of Texas School of Law and reversed a Texas trial court's decision barring Sweatt from the university. The *Sweatt* decision—just as Marshall had planned—went the full distance, declaring that separate graduate education was unconstitutional. Soon after, though, Sweatt dropped out of the University of Texas law school. His supporters emphasized the he had not been prepared for the academic demands. He went on to have a highly successful career as an organizer for the Urban League and the NAACP in Atlanta. A capable, thoughtful, professional, and politically committed person, he had been a terrible fit for the role of desegregation plaintiff and first at the University of Texas. The blame for the mismatch between plaintiff and lawsuit rests squarely on the shoulders of Marshall and the LDF.[51]

After passing the bar examination, Ada Sipuel Fisher had a long career in law and academia, and she eventually became a member of the very Board of Regents at the University of Oklahoma that had so assiduously fought against her admission. Her last act before retiring was a vote in support of an endowed professorship for Anita Hill, who in 1991 became one of the most visible black women in the nation when she bravely testified before Congress about sexual harassment she experienced while working for then Supreme Court nominee Clarence Thomas.[52]

———

Sipuel brought an unusual complement of skills to her fight with the University of Oklahoma. Coping simultaneously with white hostility and black expectation, with media exposure and fraught encounters with white officials, was a tall order for anyone, no matter how educated or committed to the principle of desegregation. The outsized demands and relentless scrutiny required a rare mix of attributes: personal ambition combined with an ability to withstand public humiliation, charisma in front of the camera and self-sacrificing patience, the appearance of openness with the black and white press corps alongside an implacable determination. Sipuel brought to this near-impossible challenge an Olympian dexterity that allowed her to navigate social and political minefields in a way that made her presence in the spotlight and at a white university seem inevitable. In a letter to Sipuel, a supporter, Mrs. J. M. B. Michelle, tried to describe her appreciation. "In my humble opinion a finer specimen of young womanhood from any angle could not have been chosen," she wrote. "Not too young or too old; not too stout or too thin . . . intelligent . . . pleasant . . . [possessing] courage and confidence in your own proposition." After trying unsuccessfully to describe Sipuel's ability to hit all the right notes, Michelle ended her letter by saying, "And what, you have the right to ask, are you trying to say? Simply this, personally I think you're wonderful! I think you are grand! Who knows but to this end you were born?"[53]

3

Girls on the Front Line

Grassroots Challenges in the Late 1940s

IN THE WAKE OF *Sipuel*, *Sweatt*, and *McLaurin*, parents and daughters began to file school desegregation lawsuits at the grade school level. Between 1947 and 1949, almost a dozen such cases were brought in Texas, Louisiana, Virginia, Kansas, Washington, DC, and elsewhere. The cases that were initiated in 1947 and continued through 1950 created a drumbeat of pressure on the LDF. Though Thurgood Marshall only took on one of these cases (*Jennings v. Hearne* in Texas), he received almost daily pleas for help; memos detailing the many warring school cases in Washington, DC; and input from NAACP lawyers in the field—especially Spottswood Robinson in Virginia and Charles Houston in Washington, DC—representing clients who wished to desegregate schools immediately. Making matters more pressing was the fact that school desegregation activists showed a commitment that was so intense, patient, and determined that the major black newspapers—chiefly the *Chicago Defender*, the *Pittsburgh Courier*, and the *Kansas City Call*—were fully supportive of these desegregation cases and gave them front page coverage.

By 1950, Marshall, who later admitted he "didn't want any of these cases," was forced to put grade school desegregation at the center of the LDF's strategy. Ever since, scholars have marveled at the NAACP's decision to go after segregated grade schools: Was it the right choice? Would it have been better if the NAACP had chosen equalization instead? Was *Brown v. Board* a beneficial or detrimental decision? These questions are asked because *Brown* is viewed as a strategic decision made by a small group of crusading lawyers. But when all of the cases that came to the NAACP's New York office— both those that did and, just as importantly, those that did not make it to the Supreme Court—are examined, it becomes clear that Marshall put off these cases for as long as he could. As early as 1948, it had become clear that if he and the LDF did not take a school segregation case to the Supreme Court, someone else would.[1]

If a lawyer unaffiliated with the NAACP took a school desegregation case to the Supreme Court, there was no good outcome. If he lost the case, it would strengthen segregated schooling and further entrench Jim Crow in the South, if not throughout the United States. If an outside lawyer won the case, the NAACP would forfeit its status as the premier civil rights organization of its time. The LDF did not make a strategic choice; it responded to developments on the ground, and the LDF's strategy was shaped by the determination of ordinary citizens to take action against the legal regime undergirding segregation in America's schools. Taking the measure of those who were coming forward, who took enormous risks and refused to back down, the LDF saw that grade school desegregation had fervent supporters. When a few southern judges began, in 1949, to show some sympathy for these cases, the LDF felt more confident that desegregation could prevail. That almost all of the early cases— the radical first attempts that earned both the biggest headlines and the most backlash—were filed on behalf of girls went unremarked upon in the official records of the NAACP.

When Marguerite Daisy Carr faced off with the principal of Eliot Junior High School in April 1947, it was the first move in what would become a three-year lawsuit. The lawsuit was the first of its kind to be filed in Washington, DC, and the first step toward what would become a full-fledged attack on segregated, unequal education in the nation's capital—a struggle that would ultimately involve all of the parents who had children at the overcrowded black school, Browne Junior High.[2]

Carr (who now goes by her married name, Marguerite Carr Stokes) was born in 1933 to parents who hailed from North Carolina. Though Marguerite's mother had a degree in education, James C. Carr Sr. preferred that she stay at home with the children. Marguerite was the youngest of five children and, by her own account, the most independent minded. "They were all dutiful, and followed the rules, and I broke 'em all." Carr Stokes describes herself as "rebellious" and a "smart aleck." Like Ada Sipuel, she courted trouble and faced the consequences head-on. "I consciously broke the rules, and [then] stopped in the yard and picked up switches, brought them in, and handed them to my father so that he could switch my legs. . . . I was just a wild child." She was—also like Sipuel—a self-professed "tomboy" and athlete. "I played basketball, football, tennis. I played all kinds of sports." Unlike Sipuel, however, she was not initially a particularly conscientious student. Today, Carr Stokes links her academic mediocrity in middle school to her own most valued attribute, independence. Her teachers had expected her to be a high achiever like her siblings. Carr Stokes remembers that her teachers would say, "'Oh, that's one of the Carr children, I know you're going to be an excellent student like your sister!' . . . And I asked my teacher . . . 'Did you ever think that I was a different person?'"[3]

Her social activism was informed by the fact that her mother, like Martha Sipuel, could have passed for white—and the difficult social tension this fact often created. "My mother," Carr Stokes explains, "was more white than most white people." Marguerite was a "towhead" as a child. When they went out, most people simply assumed they were white. They could sit anywhere they wanted, go anywhere they wanted. "Every time I went [out] with my mother I could sit anywhere I wanted to." Also, her father and uncle "had opportunities that other blacks did not have. . . . All of us were very fair, it was not that anybody passed for anything! But everybody assumed that we wanted to be white because we were fair . . . but it is just that we had privileges . . . and they had training."

If being "mixed" held privileges, looking white in public constantly threatened to cause trouble. Whatever white people assumed about the family, it was important, Carr Stokes says, never to contradict them. "The worst thing a white person can do is think that a black, a colored person, is white and they made a mistake. Rather than make that kind of mistake, most white people avoid it." That is, white people preferred a world where racial distinctions were obvious and rigid. To remind them otherwise was to court anger and even arrest. When Carr Stokes later accompanied her husband to Montgomery, Alabama, where he was stationed in the air force, the police tried to arrest the couple for race mixing. Indeed, while the snobbery of some light-skinned African Americans is well known, there were vulnerabilities for those with fair skin—emanating from both sides of the color line. As several other desegregation plaintiffs and firsts have explained, being fair skinned made them vulnerable to bullying as children by black neighbors and schoolmates. Pauli Murray, who was the descendant of slaveholders on one side of her family, recalled that her black classmates yelled at her, "You half-white bastard! You dirty-faced Jew baby! [She was not Jewish]." Charlayne Hunter-Gault, who desegregated the University of Georgia in 1961, says that she was regularly "taunted about [her] color," called "white girl," and physically bullied when growing up in Atlanta. She believes that the experience led her to "resent the whole color issue" more than most. Feeling marginalized in both white and black spaces inspired Murray and Hunter-Gault—and perhaps the Carr family as well—to point to the absurdity of racial classifications in a country where there were not two "colors" but an infinite range, and to embrace activism to remove those classifications. For Carr Stokes, fair skin was a privilege, a danger, and also a responsibility. It gave her advantages, but would later make her more vulnerable to the criticism that she "was acting white" in her attempt to attend Eliot Junior High.[4]

Browne Junior High School was built to handle 888 African American children, but had an enrollment in 1947 of 1,700. Students attended in shifts and had "double classes" with over fifty students in one classroom. At Eliot, a few blocks away, 763 white students attended a school built for 980. Marguerite's father, James Carr, was president of the Browne PTA. His son, Marguerite's brother, had gone to Browne and had suffered through the overcrowding, and the education he received was so poor that he arrived at high school unprepared. When Marguerite started at the school, James Carr decided something must be done. Carr Stokes describes her father saying that "he could not sit back and let [this] happen to any more children . . . [that] it may not change in my day . . . but the indignity would not be pushed onto his grandchildren. And he couldn't stand by any longer."[5]

In order for James Carr to file a petition, he first had to take Marguerite to Eliot Junior High and have her attempt to enroll. But Carr, despite his own sense of urgency about the conditions at Browne Junior High, would not approach Eliot or instigate a lawsuit without his daughter "making the decision" herself. He seems to have known exactly how difficult it would be for her. As Carr Stokes remembers, he painted a bleak picture of what she would have to endure:

> I had to make the decision because I was the one that was going to hurt. . . . I would be the one who would get all of the criticism,

I would be the one ostracized. I would be the one who had to suffer the consequences . . . and he spelled out what he thought would happen to me. And it truly did. . . . He just wanted me to be tough.

The next night, as Carr Stokes remembers it, she said, "Dad, we're going forward." He looked at her and said, "Are you sure?" "I'm sure," she answered. She was not, she claims, "eager" to do it, but willing. "I was" she says, "a willing vessel."[6]

The first time Marguerite and her father set out for Eliot Junior High, they did not make it. Carr Stokes recalls that "the photographers and newspapers and everybody . . . was so thick" that they turned back. Her father told her, "We're not doing it for the publicity, so we don't go today." Then he "turned the car around and went back home." The newspapers reported that the whole thing was a "hoax." The Carrs would make their sojourn the following Monday. This "school visit" has been lost to posterity, because James Carr achieved his aim and managed to avoid press attention. However, word got out in the black community. While the white students were pressed up against the windows of the school looking down on Carr as she met with the principal on the steps, on the street "a million [black] witnesses" stood by, marveling over the unprecedented spectacle of a black child attempting to walk into a white school. "All of the people who supported [James Carr], he had teachers and assistant principals and janitors and everybody else there. Everybody was standing there 'cause there was something to see. This colored person coming . . . to the white school, 'let's go see it.'" The black adult onlookers were as amazed as the white school officials and students. As Carr Stokes describes it, she was "presented" to the white principal, who turned to James Carr and said, "Now you know we can't accept her. Why are you doing this?" Her father responded simply, "Well, then reject her."[7]

James Carr, with the support of the PTA and assistance from his lawyer, Leon Ransom, filed a petition with the school board on behalf of Marguerite and others similarly situated in April 1947. The national black press was excited about the petition and the new militancy it portended on segregated schools. The headline "Aim New Blow at D.C. Schools: Parents Petition Board to Abandon Segregated Policy" graced the front page of the *Pittsburgh Courier*. "A full scale offensive against the discriminatory public school system in the Nation's Capitol was launched here," the article began, "when James C. Carr acting for Miss Marguerite Carr, his 13-year-old daughter, petitioned the District of Columbia School Board for transfer of his daughter from Browne Junior High School to one of the white junior high schools." In 1947, such a move was bold, exciting and, as far as the *Courier* knew, unprecedented.[8]

By October 1947, it was clear that the school board was not going to respond to the petition. James Carr wanted to file a desegregation lawsuit. When he chose to work with Leon Ransom, he purposely teamed up with the only Washington, DC, lawyer who was currently taking on grade school desegregation cases. Ransom earned his law degree with honors at Ohio State in 1927 and his doctorate at Harvard in 1935. Between 1935 and 1946, he worked with Charles Houston at Howard Law School, and from 1941 to 1946, he also served as assistant editor of the *Journal of Negro Education*. He had argued in front of the Supreme Court in *Chambers v. Florida*, leading to a unanimous decision against coerced confessions. Whenever William Hastie, dean of the law school, was away, Ransom served as acting dean. However, when Harry Truman appointed Hastie governor of the Virgin Islands in 1946, Ransom was passed over for the permanent position. He resigned immediately and returned to private practice. But he retained a high profile, serving as chair of the Committee for Racial Democracy in Washington, DC.[9]

While Spottswood Robinson was filing a slew of equalization suits in Virginia, and Houston was considering a range of options with other DC clients, Ransom was ready and willing to file school desegregation lawsuits immediately. In September 1947, Ransom had already filed a lawsuit on behalf of Constance Carter in Arlington, Virginia. At the beginning of the school year in 1947, Constance Carter had attempted to enroll at Washington-Lee High School "for whites." When she and her mother were turned away, they filed a lawsuit, *Carter v. School Board*, with Ransom. Filed in late September, Ransom's brief alleged that Carter, a minor represented by her mother Eleanor Taylor, was denied entrance "because of her race and color . . . [and therefore] denied equal protection of the laws secured by the Fourteenth Amendment of the Constitution of the United States." Ransom sought "a permanent injunction restraining [the school board] from denying said plaintiff . . . admission to and enrollment in the senior high school established, maintained and operated exclusively for children of public school age in said county who are not Negroes." James Carr wanted similar language for his lawsuit, and he would end up sticking with his chosen lawyer—even when members of the LDF wanted to take over the case and appeal it to the Supreme Court and when other PTA parents decided that they preferred to file an equalization suit, which they filed with yet another DC lawyer, Belford Lawson. James C. Carr Sr. was a loyal man.[10]

Marguerite Carr was officially rejected from Eliot, and Ransom duly filed the lawsuit, *Carr v. Corning*. In his brief, Ransom attacked grade school segregation directly and forcefully—years before Marshall and the LDF did so, and apparently without consulting them—saying that the plaintiff and "all other Negro Children of school age . . . on whose behalf she brings this action are arbitrarily, capriciously, wrongfully, and without color or authority of law, required to attend schools separate and apart from those provided for the white children of the District." Ransom went on to discuss at length and with equal passion Carr's request for a transfer from Browne to Eliot and how she was refused admission. He requested that Carr and "those on whose behalf she sues to enroll in and attend the school most adjacent to her and their homes . . . without regard to . . . the race or color or the students enrolled therein." The black newspapers were more thrilled with the lawsuit than they had been with the petition. "It will challenge in the courts for the first time whether there is any legal justification for the separation of the races in District schools," reported the *Chicago Defender*. "The first direct test of the legality of segregated schools . . . came when a suit was filed in District Court on behalf of 13-year old Marguerite Daisy Carr," the *Pittsburgh Courier* wrote. Carr herself was dispatched to speak with reporters. She described the overcrowding and explained why she had tried to enroll at the white school. Reporters quoted her saying that she was rejected "solely because she was a Negro."[11]

James Carr and other PTA parents pooled their resources to pay the filing fees, and the NAACP Washington, DC, branch covered the printing costs and other legal expenses. Carr Stokes remembers Ransom, Robinson, and other NAACP attorneys working on the case "over at Howard." Meanwhile, her father—who was a physical plant manager at the Pentagon—and everyone else connected with the suit lost their jobs. Carr Stokes puts it this way:

> They fired him. They fired everybody in his crew. . . . They fired every person who was part of the action. They went out of here, 'cause most of the people were out of North Carolina or Virginia or somewhere, went to their hometowns and fired all them people out of their jobs. Teachers and everything, they were all fired. Everybody was fired. . . . They weren't supposed to survive. They weren't supposed to live. They were supposed to recant, they were supposed to back off.

Those who were fired—in addition to the teachers and members of the PTA—included the members of James Carr's "crew" at the

Pentagon (some of whom were white), the workers who "ran the boilers" at the physical plant and kept "the building operating."[12]

It is possible that the firings at the Pentagon have remained hidden from the historical record because the fired workers quickly and quietly had their jobs returned to them by President Truman. Soon after the mass firing, according to Carr Stokes, the Secret Service, without any warning and under the cover of darkness, showed up at the house to pick up her father. The next thing he knew he was facing President Truman:

> [Truman] set down and asked him, "Well Mr. Carr, I've been keeping up with what's going on and want to know, now just what we can do for you?"... My father said, "well, I want everybody put back on their jobs ... and paid as if they had been there and not missed a day." [Truman] said ... "done." ... What do you want [for yourself] Mr. Carr?" "Well, they found a way to fire me, so, find a way to retire me." He drew a retirement check every month until he died, and after he died, they called to make sure he was dead ... before they cut the check off. That was Harry Truman. Nobody ever knew Harry Truman did anything.[13]

The White House did not keep a log of after-hours visitors during the Truman administration, so the story is impossible to corroborate. However, such an act would have been consistent with Truman's civil rights objectives in the late 1940s, which included the establishment of the President's Committee on Civil Rights and two executive orders issued in 1948: Executive Order 9980, which desegregated the federal workforce and Executive Order 9981, which desegregated the armed forces. Truman viewed racial segregation as a national embarrassment that weakened America's international standing. He was especially bothered by segregation in the capital, which was constantly brought to his attention by visiting foreign dignitaries. In autumn 1948, with school protests and the *Carr* case in the headlines of the Washington dailies, Truman acted in concert with Congress to create a "fact-finding committee" on segregation in Washington. A copy of the ninety-one-page report was put on Truman's desk in December 1948, and he told the press he would "read it with interest." He was also up for election in 1948 and was counting on the northern black vote to help him in what was sure to be a tight race. The spectacle of federal workers fired over a school desegregation case unfolding only a few miles from the White House was the last thing Truman needed.[14]

There is one piece of evidence that James Carr had a warm regard for the president. It is a letter in Truman's files from him, sent when Truman was considering whether or not to seek reelection in 1952 and written on the office stationary of a real estate management office where James Carr worked in the 1950s. He expressed his regret that Truman might be leaving the office, saying, "All these fancy speeches Mr. Eisenhower's included can't drown the many fine things you've done thru the years." At "this critical stage of world affairs your leadership is needed as never before," he continued. But should the president decide to leave public life, "I am sure you will carry with you the love and respect of those who want to see America remain strong and a common understanding reached by people the world over." It does sound as if the president would know, specifically, what "many fine things" James Carr was referring to. But while Truman's intervention is highly plausible, given his stance on racial segregation in 1948 and Carr Stokes's knowledge of the encounter, his actions were secret by design and her father was a private man—two facts that make this story difficult to corroborate.[15]

While the adults coped with economic retaliation, Marguerite took abuse from her classmates. After the lawsuit was filed, "I had to fight my way home every day," she recalls. "Because they . . . said I wanted, was trying to be white, that I was making things tough." However, Marguerite, as her father no doubt already knew, was not one to back down from any kind of fight. "In those days, you made appointments around on the back of the school yard . . . to discuss your disagreements. And so, I used to beat people up every day." Her fights were primarily with boys, "because girls are too timid." She did not tell her parents about what was going on because she did not want to be labeled a coward by her peers. One day, when he came to pick her up from school with her brother, her father saw her from a distance settling a "disagreement." He turned to her brother and asked, "Is that Daisy [Marguerite] over there?" "Yeah Dad," her brother responded. "That look like Daisy." Carr Stokes recalls, "I was whaling on somebody. And so they broke up the fight." Soon after, there was a school-wide assembly about fighting on school premises, and the violence stopped.

Faced with Marguerite Carr's petition, Superintendent Hobart Corning finally began to take some action to address the overcrowding. The school board hastily handed over two old "white" elementary schools: Webb, built in 1900, and Blow, built in 1906. These buildings—deemed "outmoded and obsolete" by a November 1947 report commissioned by the DC branch of the NAACP—were meant to relieve the overcrowding. But the school board provided no shuttle service to the two schools, which were fifteen and nine blocks away, respectively, from Browne. The students had to walk back and forth between these annexes in all weather and with little adult oversight. Junior high students, moreover, got little help from these schools. They needed facilities matching their age: lockers, chalk boards, and water fountains higher than their knees. The gesture of opening the two schools did more to anger parents than to alleviate their frustration. What was happening at Browne and Eliot, according to a subsequent NAACP branch report, was a citywide problem:

> The practice of releasing schools built for white pupils to Negroes follows the familiar pattern, which characterizes segregation. When Negroes move into residential areas not previously opened to them, the white residents tend to vacate their homes.

It is inevitable, therefore, that the schools in these sections soon become surrounded by Negroes and that the nearest Negro school will be overcrowded while the white school will operate below pupil capacity.[16]

On November 9, when school was already in session, Corning created chaos when he removed the white elementary students from Webb and Blow amid a concurrent protest staged by black parents in front of the two lower schools. On November 13, the Browne PTA and other citizen's organizations called a meeting to "vigorously oppose" the transfer of Browne students to the two "cast-off" lower schools. A follow-up meeting was scheduled at the Jones Memorial Church in late November for all parents of Browne Junior High children transferred to Webb and Blow. A strike was unanimously called and, on December 3, almost the entire student body of Browne stayed home. While most viewed this protest as a strike, Charles Houston, in a letter to a friend, said, "I call it a lockout by the [school] board." Buoying the spirits of the parents, perhaps, was the fact that the *Washington Post* followed every move of the striking parents and students. The articles were sympathetic, often on the first page, and, beginning in December, appearing every other day. The whole city was watching. Congressman Everett M. Dirksen, chairman of the House Committee on the District of Columbia, announced that he was sponsoring a "full report on the parent-pupil strike" and would appoint a "fact-finding" committee to look into the conditions at the Negro schools throughout the district. The report on DC schools—delivered to Congress in 1949 and commonly referred to as the Strayer Report after the lead researcher George Strayer—was damning.[17]

During the strike, there was little agreement among the parents about how to proceed. The city began to send truant officers to the homes of those on strike, and by late December James Carr and several DC lawyers were urging parents to send their children back to school. The majority of students went back to Browne, but those assigned to Webb and Blow continued to boycott. The advice they received from an experienced parent at another black school in the city was that if the students continued to use the temporary annexes, they would stay there indefinitely. A core group of around two hundred students stayed on strike full-time. A meeting was called for Christmas Eve 1947. Parents were torn between several legal possibilities, and several lawyers. The first approach—desegregation—was already before the courts in the form of Leon Ransom's brief for *Carr*. But other parents in the PTA wanted to simultaneously file an equalization lawsuit demanding that Eliot Junior High be handed over immediately for their children's use. (This idea had already been rejected by Superintendent Corning, who said it would create "racial antagonism.")[18] At the end of the meeting, it was decided that Ransom and his law firm would stay on the *Carr* case, attorney Belford Lawson would sign on for the PTA's equalization case, and both would consult with Charles Houston and James Nabrit, a professor of law at Howard University who had made a name for himself by assembling over two thousand cases for his civil rights course. It was an all-hands-on-deck, multivalent approach to the crisis of black schooling in the nation's capital.[19]

A third group of parents began to meet separately and vowed to continue striking. Initially, Nellie Greene was the organizer and spokesperson for this group. But by early January, Gardner Bishop had become the sole voice for those who wanted to continue the strike. Bishop claimed to have disliked James Carr and the middle-class members of the Browne PTA almost as much as he did the white school board. "It was Double Jim Crow," he said. Incensed at the overcrowding *and* the pretensions of the PTA lawyers, especially Lawson, he stepped up to help keep the strike going in late December 1947 and January 1948. The group that Bishop came to lead eventually incorporated as the Consolidated Parent Group, or CPG. Bishop said of his leadership, "I had more mouth than anyone else and wasn't in a [government] job so I was not afraid to speak out. Ignorant as I was, they believed in me."[20]

Bishop approached Houston after an NAACP meeting about the strike in January 1948. The strike was losing steam, and Bishop needed to find other avenues of attack. He asked Houston if he might be willing to help. Bishop remembered that Houston put his arm around him and said, "I know you Bishop, and I'd like to help." Thus began a deep friendship, in which Bishop—who had no college education—came under what he considered to be the tutelage of Houston. Houston, for his part, wanted to know all about Bishop's people on strike: "The little people," as Bishop described them. Houston was "anxious to handle the case" and offered his services for free. But first, Bishop would have to call off the strike (something that was not hard to do by January 1948), and then the CPG would have to cover the expenses associated with litigation. Houston wanted to file lawsuits up and down the educational ladder, from kindergarten to high school. Bishop wanted, above all, to fight segregated education, but Houston thought it better to file equalization suits and a suit for damages against individual board members, as he had done before at the graduate level in Missouri.[21]

While the two men shared a close friendship—Bishop's daughter, Judine Bishop Johnson, said that the two men "loved each other, it was a very close bond"—they were mismatched in terms of their immediate goals. Bishop's statements, both public and private, all centered on school desegregation. It was the promise of desegregation that excited his followers and inspired CPG parents to contribute time and money to the organization. But Houston simply could not bring himself to tackle segregation head-on. "Charles Houston didn't believe they could win a segregation per se suit because of Congressional laws," Bishop later reflected. Houston "feared he would get laughed out of court in view of Congressional support for [segregation]." Bishop and the hundreds of members of the CPG urgently wanted to tackle Jim Crow schools in the nation's capital. But in this case, Houston was a conservatizing force, trying to harness the grassroots energy for desegregation as a way to fund lawsuits for more incremental changes. Bishop and Houston filed *Bishop v. Corning* in 1948. The two plaintiffs were Bishop's daughter Judine and Barbara Jean Arnold. The lawsuit sued the members of the school board for failing to share the "surplus facilities for white pupils" with Negro students "despite overcrowded conditions in their schools." Though Houston's legal briefs were conservative, he did see them as a step on the road toward desegregation. In a letter he wrote to his personal friend Louis S. Weiss (of law firm Paul, Weiss, Wharton and Garrison), he described the school strike and his interest in the CPG as "not wholly [altruistic]. I have a son who will be four next month. Ever since I knew he was coming I have wrestled with the problem of remaining here and having him educated in a Jim-Crow system. I finally decided to stay and fight the system, believing that the legacy of courage and struggle will mean more."[22]

Discord among the lawyers representing the various parties was, perhaps, unavoidable. *Carr v. Corning* was financed by the Washington, DC, branch of the NAACP as "our test-case for integration in the public schools of the District of Columbia." But Ransom resigned from the DC branch in March 1948 because of pressure to consolidate his case with Houston's case, *Bishop v. Corning*. A legal secretary sent an urgent memo to Thurgood Marshall on March 22, 1948, stating that Ransom "demands that he retain full control of the *Carr* school case. He has stated that under no circumstances will he allow the *Carr* case to be joined with Charles Houston's case." This development may have occurred because Ransom feared his lawsuit would become an equalization case if paired with Houston's, or because of Ransom's difficult relationship with lawyers connected to Howard Law School, including Houston. Whatever the origins of the antagonism, by November 1948 NAACP-affiliated lawyers in Washington, DC, were getting nervous about *Carr*. Everyone involved with the case wanted—indeed expected—it to be appealed to the Supreme Court. To that end, several lawyers in DC—including Austin Fickling, a member of Ransom's own law firm—were lobbying Thurgood Marshall to come down and argue it himself. The case was set for argument on November 9, 1948. On November 5, Fickling sent Marshall an anxious telegram: "Carr the plaintiff insist [*sic*] on [Ransom] handling the entire case before the court. Frankly if this happens the NAACP will get no credit if the case is successful.... I suggest you come down and argue the case." Marshall sent back a formal telegram saying that if the plaintiff wanted Ransom to handle the case, then the national office could not step in.[23]

———

In the spring of 1947, just as Carr's petition was being delivered to the Washington, DC, school board, that besieged body was handed another school desegregation demand, only this time from a white girl who had been attending a black high school. Karla Galarza, the stepdaughter of Mexican American activist Ernesto Galarza, had begun attending a class in dress design at Margaret Murray Vocational School with a teacher named Miss Wharton. According to Karla Galarza, her teacher, the principal, and the students in her class had all welcomed her to the school. She remained in the class from February 2 until mid-March, when her presence in the school was reported by a "citizen" to the assistant superintendent of Negro schools, G. T. Wilkerson. According to a press release from Ernesto Galarza, Wilkerson issued "a flat order barring Karla Rosel Galarza from the Margaret Murray Washington Vocational School." This order, "supported by the Board of Education, including the three Negro members," Ernesto Galarza complained, "closes the door of the school to a white student." The board and its officials, he continued, "have extended segregation to the point where it deprives even a white citizen of equal protection under the law."[24]

Karla was born in Sacramento, California, in 1925 and moved to Washington, DC, with her mother, Mae Galarza, and her stepfather,

Ernesto, in 1936. She graduated from Washington-Lee High School in Arlington, Virginia, in 1939. In 1947, she wished to go back to school to seek training in clothing design. It is unclear how Galarza found out about Mrs. Wharton's class and whether her attendance there was based on a desire for acquiring new skills, a desire to "test the schools" (as so many black parents and students were doing), or both. A family friend claims it is doubtful that "Karla would have gone to a black school just to learn how to sew." But Galarza's daughter, Lori Pepe, points out that her mother did go on to have a career in clothing design (though, after that, political activism alongside her father-in-law). What matters is that Galarza's attendance at this school shocked the superintendent, and that Ernesto Galarza used her ejection from the school as an opportunity to publicly express his outrage at segregated education in Washington, DC, and later to file a lawsuit, *Galarza v. Board of Education*.[25]

At the time, Ernesto Galarza was an official at the Pan-American Union. He would go on to become a leading organizer of Mexican American farm labor in California, a founder of the field of Chicano studies, a Nobel Peace Prize nominee, and the famed author of *Merchants of Labor* about the Bracero Program (wherein Mexicans were allowed into the country to work only during the harvest seasons) and *Barrio Boy*, a memoir. He was the first immigrant from Mexico to get a PhD, which he earned in economics from Columbia University (the degree was awarded the same year he filed the lawsuit), and he remained committed to educational activism for the rest of his life. Karla came of age in a household that was highly political, especially on questions of race and ethnicity. Ernesto Galarza had long admired the NAACP and hoped that Mexican Americans could one day build similar institutions.[26]

Both the white and the black press found the case fascinating. The *Pittsburgh Courier* reported on the *Galarza* case alongside an article about the *Carr* case. Several white papers wrote articles about

Galarza, her family, and her desire to attend a black school. The *Washington Star*, which was hostile to the *Carr* case, interviewed Galarza at her home. In "White Girl in Colored School to Fight Transfer by Board," the paper discussed her background and intentions at length. "Let me tell you about Miss Wharton," she said to the reporter about her teacher. "She has studied in Paris and in New York. I have much admiration for her." Later in the article, Galarza said, "When school reconvenes after the spring holiday I will ignore the order and return to the Washington Vocational School."[27]

Charles Houston wanted the NAACP to take the case. He thought it would be a good addition to the Browne Junior High case and *Carr*. The *Galarza* case, he said, "Would emphasize once more the right of an individual to access all education facilities without discrimination." Everyone agreed that Ernesto Galarza should have a white lawyer, and the American Civil Liberties Union expressed interest in the case. But ultimately the LDF decided against taking it on. As legal secretary Marian Wynn Perry wrote to Thurgood Marshall, "The 'freak' aspects of this case which resulted in an inequality to a white student is, if anything, dangerous to our presentation in all segregation cases that segregation results in discrimination against Negroes." The letter that Perry sent to Ernesto Galarza telling him that the LDF would not take the case emphasized that the organization was, as of January 1948, only working on "cases on a professional-school level."[28]

Though Karla's stated reasons for wanting to attend Margaret Murray Vocational School were practical, in Ernesto Galarza's letter to the board of education, he addressed much broader political terrain. He wrote,

Both the spirit and the law of the Declaration of Independence and the Constitution have worked, through the years, toward the safeguarding of that responsible liberty of the mind on which human freedom truly rests. That liberty includes, surely, one of the fundamental purposes of education as defined by a great Southerner, Thomas Jefferson: "to observe with intelligence and faithfulness all the social relations under which he (the citizen) shall be placed."

He went on to say that one of the chief functions of modern education is "cultural interchange in our relations as a nation with other peoples."[29]

That Karla was a young woman might seem incidental to the case, had girl plaintiffs not been the overwhelming majority in such cases. In short, when Ernesto Galarza sued on behalf of his daughter, it appears that his eloquent and unequivocal statements about the civic obligations of cultural exchange were enabled by the fact that Karla was a young woman. Whether or not Ernesto Galarza would have done the same had the incident involved a son, or whether a young man would have attempted to enroll in a black school in the first place, is a matter of speculation. However, given the disproportionate number of African American girl plaintiffs, it is fair to say that the joint father-daughter desegregation lawsuit was tied to an image of racial reconciliation that was connected to Karla Galarza's identity as a girl—an identity that apparently informed the social imagination of both black and Mexican American parents.

———

After the strike ended, Gardner Bishop, now president of the CPG, filed a lawsuit on behalf of his daughter, Judine. She was not consulted but rather drafted to be a plaintiff in her father's lawsuit, and she claims that she did not profit from the experience in any way. When her father first emerged as a vocal proponent of the strike at Browne Junior High, she remembers only that she would have preferred to have been in school and that she worried about her grades suffering. "I thought school was a wonderful place. . . . I was a good student. I loved school. So at first when we went on strike I wasn't happy about that at all," Judine (now Judine Bishop Johnson) recalls. When her father explained the significance of her lawsuit to her, it came after the fact. "Those were difficult times," she remembers. "They were difficult for us as children because of what we were going through and then knowing that at home. . . . That was the only topic under discussion." Like other children of prominent civil rights leaders, Judine had been conscripted into a battle in which she would have preferred not to participate.[30]

Gardner Bishop had grown up in North Carolina. He immigrated to Washington, DC, in 1930 looking for work and had been a barber on U Street—the black business corridor of the city—since 1942. He described himself as an outsider representing the working class: "The children of prostitutes, hustlers . . . the underside of the D.C. black community." Bishop had been resisting Jim Crow since Judine was in kindergarten. On a Sunday morning in 1938, when few people were out, Bishop took her to the "whites only" playground near his home. He had just gotten her into a swing when a cop stopped him and said, "Don't you see that [whites only] sign?" Bishop told the cop, "She can't read." The cop told him he was "smart" and then took him to the station house, where he was made to pay a $10 fine.[31]

The CPG was in high gear fighting segregation in schools, parks, and libraries, but segregated education was the organization's top priority. In an interview in 1974, Bishop said nothing about the people who ran the CPG, and his version of the story made it seem as if the organization—"low income, blue-collar" as Bishop Johnson explains—materialized spontaneously in January 1948. But there was a great deal of work that went into bringing the CPG to life. Fund-raising, poster making, phone calling, door knocking, school investigating, record keeping, and everything else that goes into successful political organizing was handled by a flotilla of women, virtually none of whom have made it into the historical record and who were, almost to a person, the wives of doctors, dentists, and Howard professors. While many of the CPG's constituents were working-class parents, the organization seems to have depended upon the labor of middle-class, educated women. Because of this pairing, there are some discrepancies between Bishop's memory of the CPG and the records of the organization. For instance, whereas Bishop remembered "Chitlin' parties" to raise money, the women carefully recorded "receptions" and "delightful refreshments." There are records of flower arrangements, special awards, and thank-you notes. And while Bishop Johnson is adamant that the organization was composed of families from the less prosperous northeast section of DC, in fact most of the women working for the CPG lived in the neighborhood surrounding Howard University, in the northwest of the city.[32]

The officers of the CPG broke the city down into quadrants, in which four women oversaw fund-raising by women volunteers. Burma Whitted was responsible for the northwest section of the city; June Lewis, the southeast; Elizabeth Thomas, the northeast; and J. W. Duckett, the southwest. While the Metropolitan Baptist Church and other congregations gave sums up to $125, most of the money was raised going door-to-door and selling memberships. It cost one dollar to become a member of the CPG. Canvassers described the CPG as an organization that would "fight for integrated schools." A typical membership drive, with four neighborhoods reporting, listed one-dollar memberships sold to thirty-three women and ten men. At a meeting with the Park View PTA, the CPG made a pitch for funds. Twenty-seven women, four men, and three couples officially contributed. Another fund-raising committee was called the Doctor's Wives Action Committee Drive; listed were 108 women who contributed between one and ten dollars each. Many of these women could have been tacitly contributing for their husbands. However, as a practical, in-person, on-the-ground grassroots movement, the CPG was an organization staffed by women relying on part-time women volunteers, who in turn asked other women for memberships and donations.[33]

Gardner Bishop, though frustrated by inequalities in the schools, was most concerned about the institution of segregation. For Bishop, the effects of segregation on children were the very worst manifestation of a system that was a fundamental contradiction to American democracy, an embarrassment to the United States around the world, and a legal crime. Because segregation was criminal, he believed that the court of public opinion could be made to come to its senses. Article II of the CPG constitution reads: "The object of this organization shall be to abolish racial segregation and other discriminatory practices now imposed upon minority groups in the public schools and recreational areas of the District of Columbia." In numerous letters written to a spectrum of officials, and in pleas for donations and parental support, Bishop and the other members of the CPG come across as driven by unrelenting righteous indignation over the impact of Jim Crow on the children of DC.[34]

In his personal letters, Bishop affected the persona—not entirely unreasonable—of being the sole person awake in a capital city that has fallen asleep on the job. One letter drips with sarcasm: "To their Excellencies—the Ambassadors and Ministers Plenipotentiary accredited to the Government of the United States: May we as American citizens apologize for the recent decision of the Board of Recreation for the District of Columbia on racial segregation which discredits our nation before the world and is bound to prove embarrassing to our Government in its foreign relations." A letter dated June 1947, addressing CPG members, begins, "Do you know about the petitions? Are you helping? Have you forgotten about the children? . . . It's your fight for full freedom for the kids. GIVE THEM THAT WHICH YOU HAVE *NEVER* HAD—unsegregated schools and playgrounds. . . . Segregated schools and playgrounds are the basic roots of discrimination and prejudice." In a letter dated September 6, 1950, he addressed the board of education, saying, "Dual systems have never produced equality and the general rule is that the colored child always bears the brunt of inequalities. . . .

Why should there be different curricula for the two races? These questions always confront the colored parent and add to his confusion. How can we but question the *astuteness*, the *progressive* thinking, the *dereliction* of duty or the *competency* of those in charge!!" The urgency in Bishop's letters never waned between 1947 and 1954.[35]

What does any of this have to do with Bishop's daughter Judine? Ostensibly nothing. What is striking about Bishop's letters is how unapologetic he was about his desire to integrate. He firmly believed that black children who were cut off from whites could not function properly in "the modern world" and that not only could you "get 'em together," but that it was vital to do so. As Alonzo Smith, the son of a woman who worked extensively for the CPG, says, Bishop's frank assessment of the disadvantages of segregation upset quite a few people. They felt that their schools and communities were being maligned. Smith admits that even he (at the age of seven) and his father were somewhat amused by his mother's "militant integrationism." But Bishop's assertion that black and white youth must form social bonds with one another did not rest on the opinions of boys and men like Smith and his father. Bishop's ideas found expression in the CPG and its women members, where there seems to have been little debate about the integrationist goals of the organization. As the father of Judine Bishop, he was—like James C. Carr Sr. and Ernesto Galarza—acting on principles that fit with contemporary understandings of the appropriate roles and social obligations of girls. The father of daughters and the president of an organization composed of women, Bishop had a secure platform for his integrationist ambitions—one where he would not likely encounter the kind of ambivalence expressed by the male members of the Smith household.[36]

———

In early December 1947, when the strike at Browne Junior High was at its height, the Southwest Region NAACP issued a press release

announcing that "the second 'cease and desist' school case in less than
a week against a Texas school board was filed" when Julius Brown
"presented his daughter, Vivian Alpha Brown, 16, for registration at
the 'white' LaGrange High School and was refused." Three days earlier, about ninety miles north in Hearne, Texas, C. G. Jennings, "was
named as plaintiff with his daughter Doris Fay [sic], 13." Writing to
Thurgood Marshall about the two cases, Houston branch executive
secretary Lulu White expressed frustration that the parents would
not "let this thing alone." Nonetheless, she wrote, "you get the 'Vig-
ilanties' [sic] there ready to catch a plane and come on down with
reinforcements, because it looks like the top will blow off if another
suit is filed on this education business."[37]

The Jennings case was inaugurated in September 1947, when
thirteen-year-old twins Doris Raye and Doris Faye Jennings went
with their parents, C. G. and Ella Mae Jennings, to the white superintendent's office and attempted to enroll at the white junior high
school in Hearne. Located midway between Houston and Dallas,
Hearne was a small town surrounded by cotton fields. The girls had
attended local public schools for their elementary years. However,
the appalling building that was to serve as their junior high and high
school, called Blackshear, was unacceptable to Ella Mae and C. G.
Jennings.[38]

C. G. Jennings was a Tuskegee University graduate who had
studied agriculture under both George Washington Carver and
Booker T. Washington. After graduating, he taught math at Conroe
College, a small school just north of Houston, for a few years before
he met and married Ella Mae Kenny. Ella Mae had grown up in
Hearne and graduated from Blackshear High School as salutatorian of her class. Her twin girls were eight years old when Ella Mae
Kenny married C. G. Jennings, and he quickly became a father to
them. When she inherited a small plot of land on the outskirts of
town from her parents, the couple built a house on the property and
Jennings established himself as a contractor and business manager

for local cotton growers. According to Doris Raye (now Doris Raye Jennings Brewer), "He . . . would gather people who wanted to go to the fields and work. He would hire them and bring them back and dispense their wages . . . and he handled all the business" for a local [white] farmer. In this way, Jennings was much like James Carr—a manager in a position of some authority over workers and a leader in the community. The family also owned about thirty acres farther from the town, so Jennings did his own farming in addition to contracting.[39]

All of the Jennings children—Doris Faye, Doris Raye, and their younger siblings, Anne and Clifton Jr.—helped out on the farm, though Clifton Jr. was tasked with more farm chores than his sisters. Ella Mae Jennings worked as a maid when the girls were young. Later she worked in the home, weighed the cotton at the end of the day, and kept the books. "Mom was essentially the bookkeeper," Brewer says. "She helped keep the accounts straight and . . . [saw] to it that everybody got what they were supposed to get paid." The twins remember that, though the family did not have much money, they always had enough to eat because of the farm: "Dad would slaughter a pig and sometimes a calf," and they had "beautiful" clothes because Ella Mae Jennings was an expert seamstress. But they never had new shoes, and the family had little beyond the raw materials for what they could make themselves.[40]

Like Ada Sipuel's mother Martha Sipuel, C. G. Jennings acted as an informal broker between the black community and local white politicians. "He was very active in politics," Brewer explains, "and at that time . . . politicians, particularly white ones, came to the black churches and addressed them. . . . And if they got C. G. Jennings's endorsement, they were pretty sure they were going to win. And if he didn't endorse them, they were *not* going to win." His leadership in community affairs was an outgrowth of a "wise," even-tempered personality, generosity in times of need to both black and white neighbors, and courage in dealing with local whites. "He was very calm . . . and was not afraid of anything or anybody." Everyone, both black and white, called him "Mr. Jennings" or "Jennings"—no small accomplishment in a small town in the South, where whites universally refused to use honorifics and last names for African Americans. "Both races came to him for advice," says Brewer. Though Jennings worked with local party regulars, he took his own counsel and was in no way a bought man. As Doris Faye (now Doris Faye Jennings Alston) recalls, one time his truck broke down near a railroad crossing, and "a very prominent white man . . . came over and told him, 'You better get that out of the way.' And he, very calm, went back into his truck, got his hammer out, and chased the white man down the street." "You just didn't *do* that!" Alston exclaims. "But that was the other side of him." It was that side of him—the side that would not back down when his limit had been reached—that the twins believe inspired the lawsuit. They remember him saying, "'My children are not going to this school.' And that's how it all began."

In the mid-1940s, as new neighbors began to build around the Jenningses' plot of land on the corner, the block began to change, becoming more polyglot and diverse:

> The irony of our childhood was that we lived in what . . . began to be referred to as an integrated neighborhood. . . . There was an Italian family to our left. A white family across over there. A Mexican family over here. . . . We were just all intermingled and mixed up and we just lived together that way. . . . We played outside . . . [went] into each other's houses. When tragedies happened, the neighborhood came together. . . . Every aspect of our lives was together except for [church] and education.

C. G. Jennings insisted upon and received, with a few exceptions, respect from all members of the Hearne community, but he and Ella Mae Jennings also drilled into their daughters the values of racial openness, fairness, and the golden rule. "Instilled in us from before

I could remember," Brewer recalls, "[was] that you are as good as anybody else. And you are no better than anybody else. That you treat people like you want to be treated. And you don't judge them by the color of their skin." Alston agrees: "Planted in my mind was the fact that you . . . respect all men. You do not bow to any men. You bow only to God . . . meet people for who they are. You don't judge them by the color of their skin." Both twins describe a form of self-respect that was fundamentally intertwined with respect for others—including their white neighbors. The insistence that the girls do their best to ignore color was both a response to the unusual neighborhood in which they grew up and the aspirations that their parents had for them. They wanted the girls to "accomplish more in life than they had," to be "proud" and unapologetic about who they were, and always know that they were the equal of any person.

In 1947, the girls were slated to attend Blackshear High School—the school from which their mother had graduated and which housed grades seven through twelve. Having burned to the ground in 1946, the school was now housed in a leftover World War II camp for German prisoners of war. After the fire, the school board simply relocated the prison barracks to the site where the school had been and propped up the whole structure with railroad ties and old tires. For Ella Mae and C. G. Jennings, this state of affairs was too much to bear, and none of the other parents in town were happy with Blackshear High School either. So, C. G. Jennings suggested to the Hearne NAACP that he file a lawsuit that fall to desegregate the schools, with Raye and Faye as plaintiffs. With the support of the local branch behind him and shared outrage among black parents, the lawsuit was planned and executed within a matter of months. In order to institute the lawsuit, according to Brewer, "you had to go to the [white] school and be refused." Hence, to some degree, the confrontation on the schoolhouse steps was more of a formality—a staged encounter where all of the actors knew or could at least plan for what would happen. "Hearne's a small town," Brewer remembers, "and I don't know whether [the superintendent] was deliberately informed or whether he just got wind of it, but he knew that Dad and we were coming."[41]

The *Dallas Morning News* described the encounter this way: when the Jenningses tried to enroll at the white school, "the application of C. G. Jennings on behalf of ... Doris Fay [*sic*], 13, was refused by Supt. P. M. Hix of the Hearne Independent School District." According to Brewer, the superintendent barred their way before the group could make it into his office. As with Marguerite Carr, the white administrators would not countenance the girls walking through the front door, much less broaching the inner sanctum of the school. Brewer remembers,

> Hix met us outside the building and it was the same spiel: "If it was up to me, but it's not. It's the law".... You know, the same spiel that they give you all the time. And I think he called Dad "C. G."! ... They *knew* each other. ... He put his hand on his shoulder and said, "You know, C. G. it's not up to me" ... this sincere *hogwash*. But Dad knew it was coming. He turned around and headed for Waco [to file the lawsuit].

Calling C. G. Jennings "C. G." was a pointed departure from the norm in Hearne. It was meant to diminish him, to take away the respect that he had earned in the community. The combination of false concern and lack of culpability on the part of the superintendent particularly enraged Raye and Faye—they saw it for the "hogwash" that it was, and the encounter still riles them today. The superintendent's attempts to humiliate the family by keeping them outside the school and treating their esteemed father as some kind of dependent worthy of mock concern and condescension was a vivid, transformative experience for the twins. In this encounter on the steps, they witnessed and were subjected to the full weight of legalized, enforced segregation: the ejection from places of learning financed by all citizens' taxes, the literal barring of the school door, the inevitable humiliations inflicted on those African Americans who made claims on "white" institutions, the lies from officials who pretended to have nothing to do with the segregation they enforced. It is in these moments—anticipated by both sides and practically preordained in terms of the posture each would have toward the other—that it becomes clear why so few families willingly participated in desegregation lawsuits. Such encounters invited disdain, rejection, and white pretensions of the worst sort, not to mention the more unpredictable forms of hostility and physical danger.[42]

African American students in Hearne, like those in Washington, DC, and elsewhere, registered their frustration and support for the lawsuit by going on strike. It was reported that three hundred students stayed away from school the following day. But court cases are slow, and the strike was brief. Thurgood Marshall and Dallas attorney W. J. Durham jointly filed their complaint on November 28, 1947. It is a somewhat strained document. The words "equalization" and "integration" are nowhere to be found. Instead, Durham and Marshall emphasized the fact that the constitutional rights of C. G. Jennings, and all parents and students in Hearne similarly situated, had been violated. Taxes for "the purpose of supporting the public free school system" had been levied from plaintiff, yet he and other "Negroes [are] forced to attend one school exclusively [with] all other racial groups attending the other schools; that under the Fourteenth Amendment to the United States Constitution and the laws of the United States, the defendants . . . are required to provide educational facilities for said children without discrimination because of race or color of said children." The shortcomings of the "buildings . . . that were once used by German war prisoners" were painstakingly described: there was no fire protection, the classes were overcrowded, there was no modern equipment, and the buildings were inadequately lighted and furnished and failed to meet "the

general laws of the state of Texas for the establishment of a stan-
dardized high school." The "prayer" or request of the court was that it
enter a judgment declaring that "the policy, custom and usage of the
defendants . . . in maintaining schools . . . for Negro children . . . in
the Hearne Independent School District which are inferior to those
furnished to white children . . . is a denial of the equal protection
of laws guaranteed by the Fourteenth Amendment to the Constitution, and is therefore unconstitutional and void." The key to the
request is the word "void." If the current "customs" of the school
board were void, they would be required to cease segregating black
students immediately.[43]

The complaint, for all its radicalism, took a measured tone, especially compared to Leon Ransom's petitions of the same year and
Marshall's later briefs on grade school segregation. The Texas edition
of the *Kansas City Call*, however, breathed excitement into the case
when Marshall came down to argue it in March 1948. "NAACP
to Test Validity of Segregation" ran the headline. "The Hearne case,
sometimes called the 'Little Sweatt Case' because it constitutes an
attack on the validity of segregation on the high school level in education, was filed in federal court in Waco," the *Call* reported. It
"is another in a series of NAACP cases being launched in an attempt to eliminate segregation in education and follows exactly the
same legal theory employed in the Sweatt case." The *Dallas Morning
News* also reported that "Hearne is another attack on the segregation line growing out of the same strategy as that being used in the
Sweatt case." Marshall would have been taken aback to read that the
NAACP had launched an attack on grade school segregation; in no
way had the NAACP committed itself to such a course of action. In
fact, the organization was careful to tell those who inquired just the
opposite. Marshall, at this point, was just one of many lawyers responding to individual parents who had already tried to enroll their
daughters in white schools. That he flew down to Texas to argue the

case—as *Sweatt* was underway—says more about his commitment to the NAACP in Texas at the time. *Jennings v. Hearne* was not, as the *Call* hoped, part of a larger NAACP strategy.[44]

However, *Jennings* is historically important as the first such case that Marshall filed. He did not yet have a roster of experts to call upon, nor did he turn the trial into a showcase of segregation's ills, and the lawsuit certainly was not an all-out attack on segregation. It was, however, a start down the road toward *Briggs v. Elliott* in 1951, where Marshall argued that segregated schools were unconstitutional. Hence, the LDF's battle over segregated schooling began earlier than previously believed, and it had been brewing for a long time when the organization decided to appeal grade school education cases to the Supreme Court. This longer, slower progression makes more sense than the typical story, in which *Sweatt* was decided in 1950 and the LDF moved immediately from graduate schools to grade schools. For years, parents had been approaching white schools with their daughters, filing lawsuits against segregated schooling, and demanding legal representation. In light of this, the NAACP's pivot to grade schools after the *Sweatt* decision makes more sense. The LDF was overflowing with female grade school plaintiffs.

The Jennings twins did not testify in the ensuing trial in Waco, but they do remember being interviewed, both at the courthouse and later at home. It was a swift education in ways of the white press. "The only thing that sticks in my mind," Raye Brewer remembers, "is that . . . the reporter asked why we were doing this suit. And I said to him, 'We just want to get an education' . . . but he put it in the paper that I said, 'I just want to *get educated*.'" The reporter misrepresented her, she said, because "they did not want this intelligent black child talking in the newspaper, so they played it down." Brewer—unlike other, more successful desegregation firsts—did not save press clippings about her trial. But she did remember the nature of the misrepresentation precisely, over forty years later. The reporter, who misidentified Doris Raye as "Doris Fay," told the story this way:

Does Doris Fay Want to Go to School with White Students?

Standing in the door of her small white 3-room frame home, she crosses one foot over the other and says smilingly, "I just want to go where I can get educated."

Does she think she'd like to be in a class with young white girls her age?

"Well . . . I had rather go to school with my own friends." The school which she was going to in Hearne was not as good as the white people's school, she says.

What the reporter accurately conveyed was the directness with which Raye responded to his questions. She faced an inquiry about interracial sociality—an explosive question meant to intimidate and disarm her—with self-possession, a pleasant demeanor, a smile, and unyielding precision. She was also, appropriately enough for central Texas in 1948, cagey about the ultimate goal of the lawsuit. It was an effective performance. The confidence that the reporter conveyed testified to the fact that, as Brewer says of herself, "I looked him straight in the eye when he was talking to me."[45]

The trust that the Jennings parents had in the twins as they spoke to reporters was well placed, Brewer says, and had deep roots. "They didn't put words in our mouth," she explains. "We thoroughly understood what they were doing and why. They didn't tell us how to answer anybody. They assumed that if [reporters] asked us, we would know what to say and we did." Of those moments when the twins were speaking to the press, Faye Alston says, "That doesn't just happen. That comes from roots." Brewer agrees, "[Our parents] were pretty sure that Raye and Faye would do what was necessary when the time came. And we did . . . because the value system that they instilled in us was very strong and very deep and we had a strong sense of fairness . . . and *dignity* above all." Sounding a bit like Marguerite Carr when she said she knew how to "act in polite company," Brewer continues, "When they sent us out on *any* day they expected certain behavior of us. And we knew what that behavior was. And we knew we jolly well better do it. You know [*laughing*] the *behavior.*" The behavior—set at a higher bar for African American girls in public—was meant both to defend their dignity and to make the case for racial assimilation. Brewer and Alston also remember a communicative relationship with their parents that, again like the Carr's, was ongoing. "They explained why and what their thoughts [were] about it. They communicated with us and explained [it] to us on a level we could understand."

Also like Marguerite Carr, the Jennings twins were told that their attempt to enroll in the white school was for the sake of the whole community. "We are doing this because we are trying to get a better school for you," their parents informed them prior to their encounter with Superintendent Hix. Simultaneously they were told, "It is not really about you. It is about all the black kids." Their parents prepared them for what lay ahead by fully enlisting them in the larger purpose of equity for the race, by getting them to think of themselves as participants in a highly consequential struggle that included other students like themselves, and by convincing them of the urgency of their participation.

When assessing the effort and performance that went into Raye's smiling encounter with the press in the fall of 1948, it is important to take into account what had transpired since her case began. By that time, the pressure surrounding *Jennings v. Hearne* had been building for over a year. C. G. Jennings did not suffer from economic retaliation like James Carr or other plaintiffs: "The man for whom he was . . . managing workers didn't care what he did as long as he . . . got his cotton crops in." However, there were other dangers. The "KKK element in the area . . . decided they wanted to kill him." When the threats got specific, Jennings would sit "up all night with his shotgun across his lap, just as calm, and waited for 'em." However, people in their neighborhood were frightened, and some "had simply packed up and moved." The twins were told that, because they had filed a lawsuit claiming that Blackshear was inadequate, they could not attend the school. They were sent away for three years. For the first two, with support from local NAACP members and the Baptist Convention, they boarded at Mary Allen Seminary and College, eighty-five miles to the east in Crockett, Texas. When they were interviewed in August 1948, they were preparing to go back to Mary Allen for another school year because of the lawsuit that had been filed in their names. On the one hand, they saw their experiences of travel and boarding school as an "adventure," and believed they received a better education. On the other, Alston says, "Our lives were in danger. . . . Our parents . . . took us out of our ordinary, everyday life, and set us on this path we had to travel."[46]

The initial support for the lawsuit waned after the Hearne Independent School District built a new black high school in 1949. Without funds from the local NAACP, the Jenningses were unable to afford the tuition for Mary Allen, and the girls spent their third year away from home with an uncle and aunt in Houston, where they attended the Phillis Wheatley School. They lost not only financial but also social support, which eventually gave way to resentment. The girls returned to Hearne for their sophomore through senior years of high school, and though they maintain that they simply picked up where they left off with old friends, it was also clear that their continued support for school desegregation rankled many in the community. "There was an element that thought that we thought we were better than they," Brewer recalls ruefully. There was a sense of fighting a lonely battle of unappreciated sacrifice, incomprehension from their community, and outright hostility—feelings just like those experienced by Lloyd Gaines, Heman Sweatt, Marguerite

Carr, and those who would desegregate schools after *Brown*. Other families, Brewer says, "were not taking their children over there to that white school. They were not going to subject their children or themselves to this. In essence, [we] stood alone in this . . . and a lot of them didn't see that . . . Dad had sacrificed us to make things better for them."[47]

Even seemingly inconsequential issues—such as the academic subjects the girls chose—bothered their peers. After the lawsuit, Blackshear High School was required to offer a foreign language. The girls chose Spanish. "And there were two [of] us in there. . . . You remember Miss Blanche taught that class?" Alston asks Brewer. "Nobody, none, of the other black kids would enroll in it . . . because there was still this idea of, you don't really go too far against these white folks. You just don't challenge them." As Brewer and Alston describe it, the other students stayed away from challenging subjects at Blackshear not because they felt insecure about their academic abilities but because academic ambition would be noted by the white community and perceived as a threat. This idea is consistent with observations historians have made about rural families who did not own their own land. As Katherine Mellen Charron has written, "'Don't need no education to work the fields,' was a sentiment sometimes voiced by black tenant or sharecropping parents, especially within earshot of the white landlords on whom their livelihoods depended."[48]

In late September 1947, just after the girls' initial school visit, a white newspaper reporter caught up with Ella Mae Jennings as she was coming in from the cotton fields. The reporter asked, incredulously, "whether they really wanted their daughter in the white high school or whether the attempt to enroll her was a protest against 'inadequate school buildings.'" Ella Mae Jennings put him off with the same kind of artful noncommittal statement that her daughter would later use with the press. "We want our children to have the best education possible," she replied, "and you never know how far you can get until you try." According to the twins, this statement was a testament to her frame of mind. "That was her," Brewer says. "Don't be satisfied where you are if you can get to another place. . . . Don't ever think you've arrived. Just keep on pluggin'. It was a way of life." When Doris Raye went out to speak to the reporter in front of her house a year later, her statements were in the same mold as her mother's: open-ended, long-term, patient, and assured. Neither of the twins remembers a particular conversation about this "way of life," but it was somehow communicated to them, no doubt in ways that were both overt and implicit—and repeated often.[49]

———

None of the cases filed in 1947 and 1948 made it to the Supreme Court. James Carr elected to drop *Carr v. Corning* when lawyers insisted that Marguerite Carr be the sole plaintiff. He wanted to include everyone from the PTA who had participated—and suffered for it—to be listed as plaintiffs. Judine Bishop and Constance Carter both graduated from high school before their cases could be appealed. But these early cases helped to bring about a quiet revolution in the attitudes of both judges and school boards. Just a few years after *Carr*, *Carter*, and *Jennings* were filed, judges would become increasingly willing to acknowledge that segregated schools were discriminatory, and to say that such discrimination was unconstitutional.

When these early legal struggles were going through the courts, however, the young female plaintiffs had to have a social and political imagination that could function in the absence of any known outcome, in an uncharted public landscape. Their voices were vital for setting in motion and making possible the legal battle over the schools. It was these young women and girls—alongside activist mothers and fathers—whose willing participation in the early desegregation lawsuits paved the way for those cases that would, several years later, make their way to the Supreme Court.

4

Laying the Groundwork

Esther Brown and the
Struggle in South Park, Kansas

W HEN THE SUPREME COURT RULED on *Brown v. Board of Ed-*
ucation on May 17, 1954, the *Kansas City Call's* banner
headline, the largest the paper ever published, read simply "KILL
SEGREGATION." A few weeks later, describing a "jubilee celebration" in Kansas City, Kansas, that attracted over 150 people to
the Pleasant Green Baptist Church, the paper listed those invited
to address the crowd: McKinley Burnett, president of the Topeka
NAACP branch; Esther Brown; Robert Cotton, president of the
Kansas Technical Institute; and two local clergy members, in that
order. Brown—known to census takers as a white housewife and
to locals as a school desegregation firebrand—assumed her place
among the local dignitaries without any introduction. Her remarks
were the first words that the *Call* recorded verbatim: "Mrs. Brown
told the audience that it is the 'little people like us who bring about
such things as Monday's Supreme Court opinion. The most brilliant
lawyers couldn't have succeeded but for the help of people like you
here tonight.'"

Like Gardner Bishop in DC, Brown liberally used the term "little people"—a phrase that was not typically part of the vocabulary of local NAACP officials nor anyone else on the stage. It was characteristic of the way Brown had been speaking and thinking since she became the "guiding spirit" of the first postwar school desegregation suit in Kansas—in the semirural, unincorporated community of South Park—in 1948. Her words encapsulated her fundamental distrust of those bourgeois lawyers to whom she referred, a distrust that went back to her radical, communist youth and was reinforced by her experiences over the years it took to win the South Park case. In her many, vivid letters to the LDF over the course of the two-year battle in the courts, she referred to the lawyers in the New York office as "you people" and to the black citizens of South Park as "the people" and, at times, as "our people." She had a working-class versus middle-class, Midwest versus New York, David versus Goliath mentality—one that lent itself to remarkable feats of commitment, ambition, sacrifice, and at times what many, especially NAACP lawyers, thought was questionable risk-taking.[1]

Until her death in 1970, Esther Brown maintained that she was merely "a housewife with a conscience." She painted a deliberately humble, naïve, and conservative image that she invoked constantly in her dealings with the NAACP, reporters, her closest friends, and even her children. When historian Richard Kluger interviewed Esther Brown in the mid-1960s for his book *Simple Justice*, she said she was simply a "middle-class housewife" who was "shocked" at the conditions of the black school in South Park, just outside of Kansas City. According to Brown, her social justice awakening happened almost instantly one day in 1948 when her maid, Helen Swann, invited her to come to a school board meeting over a dispute about grade school funding in South Park, and to visit the local black elementary school, the Walker School. After viewing conditions at Walker and attending a white school board meeting, Brown was—as she described it—a "changed woman." She would spend the next several years tirelessly crusading against segregated schools, inviting the social and economic reprisals and threats of violence that were the price paid by all those who participated in early school desegregation lawsuits.

But Brown's conversion story was a ruse, one that she had refined and embroidered over the course of several decades. Brown was not a housewife—not in the sense she sought to imply. She was a one-time communist and committed radical who had been trained by some of the brightest lights on the left in the 1930s when the Communist Party USA was in its heyday. She also happened to be married and a mother. Still, Brown—and later her family—clung to the notion that she was actually an ordinary, highly feminine, private individual with extraordinary ideas about social justice. That this was Brown's story for so long speaks volumes about the ongoing stigma attached to Communist Party membership, the danger of her sustained affiliations with progressive groups during the McCarthy era, and the personal losses—both social and economic—she and her husband suffered at the hands of the Federal Bureau of Investigation (FBI) because of her radical affiliations. Her embrace of the term "housewife" also reflected, perhaps, its ongoing usefulness in her life; it was a moniker that provided a respectable platform for her interest in the plight of her black neighbors and the NAACP. Unfortunately, the housewife cover also served to obscure her impact both on the South Park case and the case it inspired, in which she also participated extensively: *Brown v. Board of Education.*[2]

Descriptions of Brown in the media do not help to round out the picture of her; they were contradictory and often suffused with incomprehension. A female friend said, joyfully, "If there were some way to plug Esther Brown into the world she would light every dark place." A male friend recalled that she was "abrasive." Lucile Bluford at the *Kansas City Call* described her as "a beautiful woman with a quiet, persuasive manner . . . gentle yet firm and persistent as she protested against those things in American life that she found wrong." Reverend E. A. Freeman, president of the Kansas City NAACP branch, thought she was a "crazy zealot," and John Anderson, Johnson County district attorney in the 1940s and later governor of Kansas, remembered thinking she was a "kook."[3]

No one really knew what to make of her. Both blacks and whites in Kansas questioned her motives and could be leery of her, and Brown understood that organizing on behalf of school desegregation made her a misfit in both communities. In this way, she shared attributes with Lucile Bluford, Ada Sipuel, and Karla Galarza. She possessed a willingness to step into the schools, organizations, and homes of the opposite race and forge interracial connections that would help others envision desegregated schooling in new ways. Brown paid attention to her role as an interracial pioneer and found meaning in her highly unusual connections with black citizens in Kansas. In the late 1940s, these activities and relationships marked her as someone unique, almost illegible; many people, including many black people, associated her with danger and stigma. The loneliness of being a racial interloper—sacrificing status in both races in order to campaign for integrated schooling—recalls the experiences of Marguerite Carr and Doris Raye and Doris Faye Jennings, and their fathers James C. Carr Sr. and C. G. Jennings. That they all experienced such heated backlash is indicative of just how radical their stance on integrated schooling was in the immediate postwar period.

Nevertheless, as segregation was challenged in DC, Texas, and elsewhere, Brown initiated, led, and held together a school strike in South Park against fierce opposition from both local whites and the local and national NAACP. The strike brought publicity and funding for a desegregation lawsuit that Brown nurtured in every way possible, again defying the many naysayers in the state, including many leaders within the NAACP. The case in South Park was, significantly, the first postwar grade school desegregation case that the NAACP actually won, and the grade school students of South Park successfully desegregated the white school in the fall of 1949.

The lawsuit—and the extensive backing it had from citizens in Kansas—provided a vital cue to the LDF's New York office about where to best put the organization's energy. It is impossible to see the Topeka case emerging without the South Park trial preceding it, and this is indeed how locals in Kansas saw the situation. It was, moreover, a case pursued almost entirely by black women and one white woman. And while the lawsuit was filed on behalf of several brave families, with an even number of girls and boys, it was a girl— Patricia Black—who was chosen to testify, setting another pattern of female participation for cases to come.

———

Born in Kansas City, Missouri, on September 19, 1917, Esther Elizabeth Swirk was the daughter of Russian Jewish parents Jennie and Ben Swirk. She had a younger brother, Joseph, born in 1920. Ben Swirk, originally Ben Skwersky, was from Zvenigorodka and Jennie was from Vilna. Both towns were within the "Pale of Settlement" in Russia: the swath of land—now Belarus, Lithuania, Moldova, and most of Ukraine—that allowed for Jewish settlements, or shtetls. Ben Swirk's date of arrival and geographic origin suggest that he was fleeing the pogroms in Russia. Swirk became a US citizen on February 27, 1917. Whether his political commitments began in Russia or the United States, Ben Swirk belonged to a host of leftist, communist, and communist front organizations, including the Workmen's Circle, the International Workers Order, and the Human Rights Club (which Esther also joined sometime in the late 1930s). His car was spotted by the FBI at a speaking event for the famous Communist Party organizer Ella Reeve "Mother" Bloor. When Jennie Swirk died in 1929, twelve-year-old Esther began to attend these meetings with her father in the evenings.[4]

By Brown's own description, she was questioning racial norms in Missouri as a first grader at Frances Willard Elementary School. In an interview with the *Kansas City Call*, Brown told Bluford that she pestered her teachers about why there were "no Negro pupils" at the school. At age thirteen, she was consumed with the Scotts-boro case—the trial of nine young black men who stood accused of raping two white women and were defended by the communist International Legal Defense and the NAACP. At Paseo High School, she complained to teachers and administrators about the exclusion of Jewish girls from high school sororities. Her parents, she maintained, were "dismayed" by her "persistent probing into the 'why' of racial and religious discriminations." But, yet again, this may be misleading. By thirteen, she was already attending a range of communist front meetings with her father and the "Scottsboro boys" were the cause célèbre of the Communist Party. What Brown did not share with Bluford was the thorough education she received in radical and leftist politics at home.[5]

Ben Swirk was a watchmaker, and if Esther's early and ongoing low-wage work is any indication of the family's finances, they subsisted on a salary that was a rung below middle class. Esther graduated from high school in 1934, facing an uncertain future amid the Great Depression. She would later tell the FBI that between 1934 and 1937 she completed course work at Northwestern and the University of Chicago, and that during the summer she worked as a salesgirl at Marshall Field's and as a social worker at Hull House in Chicago. While Esther did attend Northwestern for a semester on a fellowship from the YWCA, she neither attended the University of Chicago nor held jobs in Chicago. Her actual employment during those years was much less glamorous. In 1935, Esther was a "saleslady" in the hosiery department at Kline's department store in Kansas City, Missouri. In January 1936, she was laid off because of poor sales and placed on "extra girl" status. She was next employed at the Suzy Hat Shop, also in Kansas City, until she left in June 1936. She worked these jobs, earning about $13.00 a week, to save up enough money to attend a summer session at Commonwealth College in Mena, Arkansas.[6]

Esther's experiences at Commonwealth College—which she never publicly admitted attending—explain much of what came after. Commonwealth was one of only a few residential "labor colleges" in the United States, and the only such college in the South. Founded in 1923, the college was a "worker's school" for farmers, factory workers, and trade unionists. Located in rural Arkansas, just four miles from the Oklahoma border, the school was a radical experiment in subsistence farming, communal living, unconventional teaching methods, and radical class- and race-based "social re-vision." Reflecting on the combination of intellectual vigor and farmwork at the school, one visitor remembered that "the boys would cut a log about half in two, sit down, wipe their brows, and start talking world revolution."[7]

The school was a bastion of intellectual and political ferment. By the time Esther attended in 1936, the majority of the faculty and students were communists. The southern wing of the Communist Party would have been perhaps the only logical place for a twenty-year-old activist who was trying to simultaneously make sense of racism, anti-Semitism, and the struggles of the working class in Kansas City, Missouri. While the Communist Party USA's primary concern was organizing impoverished "toilers" of all stripes, in the South, lynching, civil rights, self-determination for southern blacks, and interracial unity were the rallying cries of the party. As the only organization in the South that held interracial meetings, it was, in historian Robin Kelley's words, "militantly antiracist and consciously interracial." Visiting speakers the summer that Esther was at Commonwealth in 1936 included Roger Baldwin, a founder of the American Civil Liberties Union; the writer Jack Conroy; and Myles Horton, founder of the Highlander Folk School, which would later become famous for its interracial organizing workshops attended by Septima Clark and Rosa Parks. For Esther, perhaps the most influential speaker at Commonwealth was Ella Reeve "Mother" Bloor. Much of the devotion to Bloor, the sanctification that was a

component of her identity as "Mother Bloor," stemmed from her total self-sacrifice and lifelong commitment to addressing child labor
and the effects of poverty on children. Her career centered on the
desperate attempts of mothers and fathers to feed, educate, and nur-
ture their children on "starvation wages."[8]

Commonwealth students traveled to join striking anthracite
coal miners in southern Illinois and textile workers in Corinth,
Mississippi. When "Commoners" participated in regional strikes,
they were regularly beaten, jailed, and escorted across state lines
by armed mobs. During this time, according to an FBI informant,
Esther "was taught how to organize the unemployed and sharecroppers" and toured Arkansas and Oklahoma, speaking with
tenant farmers and attempting to recruit them to the Communist
Party. Sharecroppers were among the most disenfranchised and
impoverished workers in the country; they were treated, as one
historian put it, "like so much human garbage." The omnipresence
of violence that was inherent in organizing farmworkers would have
tested Esther's ability to withstand dangerous conditions. And as
a young white woman speaking with mostly black tenant farmers,
she broke every rule governing race and gender in the rural South.
How she reached across lines of race, education, and social context
when speaking with farmworkers is difficult to imagine. But a few
facts can be assumed. First, witnessing some of the worst poverty
in the United States must have been searing. Second, for a white,
Jewish young woman whose political views were already sparked
by segregation, the Scottsboro case, and her own experiences with
anti-Semitism, taking part in organizing activities with black
tenant farmers must have sealed her political imagination permanently along racial lines. Finally, anything that came after—whether
dealing with the South Park school board or difficult NAACP
leaders—must have seemed tame by comparison.[9]

Like so many who attended labor colleges, Esther never went
back to a conventional university. In the late 1930s, she got a job

with the Works Progress Administration, or WPA, as a social worker interviewing clients who had applied for relief. It is unclear who contacted the FBI, but in early March 1941, the bureau began an extensive review, interviewing Esther's coworkers, friends, previous employers, and current boss. Agents reported that she had been telling relief clients who had been drafted not to report to Camp Robinson, Arkansas, because conditions there were intolerable. She alienated coworkers with her hostility toward the "British Empire" and "radical talk concerning the rights of workers to strike and tie up defense industries if this were necessary to gain their demands."[10]

Aware that the FBI was investigating her, Esther pilfered her file from her boss's office on the very day that agents arrived to read it. The agents discovered her typing up a new file. Comparing Esther's doctored file with a previous application to the WPA, the agents noted only one change: she had removed a reference to time spent in Arkansas doing "volunteer work." Agent Copeland, one of the two agents on the case, knew about Commonwealth, and he and his partner drove down to Mena to see what they could find out. The school had been prosecuted and shut down that year for failing to display the American flag and instead displaying a hammer and sickle at the entrance to the school's main building. The agents interviewed a former school official, who immediately remembered that "Miss Swirk was an attractive young Russian Jewess from Kansas City" who had attended the school for two summer terms in 1936 and 1937. Indeed, Esther Swirk had been student body president during the summer of 1936.[11]

Agent Copeland, who interviewed Esther several times in late March and early April 1941, had a reputation for being (in Esther's words) "ruthless in his manner of questioning." Whatever his methods, after he "very carefully questioned" her, Esther agreed to a sworn affidavit in which she stated that "she has never attended or been connected with Commonwealth College of Mena, Arkansas, in any capacity and that she is not, has not, and will not become a Communist." Soon after her narrow escape from the FBI, and after being fired from the WPA, Esther married her high school friend Paul Brown and assumed a highly conventional role as the wife of an enlisted man. The young couple moved to Florida, where Paul Brown was stationed. In her wedding announcement, Esther Brown stated that she had been a student at the University of Chicago and Northwestern. This would be her official story for the rest of her life.[12]

———

With a two-year-old daughter and a second child on the way, Esther and Paul Brown moved to the town of Merriam, Kansas, in 1946. (South Park is a section of Merriam.) Paul Brown worked at his stepfather's auto-body parts store in Kansas City. After her second child was born, Esther Brown hired Helen Swann to help out with the children and household chores. In later years, Paul Brown was careful to point out that Swann worked only part-time for the family. Though he was receiving a regular paycheck, Paul Brown did not make enough money to afford full-time help, and the family lived in a modest, two-bedroom home.[13]

Mary Webb—a neighbor of Swann's who would later join the desegregation lawsuit—recalled that within Merriam there was a suburban, wealthier, white area and a poorer "settlement of black people," as she called it, mostly in South Park, that was, like many semirural areas in the postwar era, not entirely segregated. In an interview, Brown recalled that whites and blacks lived "next door to each other" and passed each other's houses to go to school. When the school board finally got around to officially gerrymandering the district, they had to resort to circling the black houses with red ink because creating a contiguous line separating the races was impossible. In the poorer, more rural sections of South Park, there were no paved roads or running water, and Webb recalls using a "public well." It was a community of working-class and poor farmers, many of whom sold produce at local markets. They were, as Webb put it, "hard-working people." Women worked as maids, took in washing and ironing, and grew much of what their families ate. Men farmed or worked in quarries, on the railroad, and in plumbing, meatpacking, and construction. After holding a series of jobs, Webb's husband Alfonso—like C. G. Jennings and Gardner Bishop—had "gone into business for himself" doing construction work as a concrete contractor. He laid sewer lines and constructed patios, porches, and sidewalks.[14]

Segregation in Merriam, according to Webb, extended only to the schools, and otherwise there was "not much trouble." In the early twentieth century, black and white students attended grade school together at the Walker School. Then, in the interwar period, a new school was built for white students, the South Park School, while the black students were required to continue attending the increasingly dilapidated Walker School. After the Second World War ended, the Johnson County School Board sought approval for a bond of $90,000 to pay for a new all-white South Park School. Helen Swann—as Brown later explained—asked her opinion on the bond. Brown advised that the black parents vote against funding for the school, but they were in the minority and the bond passed. Soon after, Brown went to investigate the Walker School. She found a "tumbledown shack" of two dimly lit rooms; no cafeteria, auditorium, or gymnasium; an outdoor privy; and two teachers who were responsible for grades one through eight for fifty-seven students. Whenever there was a hard rain, the basement—where the students ate their cold lunches—flooded, which in turn shut down the heating system, contributing to pneumonia, bronchitis, and other respiratory illnesses that plagued the students throughout the school year. The Walker parents were responsible for renting a pump to get rid of the water.[15]

Brown began, she later recalled, to "talk more and listen to Mrs. Swann" about poverty, segregated schooling, and the lack of services in the black section of Merriam. However, there are some problems with this recounting. A conversation about segregation and black poverty—and eventually planning to initiate litigation—between a white employer and black maid would have been highly unconventional. White women in the 1940s were often close to the black women who worked for them. Black women, however, recall these relationships as intimate but conducted entirely for the psychological benefit of the white women they worked for. By recalling that her maid consulted her on the school bond vote, Brown painted herself as uninitiated—just an ordinary housewife who happened to be consulted by her maid on the socially explosive topic of unequal and segregated schooling. In fact, given Brown's political education and experiences, it is just as likely that she asked Swann questions about the Walker School, rather than the other way around.[16]

A former schoolteacher and the mother of five children, Swann was a determined and relentless educational activist who would see to it that all of her children went to college, with several going on to earn advanced degrees. Prior to speaking with Brown, Swann had taken her children to the South Park School and simply tried to enroll them. Afterward, Swann and Mary and Alfonso Webb approached the school board to demand that they renovate the Walker School. Unmoved, the school board recommended the black parents raise money from their churches for improvements to the Walker School. The group then contacted a Kansas City lawyer, William Towers, to represent them at the next school board meeting. The white school board responded to this action by installing a stop sign and mailbox in front of the Walker School.

It was at this point, in the winter of 1947, that Brown got involved. She and Swann decided to establish a Merriam branch of the NAACP in order to have national backing for an intended equalization lawsuit. "After hammering away at [the community] for about two months," Brown wrote in a letter to LDF lawyer Franklin Williams in what was to become a lengthy correspondence, "we formed a chapter with 37 people." By "hammering away," Brown meant canvassing and going door to door. A black woman and a white woman canvassing together for the creation of a black organization must have raised a few eyebrows. Brown recalled that although most people in the black community took what she had to say at face value and in good faith, there were always those who remained "leery" of her and her motives and "nervous" in her presence.[17]

The parents requested another school board meeting, and Towers agreed to represent the South Park families again for a fee of twenty-five dollars. Brown suggested that instead of spending the money on a lawyer, she could attend the meeting with the parents and represent them. At this juncture, Brown believed (with some arrogance), that she might have more traction with the board as a white representative for the black community. But if this was her thinking, she was quickly disabused of the notion. "Every type of propaganda and coercion was used to impress them that their school was as fitting as the new one," Brown wrote to Williams. She continued, "And after the bonds were paid off they would build the negroes [sic] a new school." The bonds were due to be paid off in thirty years. "They admitted they were prejudiced and did not want negro [sic] children going to school with theirs." She later recalled the meeting in more colorful terms. "I appeared before the most gruesome bunch of people I'd ever seen in my life," she said. "I mean these were real lynchers, by the look of it. Plaid working shirts, ignorant, didn't care about education." Virgil Wisecup, the chairman of the board of education, offered to donate light bulbs and some leftover desks from the new South Park School to the Walker School. Brown left feeling "nauseated."[18]

The white community was furious with Brown and immediately struck back. The evening after the meeting, she received a phone call from school board members telling her to "stay out of this thing." The night after that, she received an invitation to speak at a small meeting of the school board, with "no Negroes attending," during which she was invited to discuss conditions at the Walker School. Swann, who had more experience with the South Park school board, saw this gesture as a trap and advised Brown not to go. Brown, in the first of many decisions to ignore sound advice, attended the meeting anyway. When she got there, accompanied by her husband Paul, she found 250 white people amassed in the South Park School's auditorium. The assembled group had saved her a seat, right in the middle of the audience. Wisecup opened the meeting by saying, "We seem to have a racial problem in South Park all of a sudden." He then proclaimed, "N—'s in the community are determined to get into our white school." The crowd roared, shouting epithets at Brown and yelling "obscene statements." White parents took to the stage to decry against any suggestion of integration. Remarks included "If we let N—s in South Park School we'll soon have white and colored mixed babies!" "How would you feel if your child were in a Christmas play with a N—child?" and "Let's take all the N—s and send them back to Merriam, she'd like that." "After all this hoop and holler," Brown later recalled, "people began to pull their chairs away from me. And there was just a little space around *me*."

Then there was silence, and Brown realized she was expected to speak. She recalled saying, "I don't represent these people but I've seen the conditions of their school, and I know none of you would want your children educated under such circumstances. They're not asking for integration, just a fair shake." This seemingly anodyne statement was greeted with uproarious boos, name-calling, and shouts of "Go back to where you came from N—lover!" The woman sitting behind Brown tried to hit her with her umbrella and had to be restrained. A Methodist minister stood up and said that "Negroes were brought to this country as slaves [hence] the best thing we can do is meet them . . . on the basis of human beings." He was shouted down by his own congregants and told to sit down, which he did. When Brown finally got out of the auditorium, she recalled, "I was a changed woman." What changed was not her political outlook, which was already firmly in place, but her plans: she would stop at nothing less than school desegregation, not just in South Park but throughout the state of Kansas.[19]

For a full two weeks after the meeting, the Browns' phone rang twenty-four hours a day. Initially, most of her hecklers would shout epithets and hang up. A school official rang to remind her of the fate of a druggist from neighboring Shawnee County who had similarly supported the black community. He was run out of town when local merchants refused to sell his family food and citizens boycotted his drugstore. One neighbor, making a "social call," pointed to a hill just beyond Brown's house and described how the Ku Klux Klan used to burn crosses on it. Soon, callers began to threaten to burn her house down. One afternoon, coming home from a family outing, the Browns discovered the embers of a burning cross on their lawn. During these first weeks, according to Paul Brown, Esther Brown experienced her only moment of doubt. Her husband and children were probably on her mind—three people who had not asked to be a part of her dreams of social justice. But she was neither afraid nor thrown off-balance. Her experiences at Commonwealth likely provided her with the kind of fortitude she needed at this moment. It would have been in keeping with her radical education to react to unleashed repression with the impulse to organize.[20]

On April 9, 1948, Helen Swann, Alfonso Webb (now president of the Merriam NAACP), and Esther Brown made a formal demand at the annual meeting of the school board that black students be admitted to the South Park School. After they had been formally rejected, the committee resolved to sue. A. Porter Davis, president of the Kansas state NAACP, met with lawyer William Towers and the Merriam branch. Towers informed the parents that "he would have the colored children inside the new school in a month's time," at a cost of $250. Towers was confident because, officially, the law was on his side. Segregation in lower schools was only "permitted" in cities of the "first class"—those with fifteen thousand residents—but disallowed in rural and small-town school districts. Nonetheless, few school districts in Kansas were integrated, and most black schools throughout the state suffered from the same disinvestment and neglect as the Walker School.[21]

Not knowing where the money would come from but determined to file suit, the parents retained Towers and committed to raising the money themselves. However, in a demoralizing blow, Towers and Davis proceeded to ignore their telephone calls. Brown claimed that it took "almost two months of constant pressuring" to get Towers to take some action. Brown called daily, wrote daily, and made unannounced visits to the office. Towers finally filed the mandamus action before the Kansas Supreme Court in Topeka on May 25 on behalf of Harvey and Alfonso Webb, Shirley and Norbert Turner, Delores Gay, and Patricia Black. Three girls and three boys, the plaintiffs represented the children of parents who were most active in the Merriam NAACP, with the significant exception of the Swann children.[22]

To make matters more bizarre for Brown, Davis and Towers took the stage with her at a May 30 meeting at Pleasant Green Baptist Church in Kansas City, Kansas, to trumpet the possibilities of the South Park lawsuit. This meeting, billed as an update on the South Park case, brought in over 250 people and was the largest fund-raiser in the state's history for the NAACP. Despite evidence that the black citizens of Kansas were eager to take on school desegregation, both men, while officially supporting the cause, continued to delay and, in ways large and small, resist its progress. It was becoming increasingly clear to Brown and the Merriam branch that Davis and Towers did not want to pursue a school desegregation lawsuit. Both men might have been more interested in equalization. They had a wealth of political contacts in the state and may have had their own plans about how to use those connections for more school funding. Or, perhaps, they felt it was in their own interests, and in the interests of African Americans in Kansas, not to alienate what white support and political clout they had by confronting lawmakers with whom they had working relationships. A Wichita branch member later wrote a letter to Brown explaining why that branch would not pursue school desegregation. "The wealthier Negroes," she wrote, "prefer the segregated system because it means more business and jobs for them, so they think. The teachers in particular are fearful of losing their jobs if they have to compete with white teachers. They dominate the NAACP [here]." These powerful constituents no doubt influenced Davis. The Wichita branch was one of the largest and wealthiest branches in the state.[23]

The final blow came in late June 1947. On the day that Towers was supposed to be in court, Brown recalled, "I called Towers to see if I could go with him. . . . I was curious. . . . Towers wasn't even in town. He was at the Republican national convention in Philadelphia." She asked if anyone else in the office planned to go and was told "no one knew anything about it." Brown called another lawyer "to ask what happens if a lawyer was not in court on an appointed day and he said the case was dismissed. . . . I was very upset. So I called Philadelphia and located the man," a feat in itself. "And he said, [sounding] exasperated, not to worry . . . [and] 'now Mrs. Brown when you have a lawyer you have to have faith in him, the lawyer will take care of it.'" The paternalistic condescension infuriated Brown. She asked to meet with the leadership of the Kansas City branch to inform them of what had transpired. The branch leadership, she recalled, perceived her complaints to be prejudiced, and tension quickly escalated. "They interpreted this as just not wanting Towers, and here I was white, and really interfering, and that it has to be slow and that I was not to be apprehensive." She continued, "Now they appreciated the fact that I was there but they didn't want to trust me at all. What was I doing there?" This question was perhaps the most constant of her young life, from rural Arkansas in 1938 to the upper reaches of the NAACP in Kansas a decade later.[24]

Brown also believed that there was a class element at work in the reaction from Towers and the Kansas City branch to the South

Park lawsuit. This observation went unmentioned in her correspondence with the national office in the late 1940s—a correspondence in which she complained of many problems, but never class antagonism. Retrospectively, however, she put it this way: "The people in South Park were working-class people." The leadership in Kansas City was "a little more middle class and they weren't too crazy about these people in South Park. They wanted to talk about it, but let's take our time."[25]

In dealing with the stalling tactics of Davis and Towers, Brown was not without recourse. She and the South Park parents resolved to terminate their relationship with Towers and hire in his place Elisha Scott, a lawyer with a reputation in the state for taking on civil rights cases. Scott promised to pursue the case vigorously. In her first letter to the New York office, Brown asked for advice on how to deal with the delicate business of trying to replace one lawyer with another and begged the national office to take the case. "We want you people to retain [Elisha Scott] officially and work through him." She complained to Williams, "Dr. Davis was supposed to let us know if the State [branch] would retain Scott for us—we have already waited more than three weeks and still haven't heard from him." However, "if that [does] not work out," she announced, "I promised [the Merriam branch] that the Wallace Committee in Kansas would retain him. While I am 100% for the Progressive Party I feel this is a NAACP matter and we should fight it." The Progressive Party was a recently reconstituted third party with the goal of electing the left-of-center Henry Wallace president. Mentioning the Progressive Party's interest in the case was likely meant as a threat. Brown knew that the NAACP would be embarrassed if the Progressive Party got to the case before it did. Four days later, the national office loaned $250 to the Merriam branch for "for the *Webb* case."[26]

But Thurgood Marshall was annoyed. A week after the check was sent, he wrote a memorandum to Williams, saying, "I assume that all of us are in agreement that we don't like the way [the case] is presently being handled as a one-woman show and that if we are going to put money into the case, we will have to have control over it." Williams was compelled to placate his boss and vouch for Brown's integrity. "Mrs. Esther Brown, a member of the Branch," he replied, "not in an attempt to make it a one-woman show . . . but rather in a sincere desire to have the case move forward rapidly, discussed the matter with [us] at the National Convention." Brown was, Williams vouched, "one of the few militant and out-spoken members of the Branch," and he argued that her interest in the case was a boon for the organization—especially in light of a recent failure in Indiana, where a case was dropped after parents refused to pursue it. "I think this suit deserves our closest attention and greatest support possible. . . . In view of the fact that the Indiana case has fallen by the wayside, at the election of Indianapolis Branch, this suit offers us the opportunity to press this question without further delay."[27]

Brown had also managed to infuriate Towers and the Kansas State branch leadership who had recommended him. Though the letter of termination sent to Towers was signed by Alfonso Webb, president of the Merriam NAACP, everyone—including Towers, Davis, and members of the Kansas City branch—blamed Brown. "I have a terrible letter" from the Kansas City branch, Brown told an interviewer in 1965, "telling me to go to hell." She also received "a dreadful letter from Towers telling me how I interfered, I was suspicious, how wrong I was." While Brown was willing to pressure and outmaneuver male leadership on both the state and national levels, the job left her feeling isolated, angry, and hurt. That she invited the hostility of the black, middle-class, mostly male leadership of the NAACP reflects the extent of her audacity and the profound difficulty of her position as a white woman trying to push along a desegregation case, and the sheer endurance that was required. Her seemingly inexhaustible passion for the South Park case, however, should not be confused with a superhuman ability to withstand criticism and attack. In 1965, she said that she had reread the letter from Towers "a year ago and it made me boil. After twenty-five years."[28]

In the meantime, Elisha Scott initiated his own version of what an historian, describing a similar case, called "masterly inactivity." First, there was the question of money. Scott needed one hundred dollars for filing fees and his time, and the branch leadership did not have it—they already owed Towers two hundred. In October, Williams suggested to Scott that he seek "a temporary injunction pending the decision" that would allow the Walker students to attend the South Park school while the trial was going on. Later that month, Williams sent a telegram to Scott asking him if the petition had been filed. Scott telegrammed back, "Merriam case not filed. Letter follows." The promised letter never arrived. Instead, Scott informed Brown that a commissioner needed to be appointed to inspect the Walker and South Park schools for the case to proceed further. However, the commissioner—whom Scott called a "friend"—proceeded to be "sick" and incapable of conducting business for several months running.[29]

In November 1948, Scott's commissioner regained his health just long enough to request a continuance until March. Later that month, at Brown's urging, Thurgood Marshall telegrammed Scott again, this time giving him detailed instructions on how to file a petition for an emergency injunction. "Delay until March unthinkable. Understand moral [sic] of parents breaking fast. This office considers any further delay disastrous. Contact me . . . immediately." This telegram also went unanswered. December found Brown yet again writing to Williams complaining of further delays. The judge's family, one after another, had also taken ill, requiring, apparently, that the judge leave his chambers to attend to them personally. "Mr. Scott did not apply for the injunction immediately," Brown wrote. "He wanted to talk to the Supreme Court judge—as he was sitting in his office the Judge was called out as his daughter took sick. Last week

Mr. Scott made [another] appointment with the judge . . . just as he entered the judges [*sic*] office, he [the judge] received a call that his wife was very ill and for him to come home."[30]

It would have been comical if so many parents and children were not desperately awaiting progress in the case. In September, anticipating the swift ruling promised by Scott, the members of the Merriam branch had staged a walkout, refusing to attend the Walker School while the case unfolded. Classes for the forty-five students were being conducted in the living rooms of two branch members, Lucille Gay and Marva Berry. Two certified, experienced teachers, Corinthian Nutter and Hazel Weddington, agreed to take a pay cut to teach the children. "We don't have the money to pay them yet," Brown wrote to Williams in September, "but I know we can raise it." She and the South Park mothers immediately got to work raising the two hundred dollars a month required. Rosalie Parks and Mrs. Thomas Black—mother of Patricia Black, who would later testify in the case—made cupcakes, which Brown took to Kansas City and sold door-to-door, appearing, with her petite stature and youthful looks, more like a Girl Scout than an agitator. The going rate was fifty cents a dozen, and the buyers were white women whom Brown convinced of the righteousness of her cause. The women raised ninety-two dollars. Lucille Gay, who was also named in the lawsuit as mother of Delores Gay, collected old items and put on a rummage sale, raising forty-five dollars. Rosetta Taylor gave a "social." The attendees were mostly members of women's clubs such as the Eleven O'Clock Study Club, the Hallie Q. Brown Study Club (named after the founder of one of the earliest clubs for black women), and the YWCA. Rosetta Taylor's daughter, Mildred Delores Taylor, spoke to the assembled women. The event raised forty-three dollars. It was an exciting and promising time for the small band of mostly female activists.[31]

Williams, with his knowledge of the myriad delays in which lawsuits could become mired, advised Brown and the Merriam branch against a strike. Brown declined his advice. In a letter sent in late September 1948, Brown crowed about the success of the strike and "the protest schools." She credited the students as the force behind their parents' determination. "As you know the children stayed out of school," Brown wrote. "They refused to go back to the Jim Crow school—and they deserve to be commended for their action. . . . I know you felt it was not necessary to keep the children out of the school, but this little strike has really knit these people together, and has brought in families that were not interested in fighting segregated schools." Buoyed by the enthusiasm of the striking families, Brown concluded, "We feel sure of a victory."[32]

—

Meanwhile at the offices of the *Kansas City Call*, Lucile Bluford was watching the strike and lawsuit—and the activism of Esther Brown—with mounting enthusiasm. The school strike and desegregation lawsuit had all the elements Bluford relished: a brave, principled stand against a corrupt white school board, a leader who was willing to take on entrenched interests in the state (both white and black), an interracial component, and an effort in which students themselves were playing a visible role. From the first moment Bluford heard Brown speak—at a fund-raiser at Mount Baptist Church— she was an instant and fervent convert. Indeed, she printed much of what Brown had to say and explicitly endorsed her as a trustworthy, "militant" white woman:

> Mrs. Brown had spoken hardly five minutes before one got the idea that this wasn't a white woman talking but an American of the kind we have far too few. She has incurred the wrath of the people in the district where she and her family live. Mrs. Brown in her closing remarks emphasized the fact that this South Park matter was everybody's fight. . . . "We have the laws to see that justice is done

but we are doing nothing about them. We must realize that we are fighting for equality, nothing else."

Thus began a mutually beneficial connection. Bluford found a cause to which she could commit her resources, both personal—Bluford tapped allies for donations and donated twenty-five dollars herself—and professional, and Brown very much needed Bluford to vouch for her intentions to her readers in the state, even if it did nothing to change the minds of the Kansas NAACP leadership.[33]

Brown and Bluford quickly became friends, and eventually close friends. The way Bluford remembered it, Brown started to drop by the *Call*'s office in 1948. "What I remember about Esther," Bluford said, "was her coming by *The Call* early in the morning, mid-day, any time, but [mostly] early in the morning. . . . She loved to talk. She'd come by talking about what those people were doing over in S. Park." At first, Bluford was dismissive, finding Brown as incomprehensible as everyone else did. "Esther, why don't you go home and take care of your kids?" was her initial response. Brown answered, unsurprisingly, "Lucile, I can't do that, I've got to take care of this." Bluford reflected, "I never saw anyone so interested in a thing that didn't concern them personally." The two became "good friends" Bluford said, because "she'd come by often, real often." The way Brown's daughters remember it, however, Bluford was at *their* house "all the time."[34]

There was a lot to bring the two women together: a shared political passion, plotting over what became a semi-shared project, and a deep admiration on Brown's part for Bluford's professional achievements and track record on school desegregation. Brown's profound respect for Bluford leaps off the page in a line that appeared in her voluminous correspondence with Williams: "Lucile Bluford seems to think there might be hope with" a new school board member "and wants me to call him. . . . I will definitely call on him next week."

Brown rarely mentioned what others had to say and never took advice from anyone. Yet here she was, taking marching orders from Bluford. Just as important to their relationship, if not more so, was the fact that the two shared a common set of enemies. Given her publicly documented indignation with black officials who stood in the way of school desegregation, Bluford was probably just as frustrated with A. Porter Davis and William Towers as Brown was.[35]

Brown and the striking families received much-needed support, advertising, and morale from the attention lavished on them by both black newspapers in the state—the *Call* and the *Plaindealer*, which provided, in Brown's words, "terrific coverage." However, the nature of the reporting in each paper was strikingly different. The *Plaindealer* described how the parents were finally standing up for their "constitutional rights," and hewed to the usual script of describing the male professionals officially at the helm of local organizations. The paper ran stories on the careers of Towers, Davis, Scott, and the Kansas City branch under the leadership of E. A. Freeman. Brown was mentioned twice, and only in passing. Bluford at the *Call*, in contrast, discussed none of the official male leaders or lawyers in the case. Rather, she fully described the personalities and contributions of the individuals on the ground—each listed by name—who were daily participating in the strike: the teachers working in living rooms, the mothers raising funds, and the children who refused to go back to Walker. Her coverage, in short, told the story of a grassroots movement unfolding from the bottom up, rather than a top-down, male-led endeavor. It was, in this instance, the accurate story.[36]

Bluford also deployed her unique style of reporting, boldly exposing all of the ugly details. She was explicit about the dissention and disagreement within the black community. On a single page, she ran dueling articles about the different factions in the fight, just as she had done with the "Poro Law School" in 1939. On the left: "Two Pupils in Walker Building: Teachers on Duty in Nearly Empty School Quarters." The article interviewed the two teachers at the Walker School, referred to by all as "the Randall sisters," who had taught there for twenty years, and ran a large picture of the women next to the broken-down, nearly empty schoolhouse. The two women standing in the door, waiting for students who would likely never appear, made for an unsettling image. On the right side of the page, in an article entitled "Temporary Teaching for Pupils: Children Taught in Homes Pending Suit Settlement," Bluford quoted the striking parents who claimed that the two teachers at the Walker School—whose picture was one column inch away—were uncertified and unfit. That the two Walker teachers were meant to be perceived in an unflattering light is inescapable, and it is evidence of the steely resolve that Bluford had always brought to school de-segregation. Those who supported Jim Crow schools could expect to be humiliated in the pages of the *Call*.[37]

———

As Bluford raised the profile of the South Park case and the fame of its leaders grew, so too did the backlash. One family in South Park woke up in the morning to find that their cow, two calves, and a sow with eight pigs had been killed. Others were denied credit at the local store, which was owned by Virgil Wisecup, head of the school board. Mary and Alfonso Webb, whose sons were listed first on the lawsuit, suffered an attempt at arson. "We were all home that night," Mary Webb remembered, "and I happened to smell smoke, because I was right there in the kitchen.... We came out of the house. The back end of our house was on fire." It was small enough for the Webbs to put it out quickly with the help of their neighbors—"just a piddle thing" she called it. But the children, who had been dragged out of their beds and piled onto the front lawn, were rattled. Alfonso Webb remained unbowed. "My husband was a strong-willed man that believed what's right is right and he was going for it." The retalia-tion, however, did dissuade some in the community who already had misgivings. "Our own people," Mary Webb recalled, began "giving us negative feelings." As in other locales where activism against segregated schools met with sustained white resistance, many supporters backed out, convinced that they were, as Mary Webb described it, "fighting a losing cause."[38]

Conditions deteriorated for Esther and Paul Brown as well. When Brown hosted a lunch for the black families of Merriam at her home, "that was the last straw" with local whites, and the pressure to move away from Merriam became overwhelming. Once again, someone contacted the federal authorities, and FBI agents could be seen interviewing neighbors up and down the street. One of her neighbors told agents that Brown had been seen around town with Paul Robeson, the famous singer and Communist Party member. Brown knew it was only a matter of time before she was, once again, interrogated. This time, perhaps, she might not get away with a promise to reform. However, even with the FBI looking into her political activities, it is worth noting that in her public speeches Brown never missed an opportunity to inveigh against the anticommunist hysteria of the moment. In a speech at the Kansas State Association of Branches in Osawatomie, Kansas, on September 5, 1948, Brown connected postwar anticommunism with the preservation of segregation:

> We are going to have to awaken and realize that we will not get equal citizenship overnite, that we are going to have to do something ourselves. I'm afraid our gov. has lost sight of the people, yes the little people such as you and me. Hunting for communists . . . seems more important than prosecuting someone for lynching. . . . People today are even afraid to be acknowledged as liberal and progressive, to speak their minds regarding segregation and discrimination for fear of being called a Communist.[39]

Though it does not appear that Brown was still a communist in 1948, she remained unafraid to attack redbaiting. Brown's speeches during this time were far ranging. In addition to condemning anti-communist sentiment, she offered close readings of Howard Thurman's religio-philosophical book *Jesus and the Disinherited* (a work that would profoundly influence Martin Luther King) and attacked racism and inequality in broad strokes. But, like Bluford, her critiques of segregated schools were especially detailed and blistering. In words that could have easily been lifted from one of Bluford's articles in the 1930s, she said:

> We cannot rest easily with a shameful picture you know better than I—the picture of dilapidated and barren Negro school houses in most of the rural South; the poorly paid teachers, the extremely poor—or nonexistent—school transportation facilities; the scores of Southern counties where there are absolutely no high school facilities for Negroes, and the severely limited and substandard college and professional facilities.

Like Bluford, Brown was willing to describe black schools in the most unsparing language possible—an act that was no doubt upsetting to some of the educators in her audience.[40]

The biggest personal setback for Esther Brown during the strike and ongoing litigation was when her husband was fired from his job at the auto-body parts store. Returning from a business trip to Dallas, Paul Brown's stepfather informed him that a well-connected white lawyer had approached him on the train, saying that his daughter-in-law "was making waves throughout Kansas" and that he ought to "influence her" to cease her "radical activities." Paul Brown responded, "I could not force her to stop even if I so wished"—a comment that provides some insight into the dynamics of their marriage. "With that I shook his hand," he recalled, "then went to my desk and cleaned it out. Within minutes I was out on the street and practically destitute. I borrowed $100 from my father-in-law, Ben Swirk, giving the money to Esther for groceries."[41]

Paul Brown was fired in October. By the end of November, with Elisha Scott delaying the trial date and the national office insisting more and more adamantly that the branch abandon its strike and return to the Walker School, Esther Brown took perhaps her biggest risk yet: she urged the branch to continue the strike and promised that she would find the money to pay the teachers herself. Raising money became a "daily" activity, and she approached it with the same zeal and total focus that she brought to all her political commitments. She began writing to NAACP branches and churches all over the state, asking if she could address their members and congregants. "If some one will put me up for the night," she wrote, "I have a story to tell." Brown later told an interviewer that when A. Porter Davis found out that she had embarked on a speaking tour, he wrote to every NAACP branch in the state in his capacity as president, "stating 'Mrs. Brown does not represent us.'" As usual, Brown persisted nonetheless. "I went anyway because I was desperate. I had to have the money." She added, "The interesting thing about people is that there are always little people who will listen to you even when the power structure will not."[42]

Brown was humbled by the generosity of the "poor people" who contributed what they could. "No door was every closed to me. . . . They broke out the best china. . . . They fed me [and] took a chance on me." These were the same people—farmers, laborers, domestics— who first supported Ada Sipuel in her campaign to desegregate the University of Oklahoma. Indeed, they may well have been, in some instances, the very same individuals, as Sipuel traveled to Kansas on more than one occasion in the same year. The contributions, too, were in the same small denominations that Sipuel received. Brown remembered with special fondness the donations of children and teenagers. One night, in Bonner Springs, "it was raining and there were only ten children and four adults. But they gave me $10 and it was the most inspiring collection I ever made." She also remembered visiting a church in White City. "Twelve teenagers were there, [and I] raised $6.22." Helen Swann watched Brown's young children while she made these "one-night stands," and Paul Brown "put up with it." The trips were grueling. She suffered a miscarriage that fall, but did not tell her husband for fear he would put his foot down. When she came back from these rural areas, her car was covered in dust and invariably "N—lover" would be scrawled on it by the next morning.[43]

Brown formed powerful memories of these trips. Staying the night, and the role reversal of a white person entering into black homes, was so striking to her that she commented on it often. "I had been born and raised in Kansas City," she recalled, "so this was an experience . . . and I wouldn't take anything in the world for it." Here she might have been conflating events in Arkansas canvassing for the Communist Party and the similar activities involved in touring Kansas for the lawsuit. She never felt safe telling interviewers about her communist organizing activities in Arkansas, and perhaps, for Brown, this was a way to express her feelings about both experiences while keeping her radical past a secret.[44]

By December, Brown's letters to Franklin Williams had become anxious, frustrated, and "frantic," as Williams described them. The community was now stretched far beyond its ability to continue the strike. "After Dec. 6th the two women want their houses," Brown wrote. "They can't permit the children to continue using the houses as a school and you can't blame them—they have been grand. They are getting discouraged, very discouraged because of the legal delay [and] being promised one thing and then not hearing anything." A week later she wrote again, saying that she had urged Scott to file the petition "until I am almost hoarse." "This delay is killing us out here," she continued. "We can't let these people in South Park down—not only that we are letting all the interested Negro people in Kansas down. . . . The lives of a whole community are at stake and if this case is continued until March. . . these people will give up this fight."[45]

Emotions ran high as the South Park families faced the 1948 Christmas season. More families reenrolled their children at the Walker School. At a meeting where Brown was soliciting funds, A. Porter Davis told her, as she recounted to Williams, to "sit down" and be quiet, that she "didn't know what she was talking about," and that she had "no right" to contact NAACP officials in New York. He then urged the assembled group *not* to contribute. Brown must have fought back, because she described the meeting as "quite a brawl," but the very public altercation with Davis was nonetheless a setback. Brown begged Williams to straighten out Scott or to come to Kansas himself. Williams reiterated that the organization could not support a strike, that it was better for the students to go back to the Walker School, and that the NAACP did not have the money for him to travel to Kansas when it was unclear whether anything could be accomplished by the trip.[46]

Rising to the occasion, Brown made tactical decisions in late November and December that proved masterful. First, she contacted Billie Holiday's manager and asked if she could make an appeal for funds at an upcoming concert. Once again, teenagers came to Brown's aid: seventy-five Kansas City high school students volunteered to take donations. Brown had the South Park students take the stage to talk about their strike (six girls and two boys volunteered). Holiday walked off the stage when Brown came out, which hurt Brown's feelings, but later the singer agreed to pose for a picture with Brown and the children. The photo was printed in the *Call*. Soon the Kansas City (Kansas) branch, despite its initial reservations about the case, came through with the largest contribution yet—six hundred dollars—which went toward legal fees, school supplies, and teacher salaries. The large sum was most likely due to member contributions inspired by the South Park case—and Brown's description of it— rather than the inclinations of the leadership.[47]

At Brown's urging, Thurgood Marshall telegrammed Scott again. When this went unanswered, Brown tried another angle:

she suggested to Williams that he send a photographer from the NAACP's national magazine, the *Crisis*, to come out and take Scott's picture for an anticipated story on the Merriam case "to soften him up." Scott was thrilled with the positive attention and the promise of national publicity. On December 16, he filed the petition. (The injunction, however, was not granted.) Brown also convinced Williams to write a letter of appreciation to the Merriam branch to help boost their flagging spirits. Williams wrote to the branch, "I have just completed a very lengthy and full discussion of this suit with Thurgood Marshall, Special Counsel of the Association, and he agreed with me that under no conditions must we allow any further setback or delay to occur in our fight in Merriam. . . . We shall not desert the people in Merriam in this time of crisis." Encouraged, the branch voted to hang on. To keep the protest school running, Brown approached Mount Olive Baptist Church in South Park to ask if the strikers could use the building for the school. "Half the church is opposed to our fight," she confided to Williams, but ultimately they relented—like so many on the receiving end of Brown's efforts at persuasion—as long as she pledged to pay for the rented chairs and tables, janitorial services, and extra coal to heat the church on weekdays.[48]

Once again, Brown had promised to find money she did not have. She convinced Marshall to send another sum of several hundred dollars for legal fees that needed to be paid immediately. The money was wired to Davis at the Kansas state branch. Unsurprisingly, Davis attempted to keep the money for outstanding payments owed his friend William Towers. Furious, Brown drove out to Kansas City to face the man she had come to loathe. The scene took an almost absurd turn when, to resolve the dispute, a long-distance call was placed to Marshall in New York. The whole room stood listening as Marshall bellowed into the receiver: "GOD DAMN IT GIVE THAT WHITE LADY THE MONEY!"[49]

With only a few days left before Christmas, however, Brown still did not have enough to pay the teachers. With her husband out of work and her contacts tapped out, she decided to take out a personal loan. With Paul Brown's support (women could not take out loans in the 1940s without a male relative to cosign), and putting their house up for collateral, Brown secured two hundred dollars. On Christmas Eve, she made her way to the church to pay the teachers and expenses with her last dime and, finding herself in a house of worship, perhaps set aside her declared atheism to pray that the New Year would bring more success.[50]

———

And so it did. As word of the case about to be argued before the Kansas Supreme Court spread, political and financial support finally emerged from more established organizations and the men who ran them. In January 1949, Franklin Williams's article on the Merriam fight was published in the *Crisis* and brought badly needed national publicity. A retired Amherst professor sent a letter of support. Brown immediately wrote him back and asked for money. He sent one hundred dollars. The Wichita branch of the Congress for Racial Equality wrote to Williams offering to submit an amicus curiae—or "friend of the court" brief—in support of the plaintiffs. Will Maslow, director of the legal department of the American Jewish Congress in New York, contacted Sidney Lawrence, president of the Community Relations Bureau of Kansas City, to see if he might also be able to write a brief. In addition, he instructed Lawrence to provide some funding to the Merriam branch so that it would know "it is not alone in its fight." Other organizations contributing in the spring of 1949 included B'nai Brith of Kansas City, the American Veterans Committee, and the Manhattan (Kansas) Civil Rights Committee. The Topeka NAACP branch donated earlier and more than any other Kansas branch outside of the Kansas City branches. The South Park families, in the early months of 1949, also became more enthusiastic—even as the weight of maintaining the protest schools mounted—giving back to Brown some of the energy and total commitment that, as she once complained to Williams, emanated mostly from herself. Ten students who had gone back to the Walker School rejoined the striking families in February, telling the adults that the Randall sisters had lectured them constantly on the foolishness of trying to fight the school board. Thereafter, those families did "not want to think of sending their children to Walker," Brown reported.[51]

On April 4, Williams came to Topeka to argue the case with Scott. Despite the fact that the Webb boys were listed first on the complaint, Patricia Black was chosen to testify in court. Scott, perhaps worried that the testimony of a young girl would be problematic, tried to elicit a promise of truthfulness from her from the stand:

Q: You know what it is to tell the truth?
A: Yes.
Q: You know what happens to little girls that tell lies, don't you?
A: Yes.
A: You were sworn to tell the truth?
A: Yes.
Q: How old are you?
A: Eight.[52]

When asked why she was chosen to testify, Black, now known as Brandy Sebron-Kelley, echoes many of the familiar injunctions aimed at black girls to explain. "I was taught how to act," Sebron-Kelley says, and later, "I knew how to act in certain situations," and finally, "It was pushed on us kids how to act." Knowing how to act entailed, in her words, "having manners," but also "sitting up straight . . . making eye contact, being erect, and [being] nice." The phrase "certain situations" was a reference to circumstances involving white men and boys. "I was taught about sexuality," she explains. "Rape was always a possibility." When asked how such lessons were learned, she recounts a story. She was walking home with a friend one evening in

South Park when a carload of white teenage boys started following and harassing them. When she got home, her parents did not offer empathy or say anything against the obnoxious teenagers; instead they exclaimed, "You girls need to watch it!" Because of these kinds of reprimands, especially those reminding her to be always aware of herself and her surroundings, Sebron-Kelley believes she approached the witness stand with a high degree of self-consciousness and what she calls "correct conduct" already in place. Though her mother was also confident about her preparation for taking the stand, as an extra precaution she put a large, white bow on her head for the occasion. Eight-year-old Patricia protested, saying the bow was oversized, embarrassing, and unnecessary. She was overruled.[53]

By early June, the court had ruled in favor of the plaintiffs, giving the LDF its first-ever victory in a grade school desegregation case in which it had played a direct role. There would be more shenanigans on the part of the South Park school board to entice black parents to stay at the Walker School, but the Merriam branch saw to it that the parents understood they were legally entitled to send their children to the new South Park School. Not a single black child showed up to the Walker School in September 1949, and the South Park School was successfully desegregated.[54]

By this time, Brown had become famous in the state, and no one questioned her right to speak at meetings or contact the New York office. She was a member of the Council of Christians and Jews, an official spokesperson for the Missouri delegation to the Civil Rights Mobilization in Washington, DC, and, perhaps most gratifying to her, a member of the executive board of the Kansas State Conference of the NAACP Branches. She and her family moved to Kansas City, Missouri, in the fall 1949, mostly to get away from her permanently hostile neighbors in Merriam. Before she left, she raised still more funds: this time to make sure the children from Walker were well attired for their first day of school at South Park. But most importantly, the victory in Kansas sent a message to the LDF in New

York: parents and plaintiffs were willing to go the distance to see a desegregation case through to the end, despite pushback from powerful leaders in the state.[55]

As the first successful school desegregation case that the national office had a hand in, the South Park victory played a direct role in the decision to bring a school desegregation lawsuit in Topeka. The two Kansas newspapers, the *Call* and the *Plaindealer*, had made South Park famous. Brown also fondly remembered the Topeka branch—its members and its leadership—as the most hospitable and enthusiastic of all the branches when she was pursuing the case. She spoke in Topeka on more than one occasion. Lucinda Todd, one of the most vocal members of the Topeka branch, who would initiate the lawsuit there in 1950, somehow procured and kept a copy of the South Park legal complaint submitted in 1948. Todd may have been among the large crowd that showed up for the supreme court hearing held in Topeka. It appears that Todd and the Topeka branch were inspired to pursue a school desegregation lawsuit along the lines of what they saw unfold in South Park. They had ample reasons of their own for wanting to take on the segregated school system.[56]

———

For someone who left such extensive traces in the historical record, and for all the encomiums written about her on the occasion of her untimely death at the age of fifty-one, Esther Brown remains elusive. What stands out from the first moment Brown began writing Franklin Williams was her unadulterated ambition and her total commitment to school desegregation. Just two letters into her correspondence with him, she signed off saying, "We are going to win this case if it kills me, and then we are going to continue this action throughout the state." What Williams thought about this letter— from a white woman and a relative stranger—is anyone's guess, but he must have been surprised, if not a little unnerved. A white person announcing her willingness to die for racial justice in 1948—or perhaps at any time—was an oddity. He might even have questioned her sanity. Brown realized this, and, in a moment of seeming self-consciousness, later explained herself by saying that John Brown was her hero. It is to Williams's credit that he took her at her word.[57]

Those with whom she spent the most time—the black women of South Park—had little to say about her human qualities. Mary Webb, who worked closely with Brown during the difficult and intense fall of 1948, recalled simply, "The person that really came to our aid was this Mrs. Brown and because . . . she was a Jew . . . she could open doors and get in where we could not." Others referred to her in similar ways: as someone who, because she was white, had powerful contacts. Some of Brown's early feelings of distance come through in her letters to Williams, where she described those she was working with, at one point, as "the women." No doubt the aforementioned women could feel Brown's impulse to group them together. However, by 1949, Brown realized her mistake and began to describe all of the adult black women with whom she worked by first and last names, preceded by "Mrs."[58]

There were, unsurprisingly, complaints about Brown from black men. Brown mentioned in an interview that she and Elisha Scott had a very hard time finding places to meet. "Where," she queried, "do you meet to discuss [a lawsuit]? I'd take him to my home. [But] I had crosses burned on the front lawn. . . . All right, so I go into the Negro community, I go to the Negro hotel where he was staying without thinking what it looked like for me to walk into that lobby. . . . He always felt I should have known better." Brown similarly upset Helen Swann's husband, William Swann. In a letter to Paul Brown posted in November 1949, after what must have been a particularly contentious meeting, Brown wrote, "If anything happens to me, such as being shot, knifed, etc., I want you to know [that] Mr. Wm. Swann told Mrs. Black, in anger . . . that if I am not careful someone is going to shoot me. He said the white people would be waiting in ambush for me one night when I was going into South Park for a meeting." The risk she was running angered William Swann. (Tellingly, despite his wife's tireless work on the lawsuit, neither he nor the Swann children were listed as plaintiffs.) What bothered Elisha Scott and William Swann was that Brown did not pay enough attention, in their view, to the fact that she was a white woman spending much of her time in black communities. To these men, she appeared reckless, an inexperienced housewife. On the one hand, had they known that she was a career agitator with a global perspective, her presence in black communities might have made more sense to them. On the other, had they been informed of her communist past, they might have refused to work with her. She was in an impossible position in more ways than one.[59]

Brown elected—in her own way, but like so many of the women and girls involved in school desegregation—to be a broker, tacking between a broad range of actors and making it possible for disparate groups to bring about desegregation together. She was a white woman who established a black organization in Merriam, and a female leader whose job it was to confront male leaders in the state. She worked doggedly to hold professionals accountable, but was not in possession of a college or professional degree. She was in contact with the most powerful officials in the NAACP but, when the South Park suit was being fought, held no office herself. Most important, she spent the greatest number of hours during the 1948–1949 South Park fight working with black women but had never shared their particular burdens.

Because of this distance, this otherness, Brown did not always understand those she worked with and for. Perhaps her biggest blind spot concerned black male professionals in the state. A. Porter Davis was an unusually accomplished and prominent doctor, the fifty-third president of the Negro Medical Association, an entrepreneur, a member of the Chamber of Commerce, and a licensed pilot. As such, he was one of only three black men in Kansas to attend the governor's conference on education in 1948. Brown found his unwillingness to bring up segregated education at the conference reprehensible. It did not occur to her that Davis's presence at the conference was itself a form of progress, that he perhaps was protective of his accomplishments and believed he could convince lawmakers in the state to enact change in ways that did not adhere to Brown's vision. She was similarly withering in her criticism of Scott. She was especially resentful when she found out, after the South Park case was decided, that he had been settling civil rights cases out of court for a decade. Again, it did not occur to her that settling out of court might have been a mutually beneficial situation for Scott and his clients. His clients received monetary compensation, while he maintained relationships with commissioners, judges, and white lawyers in the state where he had to work for the duration of his career. Nor did Brown know that, when he took on the South Park case, Scott lost fully half of his clients, working-class white people with whom he had been building contacts for decades.[60]

In the end, it was the children of South Park who felt the most profound fondness for Brown. Brandy Sebron-Kelley says, "She was like a godmother to me, she was so kind." Sebron-Kelley remembers going to Brown's house, playing with her children, and going shopping with her. On trips to the drug store together, Brown would send her up to the counter with the money, then stand back and watch. She wanted, Sebron-Kelley says, to teach her how to stand up for herself, to learn how to deflect white hostility with "courtesies" and "nice" behavior. If the white clerk became belligerent, Brown would emerge from the background, step in, and say protectively, "She's with me."[61]

Sebron-Kelley also remembers being listened to and treated with unusual respect for a child and being liberally hugged and often complimented by "Mrs. Brown." Alfonso Webb Jr. credited Brown with changing the course of his life. "Everything just opened up for me," he effused to a reporter in a 1975 profile of Brown for the *Kansas*

City Star. "Had we not started receiving the education that we did and conversing with whites as we did, we would have suffered real drawbacks."[62]

Perhaps the most affectionate gesture was proffered by the young people of Topeka, where she would assist in funding and organizing the lawsuit that would become *Brown v. Board*. Brown became known there as "the White Mrs. Brown." The moniker carried within it all the qualities she would have appreciated. It suggested that she was central and vital to the case there, that perhaps she even stood on equal footing with the mother of the lead plaintiff Linda Brown, and that blacks in Topeka saw her for what she was—a white person who was willing, at great personal cost, to be inextricably linked to the names, and lives, of the black citizens of Kansas.[63]

5

"Hearts and Minds"

The Road to Brown v. Board of Education

IN AUGUST 1950, LUCINDA TODD wrote a letter to Walter White, president of the NAACP, asking if he would be willing to help out with a planned school desegregation case. When White wrote back saying that the national office was willing to take on the lawsuit, Todd located and recruited other plaintiffs—thirteen mothers and one father, mostly parents and children from her own block, the ten-hundred block of Jewell Avenue. These would be the plaintiffs listed on *Brown v. Board of Education, Topeka*, the lead case in a group of five such cases appealed to the Supreme Court in 1952. The cases would include *Briggs v. Elliott* (South Carolina), *Bulah v. Gebhart* and *Belton v. Gebhart* (Delaware), *Davis v. County School Board* (Virginia), and *Bolling v. Sharpe* (Washington, DC). When Todd was interviewed twenty years later, what she recalled most was a motivating anger. There were problems with her daughter Nancy's teachers, and she wanted the freedom to choose something better:

Q: How did you first get involved with the NAACP?
A: Nancy was being slighted in her schoolwork. . . . I just hit the ceiling! Oh, I was so angry . . .

Q: This must have been just after WWII?

A: I know I hit the ceiling, I was so mad . . .

Q: Mr. Burnett [the Topeka Branch president] recruited you to
    be a member of the NAACP?

A: No, he didn't recruit me! I went in and asked! I was red hot!

Q: How did you become one of the plaintiffs?

A: Because I was in there kicking and fussing!

Like other women involved in desegregation cases, Todd saw herself
not as a leader but, as Mary Webb in South Park described herself,
a "pusher." She was in the middle of things, striking wherever she
could. The urgency, as she recalls it, was in resisting the omnipresence of an unjust, enraging system. She brought the case not because
she was idealistic or unrealistic, nor because she thought that the
NAACP would win the case—in fact, she thought they would lose.
She pursued the case because fighting against segregation and for
better schools had always been part of her life.[1]

When Todd contacted the national office to request assistance
with a desegregation lawsuit in 1951, the LDF had been officially
fighting segregated grade schools for over a year, and they were more
than happy to take her case. There were two reasons for the LDF's
shift: One was its victory in *Sweatt*, which made segregated graduate
schools unconstitutional. The other reason, just as important, was
that the LDF had amassed enough evidence to know that the cli-
mate, both legal and social, around grade school cases had changed
dramatically. The LDF had been flooded with telegrams describing warring lawsuits in Washington, DC, and escalating litigation
against school boards in a number of states. Girls and their parents
had paved the way by standing up for their lawsuits in the press—
both black and white—in clear, forthright, and confident ways. As
of 1950, there had been two successful school strikes (in Washington, DC, and South Park, Kansas) and over a dozen desegregation lawsuits filed. Countless citizens had begun to engage with

their local public schools in ways that were far more determined, sustained, and demanding than before. The case in South Park had already been won. Most important to LDF lawyers, federal judges, starting in early 1950, were beginning to issue opinions that spoke directly, unequivocally, and angrily about the discrimination in the segregated school system. As Charles Houston put it in a letter to a friend in New York, "Conditions are ripe and the time is now."[2]

Parents who had been fighting the system for years suddenly learned in the early 1950s that the LDF was very interested in their school cases. Parents in Washington, DC; Topeka, Kansas; and Claymont, Delaware, found their desegregation cases embraced. Others in Clarendon County, South Carolina; Hockessin, Delaware; and Prince Edward County, Virginia, were informed that, if they were willing, their equalization lawsuits could be transformed into desegregation cases. The LDF's goal was now to appeal a group of these cases to the Supreme Court. As the national office took on these cases, something curious happened: boys began to join the girls as desegregation plaintiffs in proportion to their representation in the population at large. Perhaps more boys now joined because school desegregation cases had become normalized by 1950 and thus less conspicuous. Or perhaps the LDF went looking for some boys to balance out the girls; in some places, there is evidence that boys—and, in Topeka, a father—were consciously added to lawsuits in order to achieve gender parity and some semblance of male leadership. But even as boys joined the plaintiff lists, girls continued to distinguish themselves in one way: they were uniformly chosen to testify in court.

———

Born in Litchfield, Kansas, in 1903, Lucinda Todd was the daughter of formerly enslaved parents. Her father, C. R. Wilson, was a coal miner who spoke with a brogue and was connected to the Irish community in the area. Wilson's father was a white man, a slave owner who, Todd said, "had taken an interest in teaching him to read and seeing to it that he was educated." Todd described her father as a very intelligent man with a particular knack for biblical exegesis. Her mother, Estelle Slaughter, died when she was nine. Like her father, Lucinda Todd was an accomplished scholar and graduated from Pittsburg State University, a predominantly white school in Pittsburg, Kansas, in 1932 with a degree in education. During the summers, she taught to make ends meet, mostly in one-room schoolhouses in coal-mining towns such as Girard, Edison, and Joplin—tiny, out-of-the-way, poor communities along the border between Kansas and Missouri. When she was at Pittsburg State, she boarded with an aunt because black students were required to live off campus. From 1932 to 1938, she taught at the Buchanan School in Topeka, and though she loved teaching, she gave it up when she married Alvin Todd. During the Great Depression, teaching jobs were reserved for single women—married women, it was presumed, were sufficiently supported by their husbands. Nancy, Lucinda and Alvin Todd's only child, was born in 1941.[3]

Todd first became famous in Topeka in 1944 for boldly sitting in the white section of a movie theater and being escorted out by the police. Todd's son-in-law, Raymond Noches, remembers seeing her at Topeka High School football games. She would stand on the sidelines, as close to the players as she could get, and yell, "Hit 'em again! Hit em' harder! Harder!" These incidents reveal Todd's dominant attributes: she was courageous, pugnacious, and extremely competitive. Nancy (Todd) Noches recalls that her mother was "stern" but fair. Above all she wanted Nancy to excel in school. "Very forceful" is the way Raymond Noches remembers her. "Very interested in everything in terms of politics and integration . . . and tough. Tough, tough lady." (He also remembers being terrified of her when he asked to marry her daughter.)[4]

Parents in Topeka and its suburbs had been fighting school segregation since at least 1941. As Todd described it, the "permissive" laws of Kansas, and the integrated nature of some neighborhoods, created a "crazy quilt" system of idiosyncratic segregation. Segregation was permitted only in elementary schools, and then only in cities of the "first class"—cities with more than fifteen thousand residents. In the late 1940s, those cities were Wichita, Kansas City, and Topeka. The black and white children on Jewell Avenue in Topeka would play together on the block all weekend, and then on Monday morning a bus would come and whisk the black children away. Other Topekans remember playing baseball and other sports with white children on the fields of Lowman Hill Elementary when school was out but being forbidden to set foot on the same patch of grass when the white students were in school. Though the lower schools were segregated, Topeka High School was integrated. It was a school system and social structure so full of contradictions that everyone found it to be at best nonsensical and at worst permanently damaging to the children of both races but especially to black children.[5]

African American parents had always had to push hard for any concessions from the Topeka school board. Prior to 1938, there were no school buses, and children had to walk two or three miles to get to school. Some were sent to live with grandparents and family friends in order to be close enough to black elementary schools. School buses were provided in 1938 only after a petition drive spearheaded by Fayetta "Fay" Sawyer and her husband Daniel Sawyer, then president of the Topeka NAACP. In 1940, Ulysses A. Graham brought a suit against the school board on behalf of his nephew, Oaland Graham, to integrate the Topeka junior high schools. Black students stayed in grade school through the eighth grade, while white students went to junior high for seventh and eighth. These differing arrangements, NAACP counsel argued, meant that black students too often arrived at Topeka High School academically unprepared. Indeed, Daniel Sawyer helped bring the case and testified in it because he had been tutoring eighth graders at his dining room table for years, and the after-hours work was beginning to take a toll on him. Hence the case was an unusual hybrid: the central argument was about equalization (black students needed to be prepared for high school), while the remedy was desegregation. When the court ruled that the junior high schools of Topeka must eliminate segregation, black parents celebrated their first substantial victory in the name of bettering their children's educational prospects.[6]

Feeling that the school system was now vulnerable to judicial action, parents began, in the early 1940s, to push against the remaining segregation in the elementary schools by testing them, with their daughters: they simply brought their girls to the school office and attempted to enroll them. "In 1942 my father tested Lowman Hill School with my sister Grace when she was five," Daniel Sawyer's daughter Constance Sawyer recalled. "In 1947 they tested Lowman Hill again with my sister Mary . . . and Mary talked about how awful she felt. These people were so nasty even though she was a child." The Sawyers were not the only parents during those years to attack segregated grade schools head-on. "Now Mrs. Maude Laughton [sic] told me," Sawyer continued, "that she was sick of the whole mess and she had tried to enter one of her daughters at Lowman Hill." These wildcat attacks on segregated schools—conducted with daughters of various ages—mirror the similar, uncoordinated attempts going on throughout the South in the 1940s.[7]

The sense of optimism for most black Topekans was short-lived. *Graham v. Board of Education* sparked an ugly and corrupt backlash. No one could have imagined what was to come next, for much of what transpired was unprecedented in the state. Immediately after the state supreme court handed down its decision in 1940, the Ku Klux Klan burned a cross on the lawn of Topeka superintendent A. J. Snout, who resigned immediately. To replace him, the school board brought in Kenneth McFarland, a superintendent from Coffeyville, a town hugging the border between Kansas and Oklahoma, who had a reputation as a hard-line conservative and ardent segregationist. Teachers with any connection to the Sawyers—eight in total—were fired. Annabelle Sawyer, Daniel Sawyer's sister and a veteran teacher in the Topeka school system, never recovered. She lived out the rest of her days in penury in Alexandria, Louisiana, where members of her sorority, Alpha Kappa Alpha, did their best to find her odd jobs. She later said that the "sorority saved her life because they gave her a way to have food." The example set by these firings, and the misery exacted, had its intended effect: teachers were terrified into silence, and they eventually resisted outright any suggestion of school desegregation.[8]

The suffering in Topeka had only just begun. McFarland brought with him a right-hand man whose job it was to find new and inventive ways to punish any parents who breathed a word about desegregation, and to resegregate black students who socialized with white students under any circumstances in the Topeka junior high and high schools. The real job of the new "Director of the Four Negro Schools," was, as Lucinda Todd put it, "to keep the Negro in his place." The appointment of a new director was especially painful because the position was filled by a black man named Harrison Caldwell. "Kenneth McFarland's stooge," Todd called him, and "a Negro traitor to his group".[9]

Caldwell's first move was to make a speech at a Rotary Club meeting, composed entirely of white men, in which he stated that "Negroes were not ready for integration and that they were not ready for their rights as citizens." The speech was printed in the daily newspaper. Next, he announced that the black teachers could no longer participate in the integrated Topeka Teachers Association; they would have to form a separate, Jim Crow association. He then went to work on the high school. He designated a few tables in the cafeteria "Negro tables." Black students who were found sitting elsewhere were forced to move to a "Negro table"—an event that apparently happened with some regularity. Black girls enrolled in home economics classes were forced to find black homes nearby in which they could practice the domestic arts separately from their white classmates. The boys were relieved of their positions on sports teams and forced to travel out of town to play other black teams. The new black basketball team was dubbed, with a wink, "the Ramblers."[10]

McFarland and Caldwell then went about segregating the senior prom in the most humiliating way possible. Rather than announcing a segregated prom ahead of time—which might have inspired protest—they stopped black students at the door and diverted them to a gym at one of the black lower schools. The most bitterly resented Caldwell innovation, however, was what came to be called the "N—Bell," for newly segregated assemblies. The "White Bell" would ring first, and then the "N—Bell" second. As the white students filed into the spacious auditorium, the black students went to a small room upstairs, usually to sit through a lecture from Caldwell. "Caldwell would tell us not to rock the boat and how to be as little offensive to whites as possible," recalls Samuel C. Jackson, who attended Topeka High in the 1940s.[11]

Black students began to congregate on the second floor to complain and confide in each other. Soon, the second floor became known as the "black floor." By the mid-1950s, black students at Topeka High School, Nancy Noches recalls, sat together in the lunchroom "by choice." They preferred their own proms, Raymond Noches adds, because they found white proms to be "stiff" and the "white music" not to their taste. The Ramblers, meanwhile, became a source of so much community pride that many black Topekans argued against school desegregation in 1951 solely because they feared losing their beloved team. Lucinda Todd could hardly believe her ears when people voiced this opinion to her—an opinion that was, she said, quite common. (People made similar complaints in Wilmington, Delaware, when the schools were on the verge of desegregation: one desegregation first remembers parents worrying primarily about football players being "stolen.") To what extent McFarland won the battle by instigating de jure social segregation—or to what extent self-segregation emerged organically in the 1950s—is impossible to parse. At the very least, McFarland's regime aggravated and enlarged the social marginalization of black students at Topeka High School, thereby also increasing their sense of separateness and solidarity. By the 1950s, no one could remember a time when it had been any different at Topeka High, and thoroughly segregated academic, athletic, and social lives appeared to many students to be timeless and inevitable. The second floor at Topeka High School is called the "black floor" to this day.[12]

Todd had always had her issues with the segregated schools of Topeka, even before McFarland came to town. Her daughter Nancy—a bright, thoughtful child—had graduated from first grade at the Buchanan School unable to read. An art teacher had been assigned to her class of thirty students, and Nancy spent most of the year drawing pictures. Todd hired a former colleague to do remedial work with Nancy over the summer.[13]

A turning point for Todd came one day when she read in the newspaper that the Topeka public schools would be holding an all-lower-school music performance, with prizes given out for the best orchestras and individual musicians. Children in the black schools had not been invited to compete, on the grounds that the black schools had no orchestras. Nancy, who would later become a music therapist, played the violin and the piano and also sang. Todd was furious. "I got on the telephone and I called the supervisor and wanted to know why colored children weren't competing. I got on [the music supervisor] about not going to bat for the colored children." According to Caldwell, "Blacks didn't want music instruction, [and] could not afford instruments." Todd took her protest to the school board and won. Music instruction was added the following year to the four black elementary schools in the city.[14]

In the summer of 1948, Todd teamed up with Fay Sawyer and Daniel Sawyer to found an organization devoted to improving conditions in Topeka's schools and fighting McFarland's reign of terror. Their new organization, hatched at Todd's dining room table at 1007 Jewell Avenue, was called the Citizens Committee on Civil Rights. Their first leaflet, dating from early summer 1948, was a militant, no-holds-barred attack on the school system, and bore a striking resemblance to the mimeographed flyers that Gardner Bishop was printing up in Washington, DC, with the Consolidated Parent Group at the same moment. "The People Fight Back" was at the top of the bill, followed by "A Jim Crow Outrage." The leaflet went on to describe the actions of the "two little dictators," McFarland and Caldwell. It described a recent senior dance held at a local ballroom. When black students were, once again, turned away at the door, the memo reported, "White students stopped the dance to protest"—but to no avail. After listing some of the egregious practices of the "DIVIDE AND RULE OFFENSIVE" of the two men (their crimes were too many to list on a single page), Todd and the Sawyers wrote, "Democratic-minded Topekans have had enough! They are determined to restore fair play and democratic freedom in Topeka Schools, regardless of color." The committee announced its first mass meeting, on July 22, 1948, and ended with a plea to "PLEASE SEND MONEY OR OFFER YOUR SERVICES!"[15]

This action was enormously courageous for several reasons. First, both families had girls in the public schools. They could expect retaliation. Second, in speaking out about Caldwell's complicity with McFarland, they were making public the corrupt behavior of a high-profile professional in their own community. No matter how bad Caldwell was, there were sure to be complaints from those in the black community who disagreed with their tactics and—as in Washington, DC—felt their institutions were being publicly disparaged. Like Lucile Bluford, Esther Brown, and the Carr and Jennings families, Todd and the Sawyers were taking on a battle that did not unfold entirely along clear-cut racial lines. Their stance would be an unwelcome development for many parents.

After the July meeting, Todd and the Sawyers submitted a six-page petition. Lucinda Todd and Fay Sawyer had spent the better part of July and August canvassing Topeka, mostly on foot but sometimes in Daniel Sawyer's truck, to get signatures. Most black citizens were too frightened of reprisals to sign, but through sheer determination and relentless work, the two women succeeded in getting somewhere in the neighborhood of one thousand signatures.

The petition is a fascinating document, with an array of carefully thought-out suggestions. Many of its proposals sound prescient, and the document provides insight into Todd and the Sawyers' far-reaching political perspective—one that was simultaneously acutely aware of the difficulties black students faced in *already* integrated schools and informed by proto-feminist ideas about how to better include black women in school management to the advantage of both teachers and students. The section of the petition entitled "Colored Schools" asked that "women teachers . . . be eligible for principalships . . . because . . . the hiring of only men principals" meant that there was "a lack of opportunity for advancement," which in turn created "a general feeling of apathy which [was] reflected in [poor] preparation of colored children for secondary education." Under the heading "Mixed Junior High and High Schools," the letter made four specific demands:

1. Colored teachers in the Junior High and High Schools

2. Negro participation in all branches of High School athletics including football on the basis of merit

3. Negroes be allowed to participate in other extracurricular activities without discrimination because of race and color

4. A course in Negro History be included in the High School

The call for a "Negro History" course was twenty years ahead of its time—a demand that militant black high school students would make in the late 1960s and beyond. Here, the explanation was that "such a course would give our youth a sense of pride [and] create a wholesome respect for Negroes by the white youth."[16]

The demand to allow black students to participate in extracurricular activities based on "merit" was yet another plea to compete: "We recommended the second and third proposals" the letter states, "to make it necessary for [black students] to compete as individuals and not as Negroes and be required to come up to certain standard [sic] for eligibility." The letter is revealing. Without blaming any black member of the school system, Todd and the Sawyers successfully implied that the segregated school system (in the myriad forms it took in Topeka) erected limitations that could be fatal to the aspirations of many students and faculty alike. School segregation was, in their description, a cordon sanitaire drawn around black children and teachers. Ambition to achieve anything beyond it was impossible. As such, it choked the academic morale of those within its grip. It was not a matter of cultural exchange; rather, it was a matter of interracial competition. High schools are, after all, profoundly competitive spaces. Black students needed to compete against white students to know that they were as good as or better than white students given the chance, whether that be in debate, music, theater, literature, or any other subject. Years before the NAACP procured social scientists to testify about the impact of segregated education on children, the Citizens Committee on Civil Rights had drawn up a document detailing the effects of segregation on the self-worth of all black students, no matter how talented or protected by individual parents.[17]

The petition ended with a self-confident declaration that, in the year 1948, McFarland was rowing against the tide: "Regardless of the National trend toward integration; regardless of the fact that separation in our schools ... sets up another barrier to American unity, and hampers our leadership in world affairs, Dr. McFarland says: Separate elementary schools are here to stay and separate secondary schools are in the plans. To which Mr. Caldwell says: Amen!" To this the letter writers replied, "There is one thing we have learned however. Things and conditions don't remain static because a few well-placed people will it so. The world is in the midst of a mighty upheaval and conditions change in the twinkling of an eye." The petition's drafters had clearly taken note of the many unfolding school equalization and desegregation lawsuits around the country—Todd, for one, was an avid reader of the *Kansas City Call*.[18]

The price Todd paid for the petition was swift and steep. Just after it was submitted, Caldwell began to call Nancy's teacher away from school on "trumped up errands" and put the janitor in charge of teaching the class. Any teacher who was on friendly terms with Todd was told that she would be fired if she was to so much as be seen near Todd's house on Jewell Avenue. Some teachers continued to come over for Todd's bridge and literature clubs, as long as the blinds were closed, but most stayed away. One teacher who was a well-known friend of Todd's had her contract withheld until the day before classes started in September. Then, in fifth grade, Nancy's grades suddenly plummeted. She had always made A's, and nothing in her performance suggested any reason for being marked down, except that Linda Caldwell, Harrison Caldwell's daughter, was in Nancy's class. Linda was making straight A's. This injustice hit a nerve in Lucinda Todd that could not be calmed by a phone call or a visit to the school board. This was the moment when Todd was pushed past her breaking point. She set out to educate other parents and committed herself to taking down Jim Crow schools entirely.[19]

It was a tough sell. While some people, as Todd put it, "finally awakened to the dangers of segregation" during the McFarland administration, most thought that a school desegregation lawsuit was doomed to fail and that Todd, the Sawyers, and the Topeka NAACP branch "were a bunch of crackpots" and "radicals" for

pursuing it. But Todd, as she had already said so plainly to McFarland and Caldwell, was part of a national movement. In 1949, that
movement came to her, in the form of a visit from Walter White.
Since the better hotels were closed to blacks, he stayed at the Todd's
increasingly famous home. White's visit was a memorable event for
all race-conscious citizens in Topeka. And while the national office had put Kansas on White's itinerary for a long-planned swing
through the Midwest, it was Esther Brown who connived to make
his visit an unparalleled event—full of pomp, ceremony, a lineup of
state politicians including former governor and current state senator Arthur Capper, and conspicuous fund-raising.[20]

White's address came only a few weeks after NAACP lawyer
Franklin Williams had argued *Webb v. District No. 90* before the
supreme court in Topeka. Carl Johnson—president of the Kansas
City, Missouri, branch and one of Brown's few local male allies in the
NAACP—planned to have White speak at a black Baptist church
in late April. But Brown, already thinking of the statewide campaign
she planned to wage after the South Park decision, wanted a larger
venue in order to raise more money. "I said white people won't go
there" she recalled. "We want white people, not just Negroes." Johnson wouldn't hear of it, so Brown resorted to outright chicanery.
"When Carl went out of town I sent a telegram to Walter and signed
Carl's name to it," Brown admitted. The telegram flattered White
with the suggestion of a huge crowd, and told him that Johnson had
rented out the municipal auditorium on the grounds of the capitol
for his visit. "I'd only do this for you," she signed off. "[Your] good
friend Carl." As usual it was a brazen, high-stakes, headlong, and,
in this instance, morally questionable gamble. It was also an appeal
to White's vanity—an approach that had worked for Brown in the
past. "I rented that music hall for three hundred dollars, despite
what Carl said ... and I packed that music hall ... and Walter, he
was prestige ... he was catered to, all kinds of receptions ... he was

on the radio. Real good party . . . and we raised something like [a] thousand dollars which was unheard of in Kansas."[21]

It was a fateful event. It was "then [that] the NAACP in New York thought I was useful for something, raising money. And I was glad to do it. No question about it," Brown asserted. For Daniel Sawyer, who had been trying to drum up interest in the NAACP for decades, White's visit—the large audience and the surpassing importance of the NAACP it reflected—was the fulfillment of a long-held dream. As Constance Sawyer remembers it, "All these people were on the podium, most of whom I had never seen before. My mother and grandmother and I were sitting on the front row but Dad was sitting at the back of the auditorium. Of course he was starting to be ill by then. . . . He sat back there all comfortable with his legs stretched out, smiling." At her home, Todd found time to tell White about the dire situation in the Topeka public school system. She would later refer to their private conversation when she wrote to him in August 1951 to request that the national office assist her local branch in the school desegregation case they wished to pursue against the Topeka school board. "Dear Sir," she began, "I am Mrs. Todd, you stayed in my house when you were through Kansas. . . . I don't know if you remember our particular problems here . . . [but] our situation here has become so unbearable that the local branch has decided to test the . . . law. . . . We wonder if the national Office would help us on this case."[22]

In the late 1940s, while Brown was begging the LDF for help with the case in South Park, Thurgood Marshall was more interested in the Clarendon County, South Carolina, case, which had begun in 1947 with a simple request for a school bus. There were thirty school buses for the white children in Clarendon County, and none for the black children. The Clarendon County school board did not pay a penny for black schools. The shanty-like buildings, the coal to heat them, and school supplies were paid for by what little could be spared from the black farming community (on top of their taxes). The school board only paid the black teachers' salaries, which were a third of what white teachers made. Most rural schools only had one or two teachers for all ages and grades. The high school students, who lived within a ten-mile radius of Scott's Branch High School in Summerton, had to find their own transportation. The best place to start, local NAACP members agreed, was with the buses. It was the most obvious form of discrimination, and the least likely request to cause white backlash. Reverend J. A. DeLaine was authorized by the two churches he pastored to take up the issue with Clarendon County superintendent L. B. McCord. The request was denied. DeLaine then enlisted a friend, Levi Pearson, to file, with the assistance of a lawyer from Columbia, South Carolina, named Harold R. Boulware, a legal petition requesting that bus transportation be furnished to his three minor children, Daisy, James, and Eloise Pearson, all of whom attended the Scott's Branch High School. When the school board did not respond, Boulware filed a lawsuit, with Levi Pearson as plaintiff. *Pearson v. Board of Education* was filed on March 16, 1948.[23]

The case was thrown out of court on a technicality, and the school board's reprisals were markedly similar to those undertaken in Topeka. The principal of Scott's Branch, a veteran of eighteen years in the post, was fired and replaced with a man loyal to the school board, a man who was arrogant with the teachers and freely siphoned off cash from the school coffers. This state of affairs sparked a reaction also like that in Topeka: DeLaine and concerned parents formed a "grievance committee," which approached the school board asking for a "suitable principal" for the Scott's Branch school. Just after DeLaine submitted the petition, he was fired from his job as a teacher in a county elementary school. The committee fought back, accusing the school board of trying to set "one group against another" by offering small gifts to "better" parents and punishing those parents who spoke up. "If parents want assurance of a "BETTER DEAL," the pamphlet read, "they must stand together for the future good of their children and community."[24]

In the meantime, lawyer Boulware was in contact with the LDF in New York. In March 1949, Thurgood Marshall met with De-Laine and some of the other parents active in Columbia and told them that if they could get twenty families to commit to a lawsuit, the NAACP would bring an equalization case against the Claren-don County school board. By November 1949, DeLaine had con-vinced twenty local families to take part. At the top of the list, in alphabetical order, was Harry Briggs, plaintiff on behalf of his five minor children. Briggs was fired from the gas station where he had worked for fourteen years, and his wife was fired from her job as a maid at a Summerton hotel. Soon, all of the parents listed as plain-tiffs began to suffer reprisals. Yet, incredibly, none of them dropped out of the case. The school board offered the principalship of the Scott's Branch High School to DeLaine if he would agree to drop the suit. When he turned it down, they offered the job to his wife, Mattie DeLaine; she too declined the offer. On Sundays, Reverend DeLaine continued to preach about the "price that free men must pay in a free country for wanting their children trained as capable and respectable American citizens."[25]

Before Marshall could argue *Briggs* in Charleston, however, there was a sea change in LDF policy regarding school segregation cases; at a June 1950 meeting of civil rights lawyers convened by Mar-shall, the LDF for the first time committed itself specifically to a frontal attack on grade school segregation. There were several de-velopments that informed the timing and content of the meeting. First, the earliest encouraging judicial dissent on a grade school case came on February 14, 1950, in the ruling in the Carr case. *Carr v. Corning* had been filed in Washington, DC, on behalf of Marguerite Carr in 1947. An appeal was filed and, as expected, lost. However, there was a lengthy, encouraging dissent from Judge Henry White Edgerton. By February 1950, Carr had moved from Browne Junior High to Cardozo High School. Noting the change, Edgerton issued a detailed, scathing report on the conditions at the high school: Whereas Carr had been on a double shift at Browne, she was now on a triple shift at Cardozo. Whereas the white school close to her home sat on 11.5 acres, Cardozo occupied a site of less than one acre. School functions were "being carried on in basement rooms, corridors, assembly hall, sidewalks and public highways." Students were disadvantaged by the omission of practical subjects and by a lack of guidance and counseling. Black students in need of special services such as speech correction or remedial reading were "severely handicapped" in comparison with white students. Fire protection throughout the building was "extremely inadequate." There was not enough space, light, desks, chairs, or equipment. "It is plain," Edgerton concluded, "that pupils . . . are denied better schooling and given worse because of their color." Such distinctions had been declared "arbitrary and unreasonable" by the Supreme Court. Then, citing *Sipuel v. Board of Regents*, Edgerton wrote that the Supreme Court had recently "applied this general principle to public education" and found that it was "unconstitutional." The national black press was elated and quoted judge Edgerton's dissent at length.[26]

Two days after the ruling in *Carr*, on February 16, 1950, Robert L. Carter, assistant special counsel to the LDF, wrote an urgent memorandum describing the ruling to Marshall, who was in the midst of preparing for *Briggs*. Carter was especially keen to explain to Marshall that Edgerton dissented on the grounds not only that the schools were unequal but also "that the racial discrimination and racial segregation are unconstitutional." Austin Fickling of Ransom, Fickling, and Tate had written to Carter asking if the LDF wanted to appeal the case to the Supreme Court. "My off-the-cuff opinion," Carter wrote to Marshall, "is that if we have any basis for appeal in this case, we ought to take it up." However, the case came to an abrupt end in the summer of 1950 when James Carr refused to move ahead with his daughter acting as the sole plaintiff.[27]

The second encouraging ruling came on April 8, 1950. Leon Ransom, now working with NAACP lawyers Oliver Hill, Spottswood Robinson, and Martin A. Martin, appealed the Constance Carter case in Arlington, Virginia, *Carter v. School Board*, to the US Court of Appeals for the Fourth Circuit. On May 31, 1950, the three-judge panel reversed the lower court's decision and remanded the case for further proceedings. The three judges—John J. Parker, Morris Ames Soper, and Armistead Dobie—were a famous group. "That was some brilliant court," Marshall remembered, "maybe the three greatest judges to ever sit together." He would be looking closely at what these three judges said.[28]

What was important about the Fourth Circuit's decision was not their position on desegregation—a question they held off addressing—but their perspective on the appalling state of affairs facing black high school students in Arlington. Noting that the lower court had judged that the black high school, Hoffman-Boston, "was substantially equivalent to ... Washington-Lee," they responded that "in our view this position is untenable.... The differences between the two schools ... support the conclusion that discrimination actually exists." The justices then—like Judge Edgerton in the *Carr* case—described those differences in detail. Washington-Lee had four science laboratories, including "a physics laboratory, a chemistry laboratory and two biology laboratories." Hoffman-Boston had "only one science room in which all of the sciences given are taught." Washington-Lee had a library of 8,682 books, two music rooms, two rooms with equipment for typing instruction, two gymnasiums (one for girls and one for boys), a cafeteria, and an infirmary with seven beds. Hoffman-Boston had a library of 1,077 books, no auditorium, no space for music instruction, only a few functioning typewriters, no gymnasium, no cafeteria, and no infirmary (though one of the teachers at the school did double duty as a nurse). The differences and distinctions went on and on. The judges, all of them southerners, concluded, "This difference . . . cannot be sustained. It places a burden upon the colored student" and "deprives him of opportunities" offered to white students. Furthermore, such burdens had been found unconstitutional in *Corbin v. County School Board* (an equalization case brought by Spottswood Robinson and decided in 1949) and in *Sipuel v. Board of Regents.* "The above recital of existing conditions at the two schools," the justices concluded, is intended to "demonstrate by illustration that discrimination in the treatment accorded the students of the two races undoubtedly prevails."[29]

The judges stopped short of ordering desegregation, and Judge Parker would soon be explicit about his ongoing support for segregated schools. But the heated language of their decision registered a new sense of urgency. The moral axis of this and other judicial decisions had definitively shifted. The lengthy restating of details proving the extreme injustice of segregated schools, the explication of harm done to African American students, and the frustration and anger all indicated a new desire to remedy problems in the segregated school system that had long been ignored. That they cited *Sipuel v. Board of Regents* (*Sweatt* had not yet been handed down) reflects the justices' sense that Virginia was in violation of a Supreme Court ruling on education and needed to find a remedy immediately. And in their emphasis on racial discrimination, the justices were giving Ransom, Robinson, and Martin language to work with as they went forward with the *Carter* case. Judicial language on school desegregation cases was, by 1950, very different than it had been even a few years prior. No doubt, the fact that there were so many of these cases made the judges careful about their approach. Their rulings were part of a contentious, hard-fought, still-unfolding desegregation movement, and this was one of their more visible and consequential decisions. The judges did not want to mar their reputations by appearing obtuse or completely behind the times on such a subject.[30]

Finally, on June 5, 1950, the *Sweatt* and *McLaurin* decisions were handed down, the former desegregated graduate education and the latter made it illegal to segregate students within the classroom. It was in the wake of these rulings that Marshall called a meeting in New York, inviting as many lawyers and constitutional law professors as he could muster. The matter of a frontal attack on segregated schools was put on the table. No one disagreed about the desirability of attacking segregation per se. But there was considerable debate about how and when to do so. There was also concern about how the branches would react. Herbert Hill, director of labor affairs for the NAACP, remembered that "there was lots of resistance from the branches because real progress toward equalization was now beginning to be made in schools and other facilities like parks, libraries, and swimming pools. The dissidents said, 'You mean that you want us to oppose all this?'"[31]

The association was getting decidedly mixed signals from their constituents. On the one hand, there were the militant grade school desegregation activists such as Gardner Bishop and the Consolidated Parent Group, C. G. Jennings, James Carr, Constance Carter's mother Eleanor Taylor, Esther Brown, Lucinda Todd, and Lucile Bluford, who was doing so much for the cause as editor of the *Call*. There were the young women who had taken on the burden of approaching white schools with their parents and acting as plaintiffs. There were also the local lawyers who had drafted briefs, without the support of the national office, and had already argued that segregated schools were unconstitutional, most notably Leon Ransom, who had filed the two most high-profile lawsuits attacking segregation, *Carr* and *Carter*. On the other hand, there were the numerous parents who, while they were willing to protest unequal schools, simply wanted a better education for their children while they were still young enough to receive it, not a long, hard campaign against a long-standing Supreme Court precedent. There was power, persuasive logic, and high feeling on both sides.[32]

Marshall was, according to several colleagues, a "cautious" lawyer. His constituents, he reasoned, wanted him to win cases. He feared that taking on school segregation directly and losing could jeopardize his record. "His prevailing sense," according to Oliver Hill, an NAACP lawyer in Richmond, "was that we just couldn't afford to lose a big one." Lawyer James Nabrit remembered that Marshall thought that "if [segregation] per se lost, we'd be set back a generation." Officially, Marshall signed on at the policy meeting to go for broke and attack segregation head-on. But other lawyers in his orbit remembered having to continue to argue the merits with him afterward, and that he remained hesitant about a straightforward attack. The lawyers who worked hardest to convince him were those who were most exposed to the frustrated parents of grade school children. Robinson, who was working on a raft of school desegregation and equalization suits in Virginia, argued forcefully for immediate action. Franklin Williams, no doubt exhausted from the endless emergencies emanating from South Park, communicated his "impatience with Marshall's wariness in assaulting [segregation]" to Walter White and asked him to lean on Marshall.[33]

In May 1951, after a few procedural delays, Marshall—along with Robert L. Carter, Howard Boulware, and Spottswood Robinson—was finally ready to argue against segregated schooling in *Briggs v. Elliott.* In addition to the usual comparisons between the white and "colored" schools—funding, facilities, teacher-student ratios, available services, extracurricular programs, and transportation—the plaintiff's lawyers took the plunge and argued that segregation itself was discriminatory and thus a violation of the Fourteenth Amendment. The legal team brought in psychologist Kenneth Clark—half of the husband-and-wife research team with Mamie Phipps Clark—to South Carolina in order to test the Clarendon County students for evidence of psychological harm stemming from segregation. Clark used the famous—some would say infamous—"doll test" to gauge the children's racial self-perception.

The practice of using dolls in order to discern "racial consciousness" originated with Mamie Clark's master's thesis at Howard University, in which she argued that black children became aware of themselves as a part of a group "differentiated" from other groups very early in their development. Kenneth Clark's study of the Clarendon County children's reactions to the black and white dolls went exactly as predicted. Sixteen children were tested on doll preference. Ten students said they preferred the white doll, nine said the white doll was the "nice" doll, and eleven said that the Negro doll looked "bad."[34]

Robert L. Carter, who was in charge of expert witnesses, tried to enlist other, more well-known social scientists to help bolster Kenneth Clark's testimony. But those who had established reputations to protect were unwilling, so he had to settle for David Krech, co-author of a textbook called *Theory and Problems of Social Psychology*, and Helen Trager, a lecturer at Vassar College who had conducted research on racial attitudes of black children in Philadelphia. Both scholars were white. Krech testified that "legal segregation, because it is legal, because it is obvious to everyone, gives what we call in our lingo environmental support for the belief that Negroes are in some way inferior to white people, and that in turn, of course, supports and strengthens beliefs of . . . racial inferiority." Trager summed up her findings by stating that "the Negro children, unlike the white children, showed a tendency to expect rejection. This expectation of rejection increased sharply from five to eight years old."[35]

The social science, however, not only failed to persuade the judges, it came in for some abuse in the decision. Judge John J. Parker, writing for the majority, began by stating that the three-judge panel had found the schools in Clarendon County to be unequal. He requested that "defendants file within six months a report showing" what progress had been made in equalizing facilities. Parker went on to state that the laws of South Carolina require the establishment of separate schools for white and "Negro" children. It was a lengthy decision, citing a staggeringly comprehensive list of precedents enforcing racial segregation in schools in many states over one hundred years' time and ending with the recent decision in *Carr v. Corning*. "Only a little over a year ago," Parker wrote, "the question was before the Court of Appeals of the District of Columbia in *Carr v. Corning* . . . and the whole matter exhaustively explored . . . in an able opinion by Judge Prettyman," who wrote for the majority. Most compelling about Prettyman's decision, to Parker, was his statement that "since the beginning of human history, no circumstance has given rise to more difficult and delicate problems than has the coexistence of different races in the same area. Centuries of bitter experience in all parts of the world have proved that the problem is insoluble by force of any sort." The US Congress, Parker summed up, had "for more than three-quarters of a century required segregation. . . . The constitutional principle is the same now that it has been throughout this period; and if conditions have changed so that segregation is no longer wise, this is a matter for the legislatures and not for the courts. The members of the judiciary have no more right to read sociology into the Constitution than their ideas of economics."[36]

The dissent from Judge Julius Waties Waring was almost as long as Parker's decision. He began by asserting the absurdity of defining a certain group as "Negro" when every black person—and by inference a good many white persons—had complex and differing ancestry, and the folly therefore of trying to correctly and exactly split up students based on color. He went on to describe the progress made over the last seventy-five years by the Supreme Court in elucidating the exact nature of the equal protection clause of the Fourteenth Amendment. He cited court cases outlawing discrimination in jury selection, housing facilities, suffrage, and, of course, graduate school. Where he differed most from his colleagues was in his interpretation of the academic research. The experts "showed," he wrote, "beyond a doubt that the evils of segregation and color prejudice come from early training." From their testimony, he concluded, "it was clearly apparent, as it should be to any thoughtful person, irrespective of having such expert testimony, that segregation in education can never produce equality and that it is an evil that must be eradicated." Then, his coup de grâce: "The system of segregation in education adopted and practiced in the state of South Carolina must go and must go now. Segregation is per se inequality."[37]

Between 1948 and 1950, while Thurgood Marshall was pouring his energies into *Briggs*, grade school activists lit up the phones of lawyers in Washington, DC, Virginia, Kansas, and Delaware. In Washington, the Consolidated Parent Group, established in 1948, had continued to bring lawsuit after lawsuit, covering every grade from kindergarten to high school. Charles Houston was acting as counsel for the organization in 1948 and 1949. And while Houston was more cautious than Gardner Bishop—he asked that buildings set aside for whites be transferred to black students and for damages, as he had been doing since 1938 in *Bluford v. Canada*—the rhetoric of the CPG continued to make it clear that they wanted to take on segregation head-on. In 1949, Houston filed *Haley v. Corning* on behalf of Gloria Odessa Haley, Barbara Ann Edmonds, Bessie Boyd, Adolph Graves, and other Cardozo High School students, demanding access to buildings and equipment reserved for white students. But while Houston's strategy had not changed much, his language had. "Defendants," he said, "arbitrarily, willfully and maliciously refused to assign these surplus buildings, equipment, facilities and teaching appointments ... to the use of Cardozo High School students because of their own race prejudice." He had come some distance since declaiming, "A girl stands at the door."[38]

By 1950, Houston's health was deteriorating fast and it was necessary for Bishop to find another civil rights lawyer. Houston recommended James Nabrit, a professor of law at Howard Law School who had previously been consulted by the Browne PTA to help with the *Carr* case. In 1950, acting as counsel to Bishop's CPG,

Nabrit filed *Cogdell v. Sharpe* on behalf of Valerie Cogdell, two other girls, and one boy. The first paragraph of the complaint reads, "This is a suit for . . . a permanent injunction to restrain the enforcement, operation and execution of certain Acts of Congress which require the segregation of white and colored children in the public schools of the District of Columbia, on the ground that such Acts are repugnant to the Constitution of the United States." Nabrit was a different lawyer, with a very different approach—an approach more suited to a transformed legal and political landscape.[39]

In November 1950, Nabrit mysteriously removed Valerie Cogdell from the top of the list of plaintiffs and put Spottswood Bolling and his brother Wanamaker Bolling there instead, with three girls listed below in alphabetical order. The *Bolling* complaint is virtually identical to that filed on behalf of Cogdell. The change is highly unusual: there is no evidence in the files of the CPG or the NAACP that explains why the lead plaintiff changed. Cogdell's parents may have gotten cold feet. Or, perhaps Valerie Cogdell and the other two girls would soon graduate from high school and Spottswood and Wanamaker Bolling were younger (Spottwood was fourteen in 1953) and therefore eligible to remain on the lawsuit for the years it would be in court. Another possibility, one can speculate, is that Marshall looked at the steady stream of lawsuits filed on behalf of girls and decided to intercede. If he was going to take these cases to the Supreme Court, he needed some boys and young men out in front. It would not be difficult for Bishop and the officers of the CPG to find such a student in their large and thriving organization. If Marshall did intervene in some way, his logic would have been hard to argue with. In the event of a Supreme Court case, the general public, the judges, and the press needed to see the desire for desegregation as one that was embraced by the whole—as opposed to just the female half—of the race.

By the time the case got to the Supreme Court, Spottswood Bolling was the only plaintiff listed. The *Washington Daily News* and the *Washington Post* had been looking for Bolling for years, but he proved almost impossible to locate, much less interview. Between 1952 and 1954, he regularly dodged newspapermen and photographers who were waiting on his porch by taking a detour to the park to play baseball. When his mother, "after sitting on him all day," finally got him safely into her living room, he politely declined to offer any assessment of the case. One reporter described it this way: "[Bolling] bit his fingernails, shriveled inside his freshly-pressed tan tweed sportcoat . . . even ducked out behind the kitchen gas furnace—all to make clear he would prefer to resume watching the Notre Dame game on television, or go over to Lincoln Park and play basketball, or do anything at all but discuss a Supreme Court segregation case."[40]

In 1953, when these reporters tried to speak with Bolling, what he had to say about the case was not of critical importance. The case had already been argued in the Supreme Court and was just one of many such cases. Bolling no doubt knew this, which gave him license to evade the reporters. He would eventually become more comfortable with the public attention, but his discomfort with the press in 1953 sets in high relief the performances of girl plaintiffs with reporters in the late 1940s. The press, especially the white press, wanted to talk to these plaintiffs. They wanted to know if these young people truly wanted to desegregate white schools. Was it just their parents? Was it only the NAACP? Was there a real desire out there on the part of African American young people to attend white schools? Indeed, once black students started applying to white schools in the South in the 1960s, this would be the *only* question on the minds of most white school officials. For a plaintiff to shrink from it was perfectly natural. How does one student speak for a process that has not yet begun, that had never been tried in a segregated southern city, that would change social relations so radically? To come up with *something* with which to answer this question, one had to believe that an answer could be found, and that no matter how absurd the question was, one had a duty to answer it. Girls and young women—as we have seen—felt it was their special responsibility to find ways to address such inquiries. Bolling, evidently, did not.

Other aspects of Bolling's position as school desegregation pioneer could have been bothering him. If girls saw school desegregation as somehow linked to their responsibilities as girls, it is probable that Bolling too saw school desegregation and the performance of interracial accord that it demanded as somehow feminine and therefore something he was ill-suited for. Indeed, given how feminized the work of leading school desegregation lawsuits already was by 1952—Bolling would have known of no boys or prominent young men who were lead plaintiffs in Washington, DC, or elsewhere—it is not hard to see why Bolling might seek, instead, to distinguish himself on a neighborhood baseball field.[41]

———

In Delaware, there were two cases pending before the court of chancery—a court set aside specifically to hear equity cases—in the fall of 1951. One was filed by Sarah Bulah in Hockessin, which was ten miles from Wilmington and close to the border with Pennsylvania. Sarah Bulah sued on behalf of her grade school daughter, Shirley Bulah, in *Bulah v. Gebhart*. The second case, *Belton v. Gebhart*, was filed on behalf of Ethel Louise Belton and others similarly situated who resided in Claymont, a suburb just outside Wilmington. Initially, Sarah Bulah simply wanted a bus to get her daughter to school. In *Belton*, the story that has been told is that Howard High School in Wilmington, a black school, was run-down and hard to get to from Claymont, so parents got together and decided to sue the school board. But according to Virginia Smilack, the daughter of the Claymont High School PTA president, things happened differently. The education at Howard, according to both Smilack and Ethel Louise Belton's best friend, Janet Harmon, was excellent. The school was beloved by its students and a point of pride in the black community in Wilmington and the surrounding suburbs. The local lawyer in charge of the case, Louis Redding, had gone to Howard High School. And while in arguing *Belton* "he left no doubt that the schools were unequal, he refused to impugn the quality of teaching at Howard High School." Redding's sister, Gwendolyn Redding, taught English there. She was, according to Harmon, an inspiring teacher. Gwendolyn Redding had also been Ethel Louise Belton's teacher, and she probably recommended Belton to her brother as someone who would hold up in court.[42]

The few blacks in Claymont all lived on Hickman Row. Most revered among the black community was Miss Dyson, an elementary school teacher who held students to famously high standards and managed to elicit excellence from them all. According to Smilack, neither Superintendent Harvey Stahl nor her father as PTA president felt comfortable with the situation at Claymont High School. Both men were keeping an eye on school desegregation cases taking place in other states, and both wanted Claymont to "move forward" now, in order to get ahead of an inevitable confrontation with the residents of Hickman Row. They contacted the "person to go to," Miss Dyson. Stahl asked her if she would talk to "the community." He wanted them to sue the school district. Meetings were called and eventually the families on Hickman Row decided to participate. It was, says Smilack, "a unified effort."[43]

There were seven plaintiffs listed on the 1951 complaint, four boys and three girls. However, only Belton testified, and she became the sole plaintiff publicly identified with the case. Why did Belton testify? She was, like Spottswood Bolling, Linda Brown, Harry Briggs, and others with last names that started early in the alphabet, the first plaintiff listed. However, neither Bolling nor Brown testified. Belton—like Patricia Black in South Park—recommended herself. Belton, according to those who knew her, had a "very strong sense of right and wrong" and profound opinions about the injustice

of the situation in Wilmington. Her seriousness and sense of purpose would have appealed to Redding, who was described as a person who was "quiet, methodical," and believed in the "absolute moral
correctness" of his cause. Indeed Redding and Belton became "very
good friends" over the course of the lawsuit. Belton served as Redding's secretary after finishing high school, and they remained close
for the rest of her life. "She attended *all* the meetings about the lawsuit," says Harmon. She was, according to family members, "aggressive, intelligent, a go-getter." Harmon echoes the sentiment, calling
her "aspirational," a "go-aheader." A younger classmate says, "[Louise]
would have been my choice. She was poised, intelligent, somebody
you wouldn't be afraid to hand a microphone to. Kind of Michelle
Obama-ish—just a nice, down-to-earth person."[44]

Belton did not disappoint on the stand. The point of contention
was the burden incurred by the fact that Belton was barred from attending the white high school closest to her. In court, Redding asked
her to describe the time it took her to get from her home to Howard
High School, taking her through a series of minute, detailed questions about her commute:

> Q. Do you know how far it is from Claymont to Howard? . . .
> Q. How do you get from your home . . . to Howard? . . .
> Q. What time do you leave home? . . .
> Q. What time do you catch the bus? . . .
> Q. Where do you catch it? . . .
> Q. How long does it take you to get by bus . . . to Howard? . . .
> Q. By the time you reach Howard what time is it? . . .
> Q. So how long does it take you to reach Howard?

When this end point was reached, the next line of testimony began, "Q. Now, let's break it down again." The stultifying questions
and answers went on for several more pages. It was definitely concluded that Belton would have precisely twenty-five minutes more

to study in the morning if she attended Claymont High School. The cross-examination for the defense was brief, but telling:

> Q. If you had the extra ten minutes, or fifteen minutes, or twenty
>   minutes, you would utilize that in studying every morning?
> A. Yes.
> Q. You would?
> A. Yes.

Courtroom procedure, of course, is one of confrontation. Misconstruing, or deliberately misunderstanding, the amount of time Belton would gain—after so much testimony in order to pinpoint those very twenty-five minutes—would be disrespectful under everyday circumstances. In the courtroom, however, it was so much legal theater. At age seventeen, Belton had to learn how social intercourse proceeded in court, and she had to do so on her feet.[45]

Judge Collins Seitz surprised everyone by ordering that both Claymont and the school in Hockessin accept the plaintiffs at once. (*Belton* and *Bulah* made it to the Supreme Court because the state of Delaware appealed Seitz's ruling.) But when Belton was granted the opportunity to attend Claymont High School, she turned it down. The rest of the plaintiffs enrolled at Claymont. Those who knew Belton point to this decision with special pride. According to them, the lawsuit, the meetings, the court appearance—all of it was driven by principle rather than an actual desire to attend Claymont. Belton felt the need to make a statement about the absurdity of having to travel all the way to Wilmington because she was barred from attending school with white students. On the tenth anniversary of the *Brown* decision, *Jet* magazine asked Belton how she felt about having taken part. "I felt kind of great," she answered. "It wasn't everybody who took a stand like my mother and me."[46]

———

There was one lawsuit, among the five that would be appealed to the Supreme Court in 1952, that originated with students themselves. It started, officially, on April 23, 1951, when Barbara Johns led a student walkout at Robert Russa Moton High School in Farmville, Prince Edward County, Virginia. Moton High School was built in 1939 and was meant to hold 180 students. By 1947, the number of high school students was double what the building could hold, so the school board built three "annexes"—wood plank structures covered with tar paper. "The shacks," as they were called, leaked and were impossible to heat in the winter. The PTA at Moton High School—as in Washington, DC, and elsewhere—was very active trying to get the school board to either fix the annexes or, ideally, build a new school. Vague promises were made about finding another site and building a new school at an unnamed time in the future. Barbara Johns spoke to Carrie Stokes, president of the student body, and her brother John Stokes, the vice president. The three of them plotted what moves they could make to change their prospects at Moton High School. They began by attending school board meetings, but this got them nowhere, and by late April the three had decided to call a strike. They came up with a ploy to get the principal, M. Boyd Jones, out of the building and then called a school-wide meeting in the auditorium. Teachers were asked to leave. Remarkably, most did. Johns addressed the 450 curious students who had amassed in the auditorium. It was time, she said, that the students themselves do something about the horrific conditions in their school. The Farmville jail was too small to house all of them, and if they acted together they would not be punished. The three student leaders had prepared signs ahead of time and stowed them in the machine shop. Johns asked the students to picket in front of the building instead of going back to class. Principal Jones, when he got back to the school, officially lobbied against the strike while tacitly supporting it. (He was later fired.)[47]

As in every other locale with a school segregation fight, the question of whether the walkout and lawsuit were aimed at equalization or desegregation was fought over, understood in different ways by different participants, and later remembered as a divisive issue. Barbara Johns, Carrie Stokes, and John Stokes contacted Oliver Hill and Spottswood Robinson and asked if they would come to Prince Edward County and meet with them. At this point, the students wanted immediate improvements to Moton High School. The two lawyers went to Farmville planning to tell the striking students to go back to school and wait to see what happened in the *Briggs* case. Likely, *Briggs* would bring them some relief. But after meeting with the students and witnessing their courage and determination, the two lawyers were inspired to work with them. Hill and Robinson told them that if they were willing to file a desegregation lawsuit, the NAACP would take it on. "It seemed like reaching for the moon," Johns remembered, "but we had great faith in Mr. Robinson and Mr. Hill."[48]

Meetings were called and garnered huge turnout. One meeting to discuss the strike and the lawsuit at Moton High School brought in over one thousand people. At a meeting on May 3—with the students still out on strike—Robinson went over the details of the lawsuit. The consensus in the room seemed to be with Robinson and the NAACP. Then, in a moment that everyone remembers vividly, J. B. Pervall, former principal of Moton High School, stood up and said, "I was under the impression that the students were striking for a new building. You are pulling a heavy load, Mr. Robinson, coming down here to a county town like Farmville and trying to take it over on a non-segregated basis." An NAACP official explained that the approach had already been decided upon at a previous meeting. Then Johns got up and uttered an unforgettable statement, though people remember the exact wording differently: "Don't let Mr. Charlie, Mr. Tommy, or Mr. Pervall stop you from backing us. We are depending on you." Others remember that Johns outright called

Pervall an "Uncle Tom." Whatever the case, Johns both electrified and upset many people that night. Adults and students alike were shocked that a teenage girl had "attacked" a former principal. According to historian Kara Miles Turner, strike coleader John Stokes "recalls the strike committee later criticizing Barbara Johns for being inappropriately harsh with Pervall, a respected educator." John Stokes said that after Johns spoke, everyone was fearful of saying anything against desegregation, because "they were afraid that she was going to say something and embarrass them in the public."[49]

The striking students went back to school on May 7, and the Moton case was added to the group of cases headed to the Supreme Court as *Davis v. County School Board*, filed on behalf of 117 Moton students, listed in alphabetical order. If there was indecision in much of the community, and if, as John Stokes implied, there would have been more discussion of equalization had Johns not intervened at the meeting, the question of equalization versus desegregation became even more fraught when the Prince Edward County School Board built a new black high school, at a cost of $840,000, that opened in 1953. When *Brown v. Board* was decided in 1954, Moton High School was a better facility than the white high school, and by then African American students—as in Hearne, Texas—were voicing a desire to stay in their own school, with their own friends and their own routines. Johns was long gone. After the strike, she had to flee the county. Ironically, she was forced to move farther south—to Birmingham where her aunt lived. She finished high school there.

Johns was a leader in every way: she sought out other students and convinced them to act, she spoke in ways that captivated large audiences, and above all she had the courage to say what she thought to adults and students alike. She led the strike at Moton and then she helped lead the rest of the community to the point of making a momentous decision. She helped convince lawyers Hill and Robinson to work with the striking students, and she essentially brought to life what would become one of the five cases that convinced the Supreme Court to overturn *Plessy*. It was nothing short of extraordinary.

But there are also components of her story that overlap in important ways with earlier cases. That she remained committed to desegregation while others—even her closest compatriots—did not is especially striking when compared to earlier cases involving young women. Her steadfast commitment to desegregation stands out in a place where there were many who vocally wished for equalization. That others became angry with her was also typical. It is impossible not to think of the resentment that Marguerite Carr and the Jennings twins suffered—and without ever being vindicated by a Supreme Court decision bearing their names. The sacrifice, too, resonates with earlier cases. Johns's life was threatened and she was forced to leave her home, just like Doris Raye and Doris Faye Jennings. These girls were on the front lines of school desegregation. Their names, their faces, their reputations became inseparable from their lawsuits. As the public personas of school desegregation, they gave up what security and stability they had. Johns had stunning leadership skills. But the kind of courage, sacrifice, and verbal precision she displayed was of a part with the larger school desegregation movement. It was a movement that young women had been leading for years, and that helped make Barbara Johns both someone who was an extraordinary person and someone who was in the right place at the right time.

———

Lucinda Todd in Topeka, meanwhile, had been busy since she sent her letter to Walter White. First, she enlisted Lena May Carper, mother of her daughter Nancy's best friend, Kathy Carper, to test their local elementary schools with their daughters. Lena Carper's daughter Kathy spent every afternoon after school with her grandmother on Jewell Avenue. Lena Carper would pick Kathy up on her way home from her job as a maid. The two girls—both only

children—saw themselves as sisters more than friends, and the two
mothers were well acquainted. But Lena Carper did not sign on to
the lawsuit (and later allow her only child to testify in court) because
of personal loyalty to Lucinda Todd, nor solely because of Kathy's
arduous commute to the black Buchanan School. Lena Carper had
her own reason for wanting to take on segregated education—one
that had played a role in Marguerite Carr's pursuit of school desegregation and that would also inform the decisions of some young
women who chose to desegregate schools after *Brown*. Lena May
Carper was married to a man, a cook named Dorsey Carper, so
white-looking that his driver's license listed him as a white man.
There were incessant problems associated with Dorsey Carper's
white appearance. First, the family could not leave the house without
being harassed. Kathy (now Katherine Carper Sawyer) remembers
that they "could just be walking down the street—me, Mom, and
Dad—and cars would come by and scream 'N—lover' at Dad." This
happened "all the time." It informed every decision the family made
about how, when, and whether to go out in public. Kathy suffered
too. "Kids on the bus," she recalls, "would tease me and tell me my
dad was white. They made me cry, it was so hurtful." Being a member of a "mixed" family, as Carper Sawyer calls it, contributed to a
perspective that was skeptical of racial classifications in general. "No
one is pure anything!" she exclaims. These experiences informed the
family's desire to take on rigid racial classifications, especially in the
schools where Kathy was made to feel marginalized.[50]

First, Lena Carper and Lucinda Todd went to the white school
near Todd's home, Lowman Hill Elementary, and attempted to register Nancy. After Nancy was rejected, the two women went to the
Randolph School, the white school closest to the Carpers' home,
and tried to enroll Kathy. The two women went into the schools and
talked to the principals while the girls waited in the car. After this
exercise, Lucinda Todd and Fay Sawyer (no relation to Katherine
Carper Sawyer) sought other plaintiffs to join them. And once again

Todd and Sawyer walked the streets of Topeka to get signatures for a petition—this time to desegregate the lower schools. They managed, by one estimate, fifteen hundred signatures.[51]

Most of the plaintiffs ended up being Todd's neighbors on Jewell Avenue. There were thirteen mothers and one father who sued on behalf of their children, twenty students in all. The most difficult person to recruit, as everyone remembered it, was Oliver Brown. Fay Sawyer's daughter, Constance Sawyer, told an interviewer, "It's just true that Oliver was the most difficult one to convince." She indicated that the arduous work to retain Oliver Brown and the location of his name at the top of the list was no accident. "Most of these other folks were women . . . [and] actually there was a woman who's name would have come ahead of his [in] the alphabetizing [Darlene Brown] so they probably chose him because he was a man too." Lawyer Elisha Scott's daughter-in-law, Berdyne Scott, remembered that Oliver Brown was desperate to drop out and the NAACP was equally desperate to keep him. "Ollie wasn't involved in civic work," she recalled. "He wanted to withdraw . . . because he [was studying] to be a minister. They had to beg him to stay in the case."[52]

Lucinda Todd, in her acerbic way, communicated her frustration with Oliver Brown to a local reporter some forty years later. "Mr. Brown wasn't much for doing anything himself," she said, "but he certainly put the rest of us to work." Constance Sawyer was more generous. "Oliver was a wonderful . . . kind, kind of a shy guy. A sweet person. I can understand his reluctance . . . but he did it." This was not the first time that the LDF had worked to retain a vacillating male plaintiff. That the Topeka NAACP, in concert with the national office, went to great lengths to retain a man who was ambivalent about the lawsuit does suggest that they were especially invested in him, above and beyond the other plaintiffs, including those who signed on early and remained steadfast. If the local or national NAACP explicitly attempted to recruit and retain Oliver Brown because of his gender, no one at the LDF admitted it at the time or after the fact.[53]

The Topeka branch did everything it could to raise money for the lawsuit. Todd began to speak at regional events, and sought out suitable places for the national lawyers to stay when they came to town. Many of the lawyers simply stayed at her house. They conducted planning sessions around the same table that had been used for the Citizens Committee on Civil Rights meetings in 1948. Alvin Todd—like Esther Brown's husband, Paul—supported his wife by managing the child care while the trial was under way. In an interview in the mid-1970s, Todd credited Esther Brown's role in no uncertain terms. "I don't know if we could have done it without her," she said emphatically. "We owe her a real debt of gratitude." (Nonetheless, Nancy Noches claims her mother "didn't much like Esther Brown." She felt that Esther Brown was intruding, "like, [this] white person trying to tell us how to do things.")[54]

Why was Esther Brown considered so instrumental in Topeka? What led Todd to make the dramatic statement that the Topeka branch could not have conducted the trial without her? It does not appear that Esther Brown was on the scene prior to a few weeks before the trial. She neither canvassed for the Topeka branch nor did she attend every meeting.

What appears to have happened is this: The trial date was set for June 21, 1951. Charles Bledsoe was the local lead lawyer on the Topeka case, and Elisha Scott's two sons also worked on it. The New York office expected the Topeka branch to fund the trial, while the branch thought the New York office would cover the expenses, chiefly for the raft of specialists scheduled to testify: Dr. Horace English, psychologist, Ohio State University; Professor W. B. Brookover, department of social science, Michigan State University; Professor Max L. Hutt, psychology, University of Michigan; and Professor John J. Kane, sociology, Notre Dame. The expert witnesses were to arrive on June 23 and stay overnight in Topeka. These witnesses were an eleventh-hour surprise to the Topeka branch. All of a sudden, the local organizers had to find them hotels and foot the bill. The court date was mere weeks away when Todd wrote to Esther Brown with an urgent appeal for assistance in raising funds. "Dear Mrs. Brown," she wrote, "I was instructed to write to you about your suggestion of having . . . the ministers of Topeka [set] aside the proceeds from one of their services on June 19 for the prosecution of our case. . . . We were hoping to use what we have to finance the attorney's expenses from New York [and] of course we don't have enough. May we hear from you soon?"[55]

Esther Brown went into high gear, consulting her contacts cultivated during the South Park suit. A letter to Joe Coffman, the president of the Anti-Defamation League in Omaha, Nebraska, was typical: "The important factor in this case at the moment is money. NAACP in New York is getting on the ball, and getting all sorts of experts to testify . . . and they feel the expense should be carried by the State of Kansas. The branch in Topeka is doing a good job, but can't possibly do a $5,000 job, so I feel we all have to help." She later offered to come to Nebraska: "I feel this is something the Jewish groups will now respond to and would like to work out some method with you to raise the money." In a letter dated June 12, nine days before the trial was to start, Sidney Lawrence, president of the Community Relations Bureau in Kansas City, wrote to the Anti-Defamation League in New York desperately asking for assistance. "About two or three weeks ago it became evident . . . that [the branch] would require immediate legal and expert educational assistance. Esther Brown was appealed to in what was described as an emergency situation. She began contacting all her resources." However, at such a late hour, the sums required could not be raised locally. "I understand that a great part of the expense for this testimony is expected to be defrayed by the local groups. This is a serious problem for all those interested in the case." On May 19, Joe Coffman sent his own fund-raising letter to the Anti-Defamation League in New York. On June 20—the day before he was due to arrive—LDF lawyer Robert L. Carter wrote to Esther Brown, still unsure whether housing arrangements for himself and lawyer Jack Greenberg, as well as the expert witnesses, had been secured, or where the money would come from to pay their expenses.[56]

The trial, of course, went forward as planned. There is no evidence in Esther Brown's letters or the NAACP's records where the money came from. But the Anti-Defamation League of New York must have wired at least some of the funds to cover the costs. It appears, however, that the NAACP also took on some debt. In 1951, Carter himself was writing to branches all over Kansas asking for assistance for the appeal to the Supreme Court. "It was our belief that [the Kansas branches], like the South Carolina branches in the Clarendon County case [would] finance the suit." Later he said, "Before going out to Topeka I wrote the President of the State Conference . . . about the necessity of raising funds, but evidently they have been unsuccessful in their efforts." Carter was encountering the same obstacle that Esther Brown had encountered in 1948: A. Porter Davis. Carter was shocked at the situation in Kansas. "This may be one of the most important cases which the Association has handled, and it seems to me that our people in Kansas would want to undertake the job of defraying the expenses." The national NAACP would ultimately have to enlist the help of neighboring states to secure the five thousand dollars they needed. No doubt Esther Brown, Lucinda Todd, and president of the Topeka branch McKinley Burnett worked throughout the summer and fall to help raise the money.[57]

Unlike the South Park trial, there was little publicity for *Brown*, and the courtroom in Topeka was not even filled to capacity. It seems that Lucile Bluford believed that the true test case had already been decided, and that what came afterward was less newsworthy. Nonetheless, the trial went smoothly. Lena Carper, Lucinda Todd, and Oliver Brown all testified about the onerous and at times dangerous routes their daughters had to take to school. Neither Linda Brown nor Nancy Todd testified. Only Lena Carper's daughter, Kathy, was put on the stand. Nancy Noches remembers that she was "too shy" to do it, and Todd later said "that she did not want to put Nancy through that." Kathy Carper did not object, and her mother thought she was a good fit for the job.[58]

"I was frightened!" Carper Sawyer remembers. "When I walked into that [court] room . . . I've seen the room of course as an adult, but to me as a child, that room was enormous. And that was a *long* walk from the back to the front, to sit in that chair to testify." She proved capable and self-possessed on the stand. But she was anxious about not only her courtroom appearance but also what would happen afterward. Even though she was only nine years old, she accurately pinpointed the danger she was in. "I was worried," she recalls, "because I could hear them wondering what was going to happen." Lena Carper was particularly concerned about the reaction of Kathy's teachers, who were understandably nervous about their jobs. Kathy was relieved when the expected retaliation did not materialize. And though Kathy did not endure what Marguerite Carr or the Jennings twins did, in the lineaments of the case, her pivotal yet fleeting role within it, the personal risk and the outsized responsibility, and the requirement that she be able to speak to and in front of white adults in a tense courtroom on a matter of national importance—these characteristics fit what was becoming an emerging pattern of calling upon girls to ensure that the courtroom drama unfolded as planned. There could be no moments of childish disorder or confusion, no unwillingness to speak up clearly and resolutely. Too many overburdened lawyers and professionals had converged on that courtroom, too much money had been raised, and too much of the NAACP's reputation was at risk for a child plaintiff to hesitate or falter on the stand.

The expert testimony came next. In addition to Horace English and the other out-of-state scholars, the NAACP hoped to get local experts to testify on the conditions in Topeka's schools. They first tried to get Karl Menninger, the famous director of the Menninger Clinic, to testify, but like other men who had important political connections in the state and whose business depended on those relationships, he did not respond to requests. Jack Greenberg—a lawyer from the national office in New York—and Carter had to make do with less prestigious experts. Hugh Speer, an education professor at the University of Kansas City, and James H. Buchanan, dean at the state teacher's college in Emporia, Kansas, compared the facilities and teaching at the white and black schools. In this case, there was actually little difference between the buildings or the teacher-student ratio. The star witness for the plaintiffs turned out to be Louisa Holt, a part-time instructor at the Menninger Clinic and the University of Kansas in Lawrence. Holt was the last to testify. Asked by Greenberg if segregation had an adverse impact on the personality development of the child, Holt said, "The fact that it is enforced, that it is legal, I think, has more importance than the mere fact of segregation by itself does because this gives legal and official sanction to a policy which is inevitably interpreted both by white people and by Negroes as denoting the inferiority of the Negro group."[59]

Judge Walter Huxman ruled against the plaintiffs, saying that it was not his job but rather the job of the Supreme Court to rule on school segregation. But in his "findings of fact," an appended document, he wrote, "Segregation of white and colored children in public schools has a detrimental effect upon the colored children. The impact is greater when it has the sanction of law; for the policy of separating the races is usually interpreted as denoting the inferiority of the Negro group." The Supreme Court would quote Huxman in the body of their decision in 1954.

Hugh Speer, who testified in Topeka for the plaintiffs, called *Brown v. Board of Education* "the case of the century." Since then, historians have concurred that *Brown* is "arguably the most important Supreme Court ruling in United States history." In one stroke,

Brown overturned not only the legality of segregated education but the doctrine of separate but equal as a governing principle. The Supreme Court opinion began by acknowledging that "Negro schools" were in the process of being "equalized." Even so, Chief Justice Earl Warren wrote, "our decision cannot turn on merely a comparison of . . . tangible factors. . . . We must look instead to the effect of segregation itself on public education." The Supreme Court found that, in the act of separating black students "from others of similar age and qualifications solely because of their race generates a feeling of inferiority as to their status in the community that may affect their hearts and minds in a way unlikely ever to be undone." The decision then goes a step further to clarify its sweeping intent: "Whatever may have been the extent of psychological knowledge at the time of *Plessy v. Ferguson*, [our] finding is amply supported by modern authority. Any language in *Plessy* . . . contrary to this finding is rejected. . . . We conclude that in the field of public education the doctrine of 'separate but equal' has no place. Separate educational facilities are inherently unequal."[60]

As court decisions go, this one could easily be described as an affective decision— fundamentally about "feeling," "hearts," "minds," and "psychology." Indeed, it is exactly what school desegregation's most vocal detractors accused the project of being about in the 1940s: it is emotional. The language used by the Supreme Court establishes the central importance of creating functional, equitable, and mutually respectful social connections within the context of a modern democracy. As such, the words and deeds of young women and girls were written into the very substance of the decision. The decision seeks to establish exactly the kind of civic decency that Lucile Bluford urged her country to embrace. It reflects the social optimism of Ada Sipuel and the ambitious goals of cultural mutuality and exchange that Gardner Bishop, Ernesto Galarza, and Lucinda Todd all argued for on behalf of their daughters. The decision also contains within it the same moral conviction that inspired black girls to walk up to the doors of white schools and seek to cross the threshold—the conviction that segregated education was simply wrong. It is both a uniquely powerful and a uniquely moving opinion, and it shows how a feminine touch helped mold one of the Supreme Court's most momentous decisions.[61]

All that was left to do was to find students willing to fulfill the promise of the *Brown* decision. This, too, would fall to young women and girls.

1. Lucile Bluford (top, second from left) and other members of the Alpha Kappa Alpha sorority at the University of Kansas, Lawrence, 1930 (Courtesy of the University of Kansas Library)

2. Lucile Bluford working during her trial, *Bluford v. Canada* (Getty)

3. Ada Lois Sipuel Fisher with her mother, Martha Bell Smith Sipuel, January 15, 1948 (Courtesy of the *Oklahoman*)

4. Ada Lois Sipuel Fisher with (from left to right) University of Oklahoma dean of admissions J. E. Fellows, Thurgood Marshall, and Amos Hall, January 1948 (Getty)

5. Ada Lois Sipuel Fisher taking the bar exam in 1952 (Courtesy of the Oklahoma Historical Society)

6. C. G. Jennings, circa 1970, in Hearne, Texas (Courtesy of Doris Raye Jennings Brewer and Doris Faye Jennings Alston)

7. Doris Raye and Doris Faye Jennings in Hearne, Texas, circa 1954 (Courtesy of Doris Raye Jennings Brewer and Doris Faye Jennings Alston)

8. Esther Brown, circa 1947 (Courtesy of the Kansas Historical Society)

9. The Merriam, Kansas, NAACP branch in 1949. Patricia Black (now Brandy Sebron-Kelley) is at center. (Courtesy of the Johnson County Museum)

10. Walter White speaks at the Topeka Municipal Auditorium in 1949 (Courtesy of the Kansas State Historical Society, Lucinda Todd Papers)

11. Alvin, Nancy, and Lucinda Todd in the early 1940s (Courtesy of the Kansas State Historical Society, Lucinda Todd Papers)

12. Lena Carper and Dorsey Carper in the 1930s (Courtesy of Katherine Carper Sawyer)

13. Kathy Carper in 1951, a year before she testified in *Brown v. Board of Education* (Courtesy of Katherine Carper Sawyer)

14. Federal marshal Wallace Downs drives Gail Etienne to McDonough 19 elementary school in New Orleans, November 14, 1960 (Courtesy of the *New Orleans Times Picayune*)

15. Millicent Brown speaks with Barbara Solomon in front of Rivers High School in Charleston, South Carolina, while waiting to reenter the school after a bomb threat, September 3, 1963. The picture ran on the front page of the *New York Times*. (Courtesy of the *Charleston Post and Courier*)

16. (*Above, left to right*) Betta Bowman, Clara Kay Patin, Doretha Davis, Irma Harrison Coleman, Elaine Boyle Patin, Elaine Chustz Green, Betty Jemison Wagner, Velma Jean Hunter, and Sharon LeDuff walk into Baton Rouge High School, September 3, 1963 (Courtesy of the *Baton Rouge Advocate*)

17. (*Clockwise, from upper left*) Shirley Lawrence Alexander, Rubye Nell Singleton Stroble, Mamie Ford Jones, and Beverly Plummer Wilson in their 1965 Albany High School yearbook (Yearbook Courtesy of Nancy Presley)

6

"Take Care of My Baby"

The Isolation of the First "Firsts"

DELAWARE WAS AN EXCEPTION IN every way. In 1952, while the state's attorney general was fighting desegregation in the courts, the superintendent in Claymont, Harvey Stahl—who was from Ohio and thought segregation was "just wrong"—went ahead and invited black students who lived in his school district, just outside Wilmington, to enroll. The attorney general and the superintendent were still locked in battle the day before school started. Then, at a late hour, parents got word that Stahl had prevailed and their children would be desegregating the Claymont schools the next day. Students were shocked when their parents told them the next morning, "Go get on the bus, and go to school, in Claymont." "It hit me so fast," Carol Anderson, who was a student at the time, remembers. "Bang bang you're going, and you get up, and it's like okay we're going to a new school today." When the students arrived at the school, Pauline Dyson, their elementary school teacher and an NAACP powerhouse (and Carol and Joan Anderson's grandmother), was there to welcome them alongside the principal, vice principal, and Superintendent Stahl. The school officials wanted to welcome the new African American students to Claymont High School and Middle School.

In the late 1940s and early 1950s, some schools, wanting to begin a process that a few highly placed school officials saw as both inevitable and beneficial, began to quietly enroll black students in previously all-white schools. In Kansas and Delaware—states with active desegregation cases headed for the Supreme Court—individual black students in a few areas were encouraged by local school boards to attend "mixed" middle and high schools. In the Northeast, school officials—including those at both public and private schools—began to look for African American students who could successfully begin the desegregation process. In the South, of course, the vast majority of school boards angrily fought school desegregation with every resource available to them, and school desegregation would not begin there until the 1960s. And while northern and midwestern students experienced subtle hostility—what one first called "microaggressions"—in the Deep South, the small number of firsts who arrived in the early 1960s met constant verbal harassment and violence. But there was one aspect of the school desegregation process that all pioneers agreed upon, in both the North and South: that social isolation was the most painful aspect of their experience in formerly all-white schools.

———

The Anderson sisters—Meryl, Carol, and Joan—were the perfect image of what lawyers and NAACP officials wanted in desegregation pioneers: Their father, Leon Anderson, was the president of the Wilmington chapter of the NAACP and a doctor. Their mother, Beulah Anderson, stayed at home and brought up their six children. The girls were steeped in every manner of good breeding. "We never had to be told how to act," Carol Anderson recalls. "I mean my mom's favorite book was Emily Post." She remembers the elaborate sartorial requirements of being a young lady: "Gloves and hats . . . 'What do you mean you're going outside the house without your hat and gloves?' And we got corrected all the time. Everything, when you eat your soup you always eat away from the bowl. . . . I don't think I ever said a double negative in my whole life." The Anderson parents made sure the girls were exposed to as many cultural and sporting experiences as possible. "We took horseback riding, we took tennis, we did everything—music lessons, singing, theater." The phrase "carefully brought up" hardly does justice to the planning, the training, the "corrections," and the constant surveillance that informed their daily lives.[1]

Howard High School in Wilmington attracted the most talented black students in Delaware. The school had orchestra, theater, and athletics departments that were, far and away, superior to those offered at Claymont, which was outside Wilmington in a semirural part of the state. Carol and Joan Anderson were thrilled at the prospect of attending Howard—Carol aspired to be a professional musician and Joan dreamed of being an actress. "I looked up to the older kids at Howard," Carol recalls. "They were my idols: their poise and their talent, their command of the stage, their smartness." She was sorely disappointed at the prospect of not attending Wilmington's prestigious black high school, but her parents and grandmother did not present the prospect of attending Claymont as a choice. Carol was the youngest and most rebellious of the Anderson children, but, she says, "you didn't question your parents in those days, even me . . . though I probably did complain about it. . . . I felt I was being dragged." Carol Anderson's attitude toward desegregation mirrors that of Judine Bishop Johnson—it was a loss, an interruption of her most valued activities.

The Anderson girls' mother did not prepare them for their foray into an all-white school, but Pauline Dyson—known universally as "Miss Dyson"—as their teacher and grandmother, did. "The whole world is watching you today, so behave," Carol Anderson remembers her saying. "What else is new," she thought. "We always have to behave." Joan, who was younger and going into the seventh grade, had an easier time acclimating and making friends. Carol felt the cognitive dissonance more keenly; she was going to school with white students who thought less of her, but she also discovered that they were the children of blue-collar parents and, compared to her, culturally unsophisticated. Carol had two responses to these white students: she fought back when they demeaned her, and she began to compartmentalize her experiences at Claymont High School—to separate whatever went on at school from her true sense of herself.

When Carol arrived at Claymont High School, the white students asked her questions that reflected deep ignorance. They suspected that Carol and Joan did not follow twentieth-century Western customs and practices—that they were not even fully American. "Where do you live?" they asked, and "what do you do when you get married?" Mostly she responded with forbearance, but soon she indulged the desire "to have a little fun with them." The way you get married, she explained, is "simple—you rub your noses, and if you get the right side of the nose, you're married. But when you want to get divorced, you hit the left side—you gotta really make sure you hit the right side of the nose." Then she explained that she and her family lived in the lighthouse next to the river. "What does your father do?" they asked. "He's the lighthouse keeper on the river, of course! What else?" This was Carol's way of being "mischievous," of refusing to be a paragon of virtue in a sea of hostile curiosity. School desegregation pioneers in the 1960s would universally report that they had no choice but to push back when in a white school—both to preserve their own sanity and to survive. Desegregation firsts, when pushed to their limit, were not always nonhostile, nonaggressive, or nonviolent.

Of her ability to separate herself emotionally from the other students, Carol Anderson describes herself this way:

> Well I used to use "they" a lot in the beginning, you know, "They think I'm dumb . . . they think that I live in a. . . . *shack*". . . . But then

as I got older, I felt less about them—less concerned about them, and more concerned about my music I wanted to write . . . what I wanted to do as I got older—I started looking down the road, and I kept this separate [gestures], my home separate, and my fantasies . . . they all would be separate.

She had, by her senior year, made a virtue of necessity. Her separateness, as she sees it, helped her look to the future, nurse her ambitions, concentrate on her love of music, and tune out the rest.

Of the group of twelve students who desegregated Claymont, one young man, John Davis, left. He steadfastly refused to talk about it—at the time or since. The rumor was that he left Claymont after a "racial incident" (there were no witnesses) and joined the army. While Davis has remained silent, the experiences of another young man, Joe Douglas, who left predominantly white Topeka High School to enlist in the army in the early 1940s, might shed some light on what the young man in Delaware was feeling. Douglas made this point when reflecting on his years at Topeka High School in an interview:

Q: Were you drafted?
A: No, I joined. . . . At the time I had become totally disenchanted with the public educational system. . . . I felt like an outsider in the thing. It didn't really relate to me. That doesn't mean that every single individual that I came into contact [with] was anti-me, because I had some beautiful teachers that really related well to me. The overall system was not inclusive of me as a black student. It was very clear to me.

It is helpful to keep Douglas's comments in mind when recounting the stories of those young men who eventually left the schools they had desegregated in the South in the 1960s.[2]

Boys and girls were also treated differently as desegregation firsts. Before they ever reached the schoolhouse door, some boys were told that it was more important to go to a school that "had teachers who could relate to you as a human being" than it was to go to a school that was integrated; girls recalled their parents saying, "If you're in the classroom, they cannot keep you from learning." Boys also reported being told that it was their decision whether or not to attend a formerly white school; girls were more often prevailed upon to embark on desegregation. For young men who felt alienated in newly desegregated schools, leaving was an option. Young men could join the army or, if they were old enough, simply relocate. Young men had more mobility—and autonomy—than young women, and it allowed them to walk away from the school desegregation process when they felt it was not working for them. Girls perceived that adults expected them to succeed—academically and otherwise—in white environments. Leaving, for girls, did not feel like a choice, both because they understood their parents' expectations of them and because they had fewer alternatives.[3]

——

Harvey Stahl was not the only school official looking toward a future of integrated schools. Many school districts and private schools in the Northeast sought to begin the process of desegregation in the late 1940s. Catholic institutions—from parochial schools to universities—began the process on a national level in the 1940s as well. Catholic schools brought in black students in groups, as opposed to beginning with one or two students, and in such schools there was a robust enrollment of boys. But in public schools and other private schools, there is evidence that girls were still more likely to be the first to desegregate. Although these examples are anecdotal, in many ways they bear a resemblance to other stories of female participation in school desegregation.[4]

Camilla Church Greene desegregated a Quaker school in Brooklyn in 1948. Brooklyn Friends School had been trying to attract and retain African American students for a few years, but, as Greene puts it, "they didn't last long." Greene was the first black student to remain at the school for more than a year. Her parents enrolled her in kindergarten and she stayed through high school graduation. They wanted, she says, for her to get the best education possible. Her parents, both civil servants, were attracted to the school because of the Quaker history of abolitionism and pacifism. But what Greene found there was a wealthy student body, complete with servants, and a curriculum that had little to say about black history or experience. She remembers feeling alienated from the start. "Now I do a lot of work around racial microaggressions," Greene says of the anti-racism workshops she teaches. "If I had that terminology then, I would have been able to call [it] racial microaggressions." In kindergarten, "Timothy told me that my hair felt like a bird's nest. And someone else told me I was dirty." Later, in middle school, she recalls, she "would go back to school on Monday and find out that there had been a sleepover." The school, she recalls, was predominantly Jewish—a fact that made Greene feel more alienated and marginal because she was not part of the in-group. She did have one important, close friendship with a Jewish girl, who invited her over to her apartment and whose family supported the friendship. Greene was so young when she started at Brooklyn Friends that, she says, she had no idea why everyone was making so much of it. Everyone at her church knew she was going to the school. "And they would say, 'You're going to be a credit to the race.' And I couldn't make any sense of that except, boy, we as a race must be in trouble if I'm going to be the credit to the race." She also did not understand, at first, why the custodial staff smiled at her so much. "I wish the custodian was still alive 'cause he was just beaming when I'd come down the hall, and I wouldn't give him the time of day. For years."[5]

Her parents were determined that she remain at Brooklyn Friends no matter the price. "I would rail against them putting me there because my friends were at black schools and they were having a lot more fun than I was in terms of social things, and as I got older I used to say, 'Just take me out. Take me out,'" to no avail. Greene remembers her mother saying, "We didn't send you there to be loved. We sent you there to be educated. We love you. Get your love here." Her mother did try to alleviate some of the loneliness by enrolling her in the exclusive black youth club Jack and Jill— where Greene mostly remembers being taught how to dance—and sending her to black summer camps. But school won out over every other consideration. "One summer I went back [to school] and they wrote to my parents that I was using too much slang. And so my mother's solution to that was to keep me away from my neighborhood friends. So that when a white friend called to go to the movies, she'd say yes. And if a black friend called to go to the movies, it was no." Greene did not passively acquiesce to her mother's meddling in her friendships, and she remembers many confrontations. But her mother remained firm. She kept reminding her daughter of the importance of being "a pioneer," of the sacrifices her parents were making to pay for private school, and of the utmost importance of a good education. But most of the time, Greene felt that her existence was made up of parts that never quite fit together. Between her friends in the neighborhood and her white classmates, between the upper-class milieu of Jack and Jill and the affectionate regard of the school custodians, she felt she was living "a schizophrenic life."

Marcia Pinkett-Heller similarly found that desegregation primarily affected her sense of self. Born in 1942, Pinkett-Heller grew up in Camden, New Jersey, in a predominantly white, Italian neighborhood. The children on her block were the sons and daughters of skilled artisans from Italy. "We had cement finishers, we had plasterers, we had tile makers, we had all the people from the skilled trades who had come over from Italy." Pinkett-Heller played with the children on her block and did not think much about race. She also learned Italian. "When I was younger, the little old ladies in black, who only spoke Italian, would grab whatever kid was on the block walking by to send you to the store. So as a child I understood Italian, because that's all they would speak. And you better come from the store with the right *things*. Or else you'd get the whole cheek-pinching thing." This is not to say that Camden was less racist than other northern cities; there were still elements of southern-style Jim Crow. "There were signs," Heller remembers. "We couldn't go to the skating rink. There were signs that said, 'No Colored.' We couldn't go to the swimming pools." The next county over was Gloucester County, and blacks could not even drive through there because the Klan was so active. "We knew you did not go to Gloucester." On the one hand, Pinkett-Heller was well aware of Jim Crow, because the city and region were highly segregated. On the other, her daily life was lived among the white, Italian families on her block.[6]

As in Topeka, Camden High School was integrated while the lower grades were segregated. Pinkett-Heller's mother had been one of a handful of African Americans to graduate from Camden High School in the 1930s. She went to Glassboro University (now Rowan University) and taught in Philadelphia. In 1948, "around the time Harry Truman integrated the military," Camden school officials started to think about integrating the lower schools. "And because I lived on the block, knew all these kids . . . I was somehow selected to be the child to go into first grade at the Broadway School." Going "to the white school was sort of natural," she remembers, since she had established friendships with so many of the white children attending the neighborhood school. The only strict admonition she received from her mother before she went was that she was not, under any circumstances, to let anyone know that she knew her teacher, Mrs. Miller, outside of school. Mrs. Miller was one of her mother's sorority sisters, and she was passing for white at the Broadway

School. Pinkett-Heller was also lectured about her status as a first in terms very similar to what the Anderson sisters were told. "I was a role model and had to carry myself as a role model, because I was representing the entire colored race. So I couldn't be loud, I couldn't be rowdy. . . . I was supposed to do well in school, I was supposed to be a model of behavior."

By the time she got to middle school, there were a few more African American students, but she says she did not connect with them at the time. Her mother was what Pinkett-Heller called "classist" about education—she did not prefer white people, Pinkett- Heller explains, she just did not "want anything to do with uneducated people of color or people of non-color. First standard was education." Unsurprisingly, Pinkett-Heller was very studious. "I hung with the Jewish kids," she remembers, because they were "the smart kids group." When she got to high school, her friend group remained mostly Jewish. In "high school [it] was difficult for me to break into the black group because I had gone all the way through elementary school and junior high school with white kids. And I was closer to the Jewish kids." Pinkett-Heller did have black friends through her mother's sorority and through Camp Oak Hill, where she was a junior counselor. However, she refused to go to Jack and Jill, so she had fewer contacts in the black community than Camilla Church Greene had in Brooklyn. "Most of my friends were Jewish girls, and I had a crush on a Jewish boy, which never went anywhere, because, obviously, they were more into their identity. They knew more of who they were because . . . some of their parents had come out of the camps." Pinkett-Heller found herself drawn to Jews and Judaism precisely because of their strong identification with their ethnicity, which she felt to be lacking in her own life. "I *horrified* my mother between senior year of high school and freshman year of college," she remembers, "because I said I was going to convert to Judaism."

She would eventually find that sense of identity when she went to college at Howard University. When she got the acceptance letter—and two scholarships—her mother was thrilled. But Pinkett-Heller said immediately, "I don't want to go. I won't know how to act around *those* people. I don't know anything about colored people. I don't want to go!" Her mother prevailed, and Pinkett-Heller enrolled at Howard in 1959. In Camden, she reflects, "I didn't really know who I was.... There were times when I felt I had my nose pressed up against the glass, and I could see all these white people doing things that, for whatever reason, I couldn't do." At Howard, she took a class with the famous sociologist E. Franklin Frazier, got involved in the civil rights movement, and finally came into her own. "It was the best thing that ever happened to me ... because I finally got a sense of who I was as me."

———

While the Anderson sisters, Camilla Church Greene, and Marcia Pinkett-Heller were desegregating formerly all-white schools in Claymont, Brooklyn, and Camden—and as *Brown* made its way to the Supreme Court—school boards in the South attempted to stave off desegregation by equalizing black facilities. Journalist Ralph McGill recalled the anxious efforts: "About two years before the 1954 decree, the Deep South, with almost frantic urgency, began to do something about the much relied-on, much-ignored *Plessy* decision. To the sound of hammer and saw, and to the Wagnerian bellow of oratory in their legislative halls in behalf of emergency bond issues, the South began to build modern schools for Negroes." But it was too late. The *Plessy* era, slowly but definitively, was coming to an end.[7]

But then, in 1955, the Supreme Court gave southern legislatures unanticipated breathing room. The court's second ruling—known as *Brown II*—set no deadline for ending segregated schooling and delegated oversight of compliance to federal district and appeals courts. Those courts were to ensure that school districts complied with the *Brown* decision, in the now infamous phrase, "with all deliberate speed." The vague nature of the Supreme Court's directive provided rich soil for the political, legislative, and grassroots resistance to desegregation to grow."[8]

.   There were a few states and counties where school boards attempted to slowly, judiciously, and quietly begin the process of enrolling small numbers of black students in previously all-white schools, most notably in North Carolina and Tennessee. In Nashville, where first-grade students were declared eligible to transfer based on their proximity to white schools, a roughly equal number of male and female students were enrolled by their parents. The "Nashville Plan" was backed up by a ruling from a local judge, as well as Tennessee governor Frank Clement and Nashville mayor Ben West, who both publicly stated that they would respect the rule of law. Similarly, in Greensboro, North Carolina, the school board met on May 21, 1954—four days after the Supreme Court decision was handed down—and resolved to act in uniformity with federal law. White parents sought an injunction to prevent the school board from enrolling black pupils in all-white schools, but the decision of the board was upheld by the North Carolina Supreme Court. Harold Davis, Brenda Florence, Jimmy Florence, Daniel Herring, and Elijah Herring Jr. transferred to Gillespie Park school on September 3, 1957, and one young woman, Josephine Boyd, enrolled at Greensboro Senior High School. (Boyd encountered severe harassment; she stood at four feet ten inches and was the sole black student in a school of two thousand.) It appears that, in states that made a commitment to desegregation, where white resistance was quickly thwarted by the state apparatus and black applicants were allowed to simply choose a new school, parents enrolled their sons and daughters in roughly equal numbers.[9]

But these locales were the exception. The state of Virginia led the way in fighting desegregation when Senator Harry Byrd brought together a coalition of southern politicians to sign on to his plan for "massive resistance," famously articulated in his "Southern

Manifesto." The manifesto outlined a series of laws that could be passed by state legislatures to forestall school desegregation. Only two southern senators refused to sign: Lyndon Johnson of Texas and Albert Gore of Tennessee. As historian Clive Webb points out, both men had national ambitions that would be threatened by signing an overtly racist and legally questionable document.[10]

Southern courts largely upheld these laws, ruling that desegregation be postponed because of the danger it posed to public order. And while white protest and street violence have received a great deal of attention, it was the legislatures and courts of these southern states that effectively shut down school desegregation for years. Between 1955 and 1958, southern legislatures passed nearly five hundred laws to impede the implementation of *Brown*. By 1958, Arkansas, Florida, Georgia, Louisiana, Mississippi, North Carolina, and South Carolina all had legislation in place that could be used to close the schools if desegregation appeared imminent. Citizens' Councils—white supremacist organizations that aspired to be more respectable than the Ku Klux Klan but had the same objectives—sprouted in every county and city where black parents and students made any move to desegregate the schools. The Citizens' Councils met regularly, sharing legislative approaches, printing pamphlets on the religious imperatives of segregation, and organizing white parents and students to harass black families that attempted to gain access to white schools. In 1959, the number of school districts in the South that had desegregated was, as one historian puts it, "microscopic." In 1964, ten years after the *Brown* decision, less than 2 percent of black schoolchildren in the South were in desegregated schools.[11]

NAACP lawyers readied themselves to re-litigate school segregation. However, having successfully brought *Brown* to fruition, the organization found itself targeted for retribution in the South. Local officials demanded the names of NAACP members, and when those names were not forthcoming, southern courts banned the organization. By 1958, the NAACP had lost 246 branches in the South, and its ability to support implementation was curtailed.[12]

In 1956, mobs formed in several towns to beat back desegregation firsts. Autherine Lucy was targeted at the University of Alabama, as was a group of high school students in Mansfield, Texas. The mobs succeeded because local officials and courts failed to intervene or, in the case of Mansfield, because the governor of Texas used state troopers to bar the schoolhouse door.[13] Governors throughout the South were emboldened when President Dwight Eisenhower claimed he did not have "jurisdiction to intervene" in Mansfield.[14] Eisenhower's stance inspired Governor Orval Faubus to order the Arkansas National Guard to block the Little Rock Nine when they attempted to attend the first day of school at Central High School on September 4, 1957. The Nine's next attempt, on September 23, was famously beaten back by an enormous violent mob. Elizabeth Eckford arrived separately from the other eight firsts that day. The photo of Eckford—impeccably dressed in a white dress with black checks on the skirt—standing alone and vulnerable surrounded by enraged white people, is seared into national memory. The shameful image inspired debates over school desegregation among political philosophers that remain to this day. Hannah Arendt argued, after viewing the image of Eckford and other photographs of the violent crowd, that it was unethical if not illegitimate to "burden children, black and white, with the working out of a problem which adults for generations have confessed themselves unable to solve." It was an argument that echoed W. E. B. Du Bois's observation in 1935 that children ought not to be used as a "battering ram" against segregation. Philosopher Danielle Allen published a masterful and poignant rejoinder to Arendt in 2006 describing the productive ways in which the image of Eckford has transformed the American psyche and the historical role of young people in political movements, particularly in the civil rights movement. Historians continue to debate whether young people who participated in school desegregation and civil rights movements ought to be considered victims coping with forces outside their control or political actors in their own right.[15]

Governor Faubus effectively forced Eisenhower to federalize the National Guard and send US paratroopers to protect the Nine—six girls and three boys—when the mob violence threatened public order in Little Rock. The National Guard accompanied the Nine past the protesters into Central High, and each student was assigned a guardsman who followed her from class to class for the first few months of the school year. The verbal abuse and violence inside the school were incessant and at times life threatening. As the Nine would later learn, the siege carried out by the white students was planned and orchestrated by Little Rock's Citizens' Council, which advised the white students on modes of harassment and even armed them with projectiles and toxic chemicals. The Citizens' Council believed they could get the Nine to withdraw if the siege inside the school was sufficiently relentless and terrifying. Because this was the first major test of *Brown* in a southern city, the rest of the South was watching events in Little Rock closely, and the extreme tactics of the Citizens' Council were inspired by the sense that they were acting as a bulwark against school desegregation in the South.[16]

Only a few of the original Nine graduated. Many ended up leaving the state in fear for their lives. It was not until 1960, in New Orleans, that the next attempt was made to put black students into white schools in a southern city. The scenes in New Orleans—screaming parents, racist hand-written signs, and white male hoodlums threatening violence—were as sensational as those that were splashed across the national news from Little Rock three years prior. The original New Orleans school desegregation case, *Bush v. Orleans*, had been filed in 1952 by local NAACP lawyer A. P. Tureaud on behalf of Oliver Bush and his eight school-aged children. At the urging of Thurgood Marshall, Tureaud had suspended the lawsuit in 1953 while *Brown* worked its way up to the Supreme Court. In August 1955, after the Orleans Parish School Board took no action to implement *Brown*, Tureaud went back to court and reopened *Bush v. Orleans*. This time, he won his case, and on February 15, 1956, Judge J. Skelly Wright of the Fifth Circuit Court of Appeals in New Orleans—a Louisiana native who was about to become the most unpopular white man in the state among other whites—ruled that all state laws mandating school segregation were invalid. The Orleans Parish School Board appealed the decision all the way to the Supreme Court, which upheld Wright's ruling in May 1958. The school board successfully delayed taking any action until July 15, 1959, when Wright ordered that a plan be presented to him no later than March 1, 1960. After further wrangling and delay from the school board, Wright issued the last and final date: plans for school desegregation must be made by May 16, 1960.[17]

Superintendent James Redmond did what he could to keep the number of black students applying to white schools so low that white parents might be willing to accept a few black children without street protests or violence. Only students in the first grade could apply. They had to do so in person during a brief window of time. They also had to pass a battery of tests to determine "scholastic aptitude," "intelligence or ability," "adequacy of pupil's academic preparation," "psychological qualification," "psychological effect upon the pupil," "home environment of the pupil," "health and personal standards," and finally, "choice and interests of pupil." School officials hoped that this last category would be their coup de grâce. The question was a version of the query put to Doris Raye Jennings: "Do you want to go to school with white girls?" It was also a trap. It demanded that a six-year-old student provide *positive* reasons for transferring from her own black school to an all-white school. In Louisiana in 1960, a desire for interracial mutuality was so taboo it could neither be named nor articulated, in either direction. Nor was there any evidence that black and white children could coexist in a setting as intimate and absorbing as a school, simply because it had never been done before. Even a six-year-old knew that. For a student to say that she desired to interact with white students in any way would be both a betrayal of her own race and an immediate disqualifier in the eyes of the school board, a sign that the child before them was totally ignorant or even mentally disturbed. The answer to this impossible question, moreover, had to be delivered immediately and on the spot.[18]

Of the 135 families that applied to transfer to formerly all-white schools in New Orleans in October 1960, six children were chosen. Reportedly, one boy and one girl dropped out. The four who followed through were Leona Tate, Tessie Prevost, Gail Etienne, and Ruby Bridges. Did more girls apply than boys? Did they do better on the test? Given the preference for filing lawsuits on behalf of girls, parents may have over-selected girls when applying. But Tessie Prevost, now Tessie Prevost Williams, remembers that there "were lots of kids" who applied, including boys. Tate also remembers boys applying. Prevost Williams recalls, "I was just nonchalant about [the test]. . . . I was a very smart kid. Very outgoing. *Very* independent. And I was a child that was around grownups." Indeed, Tessie was the oldest and an only child for thirteen years, and her vocabulary and demeanor were shaped by the fact that she associated primarily with adults. Tessie lived in the Ninth Ward with her mother, father, and grandmother. Her mother, Dorothy Prevost, worked at a clothing factory. She remembers taking Tessie all over the city to expose her to as many experiences as possible, giving her dancing and music lessons, and teaching her to read early. Tessie took to memorizing whole books, and by the time she reached kindergarten she had memorized the preamble to the Constitution and the Gettysburg Address. She was frequently called upon to recite passages of scripture and poetry at her family's church, Branch Bell Baptist. "People," Dorothy Prevost remembers, "already knew who she was." The most famous of the young students, Ruby Bridges, remembers that it was clear she had done an excellent job speaking with school officials. As she exited the interview, Bridges recalls, she thought "I had done so well on the test that I was going to college."[19]

On Friday, November 11, 1960, the Orleans Parish School Board announced that the black students who had passed the test would transfer on the following Monday. In response, on Saturday, state superintendent Shelby Jackson declared Monday a statewide school holiday. On Sunday, the state legislature in Baton Rouge held a special session, passing thirty bills, including laws giving the governor the right to close integrated schools, giving the legislature the right to cut off funding for all integrated schools, and calling for teachers who taught at integrated schools to be stripped of their credentials. Late Sunday evening, Judge Wright declared all thirty bills unconstitutional. Meanwhile, the Citizens' Council of New Orleans instructed parents to remove their children if black students enrolled in their schools. Leander Perez, infamous boss of the Democratic machine in neighboring Saint Bernard and Plaquemines Parishes, donated a building he owned to be operated as a private school for grades one through three and offered to enroll students in grades four through six in public schools in Saint Bernard Parish. The principals of Frantz and McDonough elementary schools, Jack Stewart and Estelle Barkemeyer, received dueling telegrams that weekend. One was from the Louisiana state superintendent ordering them to close their schools on Monday, and the other from the US Department of Justice informing them they would be in contempt of the Fifth Circuit's ruling if they did not carry out school desegregation. US Marshals would be arriving early Monday morning to escort the students to their respective schools. The Orleans Parish School Board decided it was safer to obey federal orders, and it was announced that all New Orleans schools would be open on Monday, November 14.[20]

Tessie's father, Charles Prevost, worked at the main post office downtown and was the more political parent. Transferring Tessie to McDonough was his idea. "He just felt that this was the right thing to do," Prevost Williams recalls, "that we had a right to this."

But, she continues, "my mother was not into politics. . . . She was a very strong woman but was kind of afraid." On the night of Sunday, November 13, Dorothy Prevost remembers getting a curious call from Principal Stewart. "He called me and he said, 'Now don't let Tessie go to the school . . . in her good clothes.'" The principal said his request was based on the fact that the white students dressed casually and "were wearing flip-flops." He simply wanted Tessie to fit in. However, Dorothy Prevost—in a move that foreshadows desegregation firsts' emphatic demand for sartorial dignity and the deep meaning of clothes in school desegregation struggles—said no. "She was going to go to school [in] starch-and-iron dressing. [And] a pair of oxfords. No flip-flops."

Stewart's request was also made in an attempt to make Tessie less threatening to white parents by ensuring that she would not outshine their children. While feminine beauty was a conscious part of the assimilationist project, it was simultaneously threatening to white parents. The power struggle over clothing reflected the impossible position that school boards found themselves in: If they recruited black students who did not present well, white parents would be up in arms about the fact that unkempt, seemingly unprepared black children were infecting their school. If they admitted well-dressed, middle-class, high-achieving black students, the white students and parents would feel diminished—something that whites, particularly those at predominantly working-class schools such as Frantz and McDonough, were sensitive about. There was simply no way to resolve this tension. Hence, clothes, hair, and ribbons came to represent two opposing sides of the school desegregation project. They were deployed by firsts to represent all of the reasons why black students *should* be accepted at white schools, and yet came to stand for much of what white students and parents *resented* about black students in their schools. White school boards in general opted to admit those who looked irreproachable, were exemplary students, and spoke confidently. In so doing, however, they set off a war within their schools over self-presentation and, to a lesser extent, academic achievement.

Clothes would become one of the most relentlessly contested issues of school desegregation—a proxy battle that handed to its victors prestige in a way that exceeded academic achievement. Clothes were a way to compete with white students and win. Black parents and students saw attendance at a white school not only as a form of racial rapprochement but also a step into an arena of competition: black students had come to white schools not just to sit next to white students but to enlighten them about black ability, dignity, and even, where possible, superiority. Girls who wore attractive, clean, well-preserved clothing had a competitive advantage.[21]

The crowd at McDonough was so large it seemed that every local resident was present. The crowd was enlarged by high school students, mostly boys, from other parts of the state who took advantage of the official school holiday on November 14 to drive to New Orleans to participate in the protests. When the US Marshals arrived at Frantz and McDonough, they were relieved to see that the New Orleans police—some on horseback—were holding the crowd back from the entrance of the two schools. Still, it was like nothing any of them had ever witnessed. "The things that went on were indescribable," one federal marshal recalls. "I couldn't believe grown people would act the way they did." The crowd at McDonough, however, was not solely white and angry. While reporters on the scene trained their cameras on the white protesters, the signs they held, and their ugly chants ("Two, four, six, eight we don't want to integrate!" and "N—s go home!"), a large crowd of black citizens also assembled in front of the school. All but lost to history, this crowd of onlookers was composed of the entire population of the nearby black Harding Elementary School: teachers, students, administrators, cooks, and custodians.[22]

The crowd of African American onlookers in New Orleans is reminiscent of the crowd that came to watch Marguerite Carr walk up the steps to Eliot Junior High in Washington, DC, in 1947, and it tells us something important. The sight of these three girls walking into a white school was astonishing. It was so unimaginable that the girls might actually enter an institution from which they had been barred for over a hundred years that teachers left their posts and students were excused from class. Quite possibly, the black school officials and students came to both witness and revel in the fact that a white institution was about to be transformed instantly and irrevocably into a *public* institution that included them. Some, perhaps, came to gloat, others to stand at the ready in case the girls were attacked, and yet others simply to marvel. For many in this crowd, it must have been a moment of triumph when the girls crossed the threshold and entered the school. Like two opposing sides at a sporting event, only one crowd went home satisfied that day.

Tessie Prevost and Leona Tate saw the milling crowds and thought it was Mardi Gras. Tate recalls, "I thought a parade was coming but I had to go to school." Gail Etienne had a more accurate perspective. "I do remember going to the school," she says. "I was scared. Crowds of people saying all kinds of things. If they could get to me, I thought they was going to kill me." If the crowd outside was both amazed and incensed to see the girls walk through the entrance at McDonough, the principal and staff were apparently in shock that the girls had actually arrived. The girls were made to wait outside the principal's office for hours. To the six-year-olds, "it felt like an eternity." Tessie started to practice tumbling in the hall. "It was like they did not know what to do with us," Prevost Williams recalls. "People would pass us; they were looking at us, but then it was also like they were overlooking us—like we were invisible." The McDonough Three, as they would come to be known much later, were finally assigned to Mrs. Meyer's class. But the day continued on its bizarre and nightmarish course as their fellow students began to disappear, one by one. "All of a sudden you see children disappearing. Someone would come and just snatch a child out the classroom," Prevost Williams remembers. "By the end of the day," Tate says, "there was nobody left in the classroom but the three of us. Lasted for a year and a half." The same thing happened at Frantz Elementary, where, by the end of the day, Ruby Bridges found herself to be the only student in the school.[23]

At McDonough, cardboard was hung in all of the windows. The girls were forbidden to play outside, so they played instead under the stairwell. Mrs. Meyer was "incredibly supportive," and they had fun eating lunch in a different empty classroom every day. Walking the gauntlet of screaming protesters each morning remained a challenge, but eventually, Prevost Williams says, "I was able to just tune that out." Echoing Ada Sipuel's words to the press in 1949 almost exactly, Prevost Williams explains, "I wouldn't even hear [the] person." The bigger difficulty for the girls was when they went home. The hate mail became so overwhelming—for the McDonough Three and for Bridges—that all letters were diverted from the girls' homes to the NAACP's offices so that members could sift through them first. The death threats came in many forms, some of them darkly creative. According to Dorothy Prevost, a hearse, or "dead wagon," drove up and down her street every day for months. She lived in constant fear. "Every morning after she leave, I say a little prayer. I say, 'Lord, take care of my baby. Take care of my baby. Be with her. Stay in school with her.'" She became so anxiety ridden, she stopped eating. Eventually, she says, "my dresses went way down to my ankles." Her boss at the factory, a Jewish man, she carefully explains, quietly told her to take some time off and come back when she was ready. None of the four girls were allowed to go anywhere outside to play except their backyards. Tate had the hardest time staying indoors. "The house began to look like a jail," she recalls, and her friends began to make fun of her for being under such strict orders. "They still tease me about not being able to come out the yard," she says ruefully. "Who's the little black girl who couldn't come out they yard?"[24]

The girls also received a steady stream of supportive cards and letters, mostly from white women and children in the North. Teachers, mothers, and students would sit down and write letters to the firsts telling them they would be happy to have them in school with their children. Famous women such as Eleanor Roosevelt also wrote supportive letters as the girls learned what it felt like to be famous. When Tessie went to Washington, DC, a white woman recognized her. "That's the little girl who was walking up the steps in New Orleans!" she cried. Prevost Williams remembers, "This white lady came up . . . and told me how proud she was of me." All four women say that the letters and moments of appreciation helped them to endure the first few years.[25]

Yet life was about to get even more difficult. While Ruby stayed at Frantz for the next six years, Gail, Tessie, and Leona transferred to Semmes Elementary in the third grade. Semmes was a turn-of-the-century brick building in a white neighborhood in the Lower Ninth Ward, perched next to a Mississippi River levee that would famously collapse during Hurricane Katrina in 2005. Though the school was called Semmes Elementary, it actually housed grades one through eight. There were a few factors that rendered the girls especially vulnerable at Semmes. First, they were officially designated pioneers. After the three girls (and Bridges at Frantz) desegregated a given grade, that grade was considered officially desegregated—the opening up of formerly all-white schools literally followed their progress from grade to grade. This meant that the entire school system—if not the entire city—was watching them. For white parents, especially those in the Citizens' Council, the three girls became target number one: if they could be stopped, the whole project of desegregation might be halted, perhaps even permanently abandoned. "[The white students] didn't want to leave [Semmes]," Prevost Williams says, "and they didn't want us there. And they did everything in their power to just break us." At the same time, the national media and the US Marshals—assuming their jobs were done when the protests died down—left town. The check on violence that the national spotlight had once provided was gone. Semmes became, as Tate remembers it, "the devil's domain."[26]

Contributing to the conditions at Semmes was the fact that the girls were on the younger, smaller end of the student body. As Little Rock alum Ernest Green had observed, those who were more physically vulnerable incited the most abuse, and the third graders were subjected to astonishing violence. More shocking to them—at the time and since—was that the teachers incited their students. Prevost Williams explains:

> The teachers were no better than the kids. They encouraged them to fight us, to do whatever it took. Spit on us. We couldn't even eat in the cafeteria; they'd spit in our food—we could hardly use the restrooms. We couldn't drink out of the water faucets.... They'd punch you, trip you, kick you.... They'd push you down the steps. Gail got hit with a bat. I got hit with a bat . . . in the face. They would do spitballs.... They would put it on a slingshot. Just a little ball and they'd wet it.... It was somebody constantly doing this to you. It was just terrible. It was every day. And the teachers encouraged it.... Every day. Every day.

The repetition of the phrase "every day" is common among firsts, as if the speaker is still marveling at the duration and relentlessness of the abuse. What was survived was not simply violence and aggression but a systemic, all-encompassing, organized form of endless oppression. "The harassment was on a daily basis," Tate confirms. "It was just horrific." It is one thing to get hit; it is quite another to get hit every day. Nor was the abuse solely physical. The "N-word," Prevost Williams recalls, "doesn't mean a lot to little children. *Stupid* means more. *Dumb* means more. *Ugly* means more." There was a sixth-grade teacher, Tate remembers, "who would encourage [students] to call us names. . . . When she passed us she [put] Kleenex up in her nose as if we had an odor. She told them 'don't let them touch you cause your skin was gonna turn colors.'"

None of the Semmes firsts confided in their parents. They sensed that the pressure to perform extended to their mothers and fathers. "My dog was my therapist," Prevost Williams says. "I cried with the dog. I [would] tell him a whole lot of stuff." Strength and renewal came mostly from other women in their community, who invited them to spend the night and made them special food and clothing. Sociologist Patricia Hill Collins has termed these women "othermothers." These "othermothers," Collins writes, "have been central to the institution of Black motherhood." They were "key not only in supporting children but also in supporting bloodmothers who, for whatever reason," were unable to care for a child. In this case, the experiences that the girls were having at school were no doubt too disturbing for their "bloodmothers" to endure. Listening to their daughters' daily travails could have easily induced the mothers to pull their daughters out of the desegregation process. Many mothers may not have trusted themselves to invite their daughters to confide in them; at the same time many daughters felt that such information would place too great a burden on their mothers, many of whom were already struggling with precarious finances, long hours at low-paying jobs, or the burden of a large family. In New Orleans and elsewhere "othermothers" seem to have designated themselves responsible for firsts who needed attention, emotional support, or a boost in self-confidence. They spent time with the girls, made a fuss over them, gave them trinkets, and checked in with them daily. By so doing, they simultaneously helped the girls survive inside the schools and lifted some of the burden off the shoulders of their mothers.[27]

The girls did not, it should be noted, receive any emotional support from the NAACP. Visits from officials became a routine part of life. Thurgood Marshall and Louisiana civil rights attorney A. P. Tureaud stopped by their homes, as did future mayor of New Orleans "Dutch" Morial, but the girls felt the same pressure to keep up appearances and act the role of courageous pioneer in front of these men as they did at school. NAACP officials did offer some protection: they closely monitored the girls' grades to make sure teachers did not mark them unfairly. But the NAACP's watchful gaze was felt to be additional surveillance rather than support. A range of adults "made sure I made good grades," Tate recalls, "so I was always on my P's and Q's."

It was encouraging when a small group of other black students, around ten in total, arrived at Semmes, though they were in lower grades and "the boys didn't last," according to Prevost Williams. Conditions at Semmes radically improved for the girls when they got older—and bigger. "We got in the sixth grade," Prevost Williams recalls, "and we started to fight *back*." It worked. While there were still scuffles, by and large the white students retreated. Charles Prevost also lost patience with the way Tessie was being treated by the students and with being summoned to the principal's office to account for her behavior. When she came home with her clothes torn, he was particularly incensed. Prevost Williams recalls him saying to the principal:

> You know what? I'm not coming back here anymore for this. Now that she's retaliating it's something different. . . . I'm not coming back to this school. Don't call me back here for her fighting back. Because she was coming home [with] her clothes torn, her hair ribbons torn out of her head, and marks all over her.

Charles Prevost also confronted the father of a boy who was harassing Tessie, frightening the man so much that he left town. Leona Tate's mother began to push back as well, getting into a screaming match with a white woman who regularly confronted Leona on the sidewalk in front of the school. In these moments, the girls' parents began to act more as advocates for their daughters and less as faithful representatives for the NAACP. Competing needs—for irreproachable conduct on the one hand and for self-defense on the other—created a clashing set of demands. Parents were not, as a rule, the people desegregation firsts turned to for emotional support. But they did encourage their children to stand up for themselves, explicitly contradicting the orders of local civil rights organizations because of their deep concern for the physical safety of their children.

Symptoms of emotional burnout set in. Tessie began to develop stomach pain. At first, she felt sick whenever she passed the tree in the front of the entrance to Semmes Elementary. The smell of that tree, she says, "sticks with me to this day." Her stomach problems became chronic, and for many years she had to eat only "bland food without seasoning," which was difficult to do in New Orleans. She asked her father every year if she could leave Semmes. At first he said, "We have made a commitment to stick this out. Let's just stick this out." But she persisted and eventually he relented. She transferred to the all-black Rivers Frederick School and "it was like heaven." Still, she says, "I had so much anger in me, and when I got there, I didn't know where to target it. All the teachers knew who I was. . . . They knew what I needed and they gave it to [me]." "We just took her in," one teacher remembers, "just gave her love because we knew just what she needed." Leona Tate also transferred to Rivers and found that she could not face any more schooling after she graduated from high school. "I was gonna go to academic college, but I was like schooled out. We had just been through *so* much and I guess we had to set an example. . . . Through the years I kept saying 'I'm going back to school.' Still haven't done it."[28]

The Anderson sisters, Camilla Church Greene, Marcia Pinkett-Heller, and the New Orleans first graders—Gail Etienne, Tessie Prevost, Leona Tate, and Ruby Bridges—were all drafted into conducting school desegregation during its first stages and mostly at young ages. Given how well girls performed as plaintiffs—with school officials, lawyers, and the press—it is reasonable to conjecture that even the younger girls in New Orleans brought some of these same skills to school desegregation. The ability to talk to adults, which Ruby Bridges and Tessie Prevost Williams remember explicitly, no doubt helped them through the interview process. Their persistence in the schools, despite ongoing psychological and physical attacks, stemmed in part from their parents' investment in them as firsts. Greene's mother's admonition not to look for "love" at school but at home, and Prevost's father's invocation to "stick this out" because of his commitment to the NAACP were perceived by these girls as marching orders. Daughters listened to these directives and found a way to hold on, to last, to stay, and to survive. They could not have toughed it out if they did not believe that school desegregation was valuable. They could have—like the boys at Semmes—found a way to leave earlier. But the McDonough Three and Ruby Bridges made a moral choice to hang on for as long as humanly possible. Robert Coles, who interviewed Bridges over the course of the school desegregation process for his book *Children of Crisis* called Bridges's staying power "moral stamina." It is a term that works, too, for Tessie Prevost, Leona Tate, and Gail Etienne.[29]

Older girls who volunteered to desegregate high schools in the South were more capable of articulating what they hoped to achieve. But the younger girls' actions, and their ability to withstand warfare within the schools when others could not, should be read as a barometer of their determination, courage, ability, and strength.

7

"We Raised Our Hands
and Said 'Yes We Will Go'"

Desegregating Schools in the
Mid-1960s

U S District Judge E. Gordon West was an unapologetic segregationist and had publicly announced that *Brown v. Board* was "one of the truly regrettable decisions of all time." When West reluctantly ruled on *Davis v. East Baton Rouge* in favor of the plaintiffs in 1963, he gave the East Baton Rouge Parish School Board free rein to deter black students from applying to white schools. "There is no law, nor is there any decision of any court," he said, "which *requires* integration of public schools. The only requirement is that *forced segregation* of the public school system be abolished."[1]

The first choice that the Baton Rouge school board made was to start the desegregation process with the last year of grade school rather than the first—the opposite approach of the Orleans Parish School Board. They would begin with the twelfth grade and move down through the grades every year after. Most seniors—especially those who were poised to be valedictorian or receive other honors, precisely the students who would be eligible to transfer—would not want to give up the final year of their high school experience. The board's selection criteria were similar to Orleans Parish's. Freya Anderson Rivers, who wrote a memoir about her experience desegregating Lee High School, says that students had to have "high academic grades, stable homes that included both parents . . . good student discipline records and social and mental competence."[2]

When word came out that students could transfer, local activists Raymond Scott and Dupuy Anderson (father of eleventh-grader Freya), called a meeting at the Bethel AME Church. Murphy Bell Sr., a local activist, civil rights lawyer, and father of eleventh-grader Murphy Bell Jr., was also likely in attendance. All three men had been civil rights leaders in Baton Rouge for a decade. They had helped lead the public transportation strike in 1953—two years before the Birmingham strike—and were also involved in voter registration efforts and the lunch counter and downtown store desegregation protests, assisting local college students from Southern University. Anderson, a dentist with a thriving practice, ran for mayor of Baton Rouge in 1960; afterward, he filed a lawsuit demanding that designations indicating the color of a candidate be removed from ballots. The lawsuit was appealed to the Supreme Court, which ruled in Anderson's favor. He was, by 1963, "a legend in Baton Rouge."[3]

Doretha Davis—the first student to volunteer to desegregate—spoke at the meeting that night and was, by several accounts, so inspiring that many of the young women in attendance decided instantly that they, too, would apply to transfer. Marion Greenup recalls that at the meeting "they called people and asked them if they would consider [transferring]. And then there was a young girl, same age [as me], Doretha Davis . . . and she stood up and said she was going to do it . . . and I went 'Oh, if Doretha can do this, I can do this.'" Greenup considered Davis's stand even more extraordinary because she was "darker" and therefore had even less status. She was also financially less well-off than most of the students and families assembled. "My family wasn't wealthy," Greenup recalls, "but Doretha's family I knew had even less. So I was just so inspired by her." Davis's mother also spoke. Freya Anderson Rivers remembers, "Doretha's mother was threatened with losing her job if Doretha transferred . . . but [she] defied her employer saying, 'If that's the way you feel, I guess you'll have to fire me. My daughter wants to go, and I'm going to stand behind her.'" Davis's mother was a maid who worked for a white family. Another clue to Davis's relative poverty is visible in the list of those students applying to transfer to white schools, compiled in the summer of 1963: Doretha Davis was one of only three students who did not have a phone number.[4]

After the meeting, Marion Greenup and Freya Anderson attempted to recruit their classmates at the Southern Lab School, a private institution that was attached to Southern University. Ultimately, ten students from the Southern Lab School transferred—a fifth of the senior class. The other students came from McKinley High School and Scotlandville High School; both schools had been recently built in response to the ongoing desegregation lawsuit, although McKinley was at the end of a dead-end street that flooded regularly.

The girls' canvassing yielded few recruits. Those young women who did sign on cited a range of reasons: a desire to step forward and commit to desegregation for the good of the civil rights movement, an ambition to compete academically with whites for the good of the race, and, in only one case, the desire for a better education. Young men, on the other hand, emphasized that their decisions were made with other young men and their parents. When recounting their roles as desegregation pioneers, men, almost without exception, describe their decisions as motivated by a sense of filial duty. Murphy Bell Jr. recalls the moment he committed to desegregation this way: "[Father] asked me, and we were close, and I was going to do it for him." Men also remember that their initial deliberations were conducted in a casual way, constituting little more than a temporary diversion from their usual, teenage activities. Merrill Patin recalls making the decision with a friend:

> [We] were . . . sitting outside slumming one summer afternoon. Summer of '63. And in fact we were under a tree drinking beer and he said, "Did you hear about the schools in Baton Rouge being desegregated? . . . Let's go and register for the school. It's a big party. Everybody's going to Lee High". . . . So we hitchhiked, beer breath and all, down to the school board office and signed our name up. And then, we came back home and assume our position under the tree. *Seriously* that's what happened. I had about as much sincerity about . . . desegregating the school as I do flying to the moon.

The idea that desegregation was a fantasy recalls Carter Wesley's description of school desegregation in Texas in 1947: "As unrealistic as a little boy's notion that the boards in the tree constitute an airplane that can fly all over the world." Later, Patin thought better of it. He had a chance to star on the football team at Southern Lab. Resolving to reclaim his position at the school and on the team, he went to practice in August, two weeks before school started. "So I went to football practice," he recalls, "and that evening everybody called . . . the priests, civic leaders, everybody and their brother." After his father joined the chorus of voices and "nudged" him, Patin reluctantly committed to going.[5]

Ed Vice, who desegregated the schools in Moncks Corner, South Carolina, a few years later, described his decision in strikingly similar terms:

> I remember several of us . . . were either playing basketball or football. . . . I remember Chester Prelo, he was the one that asked the question . . . who in the group was going to go. . . . I think we stopped long enough to have that conversation. . . . I know that it

was something that [the parents] wanted us to do . . . [Later] I remember saying to myself, "Dang, what have I gotten myself into?"
You know, saying yes, in a group.

Both Patin and Vice remember that other young men were responsible for bringing up the idea, that the process was not too much
trouble or time taken out of their day, that they quickly resumed
their conspicuously male pastimes of playing sports and drinking
beer, and that they later questioned their decisions. Both convey
how casually their decision was arrived at, and how contingent the
agreement was on the voices, actions, and desires of adults. School
desegregation was enacted as a form of allegiance to elders and
friends in the black community rather than something that emanated from sincere ideals about school desegregation or race relations more broadly. Both men's desire to distance themselves from
an overt, individual commitment to desegregating schools echoes
the hesitations of the male plaintiffs before them: Lloyd Gaines,
Heman Sweatt, and Spottswood Bolling.[6]

Betta Bowman, who desegregated Baton Rouge High School
with eight other young women, also saw school desegregation as
an obligation—one that was similarly connected to her father, a
man with only a grade school education who had been working at
the Exxon oil refinery in Baton Rouge for thirty years. She put it
this way:

I felt like it was a duty. You had to be willing to go. But [it was] a
duty I wanted to do. . . . It was my time. It was my chance to help
out our own people. I had seen my daddy look down at the floor,
[the] ground, "yes sir, yes sir," all that kind of stuff. This was a big,
strong man. But this is what he had to do to make a living and to
stay out of trouble. And I remember the time when he told me,
he said, "Baby, just, just smile and do what you have to do, so you

can live." *Just live.* And it was just that change was happening. And
if you could do something to help change to happen, do it. . . . So
when the opportunity presented itself that *I* could do something,
oh yes, I was going to do it.

Bowman, like the male firsts, invoked the image of her father and a
sense of duty. However, her duty was not to him personally. Rather,
through him she found purpose in school desegregation as a form of
political and social transformation.[7]

Other women who volunteered to desegregate remember a similar sense of personal responsibility and the conviction that school
desegregation was a vital component of the larger civil rights movement. Gayle Vavasseur (now Jones) was a self-described leader at
McKinley High School. She, along with friends Marion Greenup
and Elaine Chustz (now Chustz Green), had been pushing against
segregation prior to volunteering to desegregate the schools. The
three young women had demanded to try on clothes at Rosenfield's
department store. "I'm human just like everyone else," Jones remembers saying to the clerk, "and I'm going to try this dress on." Jones
believes that her decision to desegregate Baton Rouge High was an
integral part of her identity as a student leader and activist. "I was
always strong-willed. And I didn't care what anybody else did, I just
felt that I needed to do it for my people. I *had* to participate."[8]

While Jones draws a direct line from local civil rights activism to
her decision to desegregate Baton Rouge High, Greenup describes
her decision as informed by national politics that had become increasingly heated over the spring and summer of 1963: the hundreds of lunch counter sit-ins across the nation, Martin Luther King
getting arrested and writing "Letter from a Birmingham Jail," and
the Children's March. "It was just . . . a summer of such emotional,
intense focus on the civil rights movement. . . . There was this wave
of stuff, good things and bad things were happening in the press all

the time ... and [desegregating] was part of the deal. Somebody had to do it and it might as well be me."[9]

Greenup and Jones's close friend Elaine Chustz (now Elaine Chustz Green) felt just as sure about adding her name to the list. She was told she would have been salutatorian at McKinley High School, but she did not really give that fact much thought. "My brothers and sisters thought that I was crazy," Chustz Green recounts. "When I would say, 'It's not fair that we can't try on a hat in the stores. It's not fair that we have to drink hot water when there's cold water right next to it,' they would say, 'That's just the way it is. You don't rock the boat' ... and I couldn't accept that." For her, school segregation was just as urgent and unfair as other Jim Crow injustices. "I felt like [desegregating] was my calling, that's what I had to do.... It was about justice; it was just not fair." Most of these young women had no doubts about the fundamental worth of school desegregation, did not agonize over what they would be missing at their black high schools, and viewed the historical moment as one that demanded action.[10]

Chustz Green speculates that girls and young women might have volunteered in disproportionate numbers because they were looking for leadership roles. "The feminist movement hadn't started yet," she says, "and we were going to be minor players no matter what.... In the context of where women [and] girls were socially, we would never have been put in the forefront." Had they not volunteered, they might not have found other opportunities to be prominent leaders. Like Ada Sipuel, these young women were inspired not only by a sense of obligation and individual calling but also by the opportunity to do something important and highly visible in a world and at a time when young women did not often earn much public acclaim.

The girls' determination and clarity of purpose would be necessary to get them through the ordeal of school desegregation, beginning with the task of informing their mothers. Most mothers in Baton Rouge felt hesitant about their daughters' participation for a variety of reasons. Jones's mother believed her daughter was not suited to the task. Jones's courage and outspokenness—the qualities that made her an effective activist—were, in her mother's eyes, disqualifiers. Jones remembers her saying, "It's going to be too much trouble, Gayle. It could be violent. *And I know how you are. . . .* I just don't think you're the right person for that, because you can get loud and you tell people how you feel." Gayle responded, "That's why I think I'm the right person for it." Elaine Chustz's mother was terrified her daughter might be killed and told her in no uncertain terms that she did not want her to participate. Betta Bowman's mother was also uncomfortable with the idea, though she spoke more about the possibility of losing her job as a cook at the black Eden Park Elementary School. Elaine Boyle (now married to Merrill Patin) was also a student at the Southern Lab School. She recalls that her mother "was overprotective" and that she had to be convinced. Like Gayle Jones's mother, Elaine Boyle's mother voiced doubts about her daughter's disposition, but for very different reasons: she was too sensitive and cried too easily.

In the few instances where mothers were supportive of their daughter's participation, it was articulated as support for their husbands. Murphy Bell Jr. recalls that his father encouraged him to apply, and that his mother "was one hundred percent behind my father." Freya Anderson, like Murphy Bell, had little choice in the matter—her father was too visible in the civil rights movement for him not to send his own child. More importantly, Dupuy Anderson made it clear to his daughter that he would be disappointed in her if she did not apply. Officially, Freya's mother supported Dupuy Anderson's stance. But when her husband was not at home she would privately urge her daughter to change her mind. "She told me that she did not want me to go. . . . I knew she couldn't tell Daddy that she encouraged me not to go, but she was always protecting us."[11]

Mothers of all classes in Baton Rouge were generally less supportive of their daughters acting as school desegregation firsts than mothers in other locales at other times. There are some factors that help explain the phenomenon. With the exception of Elaine Boyle's mother, most of the mothers were not directly involved in the civil rights movement in Baton Rouge. The mothers of Freya Anderson and Murphy Bell Jr. were married to activists but not activists themselves. The mothers involved in school desegregation lawsuits in the 1940s and the mothers in Albany, Georgia, in the mid-1960s experienced their political goals as a form of connection to their daughters. In Baton Rouge, however, the main players in desegregation attempts in the 1960s—involving lunch counters, movie theaters, and public transportation—were students from Southern University and the local high schools. While the 1953 bus strike had involved adults in the community, it lasted only a matter of weeks. Confrontations in Baton Rouge in the early 1960s over separate accommodations and civil rights inequities were carried out by young people. Adults, except for the prominent male leaders, were not involved in large numbers. The NAACP, which brought more adults into the movement elsewhere, was not active in Baton Rouge. And the groups that were active—especially the Congress for Racial Equality and the Student Nonviolent Coordinating Committee, or SNCC—worked primarily with college students. There was, in short, a generational divide in Baton Rouge. The exception was Boyle's mother, who housed many Congress for Racial Equality members—mostly college students from other states—and was both involved with the movement and supportive of her daughter when she decided to desegregate.[12]

The timing was also significant. Mothers in Baton Rouge had, just a few years prior, witnessed the legislative uproar that the desegregation of the New Orleans schools had ignited in the state's capital. Images of Tessie Prevost, Leona Tate, Gail Etienne, and Ruby Bridges fighting their way through hateful mobs, the need for US Marshals to accompany the girls to school, and the nasty strikes the girls provoked would have been fresh in their minds. As of the summer of 1963, moreover, little about the situation in New Orleans had been resolved. Only a small minority of the white students had returned to the lower schools that had been desegregated. Louisiana may have seemed an especially dangerous and unfruitful place to initiate school desegregation. Furthermore, watching a daughter desegregate a school may have simply been more difficult for mothers in the early 1960s than fathers. In a society where traditional gender roles were fully entrenched and remained unquestioned, mothers were primarily responsible for their children's health—physical, mental, and otherwise. Hence, they may simply have been, as their teenage daughters perceived, more "protective."

Fathers in Baton Rouge were more willing to endure the risks and more confident in their daughters' ability to handle the demands of school desegregation. Like Dupuy Anderson and Murphy Bell Sr., Reverend T. J. Jemison was a prominent leader in the community—he was a founding member of the Southern Christian Leadership Conference—and had a daughter, Betty Jemison, at the Southern Lab School who was eligible to transfer. The children of all three men applied and were accepted. The school board may have been afraid of repercussions if they rejected any one of these applicants. These men were, as a group, similar to those fathers who filed desegregation lawsuits on behalf of their daughters in the 1940s. They were respected men who represented African Americans in court (Bell), delivered the black voting bloc (Anderson), or were nationally known civil rights leaders (Jemison). Everyone in Baton Rouge knew these men. They were not to be treated as other black citizens, and their children were off-limits too. Indeed, it is possible that they had amassed so much power in Baton Rouge that they felt not only that their children would be automatically approved to transfer but that their own stature would extend to their children within white schools. This seems to have been true in Murphy Bell Jr.'s case, it should be noted, but not in Freya Anderson's.

Rita Gidroz (now Gidroz White), an honor society student at Scotlandville High School, remembers that she signed up to transfer after receiving a visit from Dupuy Anderson and Raymond Scott in the spring of 1963. Her teachers had recommended her to the two men. She was somewhat shy and soft-spoken—"I was not," she says, "a socialite" —and she did not want to transfer. But her father, who worked at the Uniroyal chemical plant, immediately warmed to the idea. "My father," she says "saw it as an opportunity for me to go to a *better* school." He also said, "If you go, well then other children will be able to go later. So it's important that you go and start. Lead the way for other kids to be able to go." He also saw it as an honor that she had been selected by her teachers and leaders in the community. Her mother, a dietician at Baker High School, a white public school, concurred with her father.[13]

Another clue to the mother-father divide on the issue of school desegregation in Baton Rouge is the fact that some fathers were approached, as the head of household, by male leaders. This meant that leaders in Baton Rouge were transacting with other men in the community in making plans for their minor children. These men were making a commitment to one another as well as doing what they believed was best for their children. Fathers may have felt an obligation to other men, particularly those in leadership positions, in ways that mothers did not. In situations where fathers encouraged daughters to participate, mothers may have felt sidelined, or perhaps more able to express their ambivalence because their husbands were doing the work of lobbying their daughters. Elaine Boyle Patin and Doretha Davis were the exception; their mothers were supportive of their decision to desegregate, but their mothers were also both single.

Despite the many and varied solicitation attempts—meetings, appeals to teachers and parents, Freya Anderson and Marion Greenup's friend-to-friend canvassing—only forty-eight students applied. One snag in the process was that some teachers and school officials actively advised students *not* to transfer, either because they thought it would be too difficult to be a first or out of a sense of personal and institutional loss. Freya Anderson Rivers remembers that

her band teacher, with whom she had a tight bond as first chair clarinet, asked her not to transfer. Murphy Bell Jr. remembers that his
track coach expressed regret about losing him. Several firsts recall
that some school friends expressed anger that they were planning to
leave. A few boys told Marion Greenup that they felt "abandoned."
Betta Bowman said that at the Southern Lab School the principal called a meeting to discuss the question of applying. "Now the
principal sat us down," as Bowman described it, "and she said it's a
big decision because . . . you are not going to be with your friends,
with the teachers you've grown to know. . . . You're the cream of the
crop. You're the best we have. And I want you to think about this
before you really leave here." No doubt this speech gave many students pause. The tug of the known and loved was surely a powerful
force, and guilt about leaving nurturing teachers may have been just
as powerful. The stakes must have felt terribly high and the sense of
duty heavy. That the principal gave this speech at all speaks volumes
about the sense of loss—of intellectual capital and talent—and the
ambivalence desegregation incited in all but the fully committed.
School desegregation represented a drain on black institutions, and
many who had worked hard to build those institutions stood by
them, over and above other civil rights goals. The pull of these opposing voices within the black community helps to explain the low
numbers of students who sought to transfer.[14]

Of the forty-eight who applied, ten were tossed out on technical-
ities. Of the remaining, twenty-eight were girls and nine were boys;
one applicant had a gender-neutral first name, Lee, and an illegible
last name. After the school board consulted the students' records,
each was called individually to the school board for an interview.
Robert Aertker Sr., deputy superintendent of East Baton Rouge
Parish, did the interviewing. When Marion Greenup and her father
walked into the room, Aertker did not even acknowledge Marion's
presence. "Just started talking to my dad about what a bad decision
this was, and how it wasn't a good thing for my father to allow me to

do, and when he finished with this intro, my father said, 'Well I suggest you talk to her, because it's her decision.'" Aertker then turned to Marion and, in a manner that was "dismissive and rude and confrontational," asked her why she wanted to transfer. Betta Bowman said of the encounter, "It looked like they were trying to talk you out of it: Why would you want to go to a white school?" Elaine Boyle Patin tells a similar story about Aertker. "He was *awful*. He did everything he could think to . . . make our parents afraid. . . . He'd ask questions like, 'Why are you sending your kid? *Why* don't you want to stay at your other school? She might be harassed.'" Pointing to discrimination within the black community and referencing Elaine's fair skin, her mother answered, "Well no more than she is at her other school because sometimes they tell her she's half white."

Greenup, Bowman, and Boyle Patin all remembered their answers to the question about why they wanted to attend Baton Rouge High, suggesting that these queries made them feel instantly on their guard. As Boyle Patin puts it, "We didn't really tell the truth." Greenup describes the questions as "contrived" and thus requiring a contrived response. "So I dreamed up reasons, like wanting to take Latin . . . something insipid like that." Bowman provided an answer that served two functions at once: it got her out of the box Aertker was trying to put her in and offered an irrefutable rationale for school desegregation:

> I told them that I just wanted to really know for myself that I was an A—or A/B student—anywhere. I didn't want to think that I was doing good at the black school. . . . I wanted to know that I was a good student anywhere I went. . . . And the only way I could determine that was [to] at least try to put myself at another school, see if I could truly comprehend . . . what they were being presented. And see if I could . . . make good grades over there. He was saying "No" [you won't make A's] . . . and I kept on thinking, *Oh yes I will. Oh yes I will.* Give me a chance.

Bowman's response would have pleased Lucinda Todd, who argued so forcefully in 1948 for the need for African American students to compete as individuals in desegregated high schools. Just as black boys yearned to compete on the sports field with white athletes, so too did young women yearn to compete in one of the few ways they were allowed, aside from clothing and beauty. Bowman saw desegregation as a stepping-stone not to the upper echelons of what Baton Rouge had to offer but to the world. She would admit no limits on achievement so that her future might be truly open.

Of the twenty-eight girls who applied, seven were rejected after the interview, and of the nine boys who applied, three were rejected. One girl, Doris Marie Carney, was rejected but appealed the decision and was accepted. This means that a quarter of the girls were rejected, and a third of the boys. Young women may have done better in the interview, but the most important factor contributing to the lopsided ratio of girls to boys was that so many more girls applied. In the end, twenty-two girls and six boys were selected to transfer.[15]

———

On Labor Day, the day before school started, an effigy of a black student was hung from one of the live oaks in front of Baton Rouge High, and a cross was burned in front of Glen Oaks High School. Of all the desegregation firsts, Freya Anderson was the most accustomed to these kinds of threats. Because her father was so well known, her home had been targeted from the moment she was assigned to Lee High School. Cars would speed down her street at night and throw rotten fruit and vegetables at her house. Dead animals were found hanging from the front porch. The Klan burned a cross in the empty lot across the street from her home. The phone was tapped. Dupuy Anderson had been subjected to this kind of harassment when he ran for mayor in 1960, and the Anderson family took it in stride.

Over the summer of 1963, Betta Bowman, who was one of the less well-off girls of the bunch, spent copious amounts of time on her wardrobe. The American Friends Service Committee—a Quaker organization working closely with Raymond Scott and Dupuy Anderson—offered to pay for fabric for those who could not afford new clothing. Looking at the picture of herself in the *Sunday Advocate* taken on September 3, 1963, Bowman said, "I made my skirt and blouse. Some of 'em had money" to buy clothes, but she had to make hers. "And I was cool and comfortable in that little skirt and blouse. Nothing was too short. We all had stockings on our legs or socks, every day." Bowman's focus on clothing was so intense at the time that she was later only able to identify former fellow students by their shoes. "That looks like Elaine [Boyle's] shoes. Yes, that's Elaine." Judging by the picture in the *Advocate*, the young women achieved something beyond just being well-dressed. Shoes matched bags, which matched dresses and skirts. The girls were not simply well turned out; they were beautiful—a fact that was at once an aesthetic and a competitive victory.

The eight girls walked as a close group on the emphatic instructions of the National Guardsmen walking just behind them. "Stay together!" they yelled, and "Keep walking!" The whole group did not yet know one another well and did not automatically fall in stride close to each other. "We had to walk that walk and by the time we got to the steps of the school, you can better believe we were together," Bowman recalled. Baton Rouge High School had a long sidewalk leading up to one of the largest buildings in the city, with live oaks on either side. Boys were hanging off the trees, yelling all kinds of things, "people jeering," Bowman said, "calling you all kind of name." One young man—who was casually chatting with the local police—had a shotgun.

There were crowds in front of all the schools that day. Firsts remember the epithets and chants. On the porch of a house across the street from Istrouma High, a sign read "Token Today, Taken Tomorrow." Nonetheless, the crowds in Baton Rouge were not nearly so large or boisterous as those in New Orleans. No one remembers exactly when they disappeared, but they did not stick around for too long. Having seen how little the crowds managed to accomplish in New Orleans—and the negative national publicity the city received—white parents, it appears, were advised against lingering in the streets. Instead, the real war was fought inside the buildings of Glen Oaks, Istrouma High, Baton Rouge High, and Lee High.[16]

The students arrived in groups via taxicabs, which the leadership decided would be the only safe mode of transportation. They were asked to arrive at their schools late, after the principals prepared the white students for their arrival. The principal at Lee High told the assembled white students that "he didn't want these N—s at the school any more than the rest of them but they would just have to make the best of it." It appears that this was the position that all four principals struck. They cast themselves as victims of a process over which they had no say. Their desire—whether born of weakness or bigotry or political pressure—to ally themselves with racists was stronger than any professional impulse they might have had to run an orderly school.[17]

When the new students reported to class and sat down, all of the white students got up from adjacent desks and fanned out toward the opposite side of the room. "So we sat down," Merrill Patin remembers, "and then everybody started pulling their chairs away. . . . I was in shock at that . . . every class I went to, it was the same thing. That was shocking, that rejection." There were a few classes where the teachers would not tolerate this behavior, but those teachers were in the minority. The firsts figured that the white students would stop moving away at some point, as it meant that there were always a few who had to stand up for the entire class. "But that continued," Merrill Patin remembers, still somewhat amazed, "for the whole year."

Notes awaited them on their lockers. "You will not live through the year," Elaine Chustz Green remembers them saying. The notes became a permanent fixture. "Sometimes they would just say 'N—s go home,'" Chustz Green says. "Other times it was, as it got closer to the [end] of the school year, 'You're not going to graduate. You won't live to graduate.'" Others remember the notes threatening to tar and feather them. They were signed by the KKK. They found their lockers defaced and inoperable. "They would stuff the locker so you couldn't open it," Boyle Patin recalls. Water was also poured through the vents, soaking all of their papers and books.

White students moved away from the black students even faster in the lunchroom. Students practically flew out of their chairs if a black student sat down at a lunch table—even if it was on the opposite end of the table from the white students. This meant two things for the black students: they could always count on having a seat—indeed, a whole table—in the crowded lunchroom, and they ate either alone or with one another. The most persistent form of verbal harassment, from the beginning until the end of the school year, was name-calling. The N-word was constant, more in the hallways than in the classrooms, but some teachers implicitly and explicitly gave white students the green light to use epithets. Freya Anderson Rivers remembers that "verbal taunts of "N—, coon and baboon" were daily, relentless. Gayle Jones remembers, "We don't want you here, N—, go home. Get your black asses off this campus." Within a few months, when none of the black students had departed from their respective schools—perhaps frustrating some white students' expectations—the harassment became violent. The hallway was the most dangerous place: "Every time you changed classes there was someone pushing you ... spitting at you," Marion Greenup recalls. The girls were constantly "being jostled and pushed around and called names." Anderson Rivers describes a similar scene: "As we walked through the halls some students bumped into us, knocking us around, forcing us to bump into the wall and into other students who pushed back." Going down the stairs one day, a boy threw a lit match into Bowman's hair. "I flew to the principal . . . but I got in trouble."[18]

The white boys, by all reports, were much more physical than white girls with the female firsts. Everyone took note of it. "Believe it or not," Jones says, "the boys were the ones who were so aggressive towards us." The girls would move away in the halls, or, as Boyle Patin puts it, "Girls may say something snotty, but I only remember guys really actually trying to hit us. . . . It was always the guys." Greenup says that it was only boys who harassed her—both verbally and physically. "There was a lot of jostling and stepping [on her heels] but not with girls; girls just didn't come on. . . . I didn't have any issues with girls." While boys physically attacking girls in the hallway may seem to violate the normal order of gender relations in an early 1960s American high school, Greenup is quick to point out that "it doesn't violate the order of white boys attacking black girls. Or white men attacking black women." For Greenup, growing up in Louisiana in the late 1950s and early 1960s, white men and boys physically assaulting black girls and women was the norm rather than the exception. This status quo was escalated and intensified by the boys and girls' intimate interaction with one another within the school building, but the violence and harassment did not stand in stark contrast to the larger context in which Greenup—and all the Baton Rouge young women—came of age.

Neither Murphy Bell Jr. nor Merrill Patin remember much physical harassment. Patin would hear epithets in the halls, but no one ever said anything to him directly "except this one little guy, just a little fella . . . just N-word this and N-word that—to my face. Eventually we got into a scuffle . . . and I finally hit him. . . . After that he was expelled [and] . . . attitudes changed—names called behind [my] back were not as frequent. Maybe it stopped." Murphy Bell Jr. does not recall any physical harassment and reports that some of the white young men spoke to him regularly. One boy even offered to be his lab partner on the first day of school. Anderson

Rivers notes the different experience she was having at Lee High compared to the three young men who were there with her, Murphy Bell Jr., Melvin Patrick, and Louis Morgan. "The guys actually had people that spoke to them and participated with them in class. They even liked most of their teachers." Two young men also spoke with Merrill Patin early in the school year at Glen Oaks—but they paid for it outside of school and later transferred. Overall, men report less hostility from both students and teachers, and far less physical harassment. The only logical conclusion is that the girls were targeted because they were smaller, more defenseless, and less threatening. Indeed, the smaller the girl, the more abuse she received. Greenup was "a skinny little person," and she experienced constant physical assaults—boys stopping her from using the water fountain, bumping up against her, spitting on her. The experiences of the smaller young women in the Baton Rouge high schools mirror exactly those of Tessie Prevost, Gail Etienne, and Leona Tate when they were the youngest and smallest students at Semmes Elementary in New Orleans.[19]

———

By November, the girls had decided to fight back. At one of their weekly meetings they planned to carry large, heavy bags as weapons. Freya—the most retaliatory of the firsts, probably because she was forced to desegregate because of her father's prominence in Baton Rouge—also resolved to carry two large, open safety pins in both hands, which she crossed under her books. When someone bumped into her, they would get jabbed with a pin. (The other girls refused to participate in this approach for fear of hurting students who had accidentally walked near them.) She also carried a small water pistol; if someone spat on her, she would shoot them so they thought she was spitting back. None of the firsts could bring themselves to actually spit back. Boyle Patin remembers the first time she hit back this way: "We were getting out of class and this guy stuck me in my behind with a pen. I'm just walking along the hall, and all of a sudden I get this thing and . . . I had books in one arm and my purse in the other arm and I was just hitting . . . everybody in sight and everybody's clearing out the path." Boyle Patin had come in for severe abuse, above and beyond what the other girls were getting. The students had initially thought she was white and didn't bother her, but when they found out otherwise they were infuriated.[20]

According to Gayle Jones, there was one "boy who made life hell [for Marion Greenup] every day." One day, Jones got between them. "Because I was large-framed and bigger, I grabbed him by the collar and put him up against the wall . . . and I'm sure I used quite a few curse words also." Greenup says admiringly, "Gayle was just fearless. She could pick somebody up and throw them against the locker. . . . If someone really gave her a hard time she would rough them up and then drag them to the office and report them for roughing *her* up. And so I really idolized Gayle." Greenup believes she would not have survived the year without Jones's protection. But she was not completely helpless. She began to tell students she was carrying a gun in her bag. "If somebody said something to me, I'd say, 'I don't think you want to mess with me, you don't know what I have.'" And if "somebody kicked me, I'd kick them back. They had to really fight me." Those boys were "nasty, bullying types," Greenup continues, "and you can't let a bully bully you. So my response was to not be bullied."

These moments were triumphs of resistance for the harassed and abused young women, and they remember them as such—with a laugh, a mischievous smile, a twinkle in their eye. This kind of resistance went against the advice of community leaders, who preached nonviolence at the students' weekly meetings. The decision to fight back was made consciously, among themselves, but no one informed the adults. There was also outright mischief and planned revenge. Jones figured out which locker belonged to the "little guy" who was tormenting Greenup. As the black students were the only ones at Baton Rouge High who actually locked their lockers, Jones opened up his locker, "took a book of his and chewed up vanilla wafers and ginger snaps and spit them in between all the pages of his book."

This tit-for-tat, low-level, never-ending war would become the norm in high schools throughout the state of Louisiana and the South. For instance, siblings Ronald Julien and Alyce Julien (now Robinson), who desegregated Donaldsonville High School about twenty-five miles downriver from Baton Rouge with a dozen other black students in 1965, came up with an ingenious plan against the white students who moved away from them at lunch. "We decided, let's just see how foolish these people really are," Ronald Julien recalls. "So we decided we would [each] sit at different tables ... and nobody would come around, so we kept stretching it until finally they were [all] standing up with their trays in their hands." The firsts at Donaldsonville High sat at individual tables for months; the white students ate lunch standing up, lining the perimeter of the lunchroom. The group undertook the same experiment on the bus, with each first sitting in a different seat, forcing the white students to stand and crowd the front and back of the bus. In a highly satisfying reversal of the Jim Crow order, they had succeeded in pushing the white students to stand while they sat. "Yeah," Ronald Julien says, not entirely sarcastically, "we had lots of fun."[21]

Freya Anderson planned a more dangerous form of revenge. On spirit day students brought confederate flags (the official flag, of course, of Lee High) to a school pep rally, each homeroom vying to have the largest flag. Freya went to the store and purchased the tiniest flag she could find. It was a paper flag attached to a toothpick—the kind used for decorating cupcakes. She brought the paper flag to the rally, held it aloft with one hand, and, using a Bic lighter with the other, lit it on fire. The flag burned up with a "poof." Murphy Bell Jr. and the two other firsts grabbed her and rushed her out of the auditorium as fast as they could. They were furious with her. It was an audacious stunt, but not unrepresentative of desegregation firsts' general attitude toward confederate paraphernalia or toward singing

"Dixie" or "Old Black Joe," as was common at white public schools throughout the South. The girls at Semmes Elementary also refused to stand for "Dixie" and the "rebel mascot"—no matter the repercussions. None of the firsts in Baton Rouge would acknowledge confederate insignia, flags, pledges, or songs. Neither would those who came after them in rural parts of Louisiana in 1964 and 1965, or in Albany, Georgia, or in South Carolina. The refusal to pay obeisance to this relic of southern identity on the part of desegregation firsts was universal.[22]

There was, however, one incident of a girl fighting back at Baton Rouge High School—an event everyone remembers—that was not viewed as a victory. Velma Jean Hunter Jackson retaliated against a white boy who had been targeting her relentlessly. Elaine Chustz Green remembers that he taunted her in the lunch line and Jackson picked her plate up off the tray and "cracked him on the head with the melamine plate. And it broke in half. . . . His tow-headed hair was filled with blood and food." Others remember variously that it was "Dress Up Day" or "Western Day" or "Senior Day." The black students were informed that they were not allowed to participate. But Jackson did anyway. Betta Bowman described it vividly:

> She had little boots to match the skirt with all the fringe on it, and the shirt with the fringe. . . . It was a beautiful outfit. Someone threw [food] on her. . . . She just took her tray and just hit the boy over the head with it. And the whole place erupted and took fight. And I never could forget that was Velma Jean. Because . . . she was a girly little girl. . . . Always pretty. And quiet. . . . She turned that cafeteria out. Sweet girl. But she turned it out. I mean, she hit him over the head with a tray, took another tray, and just kept on. . . . *He messed up her clothes.* I was in shock. *Velma?*

There are several reasons why this moment—while potentially inspiring a cheer from a contemporary audience—was upsetting for the firsts, and why it felt, within the competitive framework of the desegregated high school, like a loss. First, Jackson was trying to participate in a white celebration from which she had been explicitly barred. Black firsts constantly tested such restrictions, but they picked their battles carefully. For instance, Freya Anderson was never assigned to be first chair in clarinet, even though she was inarguably the best player in the orchestra. In response, she signed up for a regional contest where her fellow Lee High musicians were forced to listen to her. She won an award at the competition, thus proving her superiority to the larger community. Other female firsts petitioned their principals to be allowed to attend senior prom; as a result, none of the schools held proms that year. This was also considered a small victory.

Jackson was similarly testing boundaries and making a demand for inclusion, but she lost control of her emotions and her limbs when she hit the boy either so hard or so many times that he was bleeding. Jackson's response was not only uncontrolled but also disproportionate to the attack. This was exactly what her white aggressor wanted—for her to erupt in a way that would lead to a suspension; some remember that Jackson was, in fact, suspended. Jackson's attack also contravened the unspoken set of rules about competitive retaliation: that it be planned ahead of time and executed opportunistically, and that the act itself reflect strength, precision, and carefully targeted movements that humiliated white students and thus dissuaded them from complaining to authorities. Jackson's flailing and furious attack resembled loss of control more than retaliation, and as such made her—and by extension the whole group—look vulnerable. It also, unlike Alyce and Ronald Julien's lunchroom mischief, incited violence. Firsts could not afford to be rightfully accused of starting a fight on school grounds.

The most dangerous moment of the 1963–1964 school year was on November 22, when President John F. Kennedy was assassinated. The anarchic violence in Dallas incited the Baton Rouge students to be violent and anarchic themselves. The students—and some teach-ers—erupted in spontaneous glee, and all forms of order were null and void as the students cheered and celebrated in the halls, effec-tively taking over the schools in a riotous victory party. It was "mob rule," Elaine Chustz Green remembers, as the students "just broke out of their classrooms, ran into the halls screaming, 'Your N— president is dead. Now you'll have to go home.'" Rita Gidroz White reflects with indignation, "They were *rejoicing*" and saying "What'd you going to do?" Marion Greenup remembers similar threats and taunting: "'We'll get you N—s next, we got him, we'll get you.' Over and over, just cheering. . . . It was everybody, it wasn't just the stu-dents—there were teachers who were ecstatic."[23]

The firsts' initial shock that anyone could celebrate the murder of a president soon gave way to terror as the white students used the occasion—and the sense of empowerment it imparted—to close in on them and try to inflict bodily harm, or maybe kill them. At 1:00 p.m., Freya Anderson Rivers writes, "Two large white men appeared in the doorway, talked to [my teacher] then approached Murphy and me. We were told to get our things and leave with these men." As they tried to make their way down the hallway, a crowd of stu-dents formed a circle around them chanting, "We killed Lincoln, we killed Kennedy, and we'll kill anyone else who tries to help N—s!" The men—federal marshals, they later found out—surrounded the firsts by linking arms, and in this way the group managed to leave the building as the crowd became increasingly violent, brazenly throwing punches at the marshals. The students had just slammed the door of the waiting taxicab when a bucket of urine and feces was thrown at them and barely missed, hitting the door of the car. The firsts at all the Baton Rouge high schools escaped in this man-ner—and all were astonished at the sight of the marshals. No one had seen any sign of them before November 22, when they suddenly appeared, escorted the students out of their respective schools, and then promptly disappeared from view again.[24]

In Anderson Rivers's memory, it was soon after the Kennedy assassination when Velma Jean Hunter Jackson hit the white boy in the lunchroom and when Merrill Patin was briefly suspended for fighting. Violence begot violence, as such events are wont to do. But the harrowing experience did not simply frighten them. It also inspired them to redouble their efforts, to become more committed to sticking it out until the end. Even Freya, who was perhaps the most reluctant first and who, just before the assassination, was planning to go back to the Southern Lab School after Thanksgiving break, found new meaning in school desegregation and the suffering she was enduring. "I could not believe I had been so selfish," she chided herself. "Kennedy's assassination had been a wake-up call.... I was going back to avenge all the Black people that had died to get me in that damn school [and] I was going back for all the Black children who would be able to go to better schools in their neighborhoods, and schools with new books and supplies."[25]

———

It was the isolation and ostracism that firsts remember as the most eerie, unnatural, and, over time, harmful aspect of their desegregation experience. It was more painful than any physical fight, food-throwing, name-calling, or insults—even more painful than being spat on. "We didn't have the dogs," Elaine Chustz Green says. "We didn't have the water hoses ... but the [isolation] was ... insidious." Merrill Patin, recalling the total lack of interaction with his fellow students at Glen Oaks High, uses repetition to emphasize the impact of daily silence on his psyche. "No one," he says, talked to him for "the whole year. No one. No one. No one. No one. No one. No one." Rita Gidroz White recalls, "We were lonely because we were so isolated.... No one would talk to you, nobody want to sit next to you.... It was a lonely time." Gayle Jones says that the hardest thing about desegregating Baton Rouge High was that "you're thrust into a situation where nobody likes you." Freya Anderson Rivers writes that at their weekly meetings, feelings of isolation were the chief topic of conversation. "We talked about our loneliness at the white school which hurt worse than the overt violence and aggression." Elsewhere she writes, "Spending an entire day at school with no one to talk to and being ostracized was torture. . . . Even teachers did not call on you in class, which would have at least given you a reason to open your mouth." Marion Greenup concurs. "It was as if we were aliens in the room, in every room, in every classroom." Betta Bowman blamed the administration for mandating separation and for encouraging students to shun them. "It was like you were an animal to be separated from everyone else, and you weren't treated as a human being like they were." At Donaldsonville High, Alyce Julien Robinson and Ronald Julien endured more physical altercations and relentless sabotage than anyone at the Baton Rouge high schools. When asked which was worse, the fistfights or the ostracism, they both answer, immediately and in unison, "the ostracism."[26]

Most Baton Rouge firsts claim that, despite all of the hate that was directed at them, they themselves did not succumb to hate. "I felt anger," Chustz Green recalls, "as far as the administration was concerned I felt betrayal. I don't think I felt hate." She believes— as does Merrill Patin—that her Catholicism saved her from feeling hate. She also managed to transform her anger, or channel it, into a competitive drive: "[The situation] just made me madder and more determined . . . more determined to win. To overcome. To finish." Several firsts also understood, whether from conversations with their parents or on their own, that hate was a destructive emotion. "I never hated anyone," Bowman reflected, "'cause my mother [said], 'We don't hate people. . . . You're going to hurt yourself more than you hurt the other person.'" But Jones did feel hate. "If you're going to isolate me and not look at me for who I am as a person, and you hate me . . . then I'm pissed off. And I'm angry at the whole group now. . . . I literally hated white folks." Freya Anderson became, and remained, more disgusted with white people over time—her descriptions of the beehive hairstyles and makeup of working-class white girls at Lee High are scathing—but her chief response was to become depressed. She was often sick, so listless that some days she had trouble walking across the schoolyard. Aurelius Martinez, who shared a daily taxi with Greenup to Baton Rouge High, started to miss school. "He just didn't want to go," Greenup says. "We . . . had to go in and get him to come every morning. Or he wouldn't show some mornings." Martinez eventually dropped out of Baton Rouge High and left the state altogether. No one has heard from him since. The rumor is that he moved to Mexico or California.

Like Tessie Prevost and Leona Tate, most of the desegregation firsts in Baton Rouge chose not to confide in their mothers. Chustz Green says that she did not want to burden her mother "because she worried about money so much I never—I didn't tell her any of that stuff." Gidroz White says she did not confide in her mother, "'cause my mother was *soft*. And I didn't want her crying, when I would tell her things." She did confide somewhat in her father, but did not give him the full picture. "I cried a lot at night," Greenup says. "I didn't ever tell my parents, because I didn't want them to worry. Nothing was going to change, they couldn't fix it, so there was no need to worry them. . . . If you were upset with anybody, they were even more upset. So we edited." Anderson Rivers believes that if her mother found out what was going on, she would have withdrawn her from Lee High. "I never told Mama about the things we went through each day. . . . It was just too much. I think Mama would have pulled me out if she knew all the details." Hence, the isolation that the firsts felt was amplified by the restraint they had to exercise at home in front of their parents. They did confide in one another, and some talked to their siblings. Others remember their mothers' friends calling them regularly to check up on them. Yet these forms of communication provided only momentary solace, and many, like Greenup, simply cried in the safety of their own rooms, alone and at night.[27]

———

The same summer the Baton Rouge firsts were getting ready to de-segregate the high schools, Millicent Brown's father informed her that the Charleston school board had requested to see her. Her mother had been attempting to transfer her to a nearby white school since 1955. Before the meeting, twelve-year-old Brown was told only to dress nicely. "So I go in, and the whole, all-male, white, Charles-ton County School Board is sitting around a table!" They wanted to ask her if she was unhappy at her black school, did she not like her teachers, why did she want to leave her black friends? "So why would you want to leave that and go to someplace where you don't know anybody?" Brown—unprepared as she was—returned, "Because I make friends wherever I go." It was an artful response. Contained within it was every aspect of social discipline black girls had been taught to master—manners, self-possession, and a finely calibrated projection of warmth. Her answer was polite yet self-assured; it was ostensibly sweet yet full of moxie. But perhaps most importantly, her words were so simple and humane that they turned the question of sociality back onto her interlocutors—as if to say, "I don't know what *you* do when you go to a new place, but I make friends." She had checkmated the whole room.[28]

On September 4, 1963, Millicent Brown was on the front page of the *New York Times*, standing on the threshold of formerly all-white Rivers High School. Below her was a picture of one of the Baton Rouge firsts in the Istrouma High lunchroom. "School Integration Begins Calmly," the *New York Times* trumpeted on its cover. True to her word, Brown was smiling and talking to a white female student in front of their shared school, looking, for all the world to see, like two people becoming friends. Brown hates the picture because the *Times* failed to mention that the students were outside because of a bomb threat.[29]

Brown—like Freya Anderson, Betty Jemison, and Murphy Bell—was the daughter of a well-known lawyer and activist, J. Arthur

Brown, president of the Charleston NAACP. Immediately after *Brown v. Board* was decided, J. Arthur Brown tried to enroll his two daughters in public schools close to the family home. Turned away, he filed a lawsuit on behalf of his older daughter, Minerva. After Minerva graduated from high school, he simply substituted Millicent's name for Minerva's. Every year thereafter, Millicent's mother, MaeDe Brown, attempted to enroll her daughter in the public school closest to their home. For her trouble, the family had their names and address printed on the front page of the *Charleston News and Courier*.[30]

During the summer of 1963, Millicent Brown took part in what she calls the "Charleston Movement." She—alongside every member of her family—marched, picketed, and conducted sit-ins at segregated commercial and civic establishments— including swimming pools, lunch counters, and tennis courts—as well the city's newspaper to protest racist reporting. As in the Albany movement in southwest Georgia and elsewhere, it was common for whole families to protest together. "The Woods family," Brown wrote in her dissertation on the Charleston Movement, "was the most visible example of full-scale dedication to the cause. Fellow-participants dubbed Andre and Delbert, Jr. the 'most arrested' demonstrators, as they were regularly carted off to jail, released and sometimes rearrested within hours. For years the brothers competitively kept a tally of their multiple incarcerations." The protest at the *News and Courier* was particularly memorable. The group met at the Emanuel AME Church in downtown Charleston—recently made famous by the tragic, racially motivated terrorist shooting that took place there in 2016. Brown estimates a crowd of eight hundred gathered at the church in the summer of 1963 and then walked the mile-and-a-half to the newspaper plant at 134 King Street. According to the police, a "riot" ensued when NAACP officials traded words with police and a policeman pushed a demonstrator. Rocks were thrown at the police in retaliation, and the situation deteriorated into violence. The police rounded up everyone they could fit into the paddy wagon. Brown was held with other minors in the juvenile division of the city jail.[31]

These experiences informed Brown's perspective on her role as a desegregation pioneer. There was a "clear message that we had a responsibility and a role, and that this was a defining moment not only in history but in our lives. And you're expected to be out there." As for desegregating the schools, she says, "we had *years* to build up a certain righteousness about this thing, so I *knew* whatever they asked, I just knew that this was the way things [were] supposed to change." She says that her "father had always shared with us his belief that if you're going to be a civil rights leader . . . you can't ask other people's children to do things that you would not have your own children do." While her father "had a lot of respect for Martin Luther King, he also had his differences. One of them was with all the marches. . . . His children never marched. . . . If you are going to ask somebody to send their child into a situation, you had better be willing to do it yourself." She says she felt prepared to go into a white school because of her mother's intense efforts to instill "refinement" and careful "grooming" through Jack and Jill and other extracurricular experiences. "I knew I wanted to represent the race. I'm into this, I've been representing almost since birth. *What we do is represent the race.*"[32]

In many ways, Brown's experience at Rivers High School was identical to what the Baton Rouge firsts experienced. When she would walk down the hallway, students would "cringe and go to the sides, as if to say 'Ew . . . she's an untouchable'. . . . I'd be walking and the Red Sea would part. They kept this up for *three* years." Food was lobbed at her in the lunchroom. Teachers invited racist comments. She received her first D. The "boys . . . deliberately ran through the mud" to stain her clothes. At first, she felt as if she lived in "two worlds." After school, she would wait on her porch for her friends at Burke High School, the black high school, to walk by—her house was on the route most took home from the school. "I had a little boyfriend. I lived in two worlds." But then one night she went to a basketball game at Burke. "I got jeered by some black kids. Telling me, 'What are you doing here? You don't belong here. You want to be with the white kids. You want to be white.' It crushed me. I never went back to another basketball game. I really fell apart that night." It was, she says, "the girls that made me know that I was not welcome in that world." Like Marguerite Carr and some other firsts, Brown was quite fair-skinned. She may have been more vulnerable to accusations of "wanting to be white" for this reason. Some of the "fellas" kept coming to her porch to visit her after school, but after a while they, too, stopped coming by. Terrible loneliness—the great scourge of school desegregation pioneering—set in.

But there were mitigating circumstances at Rivers High School that the Baton Rouge students did not enjoy. Rivers was the school that "all the Jewish kids went to." The student body was about one-third Jewish. "The only folks who talked to me were the Jewish kids." Both boys and girls spoke to her. Not all of them, but a solid number. "The Jewish community obviously has some understanding of ostracism," Brown says, "and Rivers was a very good school for me because they *did* have that ameliorating effect." There were two girls in particular who befriended Brown. One of them, Regina Cohen, was herself marginalized, even from the Jewish students. "Regina befriended me the first year . . . and she was a total outcast. She was kind of an excitable kind of person. So her social skills were a bit off. Smart. Jewish. And she gravitated to me! She didn't have *nobody* else to talk to. And I just felt like I *wanted* her company, but I would not have chosen this child in a million years." Later, Barbara Solomon—the girl she was speaking to on the cover of the *Times*—became a real friend:

Barbara was one of the most fascinating people. In tenth grade Barbara was always in trouble. . . . She was swimming upstream. And she was part of the Jewish community, her father was the president of the bank . . . but Barbara was just her own person! And so I knew instinctively Barbara was gonna grab me and become my friend, because that was a way of tellin' people to kiss her butt. I knew that. She was rebellious. And so her immediate friendship with me—now, it grew deeper. And I grew to love Barbara, especially after high school . . . but she was an iconoclast! And so befriending me, I always thought was a political statement for her. Her parents had gone away when school opened that first day. They called her and said "Barbara, we're in New York, and we pick up the paper and you're on the front! We can't go away for a *minute*."

Brown sat with Cohen and Solomon at lunch. The two girls walked down the hall with her. Their friendship did not change the fact that she would be harassed and insulted for years by the other students, but, in Brown's words, "it tempered it differently." Just a few genuine friends made a difference.

The abuse still took a toll. Mostly, Brown did not speak to her parents about her suffering because she felt she had to always be "a champion of this cause." But one day, "probably when the guys splashed mud on me, or tripped me up in class or something . . . I remember saying, 'Mama I want to go back to Burke'—and she just said, 'Honey, you've gotta be bigger. You've gotta be bigger.' I had to hang in there." Brown—like Tessie Prevost and Freya Anderson—eventually became physically ill. "I couldn't walk from here to there without being totally out of breath. We thought I had a heart con- dition." Her parents took her to a white doctor who ran tests but could find nothing wrong. However, the doctor had a younger sister who attended Rivers High School. After talking to his sister one night at dinner, he diagnosed Brown with a nervous condition. The "nerves in my chest had just tightened up around my lungs . . . a re- sidual of the stress from three years." The difficulty breathing made Brown see her work desegregating Rivers in a new light. "That's why I hate that picture in the *New York Times*," she reflects, "because that became my *persona*. That Millicent's getting through this, and she's just *smiling* the whole time. And it was a defense mechanism! But this problem I had with breathing really brought home to me that I wasn't getting through this quite as well as I thought I was. I was taking a lot of mental abuse, a little bit of physical abuse and it was having an effect."

———

Deborah Gray was a first who was drafted to desegregate her local public school, even though she did not understand it that way at the time. The same fall that Baton Rouge and Charleston desegregated their schools, public school administrators on the Upper West Side of Manhattan carefully selected and transferred three girls from their black classes into an all-white honors program. The honors program, with classes labeled Special Progress, or SPE, was in the same building as Deborah's "mixed" school, but functioned, in effect, like a school within a school at PS 44. The SPE classes were all-white and predominantly Jewish. The other classes were almost entirely black.[33]

Deborah's mother had moved the family from their Harlem apartment to the San Juan Hill neighborhood between 61st and 64th street on the west side of Manhattan when Deborah was around five years old. The housing project they moved into was brand new, and Deborah, now Deborah Gray White, remembers being struck by how light and airy the apartment felt when she and her family moved in. The "nice little white lady" who advised Deborah's mother to move to the new housing project convinced her that the neighborhood schools would be better. From kindergarten through seventh grade, Deborah was in all-black classes. The classes were numbered one through four, with K-1 being at the top of the intellectual ability hierarchy and K-4 the bottom. It was, as Gray White describes it, "serious tracking." While she did outstanding work in grade school, Deborah "lived in the shadow of [her] brother," who was, officially, a genius. Four years older than Deborah, Otis Gray was constantly being tested for special programs and had an IQ above 160. As is so often the case with such children, he was the center of attention at home. Great things were expected of him. In high school, Otis tested into Hunter College School with a full scholarship. But he turned it down. "He didn't want to take it," Gray White remembers, and he was determined not to go. "I'm not going to go because I want to be with my friends."

Deborah Gray made up for her only slightly-less-than-genius-level abilities by going after every opportunity available to distinguish herself in school. She was in all the honor societies and student government. One year, she was selected to go to Washington, DC, with a small, elect group of students. Prior to transferring to the SPE class in eighth grade, she was outgoing and talkative in class and had many friendships in the neighborhood. Like several of the desegregation plaintiffs in the 1940s, she was also a tomboy. In her neighborhood, she remembers, "You had to exhibit confidence or get your ass kicked." After she won a street fight with a girl who had been threatening her, the tough girls left her alone and the more academically oriented girls became her friends. In seventh grade, teachers and administrators at PS 44 decided that she and two other girls—Cynthia Moore and Rosalyn Gay—should desegregate the SPE classes. Two African American male teachers and two white female teachers began the process of preparing the girls to transfer. "We met with them after school and sometimes during school, during our free period, and they talked to us about going into this class." The teachers prepared the girls both academically and mentally, and their counsel sounds much like the way parents spoke to their daughters in Kansas and elsewhere. "I can remember them saying, 'No matter what is said to you don't let it [get to you]. . . . You're smart. You can handle this.'" Deborah did not think much of it until the waning days of summer, just before the start of eighth grade, when she suddenly became apprehensive. "I got really nervous about it," she reflects, "and I can remember saying to myself, *No matter what they say, I'm just going to be on a real even keel. I'm not going to let anybody get me angry."*

At first the transition went smoothly. Deborah believed that she and the two other girls had been selected because of their proven academic merit. She committed herself to working hard and proving herself worthy of Class 8 SPE, and the white students did not immediately react with overt hostility. Then, one day at lunch, a Jewish girl named Linda expressed irritation at the fact that one of the black girls had made a perfect score on a social studies test. Deborah told her that she was jealous and "you just wish you were her." At which point Linda turned to her and said, point blank, "I don't want to be her. I don't want to be a Negro." Gray White remembers, "That cut." From that point forward, she invested herself exclusively in her friendships with Moore and Gay and tried to screen out the rest. That it was a Jewish girl who insulted her proves the simple fact that when Jews were in the majority and not ostracized, they could be just as arrogant and racist as dominant groups everywhere in the United States.

The second, more debilitating blow, came when she realized that she was still at the top of her class. "It just hit me like of ton of bricks: These kids aren't that smart.... They are only in this class 'cause they're white." Realizing that she had not, in fact, been placed in a more academically rigorous class made her doubt her own academic abilities. Deborah Gray White remembers revolving the question in her mind, constantly, of why she was there: "Well, I was chosen for some reason but not because I'm smart." She subjected herself—like the desegregation firsts in the South—to constant self-surveillance. "You start to objectify yourself, and you're standing outside yourself and looking at yourself and trying to figure out how other people are perceiving you, and you're trying to be perceived as somebody who is acceptable.... It changes your whole personality from A to Z." Her experience as a desegregation pioneer in a New York City public school was less difficult than was typical in the South on a day-to-day level—no violence, no epithets—but the effects were more insidious. In the South, firsts expected to encounter a system that was irrational and ignorant of their humanity. In New York, Deborah Gray was led to believe—because of the tutoring and special preparation—that she had achieved her place in the white SPE class. That racism rather than academic distinction lay behind the SPE classes was something that she had to figure out by herself, a fact that led her to question everything about the school and her place in it. She remembers wishing she had an adult to talk to about what she was experiencing, but no one offered a reasonable explanation.

She reacted by shutting down. Upon discerning the racial politics that lay behind the creation of the SPE classes, Gray White says, "I stopped talking. I just did." She attempted to allay the loneliness by seeking out her old friends at lunch. "I go into the lunchroom and, you have to sit with your class, and I'm on the side that has all the white kids . . . so every time I would try to skip over there, I would be found" and brought back to the SPE table. It was yet another effort at social control in the cafeteria—like Harrison Caldwell in Topeka, but in reverse.

The isolation was intensified by the fact that friends from the neighborhood reacted badly to her status as desegregation pioneer. "When I would tell my friends what class I was going into, they were like, 'Oh, you must think you're the cat's meow. You think you're better than us.'" A group of "tough girls" vowed to beat her up. Her former confidence gave way to fear: "I was scared to come out of school. . . . I was really scared." Deborah Gray enrolled in every after-school activity possible to avoid being on the streets alone when school let out. She also lost a close friend. "Gloria Fischer was my friend, and then she really turned on me." Deborah heard through the grapevine that Gloria's other friends had "convinced her that I thought I was smarter than everybody." While her black friends accused her of snobbery, the white teachers and program administrators she encountered, as she remained in predominantly white classes and went on to a predominantly white high school, often doubted her, and she found that she had to prove herself at every turn. There were a few teachers who recognized her brilliance and encouraged her to speak more in class. But other experiences proved a heavy counterweight to those few, nurturing teachers. For instance, she took a test for a summer enrichment program at the Society for Ethical Culture. When she earned an unusually high score, program administrators "had me retake the test because they could not believe that one of the black kids could . . . score what I scored." She dutifully took the test again. Like so many desegregation plaintiffs and firsts who were enlisted to do school desegregation work, she was made to feel that desegregating was not something she could consider separately from the expectations and hopes that adults (in this case, her teachers) invested in her. When she was groomed to desegregate in the seventh grade, the "experiment" as Gray White calls it, was not presented to her in a way that invited any sense of agency on her part. "I don't know that I had a choice," she says. "I never thought that I could say no. You know, unlike my brother who just said no. I didn't know that I had a choice."

———

In the early 1960s, the civil rights movement in Albany, Georgia—as in Charleston, South Carolina, and cities all over the South—took over the streets. Between 1961 and 1963, Albany was the scene of mass arrests in an uprising that was eventually dubbed the "Albany Movement." It was, perhaps, of all the local civil rights struggles of the early 1960s, the most working-class. Historian Howard Zinn called it "a populist rebellion by lower-class Negroes." In Albany, African Americans worked in the pecan factories, in the Bobs Candies factory, and as maids and groundskeepers. Just outside the city lay the famously dangerous "Terrible" Terrell County and "Bad" Baker County, where SNCC workers encountered extreme violence. Charles Sherrod, twenty-two years old, and Cordell Reagon, eighteen, arrived in Albany in 1961 to set up a voter registration office. Initially, few would speak to the young organizers. But Sherrod and Reagon quickly found their constituency: students in the local high schools and at Albany State College for Negroes. As Sherrod put it, "We drew young people from the colleges, trade schools, and high schools, and from the street." Soon there were mass meetings at Shiloh Baptist Church and Bethel AME Church. Sherrod and Reagon held workshops on the techniques of nonviolent direct action. The NAACP Youth Council, the Baptist Ministers Alliance, and SNCC formed a coalition. Local doctor William G. Anderson became president and real estate salesman Slater King (no relation to the King family of Atlanta) vice president of the new Albany Movement.[34]

At the first march, eleven people were arrested by police chief Laurie Pritchett for parading without a permit. Four hundred high school and college students marched downtown to protest, singing and chanting their way to the courthouse. Pritchett arrested all four hundred marchers. A few days later, Slater King was arrested with seventy others at a "pray-in" conducted in front of city hall. Slater King and William G. Anderson invited Martin Luther King to speak to the burgeoning movement. With Reverend Ralph Abernathy, Martin Luther King addressed a crowd of one thousand at Shiloh Baptist Church. "Don't stop now. Keep moving. Don't get weary. We will wear them down with our capacity to suffer." As the students attempted to sit in the white section at the Trailways bus station and to desegregate the city library, the public swimming pool, the bowling alley, and lunch counters, the Albany jail filled to overflowing. Chief Pritchett shipped out the extras to the Camilla jail and to the county jail in Terrell. At the Camilla jail, eighty-eight women were jammed into one cell. The few mattresses were damp, the toilet over-flowed, and the stench was unimaginable. The young activists sang their way through it. Among them were those who would become known as the Freedom Singers: Bernice Johnson (who would go on to found Sweet Honey in the Rock), Rutha Harris, Bertha Gober, and Cordell Reagon.[35]

In September 1963, a large, heterogeneous group of high school students of both genders attempted to walk into Albany High School to enroll. Pritchett met them on the steps and arrested the whole group. As Rubye Nell Singleton Stroble put it, "Child, we went to *jail*." But jail was, for virtually all of them, nothing new. Beverly Plummer (now Wilson), who would come back the following year and try again to enroll at Albany High School, had been to jail seven times.[36]

The next year, the student applicants went with Andrew Young, executive director of the Southern Christian Leadership Conference, and their mothers to the school board. Of the one hundred or so students who had tried to register at Albany High School the year before, only six came back to try a second time. All were girls. The Civil Rights Act of 1964 had been signed into law the previous July, and it was clear that school desegregation could no longer be prevented. Albany commenced the school desegregation process by admitting students to transfer in the first and twelfth grades.

The six young women who desegregated Albany High School were all civil rights veterans, and for them, school desegregation was an extension of the movement as they had been living and breathing it since 1961. They had been roughed up by the police, jailed, and had their lives threatened. Some had traveled through the rural areas surrounding Albany registering voters. Some had white SNCC organizers staying in their homes, which invited bomb threats and drive-by shootings. Mamie Ford had traveled to Saint Augustine, Florida, (an hour and thirty minutes by car from Albany) the previous June for a "wade-in" at a segregated beach and "dive-in" at the Monson Motor Lodge. When the hotel owner James Brock discovered the integrated group in the swimming pool, he poured a bottle of muriatic acid in the water. Mamie Ford (now Jones) recalls, "I couldn't breathe." A photographer caught her screaming and reaching for one of the men near her for help. Many believe that the photo, which was published in the *Washington Post* on June 19—just as Congress concluded its debate on the Civil Rights Act—helped to garner support for the bill. Jones is adamant about her agency in choosing to desegregate Albany High School. "Some people thought that we were handpicked. We were not handpicked to go to Albany High School. It was our own volition. And we were all very active in the Albany Movement. . . . It was the fabric with which our lives had been woven. . . . We raised our hands and said 'Yes, we will [go].'"[37]

Plummer Wilson similarly describes her decision to desegregate Albany High School as inseparable from her political consciousness. "Most high school seniors," she says, "wanted to graduate from where they was at; they didn't want to come over." But she did not feel that desegregating entailed a sacrifice:

> I just didn't feel like I was giving *up* something. I just felt like I had been working towards something. When you work towards something . . . for freedom, you have the right to go here, the right to stay. And I wanted to make that adjustment that I had marched for. That I went to hear Martin Luther King's speech on the March on Washington [for]. Because I was in the March [on] Washington. And this was the next step: to integrate. Why stop now? Continue.

She remembers the night before the first day of school, local lawyer and civil rights leader C. B. King (brother of Slater King) asked her if she was sure about going to Albany High. "I said, 'Well, all the work I've done was not in vain.' Because I had went to jail, I had walked many miles for voter's registration as a young teenager, so I wasn't going to stop *then*." Shirley Lawrence (now Alexander) echoes Plummer Wilson almost exactly. "I think [school desegregation] was just, for me, an automatic thing because I had gone to jail, I had marched, I had demonstrated, I had sat in. I had done everything. So, if I had not been afraid at that time, then truly I was not going to let fear set in to keep me from what I had worked for. Because I considered it something I had worked for."[38]

Rubye Nell Singleton Stroble was the only one of the six who had something to say about the fact that only six girls transferred from Monroe High School to Albany High. She looked back on it as something that was made more difficult by the low numbers of volunteers and the fact that they were all girls:

> I was *ready* to go. But of course I was [scared]. Because you've got to look at six black girls going over to a school that housed over a thousand white students that we were going to have to deal with! So it wasn't like I'm King Kong! It was six black girls! That were go- ing over there to face this monstrous task, job, whatever you want to call it . . . but *scared*—scared, no. I knew what I was going for, and that was the motivation there; just what Martin Luther King preached: equality. . . . But we didn't have not one boy, not one man. Couldn't get a man to come. Isn't that something?

The young women that went, she says, were simply strong. They came from political families and were fully committed activists. "All six that went was six strong, black young ladies. I mean, strong. Every last one of 'em. Shirley, strong. JoAnn, strong. Mamie Nell, strong. Eddie Maude, strong. Beverly and myself. All of our families played a great big part in the Albany Movement; the *family*, the en- tire family."

Beverly Plummer Wilson, Shirley Lawrence Alexander, and Mamie Ford Jones also say that the movement enveloped their families in ways that made their mothers willing to let them go to Albany High School—in contrast to the mothers in Baton Rouge. Alexander describes her mother as "old-fashioned . . . protective, she thought she could keep you from anything." But "[the movement] changed her way of thinking." Alexander's mother worked at the pecan factory and her father was a truck driver. He lost his job when she and her mother started marching, though he quickly found a new one. Once Shirley and her mother had canvassed to register voters and been to jail together, she began to trust Shirley to handle herself in any kind of situation. "My mom let us have lots of freedom when it came to the movement," she says. "We came to Atlanta for SNCC meetings . . . we would travel to D.C. with folk like [SNCC leader] Julian Bond. . . . Your parents trusted these people." Beverly Plummer's mother, who worked at the Bobs Candies factory, had also marched and gone to jail alongside her daughter, and when Beverly informed her that she was going to transfer to Albany High, her mother took it in stride. Mamie Jones says that her mother "had a sense of pride" that she had been in jail, and when it came to school desegregation, "it didn't matter whether we suffered any kind of reprisal. Many parents lost their jobs because of their students' activism, but it didn't deter our parents or us." It was a very different world from Baton Rouge.

Albany also stands apart from desegregation attempts elsewhere because there were no academic requirements, tests, or interviews. "They thought," Stroble said, "they were getting the six smartest children. No, they got the six black girls that would *go*." Alexander calls herself "a mediocre student . . . just an average student." Jones was the most academically inclined. "My academic ranking," she recalls, "was number twenty-one" out of a class of five hundred. "Prior to our graduating, they had marched according to academic rank. . . . They changed it to height."

The indignities that applied everywhere else in the South were the same at Albany High School: the relentless N-word, the students acting in animalistic ways, food thrown in the lunchroom, heels stepped on in the hallways, the attacks coming from the boys. There was one boy who put a thumbtack on Alexander's chair on and off all year. But two factors stand out. First, the meanest student was a Jewish boy. "There was a Jewish kid. He was even more vociferous [than the rest]," recalls Jones. "And his reaction, his negative interactions toward us. . . . I said, 'This is to deflect from him because they hate Jews as much as they hate me.'" But there were also people at Albany High School who spoke to the girls. By the end of the year, all six remember, there were a few students who spoke to them, though there was only one genuine friend—Virginia McKemmie, the daughter of a British doctor who worked at the military base near Albany. Like the boys who spoke to the male students in Baton Rouge, McKemmie was ostracized by the white student body. But it meant a great deal to Mamie and Shirley to have "a sincere and authentic" relationship with at least one of the students.

Because they were already seasoned activists, the girls were used to the harassment. They had been called every epithet imaginable when they marched through Albany. They were so experienced by the time they enrolled that they were able to understand Albany High School in its larger context. Jones puts it this way:

I think we all came there bigger than that high school, any of those people there. I think we came there with a sense of self-affirmation. And we brought that from our families [and] from the movement. Because we raised our hands and said "We will go". . . . My knowing why I was there and what I was there to accomplish and achieve— that was intact with me. And I left there with that intact. If anything I was strengthened by that. I'm not saying that was everyone's experience. But for me, what I brought there is what sustained me while I was there.

Alexander sums up her dedication to school desegregation similarly:

> I anticipated that I would go through a lot. I wasn't going to fool myself about that. But I was ready for even that. I was ready for whatever. Because when you've gone that far, there's no turning back. You can't turn back. . . . You say this is what you believe in, so, are you gonna run? I don't think any of us thought about running. We thought about enduring it until the end no matter what.

Epilogue

In the early 1960s, Carol Anderson—who desegregated Claymont High School with her sister Joan Anderson in 1952—was living in Chicago, where she was a social worker and member of the Oak Park and River Forest Symphony Orchestra. The small, amateur orchestra was directed by Milton Preves, conductor of the Chicago Symphony Orchestra. In January 1963, Preves, in a deliberate attempt to desegregate the Oak Park and River Forest Symphony, recruited Carol Anderson to play a concert with the all-white orchestra. After Anderson showed up for the first rehearsal, someone contacted the symphony board to complain, and the following week a board member by the name of Mrs. Palmer appeared at rehearsal and dramatically ejected Anderson. A storm of controversy quickly enveloped the small orchestra, with the *Chicago Tribune* and the black papers championing Anderson and castigating Palmer. Twenty-five members of the orchestra threatened to quit if Anderson was not reinstated, as did conductor Preves. Anderson quickly found herself a sensation, with her story appearing in the national news. Palmer was forced to invite Anderson back to the symphony when the Oak Park community sided with Preves and the other musicians, and when local religious leaders called for "racial tolerance." Palmer's olive branch extended, the press breathlessly awaited Anderson's decision.[1]

Anderson remembers being pressured on all sides, especially by her boyfriend at the time, who espoused a Black Power philosophy and urged her to boycott the orchestra as a way, in her words, "to punish" white racism. "I went to some of those meetings," she recalls, "and I'm going, well this doesn't sound right. . . . Why should everything be all black and all white? We don't live in this kind of world, we don't live in this kind of country." She decided—despite having missed practice—to play. Seven hundred and fifty people showed up to hear the concert. When asked by the *Chicago Defender* "if the pressures surrounding her appearance had upset her musically, she said, 'No. When I'm playing, I concentrate only on the music.'" Her ability to focus and compartmentalize under this kind of scrutiny, she believes, was learned on the job at Claymont. "I didn't get swayed by anybody, and I thought I handled it as well as I did Claymont . . . with dignity and poise. And I didn't get angry."[2]

She did, however, lose her boyfriend. But she found solace in the warm response of the public. "I started getting phone calls from schoolteachers, and they would say, 'the most amazing thing happened: my kids wrote about you for current events, and they want to be like you, and they said, 'She was a *lady*, she didn't scream and yell at them, she didn't use bad language, and look what happened to her! She was so nice to the bad, nasty people.'" Anderson had become a figure of racial reconciliation at a time when, she believes, the country needed it: "Right in the middle of Black Power." Anderson's rejection of Black Power was not representative. Many former desegregation firsts in the South embraced black nationalist and Black Power movements in the late 1960s. But Anderson's trajectory does presage that of other firsts in one important way: her desegregation experience at Claymont effectively set her up for more desegregation work later in life.

Firsts were often recruited to desegregate colleges, universities, and eventually the professions. In places like Baton Rouge—where everyone knew the names of those who had desegregated the high schools—elected officials reached out to firsts when they sought to desegregate universities, public school teaching faculty, and state offices. While most did not follow through with desegregating universities, many did continue the arduous work they had begun as school desegregation firsts later in life because they already knew how to do it. Desegregation, as it turns out, was not simply an experience that one survived or did not survive—a one-time test. It was, in many ways, like learning a language or how to play an instrument: a skill best acquired through early exposure and constant practice.

In the immediate aftermath, however, most firsts in the Deep South were in no mood to do any more school desegregation work. They were angry and emotionally exhausted. Many were depressed and held negative opinions of their desegregation experiences. Upon graduating from Baton Rouge High School in 1964, Elaine Chustz Green says, "I knew I could not look at another white person. That's why I went to Spelman," one of the historically black colleges and universities, or HBCUs. Betta Bowman, too, ended up at an HBCU. Lindy Boggs—wife of US House majority whip Hale Boggs and eventual US representative herself—personally recruited Bowman to desegregate Louisiana State University (LSU). But Bowman— like other black firsts at LSU—left after a year and transferred to Southern University. The vast majority of desegregation firsts went to HBCUs. Looking back, Gayle Jones says that after graduation in 1964, "I felt that it was probably a wasted year of my life. To create all of this anger in me toward another race of people." She had begun, she says, "to hate as much as they hated me." For college, she says passionately "I needed to be around my people." Jones also went to Southern University.

At Spelman, Chustz Green became part of the student movement in Atlanta, joining the restaurant sit-ins and spending time with H. Rap Brown, an organizer for SNCC who was originally from Baton Rouge—and who regularly had FBI agents tailing him, Chustz Green remembers. On summer breaks, she and H. Rap

Brown would canvass the poorer sections of Baton Rouge to help people register to vote. Millicent Brown—who desegregated Rivers High School in Charleston—went through a major transformation when she was in college in Boston. "The Black Power movement has taken over," she says of those years, "and it's just a heightened consciousness of what struggle is all about . . . and my politics are getting stronger and stronger, and I get very resentful of all that integration bullshit. And I'm just not feelin' it." She remembers a time when she met her parents at the airport, "and I had cut my hair and had an Afro. And Daddy walked by me and wouldn't talk to me." They had a difficult relationship for a few years. "My father and I [had] a couple of years where it's really kind of tough. Because I told him, 'Why do you want to use me as a guinea pig?'" Millicent Brown and Gayle Jones's anger at the toll of their desegregation work anticipated a black feminist perspective that would name and rebel against the disproportionate amount of labor black women were expected to perform in creating interracial understanding. The landmark black feminist anthology, originally published in 1981, is called *This Bridge Called My Back*.[3]

Despite the ongoing toll of desegregation work, however, virtually all school desegregation firsts held a positive perspective on the work they had done later in life. They believe that desegregation was worth the fight. They also have had successful careers, often in newly desegregated schools and offices. Plaintiffs and firsts went on to be lawyers, educators, school administrators, architects, college professors, and well-known political activists. Shirley Lawrence Alexander became a vice president at Sun Trust Bank. Marguerite Carr Stokes was one of a handful of women who graduated from Howard Law School in the 1950s, and she became an official in the Washington, DC, office of Mayor Marion Barry. Both Anderson sisters became music instructors. Doris Raye Jennings Brewer was a librarian and Doris Faye Jennings Alston a high school English teacher. Velma Jean Hunter Jackson is a dentist. Millicent Brown and Deborah

Gray White are both groundbreaking history professors. Marion Greenup is vice president for administration at the Simons Foundation, a science research institute in New York. More than a few desegregation firsts went on to become special education teachers and speech pathologists. Elaine Boyle Patin was a lawyer in the justice department in Baton Rouge, and Merrill Patin is a successful entrepreneur who runs his own pharmaceutical company. The children of firsts, moreover, often populated "mixed" schools to the extent such schools existed in the seventies and eighties. Their children went to city magnet schools, tested into gifted and talented programs, and joined small minorities of African Americans attending predominantly white schools. Many parents found themselves having to respond to all-too-familiar feelings that their children were having in these environments.[4]

As firsts in the professions, many of the school desegregation firsts also nurtured the careers of black women (and men) who came after them—mentoring them, giving them support, and acting as role models. The effect of this advocacy—proffered by firsts all over the nation—is incalculable. Anita Hill recalls how important Ada Lois Sipuel Fisher—who was by then on the Oklahoma University Board of Regents—was to her career when she became the first African American to hold a tenure-track job at the College of Law:

> As I settled into my role there, I drew on her enthusiasm. At every step she supported me, from the day I was hired, through tenure, and finally when I needed it most, when my job was threatened after I testified in 1991 at the Senate Confirmation Hearing for Judge Clarence Thomas. Her support was vocal, in both private conversations and public settings. At a university function in Norman, days after my testimony, she greeted me in her familiar enthusiastic manner. "Anita, you are my kind of woman." I knew then that I could weather the trials that lay ahead, because Ada Lois Sipuel Fisher told me I could . . . Ada Lois Sipuel Fisher was my

role-model for strength and committed leadership and my inspiration to remain hopeful. And she still is.[5]

Desegregation plaintiffs and firsts—with their many stories of prevailing and bringing change to their professions—believe their actions as school desegregation pioneers transformed the arc of American history for the better. However, many legal scholars, historians, and ordinary African Americans have grown frustrated, suspicious, and critical of the hagiography of the *Brown* ruling. Perhaps the most influential critic has been Derrick Bell, who published *Silent Covenants: Brown v. Board of Education and the Unfulfilled Hopes for Racial Reform*—a book that summarized his thinking on the subject over many years—on the fiftieth anniversary of *Brown* in 2004. In it, Bell lamented how little *Brown* had delivered, how the decision kicked off massive resistance on a scale that all but guaranteed failure, and how exhausting and demoralizing busing children to achieve racial balance in urban schools was in the 1970s. He also bemoaned how busing alienated parents who lived far away from these schools, the damage that tracking has had on black student self-perception, and the insults and hostility that black students endured in places where small groups of black students desegregated schools. Like Heman Sweatt and other anti-desegregation and pro-equalization activists going back to the 1940s, Bell invoked history to argue that *Brown* was too optimistic about disassembling intransigent racism and that it has obscured racial hatred since it was passed, massive resistance to it notwithstanding. "History as well as current events," he wrote, "call for realism in our racial dealings. Traditional statements of freedom and justice for all, the usual fare on celebratory occasions, serve to mask continuing manifestations of inequality that beset and divide people along lines of color and class." A chapter of his book is devoted to a hypothetical Supreme Court decision in which *Brown* mandated equalization instead of desegregation—a conservative decision based on precedent and that, Bell believes, would have produced better outcomes. The book both reflected and reinforced the dark perceptions about the school desegregation mandate at the turn of the twenty-first century. Nonetheless, school desegregation plaintiffs and firsts—while acknowledging this shift in thinking—see the Supreme Court decision and their role in bringing it to fruition and carrying it out as a great achievement. That American society looks radically different today than it did in the forties and fifties because of what they did.

Most of the men feel as positive as the women desegregation firsts. Charles Plummer, Beverly Plummer Wilson's younger brother, was among a wave of students who helped carry out school-wide desegregation in Albany the year after Beverly Plummer desegregated Albany High. He says of his experience desegregating a middle school, "I'm glad I went through what I went through because it made me stronger. You couldn't be shut down, because if you did, they would treat you different. But if you open up—if you could talk back and stand up, you got more respect. You learn how to be a people person. So that helped me. . . . I can interact with all kinds of people." Merrill Patin says, "I felt a sense that [desegregation] put a different view in those students at Glen Oaks, for their appreciation of a black man . . . if nothing else, I think I did that." He concludes, laughingly, "Not only were we athletic, we do know how to read, too." Heman Sweatt was among the few dissenters. At an anniversary celebration, he told a reporter that he only came to the event to make it clear he was unhappy with current developments. "I'm bothered about the low level of support blacks are giving their organizations," he said. "Maybe a little integration is a dangerous thing." James Meredith—who famously desegregated the University of Mississippi in 1962 and successfully graduated in three years—also diminished his accomplishment when he reflected on it in his autobiography. He wrote that the goal "to 'integrate' the university . . . [was] a minor and relatively timid objective." He did not see his school desegregation work as particularly valuable and believed his other forms of activism, such as his work on voter registration, were more worthwhile.[6]

For the majority of female grade school and high school desegregation pioneers, the anger and depression, over time, was supplanted by compassion, a sense of connection with all kinds of people, and a conviction that what they accomplished by attending those white schools was necessary. Sandy Couch (formerly Bernice Byrd) desegregated Claymont High School with Carol Anderson. She says of her experience there, "It made me more accepting of others, and when I say others I mean black, white, Chinese, whatever." Rita Gidroz White of Istrouma High School in Baton Rouge, says, "I think it made me a better person. And a more caring person for others . . . especially where children are concerned."

Elaine Chustz Green describes a striking degree of empathy for students. After graduating from Spelman, she moved to Detroit where she taught English in the public school system, rising through the ranks to eventually became a school principal. "That was the year after the 1967 riots in Detroit," she says. "White flight. Burned-down neighborhoods. The school was in absolute turmoil. I felt we should get combat pay. Kids were bigger than me." What she enjoyed about that time was that the students protested the lack of courses on black history and literature, so she started teaching them. "They inspired me to do it. I loved having that invitation." But her embrace of what she calls "black studies" and black nationalism as an ongoing political perspective did not diminish her profound empathy for other marginalized groups—extending even to the few remaining white students in the Detroit public schools—nor her belief in school desegregation. She explains:

> We lost white kids every year. So when it got to the point where I only had one or two white kids in the classroom, I felt such empathy. . . . I just wanted to put my arms around 'em and hug 'em. You

know, you're the only one in there, and you don't have any friends, nobody to swap notes with . . . and sometimes I would send those one or two kids to the library and just talk to my black students, one black person to another, about those two white kids . . . [whom] they needed to treat like people. Like human beings . . . they had never thought about it. . . . I told them what I went through at Baton Rouge High—they thought I was a hundred years old to have participated in that.

Given how Chustz Green was treated by the white students at Baton Rouge High, and the racist behavior of Detroit parents who were contemporaneously abandoning desegregated city schools, her empathy for white students is astonishing. But it is also characteristic of the enlarged and humane perspective that almost all desegregation firsts brought to their later experiences. Empathy—for vulnerable children especially—was, for some, both part of the healing process and evidence of an atypically expansive social and racial imagination.

Their compassion, however, does not interfere with a full understanding of the disastrous effects of post-1954 white flight from inner city schools, the failure to implement the spirit and letter of *Brown v. Board*, and contemporary resegregation of the public schools. The year 1988 is generally believed by scholars to be the high point of school desegregation, when close to half of all African American children attended a majority white school. Since then, the number of schools deemed high poverty and predominantly black has doubled. And while scholars of education have noted that integrated schools reduce the racial achievement gap and that on average students of all races do better in socioeconomically and racially diverse schools, white parents continue to press the legal system to resegregate their children. In 1974, the Supreme Court ruled in *Milliken v. Bradley* that integration could not take place across district lines, which contributed to the kind of devastation that Chustz Green had witnessed in the Detroit schools. The Supreme Court further retrenched the *Brown* decision in 2007 when the Roberts court ruled, in *Parents Involved in Community Schools v. Seattle School District No.1*, that "explicit racial classifications" could not be used to place students in specific schools. Today, many white neighborhoods are trying to secede from larger districts—especially in the Deep South—that are integrated, solely to create separate, homogenous school districts.[7]

This situation, as Millicent Brown explains, has contributed to bitterness among African American parents. "Today," she says, "nobody's particularly happy with what happened after *Brown*. The black community *damned* sure is not happy." Some in her community in South Carolina direct their anger at her because she is a prominent desegregation pioneer. "They're *saying* it: 'If ya'll had just kept your little black butts where you were . . . we wouldn't have the high drop-out rates, because the black teachers loved us . . . and they see all the problems that exist today, and their . . . explanation is 'we should never had desegregated.'" Millicent Brown responds to this challenge by saying, "I *feel* that frustration . . . but intellectually I know that keeping segregated schools was not the answer. It's the failure to really act on *Brown*" that is the problem. "America," she says, "could not be allowed to have apartheid. And somebody had to knock it and chip at it." She also says that the critiques of the post-*Brown* era are "ahistorical." "The rural experience," she says, "needs to be remembered with more accuracy." There were "too many [rural] schools that were not manned with good teachers, good black teachers . . . and so desegregation was very important for black kids who were stuck in these inferior kinds of spaces."

Elaine Chustz Green—who witnessed segregated schools on both sides of the racial divide—says simply, "Segregated schools. They are not good for kids." Schools that are segregated, she maintains, will never be equal. "Not going to happen." In Detroit, she says, "those all-black schools were so severely crippled: socially, culturally.

Some of 'em had never been outside an eight-block radius of where they lived. They probably thought that blacks were the majority in the United States because they were a majority everywhere they went." Chustz Green also sees the financial vulnerability of segregated black schools as inevitable. People who think desegregation was a mistake "didn't live under it. . . . They didn't live through it. When we lived under segregation, and the staff and students were all black, there were some advantages to that . . . but the educational resources were not sufficient. Wasn't good enough. Not to mention, the upkeep of the school building." Chustz Green had attended McKinley High School in the early 1960s before transferring to Baton Rouge High. It was a brand-new school when she went there, built to help stave off desegregation litigation. Still, she could already see the building deteriorating. "If something broke at McKinley, it stayed broke. We'd go to Baton Rouge High, if a hinge fell off they were fixing it the next day. If a window got broken, they were fixing it the next day." This was also true in Detroit. When the white students were no longer in the building, she says, the city ceased to maintain it. One of the windows broke in her classroom, and eventually she had to resort to putting an old desk over it to keep the wind and snow from blowing in.

While desegregation plaintiffs and firsts admit to the complexity of tackling the equalization versus desegregation debate, and to the broken promises of *Brown*, most are unequivocal about the larger effects that *Brown* had on the body politic. Beverly Plummer Wilson reflects, "Going to Albany High made a big difference; it had a whole big impact on the rest of the blacks and the whites. Because they had to get used to different children of a different race [and] one day they're going to have to leave school and go into a work zone and then that's when you met all kind of people. . . . People didn't know how big this thing was going to be." What previously could not be imagined had become an everyday reality. Shirley Lawrence

Alexander, also of Albany High, maintains, "I'm still excited about the fact that I did it. I'm always excited about that. I don't regret anything about going to Albany High. Not a thing. If I had to do it all over again, I'd do it that same way."

Deborah Gray White sees her school desegregation work through a political lens:

> I see that what I did and what friends of mine did and those of my generation and the so-called "only ones in the room," the first[s], that we made it possible for Barack Obama to be president.... [Today] some of these young black [students], they want to be individuals and they don't want to have to represent the group.... I can empathize with that and I don't blame them for wanting to do that. Because who the hell wants to carry the race around with you on your shoulders every single place you go? But because my generation did it and because I did it, you are able to be whoever it is you want to be. And there are some times when I just want to say "And don't you damn forget—don't you dare forget it." And when Obama says that he stands on the shoulders of others, he doesn't just stand on [the shoulders] of Martin Luther King.... He is standing on the shoulders of ordinary people like me and others who made it okay, who opened the workplace, who opened academe.... You're standing on our shoulders.

Whether speaking of social, professional, or political transformation, desegregation firsts see their actions as a significant piece of a larger whole, an arduous step forward that had vast consequences that continue to add depth, breadth, and ultimately strength to the social body of the United States. It is important that we not forget their sacrifices—the striving for a goal few could initially imagine, the hard work, the social dexterity, the loneliness—and that we acknowledge what was accomplished and by whom. To quote historian Blanche Wiesen Cook, "history tends to bury what it seeks to reject."[8] For too long the school desegregation work of young women and girls has been invisible—buried so that other, mostly male heroes could emerge. *Brown* has retained its place as a defining decision in US history, but it is time to incorporate the stories of girls and young women who were integral to the school desegregation process, beginning with the lawsuits and extending through the desegregation pioneers of the 1960s. *Brown v. Board of Education* would not have happened without their commitment and skills. When girls and young women crossed over the threshold into previously all-white schools, the meaning and purpose of those public institutions was transformed, and racial coexistence within them appeared, suddenly, neither shocking nor radical—something that was both achievable and, in the twenty-first century, a vital measure of American Democracy.

Acknowledgments

Cold-calling people to ask for interviews was the most difficult aspect of this book project. It took me hours, sometimes days and weeks, to work up the nerve to do it. However, the experience of interviewing those who answered my calls will always be that for which I am most grateful. I want to begin these acknowledgments at the moment when I got my best cold call response, the moment when this book achieved liftoff: when I called Marguerite Carr Stokes in 2008. I had just visited the District of Columbia Office of Public Records and found her marriage certificate. She was now Marguerite Carr Stokes and still lived in DC. I called, introduced myself, and said, "I see that you filed a lawsuit in 1947. Would you be willing to speak to me about it?" Marguerite Carr Stokes: "What took you so long?"

Thus began the first of many astonishing interviews with school desegregation plaintiffs and firsts. I was educated by some of the most courageous leaders then and now alive about what it meant to be on the front lines of the war that was school desegregation. It has been a privilege and an honor.

A Girl Stands at the Door took a decade to research and write. A year at the Charles Warren Center for Studies in American History at Harvard University in 2008–2009 gave me time to flesh out what was, when I arrived, merely an idea. Evelyn Brooks Higginbotham and Kenneth Mack put together a fascinating seminar on the civil rights movement that year. Evelyn Brooks Higginbotham's early excitement about the project helped me, from that time forward, whenever I went through difficult times. Kenneth Mack has been an unstinting ally over the years; he read an early and then a late-stage version of the manuscript and is responsible for some key changes that helped me to better frame the project. I benefited enormously from conversations at the Warren Center with Zoe Burkholder, Matthew Countryman, Kevin Mumford, and Thomas Guglielmo. A special thank you to Arthur Patton-Hock who so kindly put up with all my schedule changes and many logistical challenges.

Another critical year of research was funded with a grant from the Alphonse Fletcher Sr. fellowship program from the W. E. B. Du Bois Institute at Harvard University. I am grateful for conversations with Henry Louis Gates and other African American scholar-luminaries whom I met that year. When the book was in its final stages, I managed to finish it because of a grant from the American Academy of Learned Societies. The comments that arrived from ACLS reviewers were especially thoughtful and encouraged me to look beyond the twentieth-century United States to think about girls and cultural diplomacy—something I am still thinking about.

I am indebted to more archivists than I can possibly fit here, but several stand out. Christopher Harter at the Amistad Research Center in New Orleans fielded a constant stream of inquiries—from information on the McDonough Three, to questions about Amistad holdings, to how to get in touch with an actual human being at NOLA.com. He answered them all. Thank you. Theresa Noble at the Kansas State Historical Society helped me with the many different collections I worked with and more. Kathe Hambrick at the River Road African American Museum in Louisiana helped me to locate several desegregation firsts who added important small-town and rural voices to the last chapter of the book. Turry Flucker, formerly of the Louisiana State Museum, generously showed me letters sent to the desegregation firsts in New Orleans—fragile and moldy paper that required very careful handling and a full afternoon of his time. I am particularly thankful, as well, to Lisa Oppenheimer, who answered my letter and agreed to meet me in New York to go through her mother's papers, listed as the Esther Brown Papers.

I began a new job at Rutgers University when I was a few years into this project. I was thrilled to land at a place where the study of women's and gender history is at the center of the department. I am especially grateful for Deborah Gray White's comments as she heard about the many, changing iterations of this project. I was surprised when she agreed to let me interview her, and inspired by her candor.

Moving to a large, public institution was also overwhelming, and two people understood this implicitly. I am thankful for Jennifer Jones and Ann Fabian for making me feel welcome. Ann Fabian also read an article-length version of what is now this book and gave me incisive comments. At Rutgers, I have also benefited from the intellectual example and analyses of gender and race in conversation with Marisa Fuentes, Leah DeVun, and Seth Koven. Camilla Townsend generously shared a paper she had written on Native-Euro contact, and met with me for a long, edifying discussion about girls as racial intermediaries in the colonial era.

Nancy Cott has been a steadfast reader, letter writer, interlocutor, and friend—available at all hours to talk to me about my latest round of edits or obstacles in my path. Her support for this book has been unwavering and invaluable.

I was lucky to be able to present work at the US Women and Gender History Writing Group, organized by Lara Vapnek, Kristin Celello, and Vanessa May. The support of the many women in the room that day meant a great deal to me. Linda Gordon offered wonderful comments that helped me to locate where to put my emphasis in explaining my findings. Martha Hodes invited me to present at a seminar at NYU and afterward sent me a long email with suggestions. LaKisha Michelle Simmons generously agreed to read portions of the manuscript and provided excellent comments.

Thank you to Jennifer Mittelstadt for putting me in touch with her editor, Brian Distelberg, at Basic Books. Brian immediately understood what was important about this project. I will always be grateful to him for the way in which he championed the book and encouraged me to stick to what it was really about: the unheralded accomplishments of black young women and girls. Publishing with Basic involved a steep learning curve—writing for a broad audience was new to me—but it is absolutely what was best for this project and these historical actors. Editors Melissa Veronesi and Elizabeth Dana at Basic have been wonderful to work with, and I thank them both. I could not have completed a project of this scope without all kinds of assistance, research and otherwise. Brennan Sutter, Ana Saldamando, Galina Reznick, Tia Vice, Dana Glaser, Gretchen Brinson, Alicia Torres, and last but never least, Bernard Devlin have been indispensible assistants and researchers.

The diversion of good friends, who helped me to laugh and productively step away from the manuscript, has sustained me. Thank you to Deborah Reiders, Trip McCrossin, Liz McMahon, Anne Bunn, Sam Thompson, Lee Solomon, Jim Boyden, Alisa Plant, Larry Powell, Michele Orecklin, Melissa Marks, and Carolyn Happy.

From the beginning to the end of this project, I have shared every detail with two brilliant scholars and friends. Laura Rosanne Adderley was an early confidant and enthusiast who nurtured *A Girl Stands at the Door* from the ground up. Whenever I needed perspective, she always lent me her ear and her deep expertise in African Diaspora and African American history. Sharing this work with her has been a joy beyond measure. Writer Kio Stark read every page of this book, many more than once. Her sage, experienced advice kept me from making some blunders and sharpened and clarified the writing. Our discussions about the process of writing has enriched our friendship, and I am deeply appreciative of her unconditional support.

My family has been so patient and understanding when the book required both travel and long hours at my desk. Jonah and Cady—you are the delight of my life, and I thank you profoundly for saying, when I had to be away, "It's OK Mom, you are writing a book. We get it." They took their cues from their father, Stephen Sollins, who selflessly supported this book for longer than I care to quantify. I know that he put aside some of his own projects so I could finish this one—a sacrifice that he has, with the utmost grace, never mentioned. I hope to be able to repay him for his devotion in the years to come.

Archives and Collections

Albany Civil Rights Institute, Albany, GA.

Albany High School yearbook. Nancy Presley Papers. Private collection.

Anderson, Meryl. Papers. Private collection. Courtesy of Joan Anderson.

Bizzell Memorial Library. University of Oklahoma.

Bowman, Betta Jean. Papers. Private collection.

Brown, Esther. Papers. Private collection.

Brown Foundation for Educational Equity, Excellence, and Research, Topeka.

Brown, J. Arthur. Papers. Avery Research Center, Charleston.

Brown, Millicent E., Papers. Avery Research Center, Charleston.

Cagle, Bubbah. Papers. Private collection.

Consolidated Parent Group, Inc. Papers. Moorland Spingarn Research Center, Manuscript Division. Howard University.

DC Board of Education. Papers. Moorland Spingarn Research Center, Manuscript Division. Howard University.

Dobie, Armistead Mason. Papers. Arthur J. Morris Law Library, Special Collections. University of Virginia.

Dolph Briscoe Center for American History. University of Texas, Austin.

Fisher, Bruce. Papers. Private Collection.

Galarza, Ernesto. Papers. Cecil H. Green Library. Stanford University.

Greenup, Marion. Papers. Private collection.

Harry S. Truman Presidential Library, Independence, MO.

Johnson County Museum, Overland Park, KS.

Kansas Supreme Court. Court Documents. Microfilm. Kansas Historical Society, Topeka.

Kluger, Richard. Papers. Sterling Memorial Library. Yale University.

Louisiana State Museum, New Orleans.

Murray, Pauli. Papers. Schlesinger Library. Radcliffe Institute for Advanced Study. Harvard University.

National Association for the Advancement of Colored People (NAACP) records. Library of Congress.

"1964 Trail Blazers Memory Book." Velma Jean Hunter Jackson Papers. Private collection.

Noches, Nancy Todd. Papers. Private collection.

Orleans Parish School Board. Papers. Earl K. Long Library. University of New Orleans.

River Road African American Museum, Donaldsonville, LA.

Schomburg Center for Research in Black Culture. New York Public Library.

Smilack, Virginia. Papers. Private collection.

Speer, Hugh. Papers. Kansas Historical Society (courtesy of Marcia Snook), Topeka.

Todd, Lucinda. Papers. Kansas Historical Society, Topeka.

Tureaud, A. P., Papers. Amistad Research Center, New Orleans.

US District Court for the Western District records. National Archives, Fort Worth, TX.

Wieder, Alan. Papers. Amistad Research Center, New Orleans.

Will W. Alexander Library, Dillard University, New Orleans.

Notes

Introduction

1. Marguerite Carr Stokes, interview by Rachel Devlin, Washington, DC, October 23, 2008. The correct spelling is "Margurite." However, in her lawsuit, in newspaper accounts, and throughout the historical record of her case, *Carr v Corning*, her name is spelled "Marguerite." For the sake of consistency, the standard spelling, "Marguerite" is used throughout the book, with the permission of Mrs. Carr Stokes.

2. Cases filed in the late 1940s include *Carr v. Corning*, 1947, "Schools, District of Columbia, *Carr v. Board of Education*," folder 6, box B136; *Galarza v. School Board*, 1947, "Schools, District of Columbia, Galarza, Karla, 1947–1848," folder 7, box B136; *Jennings v. Board of Trustees*, 1947, "Hearne, Jennings v. Board of Trustees, 1947–1949*," folder 5, box B147; *Vivian Brown v. Board of Trustees*, 1947, "La Grange, *Brown v. Board of Trustees, 1947-1949*," folder 6, box B147, NAACP Records, Manuscript Division, Library of Congress, Washington, DC; *Webb v. School District #90*, 1948, Records of the Kansas State Supreme Court, Kansas State Historical Society, Topeka, Kansas; *Carter v. School Board of Arlington County*, 1949, "*Carter v. School Board*, Records, Briefs, Opinions, Correspondence," box 7, Armistead Mason Dobie Papers, University of Virginia Law School, Charlottesville, Virginia; John E. Rousseau Jr., "No Negro Hi. School: Child's Parents Sue St. Charles Parish," *Houston Informer and Texas Freeman*, September 13, 1947, 16; *Judine Bishop v. Sharpe*, 1948, and *Barbara Jean Arnold v. Sharpe*, 1948, folder 52, box 19-2, Consolidated Parent Group records, Moorland-Spingarn Research Center, Howard University, Washington, DC; "Negroes Plan Court Fight to End Segregation in East Side Schools," *St. Louis Dispatch*, February 8, 1949, 7.

3. Karen Anderson, *Little Rock: Race and Resistance at Central High* (Princeton, NJ: Princeton University Press, 2010), chap. 3; Melba Pattillo Beals,

Warriors Don't Cry: A Searing Memoir of the Battle to Integrate Little Rock's Central High (New York: Washington Square Press, 1995); Liva Baker, *The Second Battle of New Orleans: The Hundred-Year Struggle to Integrate the Schools* (New York: HarperCollins, 1996); Millicent Brown papers, folder 3, box 5, Avery Research Center, Charleston, South Carolina; Lowcountry Digital History Initiative, "Somebody Had to Do It: First Children in School Desegregation, http://ldhi.library.cofc.edu/exhibits/show/somebody_had_to_do_it/project _overview; Millicent Brown, interview by Rachel Devlin, Orangeburg, South Carolina, July 2009; *Davis v. E. Baton Rouge*, correspondence, 1962–1963, folder 24, box 29, A. P. Tureaud Papers, Amistad Research Center, Tulane University; Mary Royal Jenkins, *Open Dem Cells: A Pictorial History of the Albany Movement* (Albany, GA: Brentwood Academic Press, 2000), 69.

4. Recruiting and working with girls in desegregation suits involved what Rebecca de Schweinitz, in her study of NAACP Youth Councils, called a "dialectical relationship" between youth and adults. That is, parents and NAACP officials both shepherded and responded to the political concerns and abilities of youth; Rebecca de Schweinitz, *If We Could Change the World: Young People and America's Long Struggle for Racial Equality* (Chapel Hill: University of North Carolina Press, 2009), 189. For an analysis of the political abilities and actions of children and youth, see Robert Coles, *Children of Crisis* (Boston: Back Bay Books, 2003); Anderson, *Little Rock*. For a negative assessment of youth as political actors, see Hannah Arendt, "Reflections on Little Rock," *Dissent* 6, no. 1 (1959): 45–56. For a critique of Arendt and a nuanced consideration of the role of sacrifice in the black freedom movement, see Danielle S. Allen, *Talking to Strangers: Anxieties of Citizenship Since* Brown v. Board of Education (Chicago: Chicago University Press, 2006), chap. 8. In general girls joined the civil rights movement at relatively young ages. See Sheyann Webb and Rachel West Nelson, *Selma, Lord, Selma: Girlhood Memories of the Civil Rights Days* (Tuscaloosa: University of Alabama Press, 1997), 3, 11; Ellen Levine, *Freedom's Children: Young Civil Rights Activists Tell Their Own Stories* (New York: Puffin Books, 1993). On women and young women as plaintiffs in transportation cases, see Barbara Young Welke, *Recasting American Liberty: Gender, Race, Law, and the Railroad Revolution, 1865–1920* (Cambridge: Cambridge University Press, 2001).

5. Richard Kluger, *Simple Justice: The History of* Brown v. Board of Education *and Black America's Struggle for Equality* (New York: Vintage, 2004); Mark V. Tushnet, *The NAACP's Legal Strategy Against Segregated Education, 1925–1950* (Chapel Hill: University of North Carolina Press, 1987); Michael J. Klarman, *From Jim Crow to Civil Rights: The Supreme Court and the Struggle for Racial Equality* (New York: Oxford University Press, 2004), 165;

James T. Patterson, *Brown v. Board of Education: A Civil Rights Milestone and Its Troubled Legacy* (New York: Oxford University Press, 2001), 7; Jack Greenberg, *Crusaders in the Courts: Legal Battles in the Civil Rights Movement* (New York: Twelve Tables Press, 2004); Adam Fairclough, *Race and Democracy: The Civil Rights Struggle in Louisiana, 1915–1972* (Athens: University of Georgia Press, 1995); Aldon D. Morris, *The Origins of the Civil Rights Movement: Black Communities Organizing for Change* (New York: Free Press, 1984). For Kluger's influence, see "'With an Even Hand,' *Brown v. Board* at Fifty," Library of Congress Exhibition, www.loc.gov/exhibits/brown; "Courage: The Vision to End Segregation, the Guts to Fight for It," Schomburg Center for Research in Black Culture (2009–2014). For more recent reevaluations of *Brown* see "Round Table: *Brown v. Board of Education*, Fifty Years After," *Journal of American History* 91, no. 1 (2004); Charles Ogletree, *All Deliberate Speed: On the First Half-Century of* Brown v. Board of Education (New York: W. W. Norton, 2004); Mary L. Dudziak, *Cold War Civil Rights: Race and the Image of American Democracy* (Princeton, NJ: Princeton University Press, 2000); Patricia Sullivan, *Lift Every Voice: The NAACP and the Making of the Civil Rights Movement* (New York: New Press, 2009), chap. 9.

6. Thurgood Marshall, interview by Hugh Speer, 1968. Hugh Speer Papers, Kansas State Historical Society, hereinafter referred to as KSHS (unaccessioned collection, quoted with special permission from Marcia Snook).

7. "Parents Picket West Dallas School: Apply for NAACP Charter," *Kansas City Call*, September 24, 1948; "Fight for Equal Schools in Victoria Put in Lawyers' Hands Over Opposition," *Richmond Afro-American*, April 17, 1948, 5. On equalization suits, see the records of the NAACP: "Schools: Arizona, Phoenix," 1947–1948, box B135; *Sims v. Board of Public Instruction of Hillsborough County*, folder 10, box B136; *Richardson v. Board of Public Instruction of Palm Beach County*, folder 9, box B136; *Storey v. Christian County Board of Education*, "Paducah, Kentucky, 1946-1950," box B143; *W. B. Lawson v. Corpus Christi Independent School District*, folder 1, box B147; *Higgins v. Goodman* and *Butler v. Wilemon*, folder 2, box B147; *Woods v. O. H. Stowe*, folder 3, box B147; *Branch v. School Board of Greenville County*, folder 9, box B147.

8. Sullivan, *Lift Every Voice*, p. xvi and Introduction. On Charles Houston, see Genna Rae McNeil, *Groundwork: Charles Hamilton Houston and the Struggle for Civil Rights* (Philadelphia: University of Pennsylvania, 1984). On Thurgood Marshall, see Mark Tushnet, *Making Civil Rights Law: Thurgood Marshall and the Supreme Court, 1936–1961* (New York: Oxford University Press, 1996).

9. Sullivan, *Lift Every Voice*, xiv, 233–234; Tushnet, *NAACP's Legal Strategy*, chap. 2. See also Klarman, *From Jim Crow to Civil Rights*; Tushnet, *NAACP's Legal Strategy*; Sullivan, *Lift Every Voice*.

10. Neil A. Wynn, *The Afro-American and the Second World War* (New York: Holmes and Meier, 1993), 101. On the freedom movement in the 1940s, see Richard M. Dalfiume, "The 'Forgotten Years' of the Negro Revolution, *Journal of American History* 55, no. 1 (1968), 90–106; Jacqueline Dowd Hall, "The Long Civil Rights Movement and the Political Uses of the Past, *Journal of American History* 91, no. 4 (2005), 1233–1263; Harvard Sitkoff, *The Struggle for Black Equality* (New York: Hill and Wang, 2008), 11–19; Manning Marable, *Race, Reform, and Rebellion: The Second Reconstruction and Beyond in Black America, 1945–2006* (Jackson: University Press of Mississippi, 2007); Glenda Elizabeth Gilmore, *Defying Dixie: The Radical Roots of Civil Rights, 1919–1950* (New York: W. W. Norton, 2008); Martha Biondi, *To Stand and Fight: The Struggle for Civil Rights in Postwar New York City* (Cambridge, MA: Harvard University Press, 2006); Mathew Countryman, *Up South: Civil Rights and Black Power in Philadelphia* (Philadelphia: University of Pennsylvania Press, 2007); Victoria W. Wolcott charts a shift from respectability to economic self-help, nationalism, and self-sufficiency in the 1930s in *Remaking Respectability: African American Women in Interwar Detroit* (Chapel Hill: University of North Carolina Press, 2001), chap. 5; Raymond Arsenault, *Freedom Riders: 1961 and the Struggle for Racial Justice* (New York: Oxford University Press, 2011), appendix, 533–587. On young male leadership in high schools, see Countryman, *Up South*, 223–257.

11. Ada Lois Sipuel Fisher, *A Matter of Black and White: The Autobiography of Ada Lois Sipuel Fisher* (Norman: University of Oklahoma Press, 1996), xviii. Doris Raye Jennings Brewer, interview by Rachel Devlin, Newark, Delaware, 2010; Marguerite Carr Stokes, interview by Rachel Devlin, Washington, DC, 2008.

12. On young men and obligation during World War II, see Studs Terkel, *"The Good War," An Oral History of World War II* (New York: The New Press, 1984); Allan Bérubé, *Coming Out Under Fire: The History of Gay Men and Women in World War II* (Chapel Hill: University of North Carolina Press, 2010).

13. Pattillo Beals, *Warriors Don't Cry*, 44; Rubye Nell Singleton Stroble, interview by Rachel Devlin, Albany, Georgia, 2010.

14. Elizabeth A. Leech, "Activists Cite Little Progress," *Topeka Capitol Journal*, March 16, 1979, Lucinda Todd Papers, folder 3A, KSHS. For another description of events in Leake County see Derrick Bell, *Silent Covenants: Brown v. Board of Education and the Unfulfilled Hopes for Racial Reform* (New York: Oxford University Press, 2004), 100–102; Gayle Jones, interview by Rachel Devlin, Baton Rouge, Louisiana, 2010.

15. Gladys Tignor Peterson, "The Present Status of the Negro Separate School as Defined by Court Decisions," *Journal of Negro Education* 4, no.3 (1935), 351–374. On school segregation in the North and attempts at desegregation, see Thomas J. Segrue, *Sweet Land of Liberty: The Forgotten Struggle for Civil Rights in the North* (New York: Random House, 2009). On divisions within the black community over desegregation, see Tomiko Brown-Nagin, "Race as Identity Caricature: A Local Legal History Lesson in the Salience of Intraracial Conflict," *University of Pennsylvania Law Review* 151 (June 2003), 1913–1976; Brown-Nagin, *Courage to Dissent: Atlanta and the Long History of the Civil Rights Movement* (New York: Oxford University Press, 2012).

16. Tignor Peterson, "The Present Status of the Negro Separate School."

17. Stephen Kendrick and Paul Kendrick, *Sarah's Long Walk: The Free Blacks of Boston and How Their Struggle for Equality Changed America* (Boston: Beacon Press: 2004); Mae Ngai, *The Lucky Ones: One Family and the Extraordinary Invention of Chinese America* (New York: Houghton Mifflin Harcourt, 2010), 52, 55; Philippa Strum, Mendez v. Westminster: *School Desegregation and Mexican-American Rights* (Lawrence: University Press of Kansas, 2010).

18. Horace Mann Bond, "The Extent and Character of Separate Schools in the United States," *Journal of Negro Education* 4, no. 3, (1935), 321–327.

19. W. E. B. Du Bois, "Does the Negro Need Separate Schools?" *Journal of Negro Education* 4, no. 3 (1935), 328–335; W. E. B. Du Bois, letter to Yolande Du Bois, October 29, 1914, in *Letters from Black America*, ed. Pamela Newkirk (New York: Farrar, Straus and Giroux, 2009), 20-21; Tignor Peterson, "The Present Status of the Negro Separate School." On the tendency for black women to do the early, tedious, underappreciated "spade work" of civil rights organizing, see Barbara Ransby, *Ella Baker and the Black Freedom Movement: A Radical Democratic Vision* (Chapel Hill: University of North Carolina Press, 2003), 106, 118; Jeanne Theoharis, *The Rebellious Life of Mrs. Rosa Parks* (Boston: Beacon Press, 2013), 18; Belinda Robnett, *How Long? How Long? African-American Women in the Struggle for Civil Rights*, (New York: Oxford University Press, 1997), chaps. 2 and 3; Temma Kaplan, *Crazy for Democracy: Women in Grassroots Movements* (New York: Routledge, 1997). See also Bettye Collier-Thomas and V. P. Franklin, eds., *Sisters in the Struggle: African American Women in the Civil Rights-Black-Power Movement* (New York: New York University Press, 2001); Lynne Olson, *Freedom's Daughters: The Unsung Heroines of the Civil Rights Movement from 1830 to 1970*, (New York: Scribner, 2001); Dayo F. Gore, Jeanne Theoharis, and Komozi Woodard, eds., *Want to Start a Revolution?: Radical Women in the Black Freedom Struggle*, (New York: New York University Press, 2009).

20. Rockwell worked with a model for the painting. Pictures of all four desegregation firsts in New Orleans were printed in the national news. Gail Etienne wore a white bow. Ron Schick, *Norman Rockwell: Behind the Camera* (New York: Little Brown, 2009), 203.

21. On white boys attacking girls on the street in New York, see Mary White Ovington, *The Walls Came Tumbling Down* (New York: Adorno, 1969), 36. In New Orleans, LaKisha Michelle Simmons *Crescent City Girls: The Lives of Young Black Women in Segregated New Orleans* (Chapel Hill: University of North Carolina Press, 2015), 51–55; Theoharis, *Mrs. Rosa Parks*, 7; "Hurt in Playground Fracas," *Richmond Afro-American*, 1952; "High Court to Get Virginia Bus Case," *Richmond Afro-American*, December 18, 1948, 1. See also Jo Ann Gibson Robinson, *The Montgomery Bus Boycott and the Women Who Started It* (Knoxville: University of Tennessee Press, 1987), 22; Coles, *Children of Crisis*, 4; "Scout Officials Defy Hate Mob," *Richmond Afro-American*, July 10, 1948, 10; "Schools, General, California, 1945-1953," box B136, NAACP; William T. Ray, letter to Thurgood Marshall, folder 3, box B 137, NAACP; "Schools, Indiana, 1947–1949," box B137, NAACP; "Schools, Illinois, East St. Louis, 1949, folder 10, Box B 137; NAACP; "Their Eviction from White Schools to Be Grounds for Suit," *Richmond Afro-American*, February 12, 1949, 2; "East St. Louis," *The Crisis* (March 1947). School strikes and student activism were not uncommon in the late 1940s. See, for instance, Ronald D. Cohen, "The Dilemma of School Integration in the North: Gary, Indiana, 1945–1960," *Indiana Magazine of History* (June 1986), 279–302. Thanks to Zoe Burkholder for sharing this article. As Charles Payne pointed out in his study of female civil rights workers in Mississippi in the 1960s, girls and young women could not anticipate a "reprisal differential," especially when whites felt their racial privileges were threatened. Charles Payne, "Men Led, but Women Organized: Movement Participation of Women in the Mississippi Delta," in *Women in the Civil Rights Movement*, ed. Vicki L. Crawford (Bloomington: Indiana University Press, 1990), 4; Levine, *Freedom's Children*, 46. On differences in experiences of violence on the part of black women, see Kimberle Crenshaw, "Mapping the Margins: Intersectionality, Identity Politics, and Violence Against Women of Color," *Stanford Law Review* 43, no. 6 (July 1991), 1241–1299.

22. See especially Elizabeth Jacoway, *Turn Away Thy Son: Little Rock, the Crisis That Shocked the Nation* (New York: Free Press, 2007); Daniel Letwin, "Interracial Unionism, Gender, and 'Social Equality' in Alabama Coalfields, 1878–1908," *Journal of Southern History* 61, no. 3 (1995), 519–554; Jane Dailey, "Sex, Segregation, and the Sacred After *Brown*," *Journal of American History* 91, no. 1 (2004), 119–144; Hasan Kwame Jeffries, *Bloody Lowndes:*

Civil Rights and Black Power in Alabama's Black Belt (New York: New York University Press, 2009), 89; Blain Roberts, "The Ugly Side of the Southern Belle," editorial, *New York Times*, January 16, 2013, A23; Chart presented by John S. Lemasson, chief of tabulation and analysis for the State Department of Health, folder 29, box 30, A. P. Tureaud Papers, Tulane; Klarman, *From Jim Crow to Civil Rights*, 297.

23. Nell Irvin Painter, "'Social Equality,' Miscegenation, Labor and Power," in *The Evolution of Southern Culture*, ed. Numan V. Bartley (Athens: University of Georgia Press, 1988); Deborah Gray White *Are'n't I a Woman: Female Slaves in the Plantation South* (New York: W. W. Norton, 1999), 30–38; Darlene Clark Hine, "Rape and the Inner Lives of Black Women in the Middle West," *Signs* 14, no. 4 (1989), 912–920; Jacquelyn Dowd Hall, "'The Mind that Burns in Each Body": Women, Rape, and Racial Violence," in *Powers of Desire: The Politics of Sexuality*, eds. Ann Snitow, Christine Stansell, and Sharon Thompson, (New York: Monthly Review Press, 1983), 328–349; Tera W. Hunter, *To 'Joy My Freedom: Southern Black Women's Lives and Labors After the Civil War* (Cambridge: Harvard University Press, 1997); Hanna Rosen, *Terror in the Heart of Freedom: Citizenship, Sexual Violence, and the Meaning of Race in the Postemancipation South* (Chapel Hill: University of North Carolina Press, 2008); Kali Nicole Gross, "African American Women, Mass Incarceration, and the Politics of Protection," *Journal of American History* 102, no. 1 (2015), 26–28; Danielle McGuire, "'It Was Like All of Us Had Been Raped': Sexual Violence, Community Mobilization, and the African American Freedom Struggle," *Journal of American History* 91, no. 3 (2004): 906–931; Patricia Hill Collins, *Black Feminist Thought* (New York: Routledge, 2000), chap. 6; Susan K. Kahn, *Sexual Reckonings: Southern Girls in a Troubling Age* (Cambridge: Harvard University Press, 2007). For an example of a white mother's sexual anxiety about her son spending time with a teenage black girl, see Anne Moody, *Coming of Age in Mississippi* (New York: Dell, 1992). For a discussion of the fear of innocent white men being seduced by "mulattos" in particular, see Painter, "Social Equality," 56.

24. Quoted in Jeffries, *Bloody Lowndes*, 89; Alan Wieder, "The New Orleans School Crisis of 1960: Causes and Consequences," *Phylon* 48, no. 2 (1960).

25. Derrick A. Bell Jr., "Serving Two Masters: Integration Ideals and Client Interests in School Desegregation Litigation," *Yale Law Journal* 85, no. 4 (March 1976), 477; Tessie Prevost Williams, interview by Rachel Devlin, New Orleans, 2011; Pattillo Beals, *Warriors Don't Cry*, 27; Ada Lois Sipuel Fisher, *Matter of Black and White*, 54.

26. Lisa Krissoff Boehm, *Making a Way Out of No Way: African American Women and the Second Great Migration* (Jackson: University Press of

Mississippi, 2009), 48; Jacqueline Jones, *Labor of Love, Labor of Sorrow: Black Women, Work, and the Family from Slavery to the Present* (New York: Basic Books, 2010), 201; Anne Valk and Leslie Brown, *Living with Jim Crow: African American Women and Memories of the Segregated South* (New York: Palgrave, 2010), 35; Elizabeth Clark-Lewis, *Living In, Living Out: African American Domestics and the Great Migration* (Washington, DC: Smithsonian Books, 2010), 46, 97; Simmons, *Crescent City Girls*, 83; See also Judith Rollins, *Between Women: Domestics and Their Employers* (Philadelphia: Temple University Press, 1985), 168; "The culture of dissemblance," as described by Darlene Clark Hine, was also a component of domestic labor and black female survival, and was arguably at work in school desegregation encounters as well (Hine, "Rape and the Inner Lives of Black Women," 912); Deborah Gray White discusses dissemblance in *Aren't I a Woman*, 24. On symbolic gestures in asymmetrical power relationships, see Erving Goffman, "The Nature of Deference and Demeanor," *American Anthropologist* 58, no. 3 (1956), 473–502. On women and reliance on the "immutable smile," Simone de Beauvior, *The Second Sex*, trans. Constance Borde and Sheila Malovany-Chevallier (New York: Vintage, 2009), 271.

27. On black women and their "reputation for verbal aggressiveness," and on the "never-ending antagonism" between white employers and domestic workers see Jones, *Labor of Love*, 69, 112, 204; Doris Faye Jennings Alston, interview by Rachel Devlin, Newark, Delaware, July 2011.

28. Peggy King Jorde, interview by Rachel Devlin, Englewood, New Jersey, 2013; Barbara Ransby describes an encounter that Ella Baker's mother, Anna Ross Baker, had in similar terms, and says that Ella Baker described Anna Ross Baker as a "precise-spoken woman," *Ella Baker*, 21.

29. Evelyn Brooks Higginbotham, *Righteous Discontent: The Women's Movement in the Black Baptist Church, 1880–1920* (Cambridge: Harvard University Press, 1994), 196; Simmons, *Crescent City Girls*, 18, 124. See also Marcia Chatelain, *Southside Girls: Growing Up in the Great Migration* (Durham, NC: Duke University Press, 2015), chap. 2. On girls on the streets in New York, see Cheryl Hicks, *Talk with You Like a Woman: African American Women, Justice, and Reform in New York, 1890–1935* (Chapel Hill: University of North Carolina Press, 2010). On women as racial brokers, see also Glenda Elizabeth Gilmore, *Gender and Jim Crow: Women and the Politics of White Supremacy in North Carolina, 1896–1920* (Chapel Hill: University of North Carolina Press, 1996), chap. 7; Deborah Gray White, *Too Heavy a Load: Black Women in Defense of Themselves, 1894–1994* (New York: W. W. Norton, 1999); Paula Giddings, *When and Where I Enter: The Impact of Black Women on Race and Sex in America* (New York: William Morrow, 1984).

30. On the growth of role of a "pleasing personality" in women's work, see Alice Kessler-Harris, *Out to Work: A History of Wage-Earning Women in the United States* (New York: Oxford University Press, 2003) 137, 149, 177, 234; Louise Kapp Howe, *Pink Collar Workers: Inside the World of Women's Work* (New York: Putnam, 1978); Arlie Russell Hochschild, *The Managed Heart: Commercialization of Human Feeling* (Berkeley: University of California Press, 2013); Dorothy Sue Cobble, *Dishing It Out: Waitresses and Their Unions in the Twentieth Century* (Urbana: University of Illinois Press, 1991), 3: Megan Taylor Shockley, *"We, Too, Are Americans": African American Women in Detroit and Richmond, 1940–1954* (Urbana: University of Illinois Press, 2004), 29–62. On black women, nursing, and interpersonal skills, see Karen Brodkin Sacks, *Caring by the Hour: Women, Work, and Organizing at Duke Medical Center* (Urbana: University of Illinois Press, 1988). On women of color and expectations of warmth, see Rhacel Salazar Parrenas, *Servants of Globalization: Women, Migration, and Domestic Work* (Stanford: Stanford University Press, 2001). On girls and expectations of positive, cheerful personalities, see John F. Kasson, "Behind Shirley Temple's Smile: Children, Emotional Labor, and the Great Depression," in *The Cultural Turn in U.S. History: Past, Present and Future*, eds. James W. Cook, Lawrence B. Glickman, and Michael O'Malley (Chicago: Chicago University Press, 2008). On advice literature aimed at black girls in the 1940s, see Miya Carey, "'That Charm of All Girlhood': African American Girlhood and Girls in Washington, DC, 1930–1965," (PhD dissertation, Rutgers University, 2017). On the need for black girls to be "cheerful" as a form of protection, see Margo Jefferson, *Negroland: A Memoir* (New York: Pantheon, 2015), 60.

31. Mary McLeod Bethune, "A Philosophy of Education for Negro Girls" (1926) in *Mary McLeod Bethune: Building a Better World*, eds. Audrey Thomas McCluskey and Elaine M. Smith (Bloomington: Indiana University Press, 1999), 84–85. See also Joyce A. Hanson, *Mary McLeod Bethune and Black Women's Political Activism* (Columbia: University of Missouri Press, 2003). On beauty as an obligation to the race, see Maxine Leeds Craig, *Ain't I a Beauty Queen? Black Women, Beauty, and the Politics of Race* (New York: Oxford University Press, 2002); Blain Roberts, *Pageants, Parlors, and Pretty Women: Race and Beauty in the Twentieth Century South* (Chapel Hill: University of North Carolina Press, 2014); see especially the publication of the National Association of Colored Women (NACW), *Aframerican Woman's Journal*, 1945–1950; Mary McLeod Bethune, address at the National Planning Conference on Building Better Race Relationships, Washington, DC, 1944, folder 6, box 58, Ernesto Galarza Papers, Stanford University, Stanford, CA; "Mrs. Bethune Addresses Dallas Women's Council," *Kansas City Call*, April 30, 1948, 1.

Chapter 1: Roots of Change

1. *Gaines v. Canada*, 305 U.S. 337 (1938); "Victory in Missouri U. Case," *Kansas City Call*, December 16, 1938, 1; "The Victorious Youth: Gaines Has Been Brilliant and Hard-Working Student," *Kansas City Call*, December 16, 1938, 1; "M.U. Paper Says, 'Come on Gaines,': Students Say Must Follow Court Ruling," *Kansas City Call*, December 23, 1938, 1; "Missouri Editor Says Gaines Should Have Been Welcomed to Missouri U," December 23, 1938, 1; "Lloyd Gaines Disappears—Where Is He?" *Kansas City Call*, October 20, 1939, 1, 4.; "Gaines Still Missing!!" *Kansas City Call*, October 27, 1939; "Drop Lloyd Gaines Case: Plaintiff Still Missing," *Kansas City Call*, January 5, 1940; "N.A.A.C.P. Still Unable to Find Lloyd Gaines," *Kansas City Call*, March 15, 1940; "Year Has Passed Since Lloyd Gaines Vanished," *Kansas City Call*, September 6, 1940.

2. *Gaines v. Canada*; "Houston Urges Continued War on School Ban," *Afro-American*, February 11, 1939, folder 382, Pauli Murray Papers, Schlesinger Library, Radcliffe Institute, Harvard University.

3. Robert W. Tabscott, "Lucile Bluford 1911–2003, Famed Missouri Journalist," *St. Louis Journalism Review* 40, no. 317 (2010), 24–25.

4. "Bill of Rights Is Ours Too," *Kansas City Call*, October 13, 1939, 22; "Langston U. Head Quits in Day," *Kansas City Call*, October 20, 1939, 1. "Bias in Education: NAACP Attorney to Test Validity of Segregation," *Kansas City Call*, March 26, 1948; "Seek a Supreme Court Ruling on J.C. School," *Kansas City Call*, June 4, 1948.

5. Fern Ingersoll, *Interviews with Lucile Bluford*, Interview #1, May 13, 1989 (Washington, DC: Washington Press Club Foundation); Diane E. Loupe, "Storming and Defending the Color Barrier at the University of Missouri School of Journalism: The Lucile Bluford Case," *Journalism History* 16, no. 1–2 (1989), 22; Ingersoll, *Interviews with Lucile Bluford*, 3.

6. Ingersoll, *Interviews with Lucile Bluford*, 11.

7. Ibid., 9–20.

8. Terry J. Hughs, "KC Editor's Lifelong Goal Is Equality," *Kansas City Star*, May 10, 1987, 18A, Hugh Speer Papers, KSHS.

9. Ingersoll, *Interviews with Lucile Bluford*, 21.

10. Ibid., 27, 29; "Thurgood Marshall Speaks to Students," *Dillard Courtbouillon*, March 1954, p. 1–2, Dillard University Archives, New Orleans.

11. Ingersoll, *Interviews with Lucile Bluford*, 25. Pea green and pink were the Alpha Kappa Alpha colors and may have inspired Bluford's preference for her green jacket. For other interpretations of green suits and jackets, see

George Chauncey, *Gay New York: Gender, Urban Culture, and the Making of the Gay Male World, 1890–1940* (New York: Basic, 1995), 52.

12. Loupe, "Color Barrier," 29; Hughs, "KC Editor's Lifelong Goal Is Equality," 18A.

13. Loupe, "Color Barrier," 29.

14. Ibid., 55; "M.U. Rejects Woman Student" and "Nothing Will Happen When Negro Student Is Admitted to M.U.," *Kansas City Call*, February 3, 1939, 1.

15. "M.U. Rejects Woman Student" and "Nothing Will Happen," *Kansas City Call*.

16. Danielle Allen, *Talking to Strangers: Anxieties of Citizenship Since* Brown v. Board of Education (Chicago: University of Chicago Press, 2006), xxi–xxii.

17. Lucile Bluford, "Two Schools, Double Costs," *Kansas City Call*, February 10, 1939, 22.

18. Loupe, "Color Barrier," 23.

19. Jules Tygiel, *Baseball's Great Experiment: Jackie Robinson and His Legacy* (New York: Oxford University Press, 1997), 135.

20. Bluford, "Two Schools, Double Costs"; "Citizens Oppose Lincoln U. Bill," *Kansas City Call*, February 17, 1939, 1.

21. Lucile Bluford, "Missouri 'Shows' the Supreme Court," *The Crisis*, 46 (1939), 232.

22. Ibid., 242.

23. Ibid.

24. Ibid., 246.

25. "30 Students Register for Study Despite Protest of St. Louis Organizations," *Kansas City Call*, September 29, 1939, 1; "Keep Fighting," *Kansas City Call*, August 4, 1939, 1.

26. "Name Dean," *Kansas City Call*, August 4, 1939, 1; "Lloyd Gaines Disappears," *Kansas City Call*, 1, 4.

27. David Stout, "A Supreme Triumph, then into the Shadows," *New York Times*, July 11, 2009; Edward T. Clayton, "The Strange Disappearance of Lloyd Gaines," *Ebony*, May 1951, 26–27, 30–35; Lucile Bluford, "The Lloyd Gaines Story," *Journal of Educational Sociology* 32, no. 6 (1959), 242–246.

28. "Kansas Citians Hear Youth Who Won M.U. Case," *Kansas City Call*, March 3, 1939, 1.

29. Clayton, "The Strange Disappearance of Lloyd Gaines," 26–28, 30–37. See also, Daniel T. Kelleher, "The Case of Lloyd Lionel Gaines: The Demise of the Separate but Equal Doctrine," *Journal of Negro History* 56, no. 4 (1971), 262–271.

30. "Missouri U. Says 'No,'" *Afro-American*, February 11, 1939, folder 380, Pauli Murray Papers.

31. Pauli Murray, letter to Lloyd Gaines, December 18, 1938, p. 1, folder 380, Pauli Murray Papers.

32. Pauli Murray, "Who Is to Blame for Disappearance of Lloyd Gaines?" *Kansas City Call*, January 26, 1940, 1. The editorial was also published by Roscoe Dunjee in the *Black Dispatch* (Oklahoma City), folder 383, Pauli Murray Papers.

33. Murray, "Who Is to Blame."

34. On Pauli Murray's perspective on nonviolent mass protest, see Nico Slate, *Colored Cosmopolitanism: The Shared Struggle for Freedom in the United States and India* (Cambridge: Harvard University Press, 2017).

35. Loupe, "Color Barrier," 24; Tushnet, *NAACP's Legal Strategy*, 83; "Houston Urges Continued War on School Ban," *Afro-American*, February 11, 1939, folder 383, Pauli Murray Papers; Charles H. Houston, letter to Lucile Bluford, folder 2, box B202, NAACP.

36. "File Another Suit," *Kansas City Call*, October 13, 1939, 1; "Barred Student Files Damage Suit Against the University of Missouri," *Chicago Defender*, October 14, 1939, 4; "Girl Sues University of MO. for $20,000," *Chicago Defender*, November 11, 1939, 1; "Lucille [sic] Bluford Sues for $20,000," *Pittsburgh Courier*, November 11, 1939, 4.

37. Lucile Bluford, "Halted but Not Stopped," *Kansas City Call*, October 27, 1939, 22.

38. Dorothy Davis, "White Students Crowd Courtroom for Two-Day Bluford vs. M.U. Trial: Sentiment Favors Admittance of Negro to University of Missouri," *Kansas City Call*, February 16, 1940, 1, 4.

39. "White Girl Students Banished at MO. Trial," *Pittsburgh Courier*, February 24, 1940, 19; Loupe, "Color Barrier," 25.

40. On Gaines trial, see Kluger, *Simple Justice*, 202; Charles Houston, memorandum to Walter White, February 12, 1940, pp. 2–3, folder 7, box B201, NAACP.

41. Houston to White, February 12, p. 2.

42. Dorothy Davis, "She Knocks at the Door of Missouri University," *The Crisis* 47 (1940), 140.

43. "White Students Crowd Courtroom for Two-Day Bluford vs. M.U. Trial," photo caption, "We Hope You Get in—We're for You," February 16, 1940; photo caption, "White Girls Want Bluford to Win," *Kansas City Call*, February 24, 1940; Lisen J. Tammeus, "Unlocking Segregation," *The Columbia Missourian*, February 28, 1993, section G, p. 1; Chuck Davis, "Eli Steps Down for Levi at Yale," *Chicago Defender*, December 11, 1948, 15; "Yale Elects

First Negro Captain," *New York Times*, November 23, 1948, 1; "Levi Jackson Named Yale Football Captain for '49," *Washington Post*, November 23, 1948, B5; "White Girl Deplores Bias," *Kansas City Call*, April, 1948, 6. "Sends 14th Amendment Ashes to Truman," *Kansas City Call*, February 13, 1948.

44. Charles Houston, letter to Lucile Bluford, December 13, 1941, folder 1, Box B202, NAACP, Charles Houston, letter to Lucile Bluford, January 14, 1942, folder 1, box B202, NAACP.

45. "Bluford Action Denied," *Pittsburgh Courier*, June 8, 1940, 22; Lucile Bluford, "1 Year Has Passed Since Gaines Vanished," *Kansas City Call*, September 6, 1940.

46. "University of Missouri," *Chicago Defender*, April 25, 1942, 14; "Woman Editor Renews Request to Mo. 'U' Journalism School," *Pittsburgh Courier*, May 9, 1942, 24.

47. Lucile Bluford, letter to Charles Houston, March 31, 1942, folder 1, box B202, NAACP; Charles Houston, letter to Lucille [*sic*] Bluford, April 26, 1942, p. 2. folder 1, box B202.

48. Hughes, "KC Editor's Lifelong Goal Is Equality."

49. Ibid.

50. Ibid.

Chapter 2: "This Lone Negro Girl"

1. "Interview with Berdyne Scott," November 24, 1991, Brown v. Topeka Board of Education Oral History Project, p. 35, KSHS; Anita Hill, "Personal Thoughts on Ada Lois Sipuel Fisher," email to Rachel Devlin, November 22, 2017. Writing about the case in *Simple Justice*, Richard Kluger said, "By any hardheaded measure [*Sipuel*] was a setback" (p. 259). Among the general histories of the civil rights movement that describe *Sweatt* and *McLaurin* as foundational and leave out *Sipuel*, are Adam Fairclough, *Better Day Coming: Blacks and Equality, 1890–2000* (New York: Penguin, 2001); Steven F. Lawson and Charles Payne, *Debating the Civil Rights Movement, 1945–1968* (New York: Rowman & Littlefield, 2006); Adam Fairclough, *A Class of Their Own: Black Teachers in the Segregated South* (Cambridge, MA: Belknap, 2007); and Gilmore, *Defying Dixie*. While Sipuel earns a paragraph in Michael J. Klarman's six-hundred-page book, *From Jim Crow to Civil Rights*, she is not included in the abridged version, which focuses specifically on school desegregation, *Brown v. Board of Education* and the civil rights movement. A representative schema is Peter Wallenstein's: "In the late 1940s, culminating in two Supreme Court decisions in June 1950 [*Sweatt* and *McLaurin*] the NAACP won Supreme Court cases in higher education that laid the foundation for a direct

assault on segregated schools at the elementary and secondary levels." Peter Wallenstein, "Higher Education, Black Access, and the Civil Rights Movement," in *Higher Education and the Civil Rights Movement: White Supremacy, Black Southerners, and College Campuses*, ed. Peter Wallenstein (Gainesville: University Press of Florida, 2008), 9–10. For a discussion of the ongoing tendency for women to disappear from histories of black protest, see Robin D. G. Kelley, *Freedom Dreams: The Black Radical Imagination* (Boston: Beacon Press, 2002), 136–137.

2. "GOP Asserts Democrats Don't Value Negro Vote," *Chicago Defender*, March 7, 1948, 4; "Democracy and Brotherhood Discovered on O.U. Campus," NAACP press release, folder 8, box B202, NAACP; "Universities: University of Oklahoma correspondence, 1945–46."

3. "Ada Fisher Still Not in School: Girl Who Started Oklahoma Fight Is Still Waiting," *Kansas City Call*, October 29, 1948, 1. Up until the early 1960s, Ada Sipuel was widely referred to as the progenitor of the ongoing school desegregation battle. "It was a young woman who touched off the whole thing by contending in the courts that educational facilities could not be separate and yet be equal. Ada Sipuel was her name"; "Where Is the Negro After 100 Years?" *Chicago Defender*, September 29, 1962, 6. See also Charles Benjamin Robson, "The Long Struggle," in *The Angry Black South: Southern Negros Tell Their Own Story*, eds. Glenford E. Mitchell, William H. Peace III (New York: Corinth Books, 1962), 24; "Young Girl Launches Battle," *Chicago Defender*, August 3, 1946, 13; "Ada Lois Sipuel, Henry Wallace, Dixiecrats," *Black Dispatch*, January 1, 1949.

4. Sipuel Fisher, *Matter of Black and White*, 43.

5. On black armed resistance, see Timothy B. Tyson, *Radio Free Dixie: Robert F. Williams and the Roots of Black Power* (Chapel Hill: University of North Carolina Press, 2001); Sipuel Fisher, *Matter of Black and White*, 47.

6. Sipuel Fisher, *Matter of Black and White*, 49.

7. Ibid., 25.

8. Ibid., 32–33.

9. Ibid., 54–59.

10. Ibid., 74.

11. "Freedom for All; Forever," interview with Ada Sipuel Fisher, KOCO TV, Oklahoma City, Oklahoma, August 28, 1981, Walter J. Brown Media Archives and Peabody Awards Collection, University of Georgia Special Collections Library, Athens, Georgia; David Levy, "The Day the President Went Fishing," *Sooner Magazine* 18, no. 2 (1998), 27.

12. Roscoe Dunjee, letter to Thurgood Marshall, January 15, 1946, folder 8, box B202, NAACP.

13. Kenneth R. Lamkin, letter to Thurgood Marshall, July 13, 1945, folder 2, B205, NAACP; Hastie quoted in Gary M. Lavergne, *Before Brown: Heman Marion Sweatt, Thurgood Marshall, and the Long Road to Justice* (Austin: University of Texas Press, 2010), 89; A. Maceo Smith, letter to Thurgood Marshall, August 17, 1945, folder 2, box B205, NAACP.

14. Lavergne, *Before Brown*, 91

15. W. J. Durham, letter to Thurgood Marshall, January 28, 1946, folder 2, box B205, NAACP.

16. Lavergne, *Before Brown*, 92; Heman Sweatt, letter to Walter White, November 8, 1946, folder 3, box B205 NAACP; "Texas in Fight to Ban NAACP," *Chicago Defender*, October 1, 1956, 4. On the need for progressive organizations to distance themselves from communism, see Albert Fried, *McCarthyism: The Great American Red Scare* (New York: Oxford, 1996), 22–27. On Walter White's desire to purge communists from the NAACP, see Richard M. Fried, *Nightmare in Red: The McCarthy Era in Perspective* (New York: Oxford, 1991), 165.

17. Lavergne, *Before Brown*, 103.

18. Thurgood Marshall, letter to A. Maceo Smith, January 24, 1946, folder 2, box B205, NAACP; Thurgood Marshall, letter to W. J. Durham, March 8, 1946, folder 3, box B205.

19. Merline Pitre, *In Struggle Against Jim Crow: Lulu B. White and the NAACP, 1900–1957* (College Station: Texas A&M University Press, 1999), 92; Carter Wesley, letter to W. J. Durham, March 22, 1946, folder 2, box B205, NAACP; "Memorandum to the Governor's Bi-Racial Commission on the Higher Education of Negroes in Texas," Texas Council of Negro Organizations, folder 3, box B2015, NAACP; Brown-Nagin, *Courage to Dissent*, 19.

20. A. Maceo Smith, letter to Carter Wesley, March 31, 1946, p. 1, folder 2, box B2015, NAACP; Lulu White, letter to Thurgood Marshall, July 30, 1946, folder 3, box B205, NAACP; Thurgood Marshall, letter to A. Maceo Smith, March 29, 1946, folder 2, box B205 NAACP. On the campaign for equality and desegregation of universities in Texas—and the major personalities involved—see Amilcar Shabazz, *Advancing Democracy: African Americans and the Struggle for Access and Equity in Higher Education in Texas* (Chapel Hill: University of North Carolina Press, 2004).

21. Thurgood Marshall, letter to Roscoe Dunjee, February 13, 1946, folder 8, box B202, NAACP; Thurgood Marshall, telegram to Robert Carter, February 15, 1946, folder 8, box B202, NAACP.

22. Roscoe Dunjee, letter to Thurgood Marshall, March 9, 1946, folder 8, box B202, NAACP; Dunjee to Marshall, March 20, 1946, folder 8, box B202, NAACP.

23. Brief, *Sipuel v. Regents*, March 1946, folder 9, box B202, NAACP.

24. Roscoe Dunjee, letter to Walter White, June 17, 1946, folder 8, box B202, NAACP.

25. On fund-raising in Texas, see Darlene Clark Hine, *Black Victory: The Rise and Fall of the White Primary in Texas* (Columbia: University of Missouri Press, 2003), 223–224; Sullivan, *Lift Every Voice*, 247, 282–283; Lavergne, *Before Brown*, 138.

26. "UT School of Law Class Composites, 1884–1959," Tarlton Law Library Digital Collections, accessed April 2, 2013; J. Clay Smith Jr., *Emancipation: The Making of the Black Lawyer, 1844–1944* (Philadelphia: University of Pennsylvania Press, 1993), 636; "Lady Lawyers," *Ebony*, August 1947, 19–20.

27. Kenneth W. Mack, *Representing the Race: The Creation of the Civil Rights Lawyer* (Cambridge: Harvard University Press, 2012), 138, 125; "Lady Lawyers," 19; Mack, *Representing the Race*, 129–130.

28. Roscoe Dunjee, letter to Thurgood Marshall, March 13, 1946, folder 8, box B202, NAACP.

29. H. W. Williamston, letter to Earnestine Beatrice Spears, June 20, 1951; Earnestine Beatrice Spears, "Social Forces in the Admittance of Negroes to the University of Oklahoma," (master's thesis, University of Oklahoma, 1951), 31–32; Sipuel Fisher, *A Matter of Black and White*, 95.

30. Sipuel Fisher, *A Matter of Black and White*, 95–108.

31. Juan Williams, *Thurgood Marshall: American Revolutionary* (New York: Three Rivers, 1998), 178.

32. Heman Sweatt, letter to Lula [sic] White, July 25, 1946, folder 2, box B205, NAACP; Thurgood Marshall, letter to Heman Sweatt, September 30, 1947, folder 5, box B205, NAACP.

33. "Memorandum from Mr. White to Mr. Marshall," December 30, 1946, folder 3, box B205, NAACP; Carter Wesley, "Shall We Attend the Negro U.," *Houston Informer and Texas Freeman*, September 13, 1947, p. 15; Pitre, *In Struggle Against Jim Crow*, 103.

34. "Texas Governor Signs Bill for $3,000,000 Law School," *Chicago Defender*, March 15, 1947, 1; Heman Sweatt letter to Thurgood Marshall, September 19, 1947, folder 5, box B205, NAACP; Lavergne, *Before Brown*, 240. For more on Sweatt's complicated perspective on desegregation, see Heman Marion Sweatt, "Why I Want to Attend the University of Texas," *Texas Ranger*, September 1947, 20-40-41, folder "Students-Individuals, Sweatt, Heman Marion," box University of Texas Law School Archives, Dolph Briscoe Center for American History, University of Texas, Austin, Texas.

35. J. Don Davis, "NAACP Pickets Defy Segregation," *Pittsburgh Courier*, November 15, 1947, 1.

36. "Dallas Celebrates Heman Sweatt Day," *Kansas City Call*, February 25, 1950, 1.

37. Six people filed suits against the University of Tennessee in 1940: Walter E. Hardy, Clinton M. Marsh, Joseph M. Michael, Homer L. Saunders, P. L. Smith, and Ezra Totten; "Universities, University of Tennessee, Legal Papers, 1940–1941," box B204, NAACP. See also Lavergne, *Before Brown*, 117; "Memorandum to Mr. Harrington From Legal Department: For Press Release," folder 8, box B203, NAACP. A law school was established at Southern University in Louisiana in response to *Hatfield v. Louisiana State University* with an initial appropriation of $60,000. Viola M. Johnson also attempted to register at the Louisiana State University medical school in 1946. "Memorandum to Mr. Harrington from Legal Department," folder 8, box B202, NAACP. After the appropriation bill the desegregation lawsuit was abandoned; "Plan State Law School," *Pittsburgh Courier*, January 18, 1947, 1.

38. Ada Lois Sipuel, letter to Thurgood Marshall, December 23, 1947, folder 9, box B202; Thurgood Marshall, letter to Ada Lois Sipuel, December 30, 1947, folder 9, box B202, NAACP.

39. Tushnet, *NAACP's Legal Strategy*, 125; *Sipuel v. Board of Regents* 332 U.S. 631 (1948), 2.; "It's a Wonderful Constitution, Ada Says on Return to State," *Daily Oklahoman*, January 15, 1948, 1.

40. Wesley Batherok, "Negro Barred from Enrolling at University," *Daily Oklahoman*, January 15, 1946; "It's a Wonderful Constitution," *Daily Oklahoman*, 1.

41. "Well-Known Law Prospect Gives Personal Views," *Atlanta Daily World*, January 24, 1948, 1; "Oklahoma Court Order Hits White Students," *Chicago Defender*, January 24, 1948, 1; "Surprise Move in Law School Case," *Pittsburgh Courier*, January 24, 1948, 1; "Negro Student Back in State After Victory," *Daily Oklahoman*, January 15, 1948, 2.

42. "Well-Known Law Prospect Gives Personal Views," *Atlanta Daily World*, January 24; "Negro Student Back in State After Victory," *Daily Oklahoman*, January 15, 1948, 2.

43. Marjorie McKenzie, "Pursuit of Democracy," editorial, *Pittsburgh Courier*, January 31, 1948, 6.

44. "Memorandum to Mr. Marshall from Mrs. Perry," January 22, 1848, folder 10, box B202, NAACP. The words "Ada ... refused" and "rejected" appear in the following articles in the *Pittsburgh Courier*, "Surprise Move in Law School Case: Mrs. Fisher Won't Accept Oklahoma Jim Crow Set-Up," January 24, 1948, 1; "Mrs. Fisher Ignores State Jim-Crow Setup," January 31, 1948, 1; "Mrs. Fisher Rates Praise," February 7, 1948, 3; "Open New Attack on U. of Okla. Bias," February 7, 1948; "Oklahoma Bars White Man Too,"

February 7, 1948, 4; "Oklahoma Still Has School without Pupils," March 13, 1948, 5; "Kentucky Bars Negro . . . New Trial Date Set For Oklahoma," April 3, 1948, 1; "Oklahoma Fight Continues," April 3, 1948, 6; "The Courier Salutes," *Pittsburgh Courier*, February 2, 1948, 3.

45. "NAACP Lauds Truman, Blasts GOP for Failure of Congress to Act on Civil Rights: Thurgood Marshall Speaks," *Pittsburgh Courier*, July 3, 1948, 14; "Forward!" display ad, *Pittsburgh Courier*, Feb 14, 1948, 12; "The Courier Salutes," *Pittsburgh Courier*, February 2, 1948, 3; "GOP Asserts Democrats Don't Value Negro Vote," *Chicago Defender*, March 7, 1948, 4; "Kentucky Bars Negro: New Trial Date Set for Oklahoma Case," *Pittsburgh Courier*, April 3, 1948; "NAACP Lauds Truman, Blasts GOP for Failure of Congress to Act on Civil Rights," *Pittsburgh Courier*, July 3, 1948, 3.

46. Amos Hall, letter to Gloster B. Current, March 16, 1948, folder 1, box B203, NAACP; "Memorandum to Mr. Marshall from Mr. Current," June 3, 1948, folder 1, box B203, NAACP; Roy Wilkens, letter to Amos Hall, April 2, 1948, folder 1, box B203, NAACP.

47. "Despite Jim Crow Desk, Whites Greet Negro at Oklahoma U.," *Chicago Defender*, October 23, 1948, 1. The picture of McLaurin being segregated appears in Klarman, *From Jim Crow to Civil Rights*, and in the Library of Congress online exhibit, "With an Even Hand"; Kenneth Johnson, "Creed, Color, and Cooperation," WKY, November 28, 1948, folder 1, box B203, NAACP; Saul Feldman, "Negro Education Wins a Crusade at 55," *Washington Post*, June 25, 1950, B3.

48. Viola Drew Lewis, "Sipuel Jim Crowed, White Students Hot," *Pittsburgh Courier*, July 2, 1949, 4. The quote in the *Daily Oklahoman* was slightly different. It read, "I will spend the rest of my life trying to prove to Oklahoma that a mistake was made in the attempt to keep me from entering the OU law school," June 19, 1949, p. 1.

49. "Negro Students in White Dixie Colleges," *Ebony*, March 1951, 15; "Report Card," *Time*, August 20, 1951, 56; William H. Murray, *The Negro's Place in Call of Race: The Last Word on Segregation of Races Considered in Every Capable Light as Disclosed by Experience* (Tishomingo, Oklahoma, 1948), 24–25, quoted in Ruth E. Swain, *Ada Lois: The Sipuel Story* (New York: Vantage Press, 1978), 41.

50. "Sipuel Jim Crowed," *Pittsburgh Courier*, 1; "Ada Lois Is Thrilled," *Daily Oklahoman*, June 19, 1949, B18; "Ada Lois Sipuel Fisher: Address," *Report of the Annual New York Herald Tribune Forum*, October 18–20, 1948.

51. "Court Hears Sweatt Case," *Kansas City Call*, April 14, 1950, 1; *Sweatt v. Painter*, 339 U.S. 629 (1950).

52. "For Oklahoma, Anita Hill's Story Is Open Wound," *New York Times*, April 19, 1993.

53. Mrs. J. M. B. Michelle, letter to Ada Lois Sipuel Fisher, August 21, 1951, Chickasha, Oklahoma. Possession of Bruce Fisher. I am grateful to Mr. Fisher for sharing this and other personal items belonging to his mother.

Chapter 3: Girls on the Front Line

1. Lani Guinier, "From Racial Liberalism to Racial Literacy: *Brown v. Board of Education* and the Interest-Divergence Dilemma," *Journal of American History*, 9, no. 1 (June 2004), 92–118; Derrick Bell, *Silent Covenants*.

2. Marguerite Carr Stokes, interview by Rachel Devlin, Washington, DC, 2008.

3. Ibid.

4. Rosalind Rosenberg, *Jane Crow: The Life of Pauli Murray* (New York: Oxford University Press, 2017), 3; Charlayne Hunter-Gault, *In My Place* (New York: Vintage, 1992), 36, 148. Hunter-Gault desegregated the University of Georgia in 1961 with Hamilton Holmes. On the fine-grained social distinction based on color, see Willard B. Gatewood, *Aristocrats of Color: The Black Elite, 1880–1920* (Fayetteville: University of Arkansas Press, 2000); Lawrence Otis Graham, *Our Kind of People: Inside America's Black Upper Class* (New York: Harper Perennial, 1999). Young women who desegregated high schools in Louisiana describe experiences being marginalized because of their fair color; Gail Jones, interview by Rachel Devlin, Baton Rouge, Louisiana, 2011; Vervian Elaine Boyle Patin, interview by Rachel Devlin, Baton Rouge, Louisiana, 2011; Malaika Favorite, interview by Rachel Devlin, Augusta, Georgia, 2011. On the complexity of color in Louisiana in particular, see Simmons, *Crescent City Girls*, 14.

5. Marguerite Carr Stokes, interview by Rachel Devlin, Washington, DC, 2008.

6. Ibid.

7. Ibid.

8. "Aim New Blow at D.C. School Bias," *Pittsburgh Courier*, April 26, 1947, 1. "Say D.C. Bias Jams Schools, Hits Education," *Chicago Defender*, April 26, 1947, 3.

9. *African American National Biography*, 2nd ed., eds. Henry Louis Gates Jr. and Evelyn Brooks Higginbotham, "Ransom, Leon Andrew," by Peter Wallenstein (New York: Oxford University Press, 2013), 343–344.

10. Oliver Hill, Spottswood Robinson, Martin A. Martin, and Leon Ransom, complaint in *Constance Carter v. School Board of Arlington County* and

Alice Bailey v. School Board of Arlington County, pp. 6–7, MSS 78-2, box 7, Armistead Mason Dobie Papers, University of Virginia; "Negro Children Refused at White High School, Parents Differ with Board," *Kansas City Call*, September 24, 1948.

11. *Carr v. Corning*, U.S. District Court for the District of Columbia, 86 U.S. App. D.C. 173, No. 9796 (1947–1950), folder 6, box B136, NAACP.

12. Marguerite Carr Stokes, interview by Rachel Devlin, Washington, DC, 2008.

13. Ibid.

14. Jay Walz, "Attack on 'Jim Crow' Stirs Capital," *New York Times*, December 19, 1948, E7; "Report on Capital Segregation Puts Two White Dailies on Opposite Sides," *Kansas City Call*, December 24, 1948.

15. Thanks to Randy Sowell for examining the records of the US Secret Service. On Truman's civil rights record, see Donald R. McCoy, *Quest and Response: Minority Rights and the Truman Administration* (Lawrence: University Press of Kansas, 1973); Michael R. Gardner, *Harry Truman and Civil Rights: Moral Courage and Political Risks* (Carbondale: Southern Illinois University Press, 2003); James C. Carr Sr., letter to Harry S. Truman, June 5, 1952, box 372, Harry S. Truman Library, Independence, Missouri.

16. "A Statement Concerning the Proposal of the Superintendent of Schools to Transfer Certain Buildings from Divisions 1–9," November 10, 1947, box 78-44, DC Board of Education, Moorland-Spingarn Research Center (MSRC), Howard University; "A Synopsis of the Current School Fight by the Browne Parent Group for Equality of Educational Opportunity," February, 1948, folder 867, box 78-44, DC Board of Education, MSRC; "3 Seek to Halt Transferring of 2 Schools," *Washington Post*, November 29, 1947.

17. Charles Houston, letter to Louis S. Weiss, February 9, 1948, folder 6, box B136, NAACP; "Dirksen Asks for Full Report on Strike at Brown Jr. High," *Washington Post*, December 10, 1947, B10

18. "Dirksen Asks for Full Report," *Washington Post*.

19. "Summary of Discussion re School Transfer," December 24, 1949, box 78-44, DC Board of Education, MSRC.

20. Elsie Carper, "Negro Strike Plan Running into Difficulties," *Washington Post*, December 19, 1947, B1; "Negroes Assail 'Hand-Me Down' Schoolhouses," *Washington Post*, December 22, 1947; "Parents to Continue School Strike," *Washington Post*, January 5, 1948, 1; Kluger, *Simple Justice*, 516.

21. Charles Houston, compliant in *Judine Consuelo Bishop, Barbara Jean Arnold v. Marian Doyle*, no. 290-48, folder 52, Consolidated Parent Group records, MRSC, Howard University; Houston, complaint in *Eddie Andrew Gregg v. C. Melvin Sharpe*, 1949, No. 4205-49, folder 56, Consolidated Parent

Group records; Houston, complaint in *Gloria Odessa Haley v. C. Melvin Sharpe*, 1949, no. 4227-49, folder 57, Consolidated Parent Group records.

22. On Charles Houston, see McNeil, *Groundwork*. On the ways in which Houston and "the Consolidated Parent Group were one," McNeil, *Groundwork*, 190–191; Kluger, *Simple Justice*, 516–517; Houston and Ransom, longtime associates, seem to have had a heated falling out over legal strategy in their respective cases (*Carr v. Corning* and *Bishop v. Doyle*); "Browne School Strike Ends; Two Suits to Decide 'Issues,'" *Washington Post*, February 2, 1948, 1; Charles Houston, complaint in *Judine Consuelo Bishop, Barbara Jean Arnold v. Marian Doyle*; Charles Houston, letter to Louis S. Weiss.

23. Stephen Spottswood, letter to Joseph D. Lohman, December 11, 1948, folder 867, box 78-44, DC Board of Education, MSRC; "Memorandum to Mr. Marshall from Miss Perry," March 22, 1948, folder 6, box B136, NAACP; Austin Fickling, telegram to Thurgood Marshall, November 5, 1948, folder 6, box B136, NAACP; Thurgood Marshall, telegram to Austin L. Fickling, November 5, 1948, folder 6, box B136, NAACP.

24. Press release by Ernesto Galarza, April 14, 1947, folder 869, box 78-44, DC Board of Education, MRSC, Howard University.

25. John Womack, interview by Rachel Devlin, Cambridge, Massachusetts, January 2009; Lori Pepe, phone interview by Rachel Devlin, November 2009. Galarza's attempt to affiliate himself with NAACP desegregation efforts in 1947 runs somewhat counter to Nancy MacLean's description of Mexican American political endeavors prior to Title VII. Nancy MacLean, *Freedom Is Not Enough: The Opening of the American Workplace* (Cambridge: Harvard University Press, 2006); Marian Wynn Perry, memorandum to Thurgood Marshall, "In re: Washington D.C. School Case . . . Present: Ernesto Galarza, father of Karla Galarza," June 5, 1947, folder 7, box B136, NAACP; "Memorandum for American Civil Liberties Union, Re: Constitutional Questions in the Galarza Case," July 15, 1947, folder 7, box B136 NAACP.

26. Richard Chabran, "Activism and Intellectual Struggle in the Life of Ernesto Galarza," *Hispanic Journal of Behavioral Sciences* 7 (1985), 135–152; "Ernesto Galarza, Labor Aide," obituary, *New York Times*, June 24, 1984, 24; "Ernesto Galarza, Vita, 1905–1979," folder 1, box 1, Ernesto Galarza Papers, Stanford University, Stanford, California.

27. "White Girl in Colored School to Fight Transfer by Board," *Washington Star*, folder 869, box 78-44, files of DC Branch of the NAACP, DC Board of Education, MSRC; "Aim New Blow," *Pittsburgh Courier*, 1; "D.C. Court to Hear White Student Discrimination Case," *Los Angeles Sentinel*, May 8, 1947, 2; "Legal Action Near in 2 School Cases," *Pittsburgh Courier*, May 31, 1947, 4.

28. Marian Wynn Perry, memorandum to Thurgood Marshall, January 20, 1948, folder 7, box B136, NAACP.

29. Ernesto Galarza, letter to Miss Watkins (of the school board), April 3, 1947, folder 7, box B136, NAACP.

30. *Bishop v. Corning* represents a compromise on the part of Gardner Bishop. It was an equalization suit because Houston wanted to file it that way, not because Bishop preferred equalization; Judine Bishop Johnson, interview by Rachel Devlin, Washington, DC, October 2008.

31. Gardner L. Bishop, interview by Richard Kluger, August 22, 1974, file 5, group no. 759, series I, Kluger Papers, Sterling Memorial Library, Yale University.

32. Consolidated Parent Group records, folders 6, 14–17, MSRC, Howard University. On black women organizing traditions in the twentieth century, see Charles Payne, "Men Led but Women Organized: Movement Participation of Women in the Mississippi Delta," Guida West, Rhoda Lois Blumberg, eds., *Women and Social Protest* (New York: Oxford, 1990), 156–165; Jo Ann Gibson Robinson, *The Montgomery Bus Boycott and the Women Who Started It* (Knoxville: University of Tennessee Press, 1987); Belinda Robnett, *How Long? How Long? African American Women in the Struggle for Civil Rights* (New York: Oxford, 1997); Deborah Gray White, *Too Heavy a Load: Black Women in Defense of Themselves, 1894–1994* (New York: Norton, 1999); Lisa Levenstein, *A Movement Without Marches: African American Women and the Politics of Poverty in Postwar Philadelphia* (Chapel Hill: University of North Carolina Press, 2009). On women's political work in DC, see Treva B. Lindsey, *Colored No More: Reinventing Black Womanhood in Washington, D.C.* (Urbana: University of Illinois Press, 2017). On women organizing public housing, see Lisa Levenstein, *A Movement Without Marches: African American Women and the Politics of Poverty in Postwar Philadelphia* (Chapel Hill: University of North Carolina Press, 2009).

33. "Give the Child a Fair Chance;" Mrs. Francis Payne [report]; Mrs. Julis W. Harden [report]; Mrs. Chorolette [*sic*] Price [report], "Doctor's Wives Action Committee Drive for Consolidated Parent Group," "Contributors to Consolidated Parent Group from Parkview," folder 6, Consolidated Parent Group records, MSRC, Howard University.

34. Folder 1, Consolidated Parent Group records, MSRC, Howard University. For a clarification of Bishop's intentions, see Gardner Bishop, letter to Richard Kluger, circa 1975, folder 5, box 1, Kluger Papers, Yale.

35. Folders 12, 13, 17, Consolidated Parent Group, records, MSRC, Howard University. On the ways in which civil rights was cast as a public relations problem for the United States in the context of the Cold War, see Dudziak, *Cold War Civil Rights*.

36. Gardner Bishop, letter to members, June 1949, folder 12, Consolidated Parent Group records, MSRC, Howard University; Alonzo Smith, interview by Rachel Devlin, Montgomery College, Maryland, October 2008.

37. Lulu White, letter to Thurgood Marshall, December 10, 1947, folder 6, box B147, NAACP.

38. Doris Raye Jennings Brewer and Doris Faye Jennings Alston, interview by Rachel Devlin, Newark, Delaware, 2011. All quotations by Brewer and Alston are from this interview unless otherwise noted.

39. Ibid.

40. Clifton Jennings Jr., phone interview by Rachel Devlin, 2011.

41. Ray Osborne, "Negro Pupils Quit Classes: White School Denies Girl Entry," *Dallas Morning News*, September 18, 1947, 1.

42. "Public Schools Race Bar Due for July Trial," *Dallas Morning News*, March 24, 1948, 11; "Hearne Segregation Case Postponed Until September," *Dallas Morning News*, July 18, 1948, 9.

43. Osborne, "Negro Pupils Quit Classes"; *C. G. Jennings v. Hearne ISD*, Civil Case 822 (Entry 48W159, National Archives Identifier 573081, Western District of Texas, Waco Division, Record Group 21, Records of the District Courts of the United States, National Archives, Fort Worth, Texas).

44. "Bias in Education: NAACP Attorney to Test Validity of Segregation," *Kansas City Call*, March 26, 1948, 1; "Hearne School Case," *Dallas Morning News*, September 19, 1947, 2.

45. "Negro Child Bashful on School Issue," *Dallas Morning News*, August 30, 1948, 4.

46. "Bias in Education," *Kansas City Call*, 1.

47. "Hearne's New Negro School," *Dallas Morning News*, August 30, 1948, 4.

48. Katherine Mellen Charron, *Freedom's Teacher: The Life of Septima Clark* (Chapel Hill: University of North Carolina Press, 2012), 53.

49. Osborne, "Negro Pupils Quit Classes," 1.

Chapter 4: Laying the Groundwork

1. "Kill Segregation," *Kansas City Call*, May 21, 1954, 1, Lucinda Todd Papers, KSHS; "Topekans Celebrate Supreme Court Victory," *Kansas City Call*, June 18, 1954, 1; "Her Efforts Bear Fruit," *Kansas City Call*, June 17, 1949; Esther Brown, letter to Franklin Williams, December 16, 1948, folder 1, box B138, NAACP.

2. FBI, Esther Brown file, 1941, 2-MO-451, Esther Brown Papers, New York. Thank you to Lisa Oppenheimer and Susan Tucker for granting access

to Esther Brown's personal papers. The Schlesinger Library, Cambridge, Massachusetts, is the intended beneficiary of the Esther Brown Papers.

3. "The Successful Life of Esther Brown," *Kansas City Times*, May 26, 1970, Kluger Papers, Sterling Memorial Library, Yale University; Homer Wadsworth, "Eulogy of Esther Brown," May 26, 1970, Kluger Papers, Yale; "Her Light Will Shine Eternally," *Kansas City Call*, June 4, 1970, 1, Hugh Speer Papers, KSHS; "Brown, Esther," Kluger Papers, Yale; Esther Brown, phone interview by Richard Kluger, May 31, 1969, Kluger Papers, Yale.

4. The FBI reported that Ben Swirk's automobile was spotted outside a meeting hall in 1941 where "Mother" Bloor, national Communist Party official, spoke at party headquarters in Kansas City; FBI, Esther Brown file, p. 2, Johnson County Museum. See also Jean Van Delinder, *Struggles Before Brown: Early Civil Rights Protests and Their Significance Today* (New York: Routledge, 2011), 84.

5. "Mrs. Esther Brown, Twentieth Century Joan of Arc, Woman of the Week," *Kansas City Call*, April 22, 1949.

6. FBI, Esther Brown file, 1941, 2-MO-451, Esther Brown Papers.

7. Other colleges include Work People's College in Minnesota and Brookwood Labor College in New York. Both Pauli Murray and Ella Baker attended Brookwood. Ransby, *Ella Baker*, 73–74; William H. Cobb, *Radical Education in the Rural South: Commonwealth College, 1922–1940* (Detroit, MI: Wayne State University Press, 2000); Richard J. Altenbaugh, *Education for Struggle: The American Labor Colleges of the 1920s and 1930s* (Philadelphia: Temple University Press, 1990); Cobb, *Radical Education*, 125.

8. Cobb, *Radical Education*, 116; Robin D. G. Kelley, *Hammer and Hoe: Alabama Communists During the Great Depression* (Chapel Hill: University of North Carolina Press, 1990), 28; Ann Burlak, Maude White, Helen Homan, and Louise Thompson, "Mother Bloor's Girls," in *Mother Bloor 75th Birthday Book*, eds. Charlotte Todes and Sasha Small (July 1937), 20. For an analysis of Bloor's organizing style and "maternalist" rhetoric, see Kathleen A. Brown, "The 'Savagely Fathered and Un-Mothered World' of the Communist Party, U.S.A.: Feminism, Maternalism, and 'Mother Bloor,'" *Feminist Studies* 25, no. 3 (1999), 540. See also Ella Reeve Bloor, *We Are Many* (New York: International Publishers, 1940), chap. 4; Van Gosse, "'To Organize in Every Neighborhood, in Every Home': The Gender Politics of American Communists Between the Wars," *Radical History Review* 50 (1991), 109–141.

9. H. L. Mitchell, "The Founding and Early History of the Southern Tenant Farmers Union," *The Arkansas Historical Association Quarterly* 32, no. 4 (1973), 352; Lowell K. Dyson, "The Southern Tenant Farmers Union

and Depression Politics," Political Science Quarterly 88, no. 2 (June 1973), 236.

10. FBI, Esther Brown file, 2-MO-451, Esther Brown Papers.

11. Ibid.

12. Ibid.

13. Rob Roberts, "Esther Brown Was 'Little Woman Who Started' Case of the Century," *Sun Newspapers*, June 15, 2001, Johnson County Museum; Paul Brown, "Esther Brown: A Memorandum," June 15, 1994, Hugh Speer Papers, KSHS.

14. Esther Brown, interview by Hugh Speer, audiotape, March 8, 1965, Hugh Speer Papers, KSHS; Mary Webb, interview by Daryl Williams, 1995, Johnson County Museum.

15. Franklin Williams and Earl L. Fultz, "The Merriam School Fight," *The Crisis* (May 1949), 140.

16. Esther Brown, interview by Richard Kluger, Kluger Papers, Yale; Clark-Lewis, *Living In, Living Out*. See also Susan Tucker, *Telling Memories Among Southern Women: Domestic Workers and Their Employers in the Segregated South* (Baton Rouge: Louisiana State University Press, 2002).

17. Esther Brown, letter to Franklin Williams, August 30, 1948, folder 1, box B138, NAACP; Esther Brown, interview by Richard Kluger, Kluger Papers, Yale.

18. Esther Brown, letter to Franklin Williams, August 30, 1948, folder 1, box B138, NAACP; Esther Brown, interview by Richard Kluger, 1969, Kluger Papers, Yale.

19. Esther Brown, interview by Richard Kluger, 1969, Kluger Papers, Yale; Milton S. Katz and Susan B. Tucker, "A Pioneer in Civil Rights: Esther Brown and the South Park Case of 1948," *Kansas History* (Winter 1995/1996), 238; "Hear of South Park, Kas., Bias," *Kansas City Call*, June 4, 1948.

20. "Twentieth-Century Joan of Arc," *Kansas City Call*; Roberts, "Esther Brown"; Paul Brown, Speer Papers, KSHS.

21. Katz and Tucker, "A Pioneer in Civil Rights," 239; Esther Brown, letter to Edward R. Dudley, August 4, 1948, folder 1, box B138, NAACP.

22. "Seek a Supreme Court Ruling on J.C. School," *Kansas City Call*, June 4, 1948, 10.

23. "Hear of South Park, Kas., Bias," *Kansas City Call*, 11; Marian Baker, letter to Mrs. Brown, May 26, 1949, written on stationery of the Wichita Committee of Racial Equality, Esther Brown Papers.

24. Esther Brown, interview by Hugh Speer, audiotape, 1965, Hugh Speer Papers, KSHS.

25. Ibid.

26. Esther Brown, letter to Edward R. Dudley, August 4, 1948, folder 1, box B138, NAACP; Franklin Williams, telegram to Esther Brown, August 11, 1948, folder 1, box B138, NAACP.

27. "Memorandum to Mr. Williams from Mr. Marshall," August 23, 1948, folder 1, box B138, NAACP; "Memorandum to Thurgood Marshall from Franklin Williams re *Webb v. School District #90, Johnson County*," August 26, 1948, folder 1, box B138, NAACP.

28. Alfonso Webb, letter to William Towers, August 11, 1948, Esther Brown Papers; Esther Brown, interview by Hugh Speer, Hugh Speer Papers, KSHS.

29. Charles W. Eagles, *The Price of Defiance: James Meredith and the Integration of Ole Miss* (Chapel Hill: University of North Carolina Press, 2014); Franklin Williams, memorandum to Thurgood Marshall "Re: Merriam School Case," October 6, 1948, folder 1, box B138, NAACP; Franklin Williams, telegram to Elisha Scott, October 8, 1948, folder 1, box B138, NAACP; Elisha Scott, telegram to Franklin H. Williams care Walker [*sic*] White, October 13, 1948, folder 1, box B138, NAACP.

30. Thurgood Marshall, telegram to Elisha Scott, November 30, 1948, folder 1, box B138, NAACP; Esther Brown, letter to Franklin Williams, December 11, 1948, folder 1, box B138, NAACP.

31. "School Case Thursday," *Kansas City Call*, September 3, 1948 folder 1, box B138, NAACP; Mary Webb, interview by Daryl Williams, August 1994, Johnson County Museum; Esther Brown, letter to Franklin Williams, September 29, 1948, folder 1, box B138, NAACP; Esther Brown, interview by Richard Kluger, 1969, Kluger Papers, Yale; Franklin H. Williams and Earl Fultz, "The Merriam School Fight," *The Crisis*, May 1949, 140; "Merriam NAACP Branch Gives Tea," *Kansas City Call*, November 19, 1948. Dollar amounts for all events in "Financial Statement on the South Park Merriam [Case]," Esther Brown Papers.

32. Brown termed them "protest schools" in her interview with Kluger, p. 3; Esther Brown, letter to Franklin Williams, September 29, 1948, folder 1, box B138, NAACP.

33. "Hear of South Park, Kas. Bias," *Kansas City Call*.

34. Lucile Bluford, interview by Hugh Speer, Esther Brown Papers; Lucille [*sic*] Bluford, interview by Susan Tucker, June 23, 1976, Esther Brown Papers; Lisa Oppenheimer, interview by Rachel Devlin, New York City, January 18, 2017.

35. Esther Brown, letter to Franklin Williams, May 1949, folder 2, box B138, NAACP.

36. "This Is Not Even Equal Accommodations," *Plaindealer*, May 7, 1948, 1; "NAACP in Protest Against Kansas Jim Crow School Setup," *Plaindealer*, May 28, 1948, 1 (this story does mention Esther Brown, saying that the audience will receive "a scathing denunciation from Mrs. Paul Brown, white, a resident of Merriam Kansas"); "Attorney Towers Pushes Jim Crow School Case," *Plaindealer*, July 16, 1948, 1; "Attorney Elisha Scott Takes Over Merriam School Case," *Plaindealer*, August 20, 1948, 1; "Press Jim Crow Case in Merriam, Kansas," *Plaindealer*, October 8, 1948, 3; "Kans. Pres. of NAACP Branches Sees Need of Civil Rights: Dr. A. Porter Davis Speaks on State of Negroes in Kansas," *Plaindealer*, October 1, 1948, 1; "Kansas School Jim Crow Case Reaches State Supreme Court," *Plaindealer*, April 1, 1949, 1; "Rev. E.A. Freeman Pledges All Out Fight for Local NAACP," *Plaindealer*, April 29, 1; "Supreme Court Rules on South Park School; Must Admit Students," *Plaindealer*, June 17, 1949, 1.

37. "Two Pupils in Walker Building" and "Temporary Teaching for Pupils," *Kansas City Call*, October 1, 1948.

38. "Twentieth Century Joan of Arc," *Kansas City Call*; Mary Webb, interview by Daryl Williams, August 1994, Johnson County Museum.

39. "Test of Address, Mrs. Esther Brown at Kansas State Association of Branches, Osawatomie, Kansas, Sept. 5, 1948," Esther Brown Papers.

40. Ibid.

41. Paul Brown, "A Memorandum," Hugh Speer Papers, KSHS.

42. Esther Brown, interview by Hugh Speer, 1965, Hugh Speer Papers, KSHS.

43. Esther Brown, interview by Richard Kluger, p. 3, Kluger Papers, Yale; Katz and Tucker, "A Pioneer in Civil Rights," 241.

44. Esther Brown, interview by Hugh Speer, 1965, Hugh Speer Papers, KSHS.

45. Franklin Williams, letter to Carl R. Johnson, December 21, 1948, p. 2, folder 1, box B138, NAACP; Esther Brown, letter to Franklin Williams, November 28, 1948; Esther Brown, letter to Franklin Williams, (no date) circa November 1948.

46. Esther Brown, letter to Franklin Williams, (no date) circa November 1948.

47. Esther Brown, letter to Franklin Williams, November 28, 1948, p. 2; "Makes Appeal for Worthy Cause," *Kansas City Call*, November 26, 1948, 10.

48. Esther Brown, letter to Franklin Williams, December 6, 1948, folder 1, box B138, NAACP; Franklin Williams, letter to Esther Brown, November 30, 1948, folder 1, box B138, NAACP; Esther Brown, letter to Walter White, "Expenditures in the South Park-Merriam, Kansas School Case,"

April 7, 1949., p. 1, folder 2, box B138, NAACP; Esther Brown, letter to Franklin Williams, December 11, 1948, folder 1, box B138, NAACP.

49. Esther Brown, interview by Richard Kluger, Kluger Papers, Yale.

50. Esther Brown, letter to Franklin Williams, January 30, 1949, p. 1, folder 2, box B138, NAACP.

51. Laurence S. Holmes, letter to Franklin Williams, February 17, 1949, folder 2, box B138, NAACP; Will Maslow, letter to Sidney Lawrence, February 24, 1949, folder 2, box B138, NAACP.

52. Harvey and Alfonso Webb were the first plaintiffs largely because their mother, Mary Webb, played a prominent role in initiating the lawsuit; Mary Webb, interview by Daryl Williams, August 1994, Johnson County Museum; "Seeking a Supreme Court Ruling on J.C. School," *Kansas City Call*, June 4, 1948, 10; *Webb v. School District #90* (microfilm), Civil Action No. 37, 427, records of the Kansas State Supreme Court, KSHS.

53. Brandy Sebron-Kelley (formerly Patricia Black), phone interview by Rachel Devlin, April 2016.

54. *Mendez v. Westminster* was decided in 1946 in California. Thurgood Marshall submitted an amicus curiae to the court, but did not work on the brief.

55. "NAACP Speaker to Be Here March 17," *Parsons News*, March 16, 1950, Esther Brown Papers; Esther Brown, interview by Richard Kluger, Kluger Papers, Yale.

56. "Manhattan Folk Hear Talk on South Park Case; Contribute $123," *Kansas City Call*, May 20, 1949; McKinley Burnett, letter to Esther Brown, April 16, 1951, Esther Brown Papers; *Harvey Lewis Webb v. School District No. 90, Johnson County* (file 3B, Lucinda Todd Papers, KSHS).

57. Esther Brown, letter to Franklin Williams, August 19, 1948, p. 2, folder 1, box B138, NAACP.

58. Mary Webb, interview by Daryl Williams, p. 12, August 1994, Johnson County Museum.

59. Esther Brown, interview by Hugh Speer, Hugh Speer Papers, KSHS; Esther Brown, letter to Paul Brown, November 3, 1949, Esther Brown Papers.

60. "Professional News: Dr. Albert Porter Davis," *Journal of the National Medical Association* 68, no. 6 (1976), 547–548; Esther Brown, letter to Franklin Williams (no date), folder 1, box B138, NAACP.

61. Brandy Sebron-Kelley (formerly Patricia Black), phone interview by Rachel Devlin, April 2016.

62. Brian Burnes, "Esther Brown," *Kansas City Star*, circa 1975, Hugh Speer Papers, KSHS.

63. "The White Mrs. Brown," clipping, Kluger Papers, Yale.

Chapter 5: "Hearts and Minds"

1. Lucinda Todd has been called an early "enlightened discontent" (Kluger, *Simple Justice*) a "significant participant" in the Topeka desegregation battle (Lucinda Todd Papers), and an "unsung heroine" (NAACP pamphlet, Lucinda Todd Papers, KSHS) by the NAACP; Lucinda Todd, interview by Ralph Crowder (no date), *Brown v. Board of Education Topeka Oral History Project*.

2. Charles Houston, letter to Louis S. Weiss, February 9, 1948, p. 2., folder 6, box B136, NAACP.

3. Linda Laird, "Todd Was Key Figure in Struggle," *Capital-Journal*, April 18, 1993, folder 3, box 1, Lucinda Todd Papers, KSHS; Lucinda Todd, interview, p. 8–11, *Brown v. Board of Education Topeka Oral History Project*, KSHS.

4. Nancy Todd Noches and Raymond Noches, interview by Rachel Devlin, March 2013, Austin, Texas.

5. Lucinda Todd, "For the Negro Press," 1951, folder 30, box 1, Lucinda Todd Papers, KSHS; *Topeka Capital Journal*, May 13, 1979, folder 1, box 1, Lucinda Todd Papers, KSHS.

6. Constance Sawyer, interview by Jean Van Delinder, March 1992, *Brown v. Board of Education Topeka Oral History Project*, pp. 10–11, KSHS; Van Delinder, *Struggles Before Brown*, 45–46. For desegregation lawsuits prior to 1930 in Kansas, see Van Delinder, *Struggles Before Brown*, 34–44.

7. Mrs. Maude Lawton is the correct spelling; "Laughton" should be spelled "Lawton"; Van Delinder, *Struggles Before Brown*, 15–16.

8. Constance Sawyer, interview by Jean Van Delinder, *Brown v. Board of Education Topeka Oral History Project*, p. 14, KSHS.

9. Lucinda Todd, "Background for *Brown vs. Board*," p. 1, folder 36, box 1, Lucinda Todd Papers, KSHS; Lucinda Todd, interview by Richard Kluger, p. 1, Kluger Papers, Yale; Nancy Todd Noches, interview by Rachel Devlin, Austin, Texas, 2013; Citizens Committee on Civil Rights, *The People Fight Back*, folder 2B, box 1, Lucinda Todd Papers, KSHS.

10. "The Brown Case" (handwritten, no date), folder 75, box 1, Lucinda Todd Papers, KSHS; "Background for *Brown vs. Board of Education* School Case" (handwritten no date), folder 3B, box 1, Lucinda Todd Papers, KSHS. On the Ramblers, see "Todd Was Key Figure in Struggle," *Topeka Capital-Journal*, April 18, 1993, folder 3, box 1, Lucinda Todd Papers, KSHS.

11. Todd, "Background for *Brown vs. Board of Education* School Case," pp. 1–6; "Des Moines Speech by Lucinda Todd" (1952), pp. 1–4, folder 38,

box 1, Lucinda Todd Papers, KSHS; Samuel C. Jackson quoted in Kluger, *Simple Justice*, 383.

12. Nancy Todd Noches, interview by Rachel Devlin; Joe Douglass, interview by Ralph Crowder, *Brown v. Board of Education Topeka Oral History Project*, p.13, KSHS.

13. Nancy Todd Noches and Raymond Noches, interview by Rachel Devlin, Austin, Texas, 2013. On class size: "There are four elementary segregated schools with 27 teachers and about 779 pupils," Todd, "Des Moines Speech."

14. Lucinda Todd, interview, *Brown v. Topeka Board of Education Topeka Oral History Project*, p. 35, KSHS; Lucinda Todd, interview by Richard Kluger, p. 1, Kluger Papers, Yale.

15. Citizens Committee on Civil Rights, *The People Fight Back*.

16. Daniel Sawyer, letter to the Topeka Board of Education, September 13, 1948, folder 2B, Lucinda Todd Papers, KSHS.

17. Daniel Sawyer, letter to the Topeka Board of Education, September 13, 1948, folder 2B, Lucinda Todd Papers, KSHS.

18. Ibid, 5–6; "Kansas Supreme Court Will Hear Jim Crow School Case This Month," July 23, 1948, *Kansas City Call*, folder 3, Lucinda Todd Papers, KSHS; "Suit Hits Separate Schools in Kansas," *Kansas City Call*, June 6, 1951, folder 2, Lucinda Todd Papers, KSHS; "Kill Segregation," *Kansas City Call*, May 21, folder 2, Lucinda Todd Papers, KSHS.

19. Nancy Todd Noches, interview by Rachel Devlin, Austin, Texas, 2013; Lucinda Todd, interview by Richard Kluger, p. 1, Kluger Papers, Yale; Lucinda Todd, interview by Ralph Crowder (no date), p. 33, *Brown v. Topeka Board of Education Topeka Oral History Project*, KSHS.

20. Lucinda Todd, "Des Moines Speech"; Lucinda Todd, interview by Richard Kluger, circa 1970, p. 2, Kluger Papers, Yale.

21. Esther Brown, interview by Hugh Speer, 1965, audiotape, Hugh Speer Papers, KSHS; the flyer and photograph of Walter White speaking at the municipal auditorium is dated April 26, 1949, folder 3, box 1, Lucinda Todd Papers, KSHS.

22. Esther Brown, interview by Hugh Speer, 1965, Hugh Speer Papers, KSHS; Constance Sawyer, interview, pp. 18–19, KSHS; Lucinda Todd, letter to Walter White, August 29, 1950, folder 19, Lucinda Todd Papers, KSHS; Lucinda Todd, in this letter and elsewhere, mentions the date that Walter White stayed with her as 1948. However, all of the dating, from the KSHS and contemporary activists remembered Walter White's visit as taking place in 1949. It is possible that he stayed with her on another trip through Kansas that

took place in 1948 that was less well attended and about which less is known. There is no mention of a visit from Walter White in 1948 in the *Call*.

23. Kluger, *Simple Justice*, 3–15.

24. Ibid., 24.

25. Ibid., 22.

26. *Carr v. Corning* Decision, 182 F.2d 14, 86 U.S. App. D.C. 173; *Carr v. Corning, Superintendent of Public Schools et al. Brown Junior High School Parent-Teacher Ass'n et al. v. Magdeburger et al.*, Civil Action Nos. 9796, 9878, United States Court of Appeals District of Columbia Circuit; Judge Julius Waties Waring's dissent in the Briggs case, in 1951, is often celebrated as a breakthrough in the NAACP's legal battle against segregation in the schools. However, such ballast came earlier, in fact, just as the LDF lawyers were preparing for the *Briggs* trial, from Judge Henry White Edgerton, a native of Kansas and appointed to the United States Court of Appeals by Franklin Roosevelt in 1937; Leon Friedman and Richard Mark Gergel, "The Dissent that Changed America," *National Law Journal* 33, no. 45 (2011), 51.

27. Robert L. Carter, memorandum to Thurgood Marshall, folder 6, box B136, NAACP.

28. Hill, Robinson, Martin, and Ransom, complaint in *Carter v. School Board* and *Bailey v. School Board* Civil Action No. 331, pp. 6–7, MSS 78-2, box 7, Armistead Mason Dobie Papers, University of Virginia; "Negro Children Refused at White High School, Parents Differ with Board," *Kansas City Call*, September 24, 1948; Thurgood Marshall, interview by Richard Kluger, 1972, Kluger Papers, Yale.

29. *Corbin v. County School Board of Pulaski County*, Civil Action No. 5921, 1949; *Carter v. School Board*, Civil Action No. 331, MSS 78-2, box 7, Armistead Mason Dobie Papers, University of Virginia.

30. Morris Ames Soper, writing for the majority in *Carter v. School Board*, May 31, 1950, pp. 1–6, MSS 78-2, box 7; Armistead Mason Dobie Papers, University of Virginia.

31. Kluger, *Simple Justice*, 291.

32. Leon Ransom was a well-known, highly accomplished, extremely busy attorney. However, the many cases he took on exacted a toll on his health—as was the case with Charles Houston as well. The only newspaper to report this was the reliably truth-telling *Kansas City Call*. "Atty. Leon Ransom Victim of Amnesia, Nervous Exhaustion," *Kansas City Call*, March 4, 1949.

33. Belford Lawson, interview by Richard Kluger, March, 1971; Kluger, *Simple Justice*, 303; James Nabrit, interview by Richard Kluger, 1971; Kluger, *Simple Justice*, 291, 303.

34. For a discussion of the doll test, including criticism, see Robin Bernstein, *Racial Innocence: Performing American Childhood from Slavery to Civil Rights* (New York: New York University Press, 2011), chap. 5; Lawrence Nyman, "Documenting History: An Interview with Kenneth Bancroft Clark," *History of Psychology* 13, no. 1 (2010), 74–88; *Notable American Women*, volume 5, s.v. "Mamie Phipps Clark" (Cambridge, MA: Belknap Press, 2005), 125–126; Kluger, *Simple Justice*, 330.

35. Kluger, *Simple Justice*, p. 362.

36. *Briggs v. Elliott*, Civil Action No. 2657, 98 F. Supp. 529 (1951) United States District Court E.D. South Carolina, Charleston.

37. Ibid.

38. Houston did file one brief in 1949 on behalf of parents whose children had been rejected from their local kindergarten. This suit no doubt delighted Gardner Bishop, as it was a straightforward desegregation lawsuit. *Eddie Andrew Gregg v. C. Melvine Sharpe*, Civil Action 4205, 1949, folder 56, Consolidated Parents Group records, MSRC, Howard University.

39. *African American National Biography*, 2nd edition, volume 9, eds. Henry Louis Gates Jr. and Evelyn Brooks Higginbotham, s.v. "Nabrit, James Madison, Jr." (New York: Oxford, 2013), 403–404.

40. "Boy, 14, Won't Hear His Racial Case Argued," *Washington Post*, December 6, 1953; "Integration by Autumn Believed Possible by Negro Parents' Group," *Washington Daily News*, May 18, 1954, 3; "Bolling," box 19-2, Consolidated Parent Group records, MSRC, Howard University.

41. On "sex-typing," see Ruth Milkman, *Gender at Work: The Dynamics of Job Segregation by Sex during World War II* (Urbana: University of Illinois Press, 1987).

42. Janet Harmon, interview by Rachel Devlin, Wilmington, Delaware, January 2009; Virginia Smilack, phone interview by Rachel Devlin, January 2009; Annette Woolard-Provine, *Integrating Delaware: The Reddings of Wilmington* (Newark: University of Delaware, 2003), 123; *Bulah v. Gephardt*, Civil Action No. 16, 1952, and *Belton v. Gephardt*, Civil Action No. 15, 1952, folder 3, box B139, NAACP.

43. Virginia Smilack, phone interview by Rachel Devlin, January 2009.

44. Woolard-Provine, *Integrating Delaware*, 123; Janet Harmon, interview by Rachel Devlin, Wilmington, Delaware, January 2009; Brigitte Brown and Andreia Brown, interview by Rachel Devlin, San Antonio, Texas, May 2009; Sandy Couch, interview by Rachel Devlin, Atlantic City, 2009.

45. *Belton v. Gephardt* and *Bulah v. Gephardt*, 1952, folder 2, box B140, Delaware Supreme Court Legal Papers, NAACP; Kenneth W. Mack, "Rethinking Civil Rights Lawyering and Politics in the Era Before *Brown*," *Yale*

Law Journal 115, no. 2 (2005); Kenneth W. Mack, "Law and Mass Politics in the Making of the Civil Rights Lawyer, 1931–1941," *Journal of American History* 93, no. 1 (2007).

46. "Youth's Travails," *Jet*, May 1964, 20–22.

47. Kluger, *Simple Justice*, 460–461, 467.

48. Quoted in Kluger, *Simple Justice*, 477.

49. Kluger, *Simple Justice*, 479; Kara Miles Turner, "Both Victors and Victims: Prince Edward County, Virginia, the NAACP and 'Brown,'" *Virginia Law Review* 90, no. 6 (2004), 1672. See also Kara Miles Turner, "'Getting It Straight': Southern School Patrons and the Struggle for Equal Education in the Pre- and Post-Civil Rights Eras," *Journal of Negro Education* 72, no.2 (2003), 217–229; Bob Smith, *They Closed Their Schools: Prince Edward County, Virginia, 1951–1964* (Farmville, VA: M. E. Forrester Council of Women, 1996).

50. Katherine Carper Sawyer, interview by Rachel Devlin, Topeka, Kansas, 2010. All subsequent quotations from interview.

51. Lucinda Todd, "The Brown Case," folder 75, Lucinda Todd Papers, KSHS.

52. "Interview with Constance Sawyer," *Brown v. Board of Education Topeka Oral History Project*, p. 20, KSHS; "Interview with Berdyne Scott," November 24, 1991, *Brown v. Board of Education Topeka Oral History Project*, p. 42, KSHS.

53. Linda Laird, "Todd Was Key Figure in Struggle," *Capital-Journal*, folder 3, Lucinda Todd Papers, KSHS; "Interview with Constance Sawyer," *Brown v. Board of Education Topeka Oral History Project*, p. 20, KSHS.

54. Lucinda Todd, interview by Richard Kluger, p. 3, Kluger Papers, Yale; Nancy Todd Noches, interview, p. 65.

55. Lucinda Todd, letter to Esther Brown, June 5, 1951, Esther Brown Papers.

56. Esther Brown, letter to Joe Coffman, June 8, 1951; Joseph Cohen, letter to Arnold Forster, May 19, 1951; Sidney Lawrence, letter to Arnold Forster, June 12, 1951; Robert Carter, letter to Esther Brown, June 20, 1951 (all from Esther Brown Papers).

57. Robert L. Carter, letter to Herbert Bell, September 14, 1951, Esther Brown Papers.

58. Lucinda Todd, interview by Richard Kluger, Kluger Papers, Yale.

59. Hugh W. Speer, *The Case of the Century* (Washington, DC: Office of Education, US Department of Health, Education, and Welfare, 1968), 59, 87.

60. *Brown v. Board of Education, Topeka*, 347 U.S. 483 (1954); Waldo E. Martin Jr., Brown v. Board of Education: *A Brief History with Documents* (New York: Bedford, 1998), 1.

61. For a critique of the psychological nature of the approach in *Brown*, see Daryl Michael Scott, *Contempt and Pity: Social Policy and the Image of the Damaged Black Psyche, 1880–1996* (Chapel Hill: University of North Carolina Press, 1997); Martin, Brown v. Board of Education, 1.

Chapter 6: "Take Care of My Baby"

1. Carol Anderson, interview by Rachel Devlin, Portland, Oregon, 2009. All subsequent quotations by Carol Anderson are from the interview.

2. Interview with Virginia Smilak, phone interview by Rachel Devlin, 2008; "Interview with Joe Douglas," *Brown v. Board of Education Topeka Oral History Project*, p. 13, KSHS.

3. "Claymont, Cornerstone of *Brown v. Board*, published by the Delaware Heritage Commission . . . to commemorate the 52nd anniversary of the integration of Claymont High School, September 4, 1952" (pamphlet sent to Rachel Devlin by Virginia Smilak, 2009); "Interview with Joe Douglas," "Interview with Vivian Scales," and "Interview with Spencer Robinson," *Brown v. Board of Education Topeka Oral History Project*, KSHS.

4. "54 Jesuit Schools Admit Negroes: Survey Shows Trend of Catholic Order," *Kansas City Call*, February 18, 1949. Camilla Church Greene says her husband (African American) attended a predominantly white Catholic high school in the 1940s, Bishop Loughlin High School, in Brooklyn. Camilla Church Greene, interview by Rachel Devlin, Brooklyn, New York, 2013.

5. Camilla Church Greene, interview by Rachel Devlin, Brooklyn, New York, 2013. All subsequent quotations by Greene are from the interview.

6. Marcia Pinkett-Heller, interview by Rachel Devlin, New York, 2013. All subsequent quotations by Pinkett-Heller are from the interview.

7. Ralph McGill, *The South and the Southerner* (Boston: Atlantic Monthly Press, 1963), 22–23, quoted in Hunter-Gault, *In My Place*, 86.

8. Benjamin Muse, *Ten Years of Prelude: The Story of Integration Since the Supreme Court's 1954 Decision* (New York, Viking, 1964), 1–29; Clive Webb, *Massive Resistance: Southern Opposition to the Second Reconstruction* (New York: Oxford University Press, 2005), 4.

9. The school board in Nashville copied a desegregation plan in Evanston, Illinois, that had proved successful at keeping the number of desegregating students low. Newly created school zones assigned black pupils to schools near their homes, drawn up in such a way that kept the possible number of black transfer students low for each grade school formerly designated white. Further, they offered parents the option to transfer their students if he or

she was a "racial minority" at his or her new school. The assumption by the board was that "both whites and blacks," Benjamin Houston writes, "given the choice, would prefer the company of their own race." *The Nashville Way: Racial Etiquette and the Struggle for Social Justice in a Southern City* (Athens, GA: University of Georgia Press, 2012), 63–64. Gayle Hicks Fripp, *Greensboro: A Chosen Center* (Woodland Hills, CA: Windsor, 1982), chapter 8. In Charlotte, North Carolina, school desegregation also began in 1957. The students applied individually and were "handpicked for their ability and character." Three girls and one boy desegregated that year. Dorothy Counts briefly attended Harding High School. She met with so much hostility that she left, spending a year with family friends in Philadelphia. Delores Maxine Huntly desegregated the seventh grade at Alexander Junior High School "without serious incident." Girvaud Roberts (a girl) peacefully desegregated Piedmont Junior High, and Gus Roberts, Central High School, where the principal, Ed Sanders, intervened when Roberts was attacked and successfully maintained order. Frye Gaillard, *The Dream Long Deferred: The Landmark Struggle for Desegregation in Charlotte, North Carolina* (Columbia: University of South Carolina Press, 2006), 1–11.

10. Webb, *Massive Resistance*, 5.

11. Muse, *Ten Years of Prelude*, 48; Neil R. McMillen, *The Citizens' Council: Organized Resistance to the Second Reconstruction, 1954–1964* (Urbana: University of Illinois Press, 1994), xxiii; Muse, *Ten Years of Prelude*, 178; Webb, *Massive Resistance*, 8.

12. Webb, *Massive Resistance*, 6.

13. For a detailed account of events in Mansfield, see Muse, *Ten Years of Prelude*, chap. 7. On Arthurine Lucy, Muse, *Ten Years of Prelude*, 53–55.

14. Muse, *Ten Years of Prelude*, 7.

15. Arendt, "Reflections on Little Rock," 50; Du Bois, "Does the Negro Need Separate Schools?"

16. Anderson, *Little Rock*; Pattillo Beals, *Warriors Don't Cry*.

17. Liva Baker, *The Second Battle of New Orleans: The Hundred-Year Struggle to Integrate the Schools* (New York: HarperCollins, 1996), chap. 16; Alan Wieder, "The New Orleans School Crisis of 1960: Causes and Consequences," *Phylon* 48, no. 2 (1960), 122–131.

18. "Pupil Assignment Procedure," Minute Book 41: 1960–1961, October 10, 1960, p. 564, Orleans Parish School Board Collection, Mss 147, Early K. Long Library, University of New Orleans.

19. Tessie Prevost Williams, interview by Rachel Devlin, New Orleans, 2010; Dorothy Prevost, interview by Rachel Devlin, New Orleans, 2010; Ruby Bridges, phone interview by Rachel Devlin, July 2012. All subsequent

quotations by Tessie Prevost Williams and Dorothy Prevost are from these interviews unless otherwise noted.

20. Wieder, "The New Orleans School Crisis of 1960," 122–131; "Through a Crowd Bravely: The 50th Anniversary of the Desegregation of New Orleans Public Schools," Tulane University, November 13, 2010, event sponsored by the Amistad Research Center, Tulane University. Speakers included Leona Tate, Tessie Prevost Williams, and Gail Etienne.

21. On the multiple uses of clothes for keeping children in school and sparing them humiliation, see Lisa Levenstein, *A Movement Without Marches* (Chapel Hill: University of North Carolina Press, 2009), 146.

22. Former federal marshal Wallace Downs, "Through a Crowd Bravely: 50th Anniversary of School Desegregation," November 13, 2010, Tulane University, New Orleans.

23. Tessie Prevost Williams, "Through a Crowd Bravely," November 13, 2010, Tulane University.

24. Ibid.

25. Thanks to Turry Flucker for showing me these letters housed at the Louisiana State Museum, New Orleans.

26. Leona Tate, "Through a Crowd Bravely," November 13, 2010, Tulane University.

27. Patricia Hill Collins, "The Meaning of Motherhood in Black Culture and Black Mother-Daughter Relationships," in *Gender Through the Prism of Difference,* eds. Maxine Baca Zinn, Pierrette Hondagneu-Sotelo, Michael A. Messner, and Amy M. Denissen, 5th edition (New York: Oxford University Press, 2015), 315–324.

28. "Through a Crowd Bravely," November 13, 2010, Tulane University.

29. Robert Coles, *Lives We Carry with Us: Profiles in Moral Courage* (New York: New Press, 2010), 208.

Chapter 7: "We Raised Our Hands and Said 'Yes We Will Go'"

1. Fairclough, *Race and Democracy*, 334.

2. Dr. Freya Anderson Rivers, *Swallowed Tears: A Memoir* (Bloomington, IN: AuthorHouse, 2012), 170.

3. Ibid., 102–107.

4. Anderson Rivers, *Swallowed Tears*, 176; Marion Greenup interview by Rachel Devlin, Yonkers, New York, 2016. All subsequent quotations by Greenup are from the interview; Anderson Rivers, *Swallowed Tears*, 171–172.

5. Merrill Patin, interview by Rachel Devlin, Baton Rouge, Louisiana, 2011. All subsequent quotations by Patin are from the interview.

6. Edmund Vice and Anna Vice, interview by Rachel Devlin, Moncks Corner, South Carolina, 2011.

7. Betta Jean Bowman, interview by Rachel Devlin, Baton Rouge, Louisiana, 2011. All subsequent quotations by Bowman are from the interview.

8. Gayle Vavasseur Jones, interview by Rachel Devlin, Baton Rouge, Louisiana, 2011. All subsequent quotations by Jones are from the interview.

9. On the civil rights movement in the early 1960s, see Taylor Branch, *Parting the Waters: America in the King Years, 1954–1963* (New York: Simon and Schuster, 1988), chap. 20; William Chafe, *Civilities and Civil Rights: Greensboro, North Carolina, and the Black Struggle for Freedom* (New York: Oxford University Press, 1981); David Halberstam, *The Children* (New York: Fawcett Books, 1999); Charles M. Payne, *I've Got the Light of Freedom: The Organizing Tradition and the Mississippi Freedom Struggle* (Berkeley: University of California Press, 2007).

10. Elaine Chustz Green, interview by Rachel Devlin, Jonesboro, Georgia, 2011. All subsequent quotations from Chustz Green are from the interview.

11. Anderson Rivers, *Swallowed Tears*, 159.

12. Fairclough, *Race and Democracy*, chap. 11.

13. Rita Gidroz White, interview by Rachel Devlin, Baton Rouge, Louisiana, 2011. All subsequent quotations by White are from the interview.

14. Murphy Bell Jr., interview by Rachel Devlin, Baton Rouge, Louisiana, 2011. All subsequent quotations by Bell are from the interview. Betta Jean Bowman, interview by Rachel Devlin, Baton Rouge, Louisiana, 2011. All subsequent quotations by Bowman are from the interview.

15. List of thirty-eight student applicants, 1963, possession of Marion Greenup, Yonkers, New York; list of twenty-eight accepted students, "*Davis v. E. Baton Rouge Parish Sch. Bd.*, Corr. 1962–1963," folder 29, box 24, A. P. Tureaud Papers, Amistad Research Center, Tulane.

16. Anderson Rivers, *Swallowed Tears*, 201.

17. Ibid., 199.

18. Ibid., 205

19. Ibid., 212.

20. Vervian Elaine Boyle Patin, interview by Rachel Devlin, Baton Rouge, Louisiana, 2011. All subsequent quotations by Elaine Boyle Patin are from the interview. (Vervian was the name Boyle Patin used through middle school. She was known as Elaine in high school and afterward. She is listed on the group of accepted students to Baton Rouge High School as Vervian Elaine Boyle.); Velma Jean Hunter Jackson, phone interview by Rachel Devlin,

2017. Jackson says that she had to accompany Boyle Patin everywhere after the discovery was made that she was not white and act as her "bodyguard."

21. Alyce Julien Robinson and Ronald Julien, interview by Rachel Devlin, Donaldsonville, Louisiana, 2011. All subsequent quotations by Robinson and Julien are from the interview.

22. Anderson Rivers, *Swallowed Tears*, 217.

23. Ibid., 21; Marion Greenup, interview by Rachel Devlin, Yonkers, New York, 2016.

24. Anderson Rivers, *Swallowed Tears*, 224–225.

25. Ibid., 227–228.

26. Ibid., 206, 233.

27. Ibid., 219.

28. Millicent Brown, interview by Rachel Devlin, Orangeburg, South Carolina, 2009. All subsequent quotations by Brown are from the interview.

29. "Integration Begins Calmly in South Carolina and Baton Rouge," *New York Times*, September 4, 1963, 1.

30. Millicent Ellison Brown, "Civil Rights Activism in Charleston, South Carolina, 1940–1970," (Ph.D. dissertation, Florida State University College of Arts and Sciences, 1997), 186, Millicent Brown Papers, Avery Research Center.

31. Ibid., 190.

32. Millicent Brown, interview transcript, p. 4, folder 8, Millicent Brown Papers, Avery Research Center.

33. Deborah Gray White, interview with Rachel Devlin, Metuchen, New Jersey, 2013.

34. Howard Zinn, *SNCC: The New Abolitionists* (Cambridge, MA: South End Press, 1964), 123. Mary Royal Jenkins, *Open Dem Cells*; Stephen G. N. Tuck, *Beyond Atlanta: The Struggle for Racial Equality in Georgia, 1940–1980* (Athens, GA: University of Georgia Press, 2001), ch. 5; Lee W. Formwalt, *Looking Back, Looking Forward: Southwest Georgia Freedom Struggle 1814–2014* (Albany, GA: Albany Civil Rights Institute, 2014).

35. Ibid., 131.

36. Rubye Nell Singleton Stroble, interview by Rachel Devlin, Albany, Georgia, 2009; Beverley Plummer Wilson, interview by Rachel Devlin, Albany, Georgia, 2009. All further quotations by Stroble and Wilson are from these interviews.

37. "Police Club Negroes in Motel Pool," *Washington Post*, June 19, 1964. Mamie Ford Jones, interview by Rachel Devlin, Roxbury, Massachusetts, 2013. All subsequent quotations by Jones are from the interview.

38. Shirley Lawrence Alexander, interview by Rachel Devlin, Marietta, Georgia, 2011. All subsequent quotations by Alexander are from the interview.

Epilogue

1. "Rejection of Young Violinist Recalls Marian Anderson Snub," *Chicago Defender*, February 11, 1963, 3; "Barred Violinist Decides Today if She Wants to Return to Symphony," *Chicago Defender*, February 13, 1963, 3; "Barred Violinist to Play with Oak Park Symphony 'Just Once,'" *Chicago Defender*, February 14, 1963, 2; "Fifth of Oak Park Symphony May Quit Over Racial Snub," *Chicago Defender*, February 16, 1963, 1; "Report 25 Musicians Quitting Oak Park Symphony on Race Issue," *Chicago Defender*, February 23, 1963, 4.

2. Carol Anderson, interview by Rachel Devlin, Portland, Oregon, 2009.

3. The title is after Kate Rushin's "The Bridge Poem." See Cherrie Moraga and Gloria Anzaldua, *This Bridge Called My Back: Writings by Radical Women of Color*, 4th edition, (Albany, NY: SUNY Press, 2015). See also Charisse Jones and Kumea Shorter-Gooden, *Shifting: the Double Lives of Black Women in America* (New York: Perennial, 2003); Deborah Gray White, ed., *Telling Histories: Black Women Historians in the Ivory Tower* (Chapel Hill: University of North Carolina Press, 2008). For a novel describing a young black women refusing to play the role of the positive, communicative student at an elite, white school, see Lorene Cary, *Black Ice* (New York: Vintage, 1992). Carol Anderson, interview by Rachel Devlin, Portland, Oregon, 2009; "Carol Wins Cheers, Dad Flies Here for Concert," *Chicago Defender*, February 18, 1963, 1.

4. There were several desegregation firsts among the group in Baton Rouge and Albany who refused to be interviewed. It is possible—if not probable— that those firsts do not hold a positive perspective on what they achieved, or feel that revisiting their desegregation experiences would be too painful. Had they been interviewed, these firsts may have offered a more varied evaluation of the personal and societal productivity of school desegregation.

5. Hill, "Personal Thoughts on Ada Lois Sipuel Fisher."

6. Clipping, no title, no date, Lucinda Todd Papers, KSHS; James Meredith, *A Mission from God: A Memoir and Challenge for America* (New York: Atria, 2012), 16.

7. Alexander Nazaryan, "Why Johnny Can't Integrate," *Newsweek*, May 19, 2017, 26–35; Nikole Hannah-Jones, "Choosing a School for My Daughter in a Segregated City," *New York Times Magazine*, June 9, 2016. On the academic

value of diverse classrooms, see Century Foundation, "The Benefits of Socio-economically and Racially Integrated Schools and Classrooms," February 10, 2016, https://tcf.org/content/facts/the-benefits-of-socioeconomically-and-racially-integrated-schools-and-classrooms.

8. Blanche Wiesen Cook, "'Women Alone Stir My Imagination': Lesbianism and the Cultural Tradition," *Signs: Journal of Women in Culture and Society* 4, no. 4 (Summer 1979), 718–739.

Index

RACHEL DEVLIN is an associate professor of history at Rutgers University. She lives in Brooklyn, New York.

Photograph by Justine Cooper